THE OXFORD INTERNATIONAL LAW LIBRARY

The Position of Heads of State and Senior Officials in International Law

THE OXFORD INTERNATIONAL LAW LIBRARY

General Editor

SIR FRANK BERMAN KCMG QC

This series features works on substantial topics in international law which provide authoritative statements of the chosen areas. Taken together they map out the whole of international law in a set of scholarly reference works and treatises intended to be of use to scholars, practitioners, and students.

The Position of Heads of State and Senior Officials in International Law

JOANNE FOAKES

OXFORD
UNIVERSITY PRESS

OXFORD
UNIVERSITY PRESS

Great Clarendon Street, Oxford, OX2 6DP,
United Kingdom

Oxford University Press is a department of the University of Oxford.
It furthers the University's objective of excellence in research, scholarship,
and education by publishing worldwide. Oxford is a registered trade mark of
Oxford University Press in the UK and in certain other countries

First Edition published in 2014

Published in the United States of America by Oxford University Press
198 Madison Avenue, New York, NY 10016, United States of America

British Library Cataloguing in Publication Data
Data available

Library of Congress Cataloging in Publication Data
Data available

ISBN 978–0–19–964028–7

Preface

The aim of this book is to review the current state of international law regarding the position of heads of State and other holders of very senior State offices and, in doing so, to pay particular attention to recent developments in law and practice. The book is divided into five chapters, the first of which contains a general introduction and survey of the topic, together with a summary of the issues covered. Chapter 2 looks in more detail at the position of a sitting head of State, including family members while Chapter 3 considers the position of incumbent heads of Government, Ministers for Foreign Affairs, and other senior State offices who may be entitled to special treatment. Chapter 4 examines the position of former heads of State and other senior State officials who have left office. All these chapters are essentially concerned with the position of such senior officials or former senior officials in foreign jurisdictions. By contrast, Chapter 5 looks at their position before international courts and tribunals. Inevitably there is overlap between certain parts of the book and, as a consequence, some repetition from one chapter to another. In the interest of clarity, however, I judged it best not to address all such issues by cross-reference and hope that the reader will bear with me in this respect.

I owe many people much thanks for their help and support in the production of this book. Above all, I am grateful to the late Sir Arthur Watts, whose early and exemplary study of the subject was an important inspiration and invaluable source. In addition, I should like to express my gratitude to David Bentley, Sir Franklin Berman, Chanaka Wickremasinghe, Elizabeth Wilmshurst, and Sir Michael Wood who have variously provided encouragement, background material, and useful comment. Warmest thanks are also due to all at OUP who have been both efficient and patient in equal measure. Needless to say, responsibility remains entirely with the author. The book is based on information available at the end of July 2013.

Joanne Foakes

Contents

Table of Cases xi
Table of Treaties and Legislation xix
List of Abbreviations xxiii
Note on Citations xxv

1. Overview and General Principles 1
   1. Introduction 1
   2. Summary of Key Issues 4
   3. Types of Immunity 7
   4. Justifications for Special Treatment 10
   5. Historical Background and Context 12
      Early theories 12
      Formulation of a general rule 15
      State immunity: the absolute doctrine 16
      State immunity: the restrictive doctrine 16
   6. Applicability of Rules of International Law Generally 18
      Customary international law 18
      Endorsement of specific rules by ICJ or other international courts or tribunals 22
      Endorsement of specific rules by national courts 24

2. Heads of State 29
   1. Constitutional Forms and Titles 29
   2. Internationally Relevant Powers 36
      The power to make war and peace 37
      The treaty-making power 38
      Appointment and reception of diplomatic representatives 40
      Ius repraesentationis omnimodae 41
   3. Recognition 42
      General principles 42
      Constituent territories of federal States 46
      Deposition and exile 48
      Role of the Executive: sitting heads of State 53
      Role of the Executive: former heads of State 55

4. Protection, Privileges, and Immunities 58
Freedom of movement 58
Freedom of communication 60
Dignity 61
Protection 74
Inviolability 76
Immunity from suit before foreign courts 80
Immunity of property 98
Exemption from dues and taxes, and customs duties 101
Families and Members of the Entourage 102

3. Heads of Governments, Foreign Ministers, and Other Senior State Representatives 110
(A) Heads of Governments and Foreign Ministers 110
1. Internal Forms and Titles 110
2. Internationally Relevant Powers 112
3. Recognition 113
4. Protection, Privileges, and Immunities 114
5. Families 126
(B) Other Senior State Representatives 128
1. Personal Immunities 128
2. Special Missions 133

4. Position After Loss of Office 136
1. General Principles 136
Relationship with State immunity 137
State immunity and State responsibility 139
Comparison between criminal responsibility and civil liability 141
2. Acts performed in an Official Capacity 142
What is an official act? 142
Criminal proceedings 147
Civil proceedings 166
Necessity for functional immunity to be invoked 172
3. Private Acts 175

5. International Responsibility of Heads of States and Other Senior State Representatives 179
1. State Responsibility 179
2. Individual Responsibility 181
History and general principles 181
The Nuremberg International Military Tribunal 183

The Tokyo International Military Tribunal 185
Relevant international conventions 186
3. International Courts and Tribunals 188
The International Criminal Tribunal for Yugoslavia 188
The International Criminal Tribunal for Rwanda (ICTR) 191
The International Criminal Court (ICC) 191
4. Hybrid Courts and Other Internationalized Domestic Courts and Tribunals 193
The Special Court for Sierra Leone (SCSL) 194
The Extraordinary Chambers of Cambodia 195
The Special Tribunal for Lebanon (STL) 196
Other internationalized tribunals 196
5. Immunities before International Courts 197
Personal immunity 197
Immunity before the ICTY and ICTR 198
Immunity before the ICC 199
Immunity before the SCSL 203
6. Conclusion 204

Selected Bibliography 207
Index 213

Table of Cases

INTERNATIONAL COURTS AND TRIBUNALS

European Court of Human Rights

Association SOS Attentats v France, 4 October 2006 (App No 76642/01) 2006 BYIL 77 45
Colombani and Others v France (App No 51279/99), 25 June 2002 70
Kalegoropoulou and Ors v Greece and Germany (App No 59021/00) ECHR Rep 2002-X 417, 129 ILR 537, 12 December 2002 170
McElhinney v Ireland [2001] 34 EHRR 322, 123 ILR 73 165
Ould Dah v France, Decision on Admissibility (App No 13113/03), 17 March 2009, [2009] 48 ILM 869 158

European Court of Justice

Hungary v Slovakia (C-364/10) Judgment 16 October 2012 58

'International Arbitral Tribunals'

Mallen (Mexico v United States), (1927) 4 RIAA 173 .... 143, 145
Rainbow Warrior (NZ v France)(1986), 74 ILR 241 161

International Court of Justice

Aegean Sea Continental Shelf Case (Greece v Turkey) [1978] ICJ Rep 3 113
Armed Activities on the Territory of the Congo (DRC v Rwanda) (Jurisdiction and Admissibility) (2006) ICJ Rep 6 .... 41, 128
Arrest Warrant of 11 April 2000 (DRC v Belgium) Judgment ICJ Reports 2002, 128 ILR 60 .... 5, 10, 21, 22, 25, 26, 35, 48, 63, 76, 81, 96, 112, 120, 121, 123–8, 131–3, 136, 149, 153, 157, 171, 176, 181, 197, 203
Case Concerning Application of the International Convention on the Elimination of All Forms of Racial Discrimination CERD (Georgia v Russian Federation) (2011) ICJ Rep 70 32
Case Concerning the Application of the Genocide Convention Preliminary Objections (1996) ICJ Rep 4 39
Certain Criminal Proceedings in France (Republic of the Congo v France) Provisional Measures Order [2003] ICJ Rep 70 42
Certain Criminal Proceedings in France (Congo v France) (2003) ICJ 102 ...... 23, 66, 80, 129
Certain Matters of Mutual Assistance in Criminal Matters (Djibouti v France) [2008] ICJ Rep 177 ....7, 23, 49, 57, 63–5, 79, 122, 129, 136, 159, 160, 173, 175
Genocide Convention Case (1951) ICJ Rep 15, 18 ILR 364 41
Jurisdictional Immunities of the State (Germany v Italy) [2012] ICJ Rep 10, 24, 139, 152, 154, 165, 170
Land and Maritime Boundary between Cameroon and Nigeria (2002) ICJ Rep 89 40
Legal Status of Eastern Greenland (Denmark v Norway) PCIJ Rep Series A/B No 53/71 .... 38, 40, 113
Maritime Delimitation and Territorial Questions between Qatar and Bahrain (1994) ICJ Rep 112, 102 ILR 1 .... 40, 113
Nuclear Tests cases (Australia v France, New Zealand v France) (1974) ICJ Rep 267 ...... 38, 40

Questions relating to the Obligation to Prosecute or Extradite (Belgium v Senegal) ICJ Rep 20 . . . . . 3, 155
Western Sahara Case ICJ Rep (1975) ICJ Rep 12 29

International Criminal Tribunal for Rwanda

Prosecutor v Kambanda, ICTR T Ch I 4 September 1998, ICTR A Ch 19 October 2000 191

International Criminal Tribunal for the former Yugoslavia

Prosecutor v Blaskic, Judgment on the Request of the Republic of Croatia for Review of the decision of Trial Chamber II, (IT-95-14-AR 108) Appeals Chamber, (1997) 110 ILR 607 . . . . . 23, 137, 149, 154, 162, 205
Prosecutor v Krstic, Decision on Application for Subpoenas, (IT-98-33-T) Appeals Chamber 17 September 2003 198
Prosecutor v Milutinovic, Reasons for Decision dismissing Interlocutory Appeal Concerning Jurisdiction over territory of Kosovo, (IT-99-37-AR72.2, A Ch.) 8 June 2004 189
Prosecutor v Tadic, Decision on the Defence Motion for Interlocutory Appeal on Jurisdiction, Appeals Chamber (IT-94-I-AR72 70) 105 ILR 159, (1996) 35 ILM 32 189
The Republic of Macedonia, (IT-02-55-Misc.6,T.Ch I) 4 October 2002 189

International Military Tribunals

Goering (1946), Nuremberg International Military Tribunal, Judgment and sentences (1947) 41 AJIL 172 184
In Hirota and Others, Re (1948) Tokyo Military Tribunal, Ann Digest, 15 (1948) 356, 373–4 185

Special Court for Sierra Leone

Prosecutor v Taylor, Case No SCSL-2003-01-1 ICL 25 (Appeals Chamber 2004) Decision on Immunity from Jurisdiction 195

NATIONAL JURISDICTIONS

Australia

Minister for Foreign Affairs and Trade & Ors v Magno & Anor [1992]101 ILR 202 71
Thor Shipping A/S v The Ship 'Al Duhail' [2008] FCA 1842 92

Austria

Dralle v Republic of Czechoslovakia (Austria) 17 ILR 155 17
Nobili v Charles II of Austria, Ann Digest, I (1919–22) No 90 . . . . . 89, 90
Prince of X Road Accident Case (1964) 65 ILR 13 (Austria, Supreme Court) 83, 97
W v Prince of Liechtenstein & Ors, Austria Supreme Court, 15 February 2001, Oxford Reports on International Law, ILDC, 1 . . . . . 83, 91, 106

Belgium

Charron v Evans et gouvernment Belge (1915–16) 11–12 RDIP 208–14 50
Mobutu v SA Cotoni (1988) 91 ILR 259 (Civil Court of Brussels) 92, 99, 106
Sharon and Yaron, Re (2003) 127 ILR 110, Belgium (Court of Cassation (Second Chamber)) (2003) 42 ILM 596 . . . . . 25, 124, 155

Canada

Bouzari v Islamic Republic of Iran, 124 ILR 428 (Ontario Superior Court of Justice, 2002) and 128 ILR 586 (Court of Appeal for Ontario, 2004) . . . 141
Jaffe v Miller and Others, 95 ILR 446 (Ontario Court of Appeal 1993) . . . 144
Schreiber v Canada (Attorney General) 2002 SCC 62, paras 32 and 35–6 (Can SC 2002) . . . 164

France

Ali Ali Reza v Grimpel, (Court of Appeal of Paris, 1961) . . . 123
'Donald Rumsfeld Case', Decision of Public Prosecutor, Paris Court of Appeal, 27 February 2008 . . . 157
Emperor of Austria v Lemaitre, Paris, Ct of Appeal, 15 March 1872, JDI (1874) . . . 32, 85
Farouk, Ex King of Egypt v SARL Christian Dior (1957) 84 JDI 716 (Cour d' Appel de Paris 1957), A-C Kiss vol III (1965) 271, (1957) 24 ILR 228 . . . 92, 176
Ghadaffi, (no 1414 2001), 125 ILR 456, 490 (France: Cour de cassation) . . . 24, 82
Heritiers de L'Empereur Maximilien de Mexique v Lemaitre, French Court of Appeal, Dalloz II (1873) 24, 15, 4, 1872, Clunet I (1974) 32 . . . 91
Investigation of Assets Re 'Bien Mal Acquis' Case, Transparency International, partie civile, (Court of Cassation) Case No 6092, decision of 9 November 2010. . . . 67, 68, 80, 100
Isabelle de Bourbon v Mellerio (1874) 1 JDI 32 (France, Cour de Paris, 1872) . . . 89
Jean Desses v Prince Farouk et Dame Sadek (1964) 91 JDI 285 (Tribunal de la Seine, 1963), 65 ILR 37 . . . 92, 176
Jean Francois N'Dengue, Re (Versailles Court of Appeal) Chambre de l'instruction, 10eme chamber section A, judgment 20 June 2007 . . . 135
Ministere Public v Dlle Masset A-C Kiss, Repertoire de la pratique francaise en matiere de droit international public (1965) iii, 269 (France, Cour de Paris, 1870) . . . 85
Mobutu and Republic of Zaire v Societe Logrine (Court of Appeal of Paris 1994) . . . 90
Wiercinski v Seyyid Ali Ben Hamond (1917) 44 JDI 1465 (France, Tribunal civil de la Seine, 1916) . . . 89

Germany

Centre for Constitutional Rights et al v Donald Rumsfeld et al, Decision of German Federal Prosecutor, 10 February 2005, (2006) ILM 119 . . . 157
Church of Scientology Case, (Supreme Court 1978) 65 ILR 193 . . . 166, 167
Dover Castle (1922) 16 AJIL 704 . . . 183
Former Syrian Ambassador to the German Democratic Republic, (Federal Constitutional Court, 1997)115 ILR 595, [1998] AJIL 74 . . . 144
Honecker, Re, (1984) 80 ILR 365 . . . 24, 81
Landovery Castle, (1922) 16 AJIL 708 . . . 183
Tabatabai, Re (1978) 80 ILR 389 . . . 146
The Staschynskij, Case 18 FRG Bundesgerichtshof 1962 . . . 162

Greece

Margellos v Federal Republic of Germany (A.E.D) Special Supreme Court 6/2002 129 ILR 525 . . . 170

Hong Kong

Democratic Republic of the Congo v FG Hemisphere Associates [2011]147 ILR 376; PRC HKSAR CFA (2011) . . . 17

India

Maharaj Indrajitsinghji Vijaysinghji v HH Maharaja Rajendrasinghji Vijaysinghji (1955) 22 ILR 244 93
Mandalsa Kumari v Ramnarin (Private) Ltd (1958) 27 ILR 109 93
Rewa Shankar v Narasinghji Maharaj (1957) 24 ILR 229 99
Thakore Saheb Khanji Kashari v Gulam Rasul Chandbhal (1955)22 ILR 253 97

Ireland

McElhinney v Williams and Her Majesty's Secretary of State for Northern Ireland [1995] 104 ILR 691, 703 (Ireland SC) 164

Israel

Attorney General of Israel v Eichmann, 36 ILR 5 (District Court of Jerusalem 1961) . . . 149, 150

Italy

Ferrini v Federal Republic of Germany, (Court of Cassation, 2004) 87 RDI 539 152
General Prosecutor of Milan v Adler and Ors (Case No 46340/2012) ILDC 1960 (2012) 27, 148
Italy v DM (Djukanovic), ILDC 74 (2004) 46, 53, 56
Italy v Lozano (Case No 31171// 24 July 2008) ILDC 1085 (2008) 27, 148

Malasyia

Village Holdings Sdn Bhd v HM the Queen in Right of Canada (1987) 87 ILR 223 87

The Netherlands

Bouterse, Bouterse Re, Hof Amsterdam, 20 November 2000, NJ 2001, 51, (2001) 32 Netherlands Yearbook of International Law 97–118 . . . . . 151, 155
Church of Scientology in the Netherlands Foundation and Ors v Herold and Heinrich Bauer Verlag [1978] 65 ILR 193, 380 166
HH and HJ and Sebastien Nzapali, decision of 7 April 2004 (District Court of Rotterdam) 158
JAM v Public Prosecutor, Netherlands Supreme Court, 21 January 1969, YBIL (1970) 222, 73 ILR 387 63

New Zealand

Fang v Jiang [2007] NZAR 420 HC NZ 27, 170
R v Mafart and Prieur 74 ILR 241 161
Wakim v Ya'alon, Ex parte Application for issue of arrest warrant to arrest General Moshe Ya'alon (District Court, Auckland, Civ-2006-004) 27 November 2006. . . . . 155, 158

Philippines

Holy See v The Hon Eriberto U Rosario Jnr as Presiding Judge of Regional Trial Court of Makati, Branch 61 and Starbright Sales Enterprises Inc (Philippines Supreme Court) cited by ILC Special Rapporteur Kolodkin in Third Report on Immunity of State Officials from Foreign Criminal Jurisdiction (A/CN.4/646 24) May 2011 53

Senegal

Habre, Re (Court of Appeal of Dakar) 4 July 2000, Court of Cassation, (20 March 2001); 125 ILR 569 . . . . . 3, 155, 196

Spain

Fidel Castro, Re (Case No 1999/2723 Audiencia Nacional 1999), (1999) 32 ILM 596 82

Paul Kagame, Re (Audiencia Nacional Ruling of 6 February 2008), discussed J Int Crim Justice (2008) 6(5)1003-1011 .... 24, 83
Sala v Kabarebe, Indictment, IDLC 1198 (2008) 159

Switzerland

Evgeny Adamov v Federal Office of Justice, Swiss Federal Tribunal, No 1A.288/2005, Judgment of 22 December 2005 .... 25, 129, 177
'FN Case', Military Court of Appeal, 1A of 26 May 2000 and Military Court of Cassation of 27 April 2001 158
Habib Ammar, Re, Decision of Attorney General of Canton of Geneva, 23 September 2003 156
Khaled Nezzar, Re decision 25 July 2012, Swiss Federal Criminal Court 130
Marcos and Associates v Chambre d'accusation, Geneva (1987) 82 ILR 53 177
Marcos and Marcos v Federal Department of Police (1989 Swiss Federal Tribunal) 102 ILR 198 .... 11, 81, 103

United Kingdom

Apex Global Management Ltd v Fi Call Ltd and Ors (11 June 2013) EWCA Civ 642, [2013] WLR (D) 228 .... 33, 94, 107, 125
Arantzazu Mendi, The [1939] AC 256 47
Aziz v Aziz & Sultan of Brunei (11 July 2007) EWCA Civ 712 .... 4, 63, 68, 69
Barak, Ehud, Re (City of Westminster Mag Ct) 2009, unreported 26, 130
BCCI v Price Waterhouse (No 4) [1997] 4 All ER 108, 111 ILR 604 .... 46, 87, 94
Bo Xilai, Re, 128 ILR 713 (Bow St Mag Ct) 8 November 2005 .... 26, 130, 131
British Arab Commercial Bank Plc v The National Transitional Council of the State of Libya (25 August 2011) EWHC 2274 47
Buttes Gas and Oil Co v Hammer [1982] AC 888 86
de Haber v Queen of Portugal (1851) 17 QB 171 .... 15, 85
Duff Development v Kelantan [1924] AC 797 46
Duke of Brunswick v King of Hanover (1848) 2 HL, Cas 1 .... 15, 85, 86, 89, 142
Gaekwar of Baroda State Railways v Hafi Habib-ul-Haq, Ann Digest 9 (1938-40) no 78 (18 March 1938, PC) 97
Gorbachev, Re, (City of Westminster Mag Ct) 30 March 2011, unreported ; BYIL (2012) 570 .... 133, 157
HRH Sultan of Pahang v SSHD (25 May 2011) EWCA Civ 616 .... 47, 48
Haile Selassie v Cable and Wireless Ltd (1939) Ch 182 51
Haile Selassie v Evening Standard Co Ltd, *The Times* 28 July 1938 70
Harb v King Fahd Abdul Aziz [2005] EWCA Civ 632, [2006] 1 WLR 578 (CA) 4, 63, 68
Her Majesty's Advocate v Al Megrahi (High Court of Justiciary), Camp Zeist Case No 1475/99 161
Holland v Lampen-Wolffe [2000] 1 WLR 1573, [2000] 3 All ER 833 .... 137, 146
I Congreso del Partido [1981] 2 All ER 1064, 64 ILR 307 17
Ionian Ships, The (1855) 2 Ecc & Ad 212, 1 BILC 635 37
Jones v Ministry of Interior of the Kingdom of Saudi Arabia [2006] UKHL 26, [2007] 1 AC 270, [2006] 2 WLR 70, 129 ILR 713 .....9, 27, 139, 141, 152, 169, 170, 171
Khurts Bat v Investigating Judge of the German Federal Court and others [29 July 2011] EWHC 2029 (Admin) 26, 129, 134, 162
Kuwait Airways Corpn v Iraqi Airways (Nos 4 & 5) [2002] 2 AC 883; 125 ILR 608 47
Littrell v USA (No 2) [1995] 1 WLR 82 146
Mbasogo, President of the State of Equatorial Guinea and Another v Logo Ltd and Others [2005] EWHC 2034 (QB), (2006) EWCA Civ 1370 87
Mighell v Sultan of Johore [1894] 1 QB 149 .... 16, 90, 98

Mofaz, Re, 128 ILR 709 (Bow St Mag Ct) 12 February 2004 . . . . 25, 130
Mugabe, Re (Bow St Mag Ct) 14 January 2004, unreported but see (2004) 53 ICLQ 769-70 . . . . 24, 82
Occidental Exploration & Production Co v Republic of Ecuador, (2005) EWCA Civ 1370, [2006] QB 432 87
P v P (Diplomatic Immunity and Jurisdiction), 22 January 1998, [1998] Times LR 119; 114 ILR 485 . . . . 146, 147
Piracy Iure Gentium, Re [1934] AC 586 181
Planmount Ltd v Republic of Zaire [1981] 1 All ER 1110, 64 ILR 268 17
Pocket Kings Ltd v Safenames [2010] Ch 438, (EWHC) 2009 47
Propend Finance Pty Ltd v Sing [1997] 111 ILR 611(CA) 11, 138, 167, 169
Rani Amrit Kunwar v Commissioner of Income Tax, 21 December 1945, (1955) 22 ILR 680 103
R v Bow Street Metropolitan Stipendiary Magistrate ex parte Pinochet (No 1 [2000] 1 AC 61, HL), 119 ILR 49 . . . . 55, 56, 93, 137, 148
R v Bow Street Metropolitan Stipendiary Magistrate, ex parte Pinochet Ugarte (No 3) [2000] 1 AC 147, HL, 119 ILR 135 . . . . 3, 7, 18, 24, 26, 55, 81, 93, 137, 144, 148, 150–4, 164, 170, 203
R v Commissioner of Police for the Metropolis CO/129/2000, unreported, *The Times*, 20 October 1999 73
R v Jones [2006] UKHL 16, 132 ILR 668 181
R v Lambeth Justices, ex parte Yusufu [1985] Crim LR 510, [1985] Times LR 114 161
R v Roques, Acquittal by Chief Metropolitan Magistrate, 1 August 1984, unreported 71
R (on the application of Alamieyeseigha) v Crown Prosecution Service [2005] EWHC 2704 (Admin); ILDC 93 (2005) 48
Republic of Haiti v Duvalier [1990] 1 QB 202 178
Republic of Italy v Hambros Bank Ltd [1950] 1 Ch 314 101
Republic of Somalia v Woodhouse Drake & Carey (Suisse) SA, The Mar [1993] 1 QB 54, [1993] 1 All ER 371 45
Salaman v Secretary of State for India [1906] 1 KB 613, 1 BILC 594 (CA) 36
Sayce v Ameer, Ruler of Bahawalpur State [1952] 2 QB 90
Sierra Leone Telecommunications Ltd v Barclays Bank Plc [1998] 2 All ER 821 45
Statham v Statham and the Gaekwar of Baroda [1912] P 92 90
Sultan of Johore v Abubakar Tunku Aris Bendahar [1952] AC 318, 19 ILR 192 . . . . 46, 99
Trendtex Trading Corpn Ltd v Central Bank of Nigeria [1977] 2 WLR 356, 64 ILR 122 . . . 17, 94
Zoernsch v Waldock [1964] 1 WLR 675 (CA) 11, 167
Zog, King of the Albanians v Sunday Pictorial Newspapers (1920) Ltd, *The Times* 28 May 1943 70

United States

Ahmed v Magan, No 2:10-cv-34 SD Ohio 15 Mar 2011 (US District Court for Southern District of Ohio) ;US Digest 2011. 344 174
Al Hassan v Al Nahyan, No 09-01106 (C.D Calif) 17 September 2010 (unreported) 84
Alicog et al v Kingdom of Saudi Arabia et al 860 F Supp 379 (District Court for the Southern District of Texas, 1994) 84
Anonymous v Anonymous (1992) 581 NYS 2d 776 90
Balcero Giraldo v Drummond 808 F Supp 2d (DDC 2011);US Digest 2011 346-9; No 11-7118 (Ct of Appeals DC Cir 23 October 2012) 172
Belhas v Ya'alon, 515 F 3d 1279, (US Court of Appeals DC Cir 2008) 27, 171, 172
Boos v Barry [1988] 485 US 312 73
Caroline and McLeod Cases (1938) 32 AJIL 82 138

Chong Boon Kim v Kim Yong Shik and David Kim (1963) 81 ILR 604, (Ct of Appeals 1st Circ), (1964); 58 AJIL 186 . . . . . 25, 123
Chuidian v Philippine National Bank 912 F 2d 1095 (1990) 58
Daventree Ltd v Republic of Azerbaijan No 2-6356 (S.D.N.Y) 10 March and 15 October 2003; US Digest 2003, 571 . . . . . 84, 123
Doe 1 v Archdiocese of Galveston-Houston, Civ Action No H-05-1047 (SD Tex) 30
Doe v Ernesto Zedillo Ponce de Leon (Suggestion of Immunity of 7 September 2012 in respect of former President of Mexico) No 3: 11-cv-01433-AWT, 18 July 2013, US District Ct, District of Connecticut; US Digest 2012, 345 . . . . . 57, 142, 145
Doe I v State of Israel, 400 F Supp. 2d 86 (DC 2005) 123
Estate of Silme G Domingo v Ferdinand Marcos (1983) 77 AJIL 305 107
Filartiga v Pena-Irala 630 F.2d 876 (Ct of Appeals 2nd Cir 1980) 171
First American Corpn v Al-Nahayan 948 F Supp 1107 (1996), 121 ILR 577 . . . . . 58, 84, 88
Fotso v Cameroon et al, No 12-01415 (D Ore. 2012); US Digest 2012 346 84
Guevara v Peru and Ors 468 F.3d 1289 (11th Circ 2006) ILDC 804 (US 2006) 140
Guinto v Marcos (1986) 654 F.Supp 276 86
HRH Prince Turki Bin Abdulaziz v Metropolitan Dade County (1984) 741 F.2d 1328 105
Habyarimana v Kagame 696 F 3d 1029 (10th Cir 2012);US Digest 2011, 349-51 and US Digest 2012, 333–36 . . . . . 24, 54
Hatch v Baez, 7 Hun 596 (NY Sup Ct 1876) 7, 166
Herbage v Meese, 747 F Supp (DC Cir 1990); 98 ILR 101 144
Hilao v Estate of Ferdinand Marcos (1994) 25 F.3d 171 171
Islamic Republic of Iran v Pahlavi (1984) 81 ILR 557 178
Jean-Juste v Duvalier (1988) No-86-0459 Civ (US District Court), SD Fla, (1988) 82 AJIL 594 176
Jimenez v Aristeguieta 311 F 2d 547 (Ct of Appeals 5th Cir 1962) 18, 31, 145, 176
Junquist et al v Sheikh Sultan Bin Khalifa Al Nayhan et al, 940 F.Supp 312 (US 1996) 107
Kadic v Karadzic (1995) 34 ILM 1592, 70 F.3d 232, 245 (2nd Circ 1995) 43, 143
Kendall et al v Kingdom of Saudi Arabia et al (1966) 60 AJIL 100 84
Kilroy v Windsor, Prince of Wales 1978 Digest of US Practice in International Law 641, 81 ILR 605 . . . . . 105, 133
Kiobel v Royal Dutch Petroleum Co 133 S.Ct. 1659 (2013) 171
Kline v Cordero de la Madrid 546 NYS 2d 506 (New York State Ct of Appeals 1989) 107
Kline v Kaneko685 F.Supp 386 (District Court for the Southern District of New York, 1988) 101 ILR 497 107
Lafontant v Aristide 844 F Supp 128 (District Ct for Eastern District of New York 1994); (1994) 88 AJIL 528–32; 103 ILR 581 . . . . . 18, 24, 31, 43, 44, 53, 54, 90, 93
Letelier v Republic of Chile 488 F Supp 665 (DDC 1980); 63 ILR 378; 79 ILR 561 . . . . . 16, 164
Leutwyler v Queen Rania Al- Abdullah184 F.Supp.2d 277, 280 (SDNY 2001) 107
Li Weixum v Bo Xilai 568 F Supp 2d 35 (DCC 2008) 25, 133
Mamani et al v Sanchez de Lozada and Sanchez Berzain (US Ct of Appeals 11th Cir 29 August 2011) 171
Manoharan v Rajapaksa F Supp 2d 2012 WL 642446 (US Ct of Appeals DDC) 9 February 2012; US Digest 2012 339-45 . . . . . 24, 54, 84
Matar v Dichter, 563 F.3d.9 (2nd Circ, 2009) 27, 58, 171, 172
McLeod and Caroline Cases (1938) 32 AJIL 82 138
O'Hair v Wotjyla 81 ILR 607; (District Ct for District of Columbia, 1979) 30, 86
Republic of the Philippines v Marcos (nos 1 & 2) 806 F 2d 344 (Ct of Appeals 2nd Cir 1986) 665 F Supp 793 (District Ct for Northern District of California, 1987) 178
Rhanime v Solomon, No 01-1479 (D.C.D 15 May 2002) 25, 125

Rosenberg et al v Lashkar- e- Taiba et al, Nos 10-05381, 10-05382, 10-05448, 11-03893 (District Ct for Eastern District of New York 2012); US Digest 2012, 231 . . . . . 58, 146
Saltany v Reagan 886 F 2d 438 (Ct of Appeals DC, 1989); 80 ILR 19 and 87 ILR 680 . . . . . 5, 25, 123, 124
Samantar v Yousef 130 S Ct 2278 (2010); US Digest 2010, 397–428 . . . . . 57, 139, 168, 172–3
Schooner Exchange v McFaddon (1812) 7 Cranch 116, (1812) 11 US 116 . . . . . 15, 62, 89, 99
State of Russia v National City Bank of New York, Ann Digest, 7 (1933–34), No 26 113
Tachiona v Mugabe 169 F.Supp 2d 259 (District Ct for Southern District of New York, 2001) 24, 25, 54, 79, 93
Tachiona v United States 386 F.3d 205, 2004 Ct of App (2nd Cir 6 Oct 2004) 78, 125
Tawfik v Al Sabah, 2012 WL 3542209 (District Ct for Southern District of New York, 2012); US Digest 2012 345 84
Underhill v Hernandez 168 US 250 (S Ct, 1897) 166
United States v Al-Nashiri, Opinion of Judge of Military Commission of 17 February 2012; US Digest 2012 347-8 82
United States v Classic 313 US 299, 326 (1941) 143
United States v Noriega, 746 F.Supp 1506, (1990) 99 ILR 145 . . . . . 31, 44, 176
Wei Ye v Jiang Zemin 383 F 3d 620 (7th Cir 2004) 24, 54, 65, 79
West v Atkins 487 US 49 (1988) 143
Xuncax v Gramajo (1995) 886 F.Supp 162 171
Yousef v Samantar, 699 F 3d 764 (4th Cir 2012); US Digest 2012, 324 173

Table of Treaties and Legislation

INTERNATIONAL INSTRUMENTS

Agreement between the United Nations and the United States Regarding the Head Quarters of the United Nations 1947
- s 11 60
- s 12 60

Charter of the Tokyo Tribunal 1946
- Art 6 186

Code of Offences Against the Peace and Security of Mankind 1954 (Draft) (A/2693 & (1954) 45 AJIL Supp, 123), Art 1 187

Convention Against Torture and Other Cruel, Inhuman or Degrading Treatment or Punishment 1984 (1465 UNTS 113) (UNCAT) 57, 143, 151, 152, 156, 187
- Art 1 187
- Art 14 . . . . 169, 170

Convention for the Protection of All Persons from Enforced Disappearance 2006 187
- Art 2 153

Convention on the Elimination of All Forms of Discrimination Against Women 1979 (GA Res 34/180; UNTS, Vol 1015, 243) 33

Convention on the Prevention and Punishment of Crimes Against Internationally Protected Persons, including Diplomatic Agents 1973 . . . . 21, 65, 75, 120, 129
- Art 1(1)(a) 104, 119
- Art 1(1)(b) 109, 126
- Art 2(3) 62

Convention on the Suppression and Punishment of the Crime of Apartheid 1973 187

European Convention on Human Rights and Fundamental Freedoms 1950, Art 10 70

European Convention on State Immunity 1972, Art 31 165

Genocide Convention 1948 188
- Art IV 186

Geneva Conventions 1949 . . . . 187–91, 195
- Art 3 194
- IV Art 147 . . . . 25, 130
- Additional Protocols 1977 187
- Additional Protocol II 194

Geneva Convention on the High Seas 1958
- Art 15 182
- Art 19 181

International Convention on the Elimination of All Forms of Racial Discrimination 1966 32

International Covenant on Civil and Political Rights 1966 (ICCPR), Art 19 64

International Law Commission Articles on State Responsibility 2001 (ILC Articles) 165
- Art 1 179
- Art 2 179
- Art 2.2 141
- Art 3 . . . . 132, 144
- Art 4 . . . . 139, 179
- Art 5 . . . . 139, 180
- Art 7 . . . . 143, 145, 180
- Art 12 141
- Art 19 . . . . 141, 180
- Art 40.2 180
- Art 41 180
- Art 41.2 50
- Art 58 180

Law of the Sea Convention 1982 (UNCLOS)
- Art 99 181
- Art 101 182
- Art 105 181

New York Convention on Special Missions 1969 . . . . 93, 115
- Art 7(2) 113
- Art 21 . . . . 113, 125, 129
- Art 21(1) 20, 21

Art 21(2) 21, 116
Art 25 120
Art 25(2) 119
Art 27 117
Art 28 . . . . 60, 118
Art 29 . . . . 62, 63, 118, 120
Art 30 119
Art 31 . . . . 122, 125
Art 32 126
Art 33 101
Art 34 126
Art 35 . . . . 101, 126
Art 39 126
Art 39(1) 103, 104
Art 41 . . . . 89, 97, 98

Nuremberg Charter 1946 186

Resolution of L'Institut de Droit International on Immunities from Jurisdiction and Execution of Heads of State and of Government in International Law, Thirteenth Commission, 26 August 2001
Art 3 91
Art 4(1) 100

Statute of the International Criminal Court 1998 (ICC Statute) 187
Art 5(1) 192
Art 11 192
Art 12(3) 192
Art 13 200
Art 13(b) 192
Art 27 193
Art 27(2) 195, 197, 199, 204
Art 33 141
Art 86 199
Art 89 199
Art 98(1) 193, 199, 200, 205
Art 120 199

Statute of the International Criminal Tribunal for Rwanda 1994 (ICTR) 191, 194, 198, 201, 202
Art 1 191
Art 3 191
Art 4 191
Art 6 191
Art 8(1) 191

Statute of the International Criminal Tribunal for the Former Yugoslavia 2009 (ICTY) . . . 191, 194, 198, 201, 202
Arts 2–5 189
Art 7 . . . . 189, 191
Art 42 190

Statute of the Special Court for Sierra Leone 2002 (SCSL) 203–4
Art 2 195
Art 20 194

Treaty of Friendship Bhutan/India 1949 . . . 34

Treaty of Friendship Bhutan/India 2007 . . . 34

Treaty of Rome 1957 39

Treaty of Versailles 1919, Arts 227–229 . . . 183

United Nations Charter 1945
Ch VII 189, 192, 196, 198, 200, 203
Art 7 184
Art 25 198
Art 41 198
Art 49 198
Art 103 198

UN Convention on Jurisdictional Immunities of States and Their Property 2004 . . . . 17, 86
Art 2(1)(b) 97, 139
Art 2(1)(b)(i) 20, 86, 167
Art 2(1)(b)(iv) 20, 23, 27, 86, 139, 167
Art 3 . . . . 88, 99
Art 3(2)(b) 20
Art 7 98
Arts 7–9 97
Art 8 98
Art 12 164
Art 13 . . . . 99, 100
Art 14 100
Art 16 100
Art 21(2) 115

Vancouver Resolution on the Immunities from Jurisdiction and Execution of Heads of State and of Governments in International Law 2012, Art 2 82

Vienna Convention on Consular Relations 1963 19

Vienna Convention on Diplomatic Relations 1961 (VCDR) . . . 18–19, 62, 129
Art 22 . . . . 72, 77
Art 22.2 71
Art 25 77
Art 27 60
Art 28 77
Art 29 . . . . 19, 64, 65, 68, 72, 74, 75, 77, 79, 118
Art 31 . . . . 83, 88, 99
Art 31.1 92
Art 31.1(a) 99
Art 31.1(c) 92
Art 32 . . . . 89, 98

Art 32.1 97
Art 34 101
Art 36 101
Art 37 95
Art 37.1 . . . . 104, 105, 127
Art 37.4 109
Art 39 . . . . 140, 147
Art 39.2 . . . . 9, 84, 137, 140, 143
Art 41.2 112
Vienna Convention on the Law of Treaties 1969 (1155 UNTS 331)
Art 2.1(a) 38
Art 7 129
Art 7.2 . . . . 39, 113, 115
Art 7.2(a) 39, 97
Art 46 38
Art 46.2 38
Art 53 181

NATIONAL LEGISLATION

Australia

Diplomatic Privileges and Immunities Act 1967 92
Foreign States Immunity Act 1985
s 6 165
s 36(1) 92, 93, 99, 104–5

France

Act of 29 July 1881, s 36 70

Israel

Torture Victim Protection Act 1992 (Pub Law 102-256) 171

Japan

Constitution 1889, Art 1 42

Malaysia

Constitution 1963, Art 32 34

Netherlands

Criminal Code 2005, Art 118 69
Penal Code 1858 .183

Singapore

State Immunity Act 1979, s 19(2)(a) 165

Spain

Law of Succession 1947 33

Switzerland

Swiss Criminal Code 1937, Art 296 50

United Kingdom

Act of Association 1584 . . . . 13, 14
Aircraft Security Act 1982 161
Coroners and Justice Act 2009, s 73 69
Criminal Justice Act 1988, s 134 57
Diplomatic Privileges Act 1964 . . . . 8, 77, 93, 137
s 4 55
Diplomatic Privileges (Extension) Act 1941 50
Geneva Conventions Act 1957, s 1 . . . 26, 130
Immigration Act 1971 59
International Criminal Court Act 2001
s 23 199
s 23(4) 200
Matrimonial Causes Act 1973 68
Police Reform and Social Responsibility Act 2011, s 153 157
Regency Acts 1937–1953 32
State Immunity Act 1978 . . . . 86, 93, 138
s 14(1) 139, 167
s 14(5) 47
s 16(2) 165
s 20 . . . . 8, 47, 77, 94, 99, 109, 116
s 20(1) 55, 59, 104, 109
s 20K 68

United States

Act for the Protection of Foreign Officials and Official Guests of the United States 1972 (1973) 67 AJIL 622 .69
Foreign Sovereign Immunities Act 1976 (FSIA) 58, 93

List of Abbreviations

AC	Appeal Cases (Law Reports)
All ER	All England Law Reports
ADIL	Annual Digest of Public International Law
AJIL	American Journal of International Law
ATS	Alien Tort Statute
BDIL	British Digest of International Law
BYIL	British Yearbook of International Law
Can YIL	Canadian Yearbook of International law
CAVV	Commissie van advies inzake volkenrechtelijke Vraagstukken / Advisory Committee on Issues of Public Law (Netherlands)
Ch	Chancery Division
DPA	Diplomatic Privileges Act
DRC	Democratic Republic of the Congo
ECHR	European Convention for the Protection of Human Rights and Fundamental Freedoms
ECtHR	European Court of Human Rights
ECJ	European Court of Justice
EJIL	European Journal of International Law
EWCA	England and Wales Court of Appeal
EWHC	England and Wales High Court
FCO	Foreign and Commonwealth Office
FRY	Federal Republic of Yugoslavia
FSIA	Foreign Sovereign Immunities Act
F.Supp	Federal Supplement
HKCFA	Hong Kong Court of Final Appeal
HL	House of Lords
ICC	International Criminal Court
ICCPR	International Covenant on Civil and Political Rights
ICJ	International Court of Justice
ICLQ	International and Comparative Law Quarterly
ICTR	International Criminal Tribunal for Rwanda
ICTY	International Criminal Tribunal for the Former Yugoslavia
ILC	International Law Commission
ILDC	Oxford Reports on International Law in Domestic Courts
ILM	International Legal Materials
ILR	International Law Reports
IMT	International Military Tribunal (Nuremberg)
JICJ	Journal of International Criminal Justice
LQR	Law Quarterly Review

MPEPIL	Max Planck Encyclopaedia of Public International Law
NGO	Non-Governmental Organization
NYIL	Netherlands Yearbook of International Law
NZLR	New Zealand Law Reports
PCIJ	Permanent Court of International Justice
PTC	Pre-Trial Chamber
PD	Probate, Divorce and Admiralty Division
QB, QBD	Queen's Bench Division (Law Reports)
RBDI	Revue Belge de Droit International
RdC	Recueil de Cours
RDIP	Revue de Droit International Prive
RGDIP	Revue generale de droit international publique
RIAA	Reports of International Arbitral Awards
SCR	Security Council Resolution
SCSL	Special Court for Sierra Leone
S.Ct	Supreme Court
SIA	State Immunity Act
STL	Special Tribunal for Lebanon
TVPA	Torture Victim Protection Act
UKMIL	United Kingdom Materials in International Law
UKTS	United Kingdom Treaty Series
UNCAT	United Nations Convention Against Torture
UNCLOS	United Nations Convention on the Law of the Sea
UN Doc	United Nations Document
UNMIK	United Nations Interim Administration Mission in Kosovo
UNTAET	United Nations Transitional Administration
UNTS	United Nations Treaty Series
VCCR	Vienna Convention on Consular Relations
VCDR	Vienna Convention on Diplomatic Relations
VCLT	Vienna Convention on the Law of Treaties
VJIL	Virginia Journal of International Law
WLR	Weekly Law Reports
YBILC	Yearbook of the International Law Commission
YLJ	Yale Law Journal
ZANU-PF	Zimbabwe African National Unions-Patriotic Front

Note on Citations

Citations generally follow OSCOLA (*Oxford Standard for Citation of Legal Authorities*) (revised 2005) at <http://denning.law.ox.uk/published/oscola.shtml>.

Where very recent or unreported cases are concerned they may be most conveniently available via the internet and the URLs of the relevant websites are given.

1

Overview and General Principles

1. Introduction

In recent years the legal position of heads of State and other very senior State representatives has received considerable attention from national and international courts, writers, and practitioners. So much so that it is no longer necessary to preface a study of the subject with the kind of remarks made by Sir Arthur Watts in his early and influential monograph. There he noted that it might, at first sight, seem a somewhat narrow and specialized topic, concerning directly as it does a relatively small group of individuals but added, with impressive perception, that it was worth a closer look than it is often given.

Since 1994 when that monograph was published, the subject has become one of increasing practical concern for both States and individuals in a variety of contexts. As Watts noted, 'To a much greater extent than was formerly the case, senior State representatives are active participants on the international stage, often travelling outside their own States, and being frequently involved in the conduct of international relations'.[1] This trend has continued so that ad hoc high-level meetings now play a regular part in diplomatic activity.[2] In addition there are numerous routine periodic meetings and 'summits' within the framework of various international organizations and other less formal State groupings. In such cases, attendance by heads of State, heads of government and Foreign Ministers may be required but they can also involve a variety of other government ministers and senior officials, for example, within the context of the European Union. Developments in transport and communications have also meant that private travel by heads of State and other high-level State officials and their families has become far more frequent than it was. It is now common for such persons to take regular and often well-publicized visits abroad for such purposes.

[1] Sir A Watts 'The Legal Position in International Law of Heads of States, Heads of Governments and Foreign Ministers' (1994) 247 III Recueil des cours 19.

[2] 'When you become Prime Minister, the first thing they do, after telling you how to launch the nuclear bomb, is to take your passport from you and then the rest of the time trying to get you to travel around the world.' Tony Blair, speaking to the Labour Party Conference in 1998.

Other factors have played their part: an increased media scrutiny of high-level State representatives and their families; the rapid growth of internet communications; and a growing tendency to personalize political affairs. Heads of State and other senior representatives may encourage such attention by travelling with spouses and other family members who may, themselves, participate in separate visits and activities on the international stage. A further complication is the fact that many former heads of State, heads of Government, and other senior representatives remain active in the international sphere long after retirement or loss of office. Sometimes, such activities are carried out under the auspices of a particular international organization but in other cases may be performed more informally in an ad hoc capacity.

All these factors have to be set against a background in which international law, itself, has changed and expanded into new fields. New fields such as the protection of human rights and the development of international criminal law are of particular relevance and are symptomatic of the way in which international law has had to accommodate the needs and demands, not only of States, but also non-State actors, including individuals and non-governmental organizations (NGOs). Such non-State actors have their own agenda which does not necessarily accord priority to the traditional objectives of the old State-centred system. In the words of a former judge of the International Court of Justice (ICJ), 'International law is deepening as well as broadening, for it is now being invoked by corporations and human rights activists in their own courts and in foreign courts'.[3] Of particular note has been the development of principles permitting (and, in some cases, requiring) the exercise by States of extra-territorial jurisdiction in relation to certain international crimes.[4] National case law has often reflected a tension between the rules conferring immunity on foreign States and their officials and principles of human rights.

The position in international law of heads of State and other senior State representatives has been one of the issues at the heart of this debate and, together with the position of other more junior foreign State officials, has become a common feature in national court cases around the world. It is often said that the establishment of the International Criminal Court (ICC) and the ad hoc international criminal tribunals,[5] together with a number of high

[3] Rosalyn Higgins, *Problems and Process: International Law and How We use it* (Oxford University Press, 1994).

[4] See Weller, 'On the Hazards of Foreign Travel for Dictators and other Criminals' (1999) 75(3) International Affairs 599 where he notes: 'As many of the most grave offences to which universality attaches can typically be executed only by state officials, the process of the gradual expansion of legal universalism has obvious implications for the doctrine of immunities from jurisdiction.'

[5] See the trial of Serbian leader Slobodan Milosevic before the International Criminal Tribunal for the Former Yugoslavia (ICTY); the conviction of the former President of Liberia, Charles Taylor, before the International Court for Sierra Leone; the conviction of Rwanda's former Prime Minister,

profile criminal prosecutions of former foreign leaders in national courts,[6] reflects a growing belief that heads of State and other very senior officials should be held accountable for serious violations of international humanitarian and human rights law. Moreover, there has been an increasing number of cases in which private litigants have sought to bring civil claims against States, heads of State, and other senior State officials in foreign jurisdictions. The right of access to a judicial remedy has been a particular focus in such cases.

It has been argued that international law is now at a stage where immunity should no longer apply in relation to serious international crimes. By contrast, others have emphasized the political and practical difficulties inherent in allowing national courts to serve as a tool for the transnational enforcement of penalties or damages for crimes committed abroad by the leaders and officials of foreign States. The resulting controversy has led the International Law Commission (ILC) to include the topic 'Immunity of State officials from Foreign Criminal Jurisdiction' in its work programme.[7] The matter has also been the subject of a review by the US State Department[8] and has prompted several other inquiries and reviews within a variety of governmental and non-governmental contexts.[9]

More generally, national courts and governmental authorities have frequently been faced with questions relating to the legal status, privileges, protection, and 'dignity' of foreign heads of State and their families. In recent

Jean Kambanda, before the International Tribunal for Rwanda (ICTR); and the indictments of the serving President Omar Al Bashir of Sudan and the Libyan leader, Muammar Gadaffi, by the ICC. Laurent Gbagbo was also indicted while he was still President of Cote d'Ivoire and is currently in ICC custody awaiting trial. In addition, the Kenyan President Uhuru Kenyatta is currently facing trial before the ICC.

[6] See eg *R v Bow Street Metropolitan Stipendiary Magistrate, ex parte Pinochet Ugarte (No 3)* [2000] 1 AC 147 (UKHL, 24 May 1999) and proceedings in Belgium against the former President of Chad, Hissene Habre. Belgium has sought to extradite Habre from Senegal where he may also face charges and the ICJ has now ruled that Senegal must extradite or prosecute him without further delay—*Questions relating to the Obligation to Prosecute or Extradite (Belgium v Senegal)* (2012) ICJ Rep.

[7] See Report of the ILC on the Work of its 63rd Session, UN GAOR, 66th Session, para 8, UN Doc A/C.6/66/L.26 (8 November 2011) (draft resolution by the Sixth Committee). Roman Kolodkin, the Special Rapporteur, submitted three reports on the topic. See Preliminary Report, UN Doc A/CN.4//601 (29 May 2008); Second Report, UN Doc A/CN.4/631 (10 June 2010); and Third Report, UN Doc A/CN.4/646 (24 May 2011). See also ILC Secretariat Memorandum, 'Immunity of State Officials from Foreign Criminal Jurisdiction' (31 March 2008,) UN Doc A/CN.4/596). At its 3132nd meeting on 22 May 2012, the Commission appointed Ms Concepcion Escobar Hernandez as the new Special Rapporteur and she has submitted two reports—Preliminary Report, UN Doc A/CN.4/654 and Second Report, UN Doc A/CN.4/./L.184.

[8] See Koh, 'Foreign Official Immunity after Samantar: A United States Government Perspective' (2011) 44 V and J Transnational L 1141, 1152.

[9] See eg *Advisory Report on the Immunity of Foreign State Officials* (No 20 The Hague, May 2011) produced by the Advisory Committee on Issues of Public International Law (Commissie van advies inzake volkenrechtelijke vraagstukken CAVV) at the request of the Netherlands Foreign Minister. See also decision by the African Union to consider seeking an advisory opinion from the ICJ regarding immunities of State officials under international law (see Summit of Assembly of African Union 23–30 January 2012).

years, such cases have covered a wide range of issues including: whether a head of State is entitled to a private hearing for a preliminary plea of immunity in connection with divorce proceedings brought against him;[10] the extent to which a court should be prepared to redact its judgment in order to spare a head of State personal embarrassment;[11] whether the arrest and detention abroad of a head of State's son infringed any rules of customary international law or international comity or courtesy; and whether the wife of a head of State on a private shopping trip abroad should be immune from prosecution.

2. Summary of Key Issues

This study will examine the special treatment, including jurisdictional immunities, privileges, and protection to which heads of State and other high-level State representatives are entitled under international law. In the case of heads of State, this will entail a wider consideration of the position of their family members and members of their entourage. Other aspects of their position are also addressed, for example the various constitutional forms and titles by which such individuals may be identified and the specific powers usually vested in them which have particular relevance for international law. The last section of this book looks at the position of heads of State and other very senior officials before international courts and tribunals, although the main focus is on the often controversial and sometimes ill-defined rules of international law regarding their treatment in foreign jurisdictions.

Any analysis of these rules and their development must also consider a much broader range of jurisdictional immunities relating to States, diplomatic agents, and persons on special mission; all of which are closely interlinked.[12] In order to fully understand how such rules operate in practice, it is also necessary to touch upon questions relating to the recognition of foreign States and governments and the role played by the executive in determining the status of their representatives.

It has long been recognized that a sovereign or other head of State is entitled to extensive privileges and courtesies appropriate to his or her status and dignity when present in the territory of another State and, more generally, to a broad personal immunity from the jurisdiction of that State, including

[10] *Harb v King Fahd Bin Abdul Aziz* [2005] EWCA Civ 632.

[11] *Aziz v Aziz and Sultan of Brunei* [2007] EWCA Civ 712.

[12] See Memorandum by the ILC Secretariat (n 7 above), para 17: 'the various immunities have all followed a varied, albeit interconected historical trajectory'.

absolute inviolability and immunity from criminal prosecution. The position with regard to heads of Government and Foreign Ministers was less fully developed,[13] although the ICJ has now ruled that a Foreign Minister and (by implication) a head of Government are entitled to the same inviolability and extensive jurisdictional immunity as a head of State.[14]

In many respects, therefore, the position of heads of Government and of Foreign Ministers can be discussed by reference to the position of heads of State.[15] However, given the slightly different historical development and rationales underlying their treatment, it is convenient to first consider the position of heads of State and then, in a separate section, consider the particular rules as applied to heads of Government and Foreign Ministers.[16] The wording of the ICJ judgment in the *Arrest Warrant* case suggests that personal immunity may extend beyond Foreign Ministers to other very senior State representatives, but the criteria on which it is suggested such an extension may be made is potentially very broad and has been the subject of criticism.[17] In discussion within the ILC it has been proposed that the circle of persons entitled to such immunities should be limited to the 'troika' of head of State, head of Government, and Minister for Foreign Affairs.[18] This proposal is reflected in the draft articles adopted so far.[19] It is clear, however, that opinion on this issue remains divided within the ILC and among States generally. It is, therefore, convenient to include in the section dealing with heads of Government and Foreign Ministers some consideration of the position of other very senior State officials.[20]

Part 2 of this book is concerned with the position of serving heads of State and Part 3 with serving heads of Government and Foreign Ministers

[13] See Watts, 'The Legal Position in International Law of Heads of States, Heads of Governments and Foreign Ministers' (1994) 247 III Recueil des Cours 20.

[14] *Arrest Warrant of 11 April 2000 (DRC v Belgium)* (2002) ICJ Rep 3. See also the US case *Saltany v Reagan and others* (1988) 80 ILR 19; affirmed (1989) 87 ILR 680.

[15] Nowadays these three are often referred to as the 'troika', picking up a term used by the ILC Special Rapporteur, Roman Kolodkin (see n 7 above).

[16] See section 3 below.

[17] See Akande and Shah, 'Immunities of State Officials, International Crimes, and Foreign Domestic Courts' (2010) 21 EJIL 815.

[18] Second Report of ILC Special Rapporteur, Concepcion Escobar Hernandez, UN Doc A/CN.4/661.

[19] See Second Report of ILC Drafting Committee, UN Doc A/CN.4/L.814. Draft Article 3 provides that: 'Heads of State, Heads of Government and Ministers for Foreign Affairs enjoy immunity ratione personae from the exercise of foreign criminal jurisdiction'.

[20] See Second Report of ILC Special Rapporteur, Roman Kolodkin, on 'Immunity of Senior Officials from Foreign Criminal Jurisdiction' (n 7 above), which noted broad agreement within the ILC that immunity *ratione personae* is enjoyed '*at least*, by Heads of State and Government and also by Ministers of Foreign Affairs', ILC 62nd session, A/CN.4/631 (my italics).

respectively. Both sections examine the special treatment and immunities to which such persons are entitled in foreign jurisdictions while they are in office. Part 4 is also concerned with the position in foreign jurisdictions but considers the position of such persons after loss of office. Inevitably this also entails a much broader consideration of the position of all State officials to which the same principles of functional immunity apply. Part 5 looks at the position of heads of State and other senior State representatives, both incumbent and after loss of office, in regard to international courts and tribunals.

Some of the key questions addressed are:

(i) Is the personal immunity enjoyed by serving heads of State, heads of Government, and Foreign Ministers absolute? Or, is it subject to any exception, for example in relation to civil proceedings for private acts?

(ii) Does it make any difference in regard to the above if the head of State, head of Government, or Foreign Minister is on an official visit or private visit to the forum State?

(iii) Do States still have a duty to protect the dignity of a foreign head of State? If so, what does this mean in practice? Does such a duty extend to heads of governments and other very senior State representatives?

(iv) To what extent, if any, and on what basis may family members or members of a head of State's official entourage be entitled to special treatment?

(v) What other high-level State representatives, if any, may be entitled to personal immunity?

(vi) What is the position of a former head of State or other very senior State representative after leaving office? In particular, are there any exceptions to the immunity generally enjoyed by all State officials in relation to acts performed in their official capacity, for example in relation to: (i) international crimes; and (ii) crimes committed in the forum State?

(vii) It is generally accepted that, after leaving office, a head of State will no longer enjoy any immunity in relation to private acts, but how does one draw the line between such acts and acts carried out in an official capacity?

(viii) Is it necessary for the State of the former head of State, or Government or other senior representative to raise the plea of immunity *ratione materiae* in order for it to apply? Or does international law require the municipal court to consider the matter of its own motion?

(ix) What is the position of former and incumbent heads of State, heads of Government, and other very senior State officials before international courts and tribunals?

3. Types of Immunity

Broadly speaking, heads of State and other very senior Government officials enjoy two basic types of immunity. The first is personal immunity or immunity *ratione personae*, which is enjoyed by heads of State, heads of Government, Foreign Ministers, and, possibly, although this remains doubtful, a very narrow category of other high-ranking State representatives by virtue of their office. This immunity is sometimes referred to as status immunity and can be wide enough to cover both official and private acts but will lapse when the office-holder concerned leaves office. The second type of immunity is subject-matter immunity (sometimes referred to as functional immunity or immunity *ratione materiae*), which attaches to the official acts of all State officials. Such immunity is determined by reference to the nature of the acts in question rather than the particular office of the official who performed them. As such it covers a narrower range of acts but a much wider range of actors—all State officials. It can also be relied on by persons or bodies who are not State officials or organs but who acted on behalf of the State. Moreover, because such immunity relates to the nature of the act in question rather than the office itself, a former State official, including a former head of State or head of Government, can claim the benefit of such immunity even after he or she has left office.[21]

Both types of immunity are derived from sovereign or State immunity and only the State of the office-holder concerned may waive those immunities.[22] Indeed, immunity *ratione materiae* is an integral part of the body of international legal rules on State immunity which govern the immunity of the State itself from the jurisdiction of a foreign State. A plea of immunity *ratione materiae* is essentially a plea by a State that the act of its official or former official was an act of the State itself and, therefore, one for which it is responsible.[23] As such it applies to all serving and former State officials in respect of acts performed

[21] In an early decision, the appellate division of the New York Supreme Court held that the former President of the Dominican Republic was entitled to immunity from US jurisdiction for his official acts. See *Hatch v Baez*, 7 Hun 596 (NY Sup Ct 1876).

[22] See *R v Bow Street Metropolitan Stipendiary Magistrate, ex parte Pinochet Ugarte (No 3) (Pinochet (No 3))* (at n 6 above) where Phillips LJ commented, 'It is common ground that the basis of the immunity claimed is an obligation owed to Chile, not to Senator Pinochet. The immunity asserted is Chile's'. See also the *Arrest Warrant* case (n 14 above) where the ICJ emphasized that the question was whether the rights of the DRC had or had not been violated by the issue of the warrant in respect of its Foreign Minister.

[23] See *Certain Matters of Mutual Assistance in Criminal Matters (Djibouti v France)* (2008) ICJ Rep,177 at 244, para [196], where the Court declared that 'the State notifying a foreign court that judicial process should not proceed, for reasons of immunity, against its State organs, is assuming responsibility for any internationally wrongful act in issue committed by such organs'.

by them in their official capacity. By contrast, personal or status immunity (which also belongs to the State) has developed an autonomous character and is now treated as more akin to diplomatic immunity.[24] As noted above, it may extend to acts performed in a purely private capacity.

The fact that the immunity *ratione materiae* to which all State officials are entitled has been viewed as an integral part of the general rule on State immunity raises a question as to whether such immunity must be entirely co-extensive with that of the State. The development of the restrictive doctrine,[25] with its established exceptions to the immunity of the State itself, might suggest that the distinction between acts carried out in the exercise of sovereign authority (*iure imperii*) and acts of a private character (*iure gestionis*) should be applicable to situations involving the immunity of officials as well. It is clear that acts carried out by an official in a purely private capacity do not attract subject-matter immunity. But what about commercial acts or other acts of a private law character performed by an official in his or her official capacity? It has been argued that an official acting in his official capacity in performing an act *iure gestionis* (eg entering into a contract for the purchase of official goods) for which the State has no immunity, should nevertheless enjoy subject-matter immunity in respect of that act.[26] One of the purposes of immunity *ratione materiae* is to ensure that an individual official is not held responsible for acts which are, in reality, those of the State and adherents of this analysis could assert that it was, therefore, serving one of its key purposes in being applied in this way.

If, however, functional immunity is seen as linked indissolubly with that of the State itself it is difficult, as a matter of logic, to argue for its continued existence in such circumstances. Another way of looking at the matter would be to focus instead on the question of attribution rather than immunity. Such a question should always precede any question of immunity *ratione materiae.* If the act concerned is imputable to the State (even where it has not expressly ordered or sanctioned it) and the State is immune, then immunity *ratione materiae* should normally apply to the official. If, on the other hand, the State is not immune then immunity *ratione materiae* which is derived from the immunity of the State itself cannot arise. There may remain, however, a question as to whether the individual official can be held responsible for the act concerned—in other words, whether he or she is a proper defendant in the case. If not, the correct action in the circumstances would be to strike out the proceedings against the State official and proceed against the State itself.

[24] See eg s 20 of the UK State Immunity Act 1978 which provides that the Diplomatic Privileges Act 1964 shall apply with the necessary modifications to a sovereign and other head of State as it applies to the head of a diplomatic mission.

[25] See 16–18 below.

[26] See Memorandum by the ILC Secretariat (n 7 above), para 161.

This is in contrast to the position of a diplomat or former diplomatic agent whose position is governed by the separate specialized regime established by the Vienna Convention on Diplomatic Relations.[27] Under Article 39.2 of the Convention, a diplomat whose functions have ceased nevertheless remains entitled to immunity with respect to acts performed in the exercise of his functions as a member of the mission and this is so even where the sending State itself would not enjoy immunity. The scope of such immunity is, however, relatively narrow compared to the functional immunity enjoyed by all State officials in that it exists only in regard to the jurisdiction of the receiving State.

It could be argued that it does not matter very much whether subject-matter immunity is regarded as an integral and inseparable part of State immunity itself or as a discrete immunity which may be applied even in cases where the State itself has no immunity, provided the end result is the same—the State official is not held responsible for an act which was, in reality, that of the State. But when the question of whether or not an exception to such immunity has emerged is considered,[28] these different analyses can assume a greater significance particularly with regard to civil proceedings. If an individual official can enjoy immunity *ratione materiae* in respect of an act for which the State itself is not immune then, conversely, can it be argued that the State is immune in regard to a particular act for which the individual is not? In *Jones v Ministry of Interior of the Kingdom of Saudi Arabia*[29] the House of Lords was not convinced. In that case various claimants brought civil actions in the United Kingdom against Saudi Arabia and a number of Saudi State officials, including two police officers, the deputy governor of a prison, and the Minister of the Interior, alleging, amongst other matters, that they had been the victims of systematic torture. The Court of Appeal dismissed the claim against the Saudi Arabia on the ground of State immunity. It also dismissed all the non-torture claims against the individual defendants on the same basis but allowed the case to proceed against them on the torture claims. On appeal, the House of Lords criticized this as a departure from established practice, noting:

> A State can only act through servants and agents; their official acts are the acts of the State; *and the State's immunity in respect of them is fundamental to the principle of immunity*. This error had the effect that while the Kingdom was held to be immune, and the Ministry of the Interior, as a department of the Government was held to be immune, the Minister of Interior (the fourth defendant in the second action) was not, a very striking anomaly.[30] (my emphasis)

[27] 18 April 1961 500 UNTS 95.
[28] See Part 4 below.
[29] [2006] UKHL 26, [2007] 1 AC 270.
[30] Per Lord Bingham at para [30].

Functional immunity shares the same procedural character as immunity *ratione personae*. As such it is merely a bar to the exercise of jurisdiction and not a defence on the merits.[31] Attempts to characterize it as a separate immunity from that of the State in the manner described above could, therefore, suggest misleadingly that it is a substantive defence whereas, in reality, it has no bearing on the responsibility of the State official and cannot remove the latter's liability, whether criminal or civil, if such liability exists.

4. Justifications for Special Treatment

A number of different theories have been advanced in support of the grant of immunities to heads of State and other high-ranking government officials. Both types of immunity are ultimately derived from prevailing theories as to the independence and equality of States and the resulting acceptance that no State should claim jurisdiction over another.[32] In *The Parlement Belge* case, Brett LJ referred to the obligation of 'every sovereign State to respect the independence and dignity of every other sovereign State'.[33] More recently in *Jurisdictional Immunities of the State (Germany v Italy)*, the ICJ described the sovereign equality of States as 'one of the fundamental principles of the international legal order'.[34]

Broadly speaking, both types of immunity have developed to enable officials to carry out their public business effectively free from interference by the exercise of jurisdiction by another State and thereby secure the orderly conduct of international relations. In *Re Honecker*, the Supreme Court of the then Federal Republic of Germany noted pragmatically that the immunity of a head of State under international law is 'primarily granted in the mutual interests of States in enjoying undisturbed bilateral relations'.[35] Over the years this has been further refined into a theory of functional necessity by which the immunities are justified as necessary for the official to perform his functions. The ILC has noted that it is this theory which appears to be 'gaining ground in modern times'.[36] In 2001, the Institute of International Law adopted a

[31] See Joint Separate Opinion of Judges Higgins, Kooijmans, and Buergenthal in *Arrest Warrant* (n 14 above), para [74].

[32] Often expressed as the principle *par in parem non habet imperium* or *par in parem non habet jurisdictionem*. See Jennings and Watts, *Oppenheim's International Law* (9th edn, Longman, 1992) 441.

[33] (1880) 5 PD 197 at 214–15.

[34] (2012) ICJ Rep 12, para [57].

[35] See FRG (1984) 80 ILR 366.

[36] In the *Arrest Warrant* case (n 14 above), the ICJ confirmed that Foreign Ministers were entitled to immunity in order to ensure the effective performance of their functions on behalf of their

resolution on the immunities of heads of State and of Government, the third preambular paragraph of which reads:

Affirming that special treatment is to be given to a Head of State or a Head of Government, as a representative of that State and not in his or her personal interest, because this is necessary for the exercise of his or her functions and the fulfilment of his or her responsibilities in an independent and effective manner, in the well-conceived interest of both the State or the Government of which he or she is the Head and the international community as a whole.[37]

There are, however, important differences between the two types of immunity in this respect. Personal immunity, which, as indicated above, is restricted to a very limited category of high State officials, is also linked in its origin with notions as to the inherent dignity and majesty of sovereigns and their close identification with the State itself both as chief organ of that State and its representative in all external relations. This theory is founded on the premise that the office-holder concerned personifies the State itself. A Swiss court acknowledged the mixed elements of the rationale, stating that 'customary international law grants such privileges *ratione personae* to heads of State as much to take account of their functions and symbolic embodiment of sovereignty as by reason of their representative character in inter-State relations'.[38] By contrast, immunity *ratione materiae*, which may apply to all officials of whatever rank, rests on the practical rationale that an individual official should not be held responsible for acts which are, in reality, those of the State and also prevents the circumvention of the immunity of the State through proceedings brought against the official who acted on behalf of that State.[39]

respective States and noted that immunity and inviolability 'protect the individual concerned against any act of authority of another State which would hinder him or her in the performance of his or her duties' (para [54]).

[37] *Immunities from Jurisdiction and Execution of Heads of State and of Government in International Law* (Institute of International Law, YB (vol 69 2000–01) 743).

[38] *Marcos and Marcos v Federal Department of Police* (1989) 102 ILR 198, Swiss Federal Tribunal.

[39] See *Zoernsch v Waldock* [1964] 1 WLR 675 at 692, CA (per Diplock LJ): 'A foreign sovereign government, apart from personal sovereigns can only act through agents, and the immunity to which it is entitled in respect of its acts would be illusory unless it extended also to its agents in respect of acts done by them on its behalf.' This aspect of the rule was also summed up in the statement of the UK Court of Appeal in *Propend Finance Ltd v Sing* (1997) 111 ILR 611 at 669 to the effect that State immunity 'would be undermined if employees, officers or… "functionaries" could be sued as individuals for matters of State conduct in respect of which the State they were serving had immunity' so that officials should be protected 'under the same cloak as protects the State itself'.

5. Historical Background and Context

Early theories

The rule that a sovereign or other head of State is entitled to broad immunity from the jurisdiction of another State took some time to develop. Early theories as to the scope and nature of sovereign power and the status of the monarch were heavily influenced by mystical and quasi-religious ideas. A notable and prevailing doctrine was that of the king's two bodies.[40] A king's natural body was his physical body, subject to decay and mortality, but accorded certain dignities that were absolute. His body 'politic' was a more mystical entity, inextricably linked with his natural body, but, unlike that body, immortal and, therefore, capable of passing from one individual monarch to his anointed successor, all the while enjoying certain temporal powers and privileges. All this was, of course, overlaid by a belief in the sovereign's divine appointment, illustrated most powerfully by the belief that a monarch's very touch possessed the power of sacred healing.

However, the development of modern rules of international law regarding the special position of heads of State and other very senior State representatives is intimately bound up with the development of the territorial State itself. The growth of an international system of states, unequal in power, but each claiming to be independent and each to exercise an exclusive jurisdiction within defined territorial limits, was a prerequisite for the development of such rules. Theories relating to the independence of such states from external control and the need to promote and protect the channels for friendly international relations between those states inevitably played a part in that development but, more important, in the early stages, was the complete identification of the sovereign with the State itself. The former embodied the latter and no very clear distinction was made between the two.[41] In this respect Louis XIV's frequently quoted phrase '*L'Etat, c'est moi*' provides an apt description. In certain respects the State was seen almost as the property or sacred charge of the monarch and it was the monarch's personal attributes of sovereignty which gave his State the quality of being a sovereign State rather than the other way round.

[40] See Kantorowicz, *The King's Two Bodies: A Study in Mediaeval Political Theology* (Princeton, 1997).

[41] Watts, 'The Legal Position in International Law of Heads of States, Heads of Governments and Foreign Ministers' (1994) 247 III Recueil des Cours. Watts emphasizes the essentially personal quality of international relations at the stage when sovereign States were mainly absolute monarchies and the fact that, as a result, issues of sovereign immunity were mainly concerned with protecting the position of the Head of State, just as diplomatic immunities were a matter of protecting his envoy.

It was, therefore, the closeness of the relationship between State and ruler that prompted the gradual development of rules of customary international law governing the treatment to be accorded to a foreign sovereign and, in a separate but closely related strand of law, to his diplomatic envoy. As early as 1584, the international jurists Gentili and Hotman, who had been consulted by the council of Queen Elizabeth I of England as to the position of Mendoza, the Spanish Ambassador, had advised that the latter's involvement in a conspiracy for the overthrow of the queen was not subject to the jurisdiction of English law but must be referred for punishment to his own sovereign. Mendoza was, accordingly, merely required to leave the country. In the following year, Gentili published his treatise *De Legationibus*[42] in which he confirmed his view that an ambassador was absolutely exempt from the local criminal jurisdiction of the State to which he is sent and that even if he conspires against the sovereign to whom he is accredited, his punishment can only be expulsion. The close relationship between diplomatic immunity and head of State immunity is also noted in the work of Hugo Grotius who wrote that an ambassador represents the majesty of the sovereign by whom he is sent, whose power is not limited by local jurisdiction.[43] In practice, it took many years for the international rules on such matters to stabilize and be applied with a reasonable degree of consistency by States.

One of the earliest and most famous trials of a foreign sovereign (or former foreign sovereign) occurred in England in 1586. This was the trial of Mary, Queen of Scots, which is sometimes given as an example of a case which pre-dates any clear acceptance of the rules governing the special treatment of foreign sovereigns. As we have seen, however, such theories were beginning to emerge and the trial provides a fascinating insight into the debates and practical concerns surrounding issues of sovereign power and immunity at the time. Mary had been deposed by her subjects and fled to England where she was detained for 19 years. Eventually she was accused of complicity in a plot to overthrow Queen Elizabeth and it was proposed to bring her to trial under an Act of 1584 which had been passed for the protection of the life of the English queen.[44] It was clearly considered to be advisable or, indeed,

[42] Alberici Gentilis, *De Legationibus*.

[43] Grotius, *De iure belli ac pacis*, Book II, Ch XVIII, sect 4. See also Memorandum by the ILC Secretariat (n 6 above), para 19.

[44] This was the Act of Association, drafted by Elizabeth's Privy Council, led by her Secretary of State, Sir Francis Walsingham. It was, in essence, a written oath signed by thousands of the queen's most important male subjects who bound themselves to 'love, fear and obey' their queen and to 'prosecute, suppress and withstand' all her enemies no matter what 'nation, condition or degree' they may have been. It further specified that anyone who took Elizabeth's life, or even 'procured' its taking, could never later succeed to the English throne. It did not refer expressly to Mary but paved the way

necessary to pass such an act and also notable that the trial did not proceed in the ordinary way by jury or before the House of Lords. Instead, a special body of Commissioners was appointed ad hoc.

The Act of Association and appointment of a special Commission may indicate some misgivings as to the propriety of proceeding against an anointed foreign sovereign in respect of a breach of local territorial law. However, Mary's situation was exceptional and does not provide an ideal model in this regard. The crime alleged had been committed on English territory and there was an argument that she was no sovereign at all given that she had been forced to flee her country and been replaced on the throne of Scotland by her young son.[45] There was also the question as to whether Mary could claim the status of an independent foreign sovereign given the nature of Scotland's relationship with England and the title still claimed by the kings of England as 'superior lords' of the kingdom of Scotland.[46] Finally there was the simple fact that Mary was a woman. At that time, women's subordinate status in society was difficult to reconcile with the majesty and supremacy of the monarchy. Again this was not something expressly acknowledged at her trial but may have played some part in easing the minds of those witnessing the trial of a foreign monarch.

All these factors did not prevent Mary, who was not permitted counsel, from relying heavily on her royal status and dignity in her contacts with the Commissioners. From Mary's point of view, the whole notion of a trial was inappropriate. She is reported as remarking 'it seemeth strange to me, that the Queen should command me as a subject to appear personally in judgment. I am an absolute Queen, and will do nothing which may prejudice either mine own royal majesty, or other princes of my place and rank, or my son'. She dismissed the Act of Association—this 'late law, upon which the authority of [the Commission] wholly depended'—as 'unjust, devised of purpose against her' and, most important, 'without example'. At the trial, Mary claimed that she was 'no subject' and 'considering that by such an acknowledgment she should both prejudice the height of regal majesty, and withal confess herself to be bound by all the laws of England, even in matter of religion'.[47]

for her eventual trial and was clearly drafted with her in view. It may also have been mindful of the advice tendered in the *Mendoza* case (see Denza, Diplomatic Law, 3rd ed 2008 (OUP) at p 257) and anxious to provide some clear legal foundation for the prosecution of the queen's enemies, even where such persons enjoyed sovereign status.

[45] This was not an argument the Commissioners chose to advance, which was not surprising given the unwillingness to admit the right of subjects to depose their ruler. Elizabeth had forbidden her ambassador, Sir Nicholas Throckmorton, to be present at the coronation of James VI.

[46] This was not made explicit at Mary's trial but had been specifically pleaded at a much earlier Commission set up in York to look into the complaints made against her by her subjects.

[47] See Lewis, *The Trial of Mary Queen of Scots: A Brief History with Documents* (Bedford/St Martins, 1999).

In denying Mary's claim that she was not subject to the laws of England, the Commission placed great weight on the special and very grave nature of the crime of which she was accused and did not seek to refute her royal status.[48]

Formulation of a general rule

As principles concerning the independence and sovereign equality of modern States became more firmly established, so too did the recognition of the immunities of heads of State at least as regards conduct involving matters of sovereign or governmental authority. It became generally accepted that the exercise of jurisdiction over such conduct by foreign States or sovereigns was incompatible with their dignity and, as such, inconsistent with international courtesy and the proper conduct of international relations.[49] The formulation of a general rule of State immunity was thus intimately linked with the established privileges and immunities of personal sovereigns and their diplomatic envoys. This was expressed clearly in *The Parlement Belge* by Brett LJ:

> That as a consequence of the absolute independence of every sovereign authority and of the international comity which induces every sovereign State to respect the independence of every other sovereign State, each and every one declines to exercise by means of any of its courts, any of its territorial jurisdiction over the person of any sovereign or ambassador of any other State....[50]

With the emergence of constitutional Government there was some debate as to whether the immunities pertaining to the individual sovereign were linked exclusively to monarchs and other hereditary rulers. However, in 1891, the Institut de Droit International declared that the same rules which applied to the foreign State should apply to both personal sovereigns or other heads of State.[51] This approach has been largely reflected in subsequent State practice.[52]

[48] See statement reportedly made by Sir Christopher Hatton: 'You say you are a queen; be it so. But in such a crime the royal dignity is not exempted from answering, neither by the Civil or Canon law nor by the Law of Nations nor of nature. For if such kind of offences might be committed without punishment, all justice would stagger, yea, fall to the ground.'

[49] *Duke of Brunswick v King of Hanover* (1848) 2 HL Cas 1; *de Haber v Queen of Portugal* (1851) 17 QB 171. See also *Oppenheim's International Law* vol 1 (9th edn, 1992) 1037–8.

[50] (1879–90) 5 Prob Div 197, CA, Brett, James, and Baggally LJJ. See n 28 above. See also *Schooner Exchange v McFaddon* (1812) 7 Cranch 116.

[51] (1885–91) II ADI 1181 at 1194. This was based on reasoning that an individual who was head of State, whether of a monarchy or of a republic, represented the State in external affairs and must, therefore, be equally entitled to immunity. See Fox, *The Law of State Immunity* (2nd edn, Oxford University Press, 2008) 204.

[52] But see Jennings and Watts, *Oppenheim's International Law* (9th edn, Longman, 1992) 1042, para 454, where it is noted that there may still be some support for distinguishing between monarchs and presidents as regards immunity from jurisdiction on private visits because presidents lack the personal quality of sovereignty.

State immunity: the absolute doctrine

The formulation of a general rule of State immunity was initially founded on the absolute doctrine whereby a foreign State or sovereign could not be impleaded regardless of the nature of the act complained of.[53] This approach was adhered to by the English courts and others until the 1970s. In practice, this meant that there was often little need to make any reasoned distinction between the personal immunity from jurisdiction enjoyed by a head of State and the immunities enjoyed by such a head as an organ of the State itself or in respect of acts carried out on its behalf. The absolute nature of the general rule meant that trading, commercial, and other activities of a private nature were included within its bar, whether the State was directly or indirectly impleaded through its sovereign or other head of State. In this way the extensive personal immunity to which a head of State was entitled under international law was largely congruent with that enjoyed by the State itself and courts sometimes failed to make any clear distinction between the two. In *Mighell v Sultan of Johore*[54] a claim for breach of promise of marriage was brought against the Sultan who, when the alleged contract was made, had been living in England under the name of 'Albert Baker'. A certificate from the Colonial Office confirmed that the Sultan was the head of a sovereign State and on this basis the Court of Appeal ruled that the defendant was immune. It was argued that the Sultan had not been acting in a public capacity in making the alleged contract but the Court held that *The Parlement Belge* was clear authority for the fact that the Sultan's immunity could only be removed by his express submission to the jurisdiction. This somewhat broadbrush approach to a head of State's immunity became untenable once the restrictive doctrine of State immunity began to take hold.

State immunity: the restrictive doctrine

Growing dissatisfaction with the application of the absolute rule, particularly in the sphere of commercial activities by States, led many States to adopt a more restrictive approach to immunity, permitting the exercise of jurisdiction over non-sovereign acts. It could be argued reasonably that such a change did not challenge the fundamental principle of the sovereign equality of States given that acts of an inherently sovereign character remained immune.[55]

[53] For general historical survey, see Sucharitkul, *State Immunities and Trading Activities* (Stevens and Sons Ltd, UK, 1959) 3–23.

[54] [1894] 1 QB 149.

[55] But the development of a distinct exception to State immunity in respect of certain torts or delicts committed by a foreign State in the territory of the forum State does not appear to respect this distinction. See eg *Letelier v Republic of Chile* 488 F Supp 665 (DDC 1980). However, the exception

In some countries this happened at a comparatively early stage.[56] In 1952, the US Government proclaimed in the Tate letter[57] that the increasing involvement of States in commercial activities made a change necessary and that it would henceforth follow the restrictive doctrine. Change took a little longer in the United Kingdom, but following some confusion and divergence in approach between individual judges, the Court of Appeal unanimously affirmed its acceptance of the restrictive doctrine[58] and this was reaffirmed in later cases by the House of Lords.[59] A significant number of States have now accepted the restrictive approach and in some jurisdictions this has been reflected in domestic legislation.[60] However, the restrictive approach was not universally adopted and many countries continued to adhere to the theory of absolute immunity, most notably the former Soviet Union and States in Eastern Europe.[61] It was not until 2004 that it proved possible to adopt the UN Convention on Jurisdictional Immunities of States and Their Property, which reflects the restrictive approach to immunity.[62]

As far as head of State immunity is concerned, the key element in the development of the restrictive doctrine was the resulting necessity for national courts to distinguish between acts of a sovereign or public nature and those of a private nature. It was no longer possible for such courts simply to dismiss a claim on the basis of the absolute immunity of State and/or sovereign regardless of the nature of the act. Inevitably this encouraged a greater focus on the nature of the act itself and on the type or types of immunity engaged. In practice, it may be difficult to distinguish between acts carried out by a State in the exercise of sovereign authority (*iure imperii*) for which it is immune and those performed *iure gestionis* which do not attract such immunity. Similarly, it can be difficult to distinguish between acts performed by a head of State in his

is usually very narrowly drawn and based upon the common sovereign interests of States in being able to regulate matters within their own territory.

56 *Dralle v Republic of Czechoslovakia* (Austria) (1950) 17 ILR 155. See also Italy and Belgium.

57 (1952) 26 Department of State Bulletin 984.

58 *Trendtex Trading Corpn Ltd v Central Bank of Nigeria* [1977] 2 WLR 356, 64 ILR 122.

59 *I Congreso del Partido* [1981] 2 All ER 1064, (1981) 64 ILR 307. See also *Planmount Ltd v Republic of Zaire* [1981] 1 All ER 1110, (1981) 64 ILR 268.

60 See eg the US Foreign Sovereign Immunities Act 1976 and the UK State Immunity Act 1978, both of which provide for a general rule of immunity from the jurisdiction of the courts together with a list of exceptions to such immunity.

61 China indicated recently that it still adheres to the absolute doctrine. See *Democratic Republic of the Congo v FG Hemisphere Assoc* [2011] HKCFAR 41 at para [211] although this is difficult to reconcile with the fact that it spoke in favour of adoption of the 2004 Convention in the UN Sixth Committee and signed it on 14 September 2005.

62 It is important to note, however, that although the Convention addresses the immunity *ratione materiae* of heads of States and other representatives of a State acting in that capacity, it does not deal with immunity in respect of criminal proceedings and does not apply where there is a special immunity regime, including immunities *ratione personae*.

official capacity which are covered by personal immunity (and usually also by immunity *ratione materiae*) and those performed in his personal capacity for which only personal immunity may protect him. However, as Watts noted in his study on the subject, 'the principle remains sound, even if its practical operation may be untidy'.

Particular difficulties in this respect have arisen in relation to acts of a head of State or other high official which may be characterized as unlawful or criminal.[63] It has been argued that such criminal acts cannot be official acts and must, by their very nature, be regarded as performed in a personal capacity.[64] Conceptually, however, such an argument is not without difficulty because it is clear that a head of State can, in the course of his public functions, engage in criminal conduct. It is therefore difficult to reconcile such an argument with the classic restrictive doctrine which rests on the distinction between public and private acts. So far as serving heads of States and other high officials are concerned, these uncertainties have prompted a renewed emphasis on the very broad personal immunity to which such persons are entitled while in office.[65]

6. Applicability of Rules of International Law Generally

Customary international law

Both types of immunity have remained largely uncodified and the principal source of the immunity of heads of State, heads of Government, and other high State representatives is customary international law. If a particular rule is to attain the status of customary international law there must be widespread State practice to support the rule, coupled with clear evidence of a belief on the part of the States concerned that such practice is required by international law.

The absence of codification is in sharp contrast to the position with regard to other immunities, most notably diplomatic immunities. These rules, which are concerned with the privileges and immunities of diplomatic missions and their staff, are set out in the Vienna Convention on Diplomatic

[63] Such acts can give rise to both criminal and civil proceedings (for damages resulting from the alleged crimes).

[64] See *Jimenez v Aristeguieta* (1962) 33 ILR 353 where in extradition proceedings a US appeals court rejected the former Venezuelan head of State's argument that the acts in question (various financial crimes) were carried out in his official capacity.

[65] *Lafontant v Aristide* (1994) WL 20798 (EDNY), noted in (1994) 88 AJIL 528–32. See also Memorandum by the ILC Secretariat (n 7 above), para 95 and fn 223, where it is noted that the publicity surrounding high profile cases such as *Pinochet* 'which technically fall under the scope of immunity *ratione materiae* has triggered an increased interest in the issue of immunity *ratione personae*'.

Relations (VCDR),[66] which was adopted in 1961. The Convention has been described as one of the most successful examples of codification ever seen and a 'cornerstone of the international legal order'.[67] It does not deal with the personal privileges and immunities of the head of State or other non-diplomatic high-ranking officials, although it has been stated that, at least as far as the head of State is concerned, its provisions ought to be taken as the minimum standard to be afforded.[68]

The success of the 1961 Vienna Convention rests on two factors: first, the long period preceding adoption of the Convention during which States had of necessity to develop and stabilize rules and procedures for the exchange and treatment of envoys; secondly, the existence of reciprocity as a direct and effective sanction promoting a high standard of observance by States. Such factors have been less compelling in the case of special missions given their temporary ad hoc nature and this may go some way to explain the comparatively low level of support for the later 1969 Convention on Special Missions. The absence of such factors has been even more marked in the case of the personal immunities of heads of State and other high officials. In practice, there has been little opportunity to develop any consistent practice on the subject.[69] In the past, heads of State and other senior officials travelled rarely and, when they did, it was unusual for an incident to occur. The cases that do exist are often old and date from a time when national courts made little distinction between what was then the absolute immunity of the State and that of its head. Nevertheless, the fact that international law requires heads of State to be accorded special treatment has been widely acknowledged by international jurists[70]

[66] See also the Vienna Convention on Consular Relations 1963.

[67] Denza, *Diplomatic Law* (3rd edn, Oxford University Press, 2008) notes how the Convention has stabilized the law on diplomatic immunities: 'The Vienna Convention has become a universal Convention, and its provisions, even where at the time of their adoption they clearly marked progressive development of custom or resolved points where practice conflicted, are now regarded as settled law.'

[68] *Satow's Diplomatic Practice* (ed. Roberts) (6th edn, 2009) 175 at 12.1. Watts also admits that the argument that the legal position of a State's ambassador should afford at least a minimum standard for that of the head of State is a compelling one but warns that there are some important differences between an ambassador's circumstances and those of a head of State. See also *Djibouti v France* (n 23 above) (para [174]) where the ICJ noted that the rule of customary international law reflected in Art 29 of the VCDR in regard to diplomats was also necessarily applicable to heads of State.

[69] 'People such as heads of States tend to conduct themselves with discretion, and relevant judicial decisions and publicly known State practice are relatively scarce. Furthermore, much of such legal authority as there is belongs to former times when attitudes to sovereignty and the role of the State differed from those which now prevail': Watts (1994) 247 III Receuil des Cours 1.

[70] See Memorandum by the ILC Secretariat (n 6 above), para 99. See also bibliographical references cited in fn 240 of the Memorandum.

The relative scarcity of early judicial decisions and publicized State practice means, however, that it has often been difficult to identify the precise contours of the rules governing such treatment. A number of international instruments have implied the existence or made specific reference to customary international law rules on this subject without elaborating further as to their content.[71]

The 2004 UN Convention on the Jurisdictional Immunities of States and Their Property included heads of State within the definition of the State itself.[72] By doing so, it extended expressly to such persons acting in their public capacity the immunities which the State itself enjoys under the Convention. The Convention, however, does not cover the immunities *ratione personae* enjoyed by foreign sovereigns or other heads of State and, in an express reference, makes it clear that the existing customary law on the subject is left untouched.[73] The same article also provides expressly that the Convention is without prejudice to the privileges and immunities enjoyed by a State under international law in relation to diplomatic missions, consular posts, special missions, and missions to international organizations and conferences. There is no mention of immunities *ratione personae* enjoyed by heads of Government, or Foreign Ministers.[74] Similarly, the savings provision makes no reference to members of the family of a head of State forming part of his household or his personal servants, although the relevant commentary does state that:

> The present articles do not prejudge the extent of the immunities which are granted by States to foreign sovereigns or other heads of State, their families or household staff, which may in practice also be extended to other members of their entourage.[75]

The New York Convention on Special Missions, which was adopted in 1969, accords extensive privileges and immunities to special missions and their members and the definition of special missions is in terms sufficiently wide to include official visits by a head of State to another State. Article 21(1) refers expressly to missions led by a head of State, although puzzlingly appears to distinguish between such missions and those led by other persons of high

[71] See 2001 Institut De Droit International resolution on 'Immunities from Jurisdiction and Execution of Heads of State and of Government in International Law'.

[72] Article 2(1)(b)(i) and (iv).

[73] Article 3(2): 'The present Convention is without prejudice to the privileges and immunities accorded under international law to heads of State *ratione personae*.'

[74] Although it should be noted that several members of the ILC were in favour of broadening the scope of para 2 to expressly include heads of Government, Ministers for Foreign Affairs, and other high officials. See CN.4/SR.2115, 2117, 2118, Summary records of 2115th, 2117th, and 2118th meetings, YBILC 1989, vol 1. Tomuschat, for example, suggested adding 'or other government officials' after 'heads of State' in order to take account of the applicable rules of international law and leave open the possibility that there were others to whom such privileges and immunities extended.

[75] Commentary to draft Art 4 adopted on first reading, YBILC 1986, vol II(2), para 7.

rank which are covered by Article 21(2). The latter expressly provides that those other 'high ranking persons' are to enjoy 'in addition to what is granted by the present Convention, the facilities, privileges and immunities accorded by international law'. By contrast, Article 21(1) merely refers to heads of State as enjoying such facilities, privileges, and immunities as are accorded to heads of State on an official visit, without specifying that they may be in addition to those granted by the Convention.[76] Support for the Convention has been relatively limited and it must be doubtful whether all of its provisions can be regarded as reflecting customary international law. Its value, however, as evidence of the latter's general content should not be underestimated.

Another relevant Convention is the Convention on the Prevention and Punishment of Crimes Against Internationally Protected Persons, including Diplomatic Agents, which was adopted in 1973. The definition of 'internationally protected persons' includes heads of State and 'any member of a collegial body performing the functions of a Head of State under the constitution of the state concerned'.

In 2007, the ILC decided to include the topic 'Immunity of State Officials from Foreign Criminal Jurisdiction' in its programme of work.[77] As the title indicates, the scope of its work is limited to the immunities enjoyed by State officials from criminal jurisdiction and, in 2013, it adopted three draft articles, one of which declares that a head of State, head of Government, and Minister for Foreign Affairs enjoy immunity *ratione personae* during their period of office. It is also noted that the cessation of such immunity *ratione personae* on departure from office is 'without prejudice to the application of the rules of international law concerning immunity *ratione materiae*'.[78]

[76] Watts explains that the ILC's draft articles had used the same 'in addition' formula for both heads of State and other high ranking persons but that this had been deleted by the General Assembly, noting that the implications of this are unclear. In a footnote, however, he speculates that it may be because the entitlement of a head of State under international law should be given effect without regard to the Convention or because the entitlement concerned so far exceeds anything conferred by the Convention that such a reference would, in practice, be meaningless. See (1994) 247 III Recueil des Cours 39.

[77] See n 7 above.

[78] See draft Art 3 (A/CN.4/). It was, however, clear from the report of the Chairman of the Drafting Committee that opinions within the Commission were divided, with some members preferring that such personal immunity be limited to heads of State and Government and questioning whether a Minister for Foreign Affairs was entitled to such immunity under customary international law and others arguing, by contrast, that such immunity should extend beyond the three office holders of the 'troika' identified by the ICJ in the *Arrest Warrant* case.

Endorsement of specific rules by ICJ or other international courts or tribunals

Immunity ratione personae

In the *Arrest Warrant* case,[79] the ICJ stated that 'in international law it is firmly established that certain holders of high-ranking office in a State, such as the head of State... enjoy immunity from jurisdiction in other States'. It confirmed that serving Ministers for Foreign Affairs enjoy immunity from jurisdiction *ratione personae* to the same extent as heads of State, in particular personal inviolability and immunity from criminal jurisdiction. Such immunity covers both private and official acts and would, therefore, extend to acts performed before a Foreign Minister had assumed office. Strictly speaking, the Court's ruling is confined to the immunities enjoyed by a Foreign Minister but it seems clear from the Court's findings that similar immunities must also apply, *a fortiori*, to heads of Government. The Court upheld the DRC's complaint that the issue of an arrest warrant was a violation of the immunity which a Foreign Minister enjoys under international law. It based its conclusions on the functions exercised by a Foreign Minister in the conduct of a State's international relations, in particular his responsibility for his Government's diplomatic activities. It noted that such functions required him to represent his government at international negotiations and meetings; to communicate constantly with his Government, representatives of other States, and diplomatic missions around the world; and to travel freely. It also noted that a Foreign Minister, simply by virtue of his office, has the power under international law to act on behalf of and to bind his State at the international level, for example in treaty relations. The wording of the judgment left open the question as to whether there may be other holders of high-ranking office in a State who may enjoy such personal immunities.[80] The Court's reasoning would suggest that, if so, such persons would have to carry out representative, international functions analogous to those of a head of State, head of Government, or Foreign Minister. This question and others, including the court's obiter comments on immunity *ratione materiae*, are discussed in the later sections of this book.

[79] n 14 above.

[80] *Arrest Warrant* case (n 14 above), para 51: 'in international law, it is firmly established that as also diplomatic and consular agents, certain holders of high-ranking office in a State, such as the Head of State, Head of Government or the Minister for Foreign Affairs, enjoy immunities from jurisdiction in other states both civil and criminal.'

In *Djibouti v France*[81] the ICJ considered, inter alia, a complaint by Djibouti that France had violated the jurisdictional immunity and/or inviolability of three of its state officials, including the head of State. In doing so, it reaffirmed the personal immunity from foreign criminal jurisdiction of a serving head of State. It appeared to accept, however, that the other two officials, the *procureur de la Republique* and the head of national security respectively, were not entitled under international law to such immunity. It did not address the question in sufficient detail to throw any further light on the precise criteria which may qualify an official for such personal immunity. It would appear, however, that high rank alone is not sufficient and that the functions of such an official must have some international character.

Proceedings were also instituted before the ICJ by the Republic of the Congo in response to a French criminal investigation directed against various Congolese officials, including the President, the Minister of the Interior, the Inspector-General of the Congolese Armed Forces, and the Commander of the Presidential Guard.[82] The Republic of the Congo contended, inter alia, that the steps taken by the French authorities in the investigation, which included a request through the diplomatic channel by the investigating judge to obtain evidence from the President, constituted 'a violation of the criminal immunity of a foreign Head of State—an international customary rule recognized by the jurisprudence of the Court'. In an interim order, the Court declined to indicate any provisional measures on the ground that, on the facts before it, there was no risk of irreparable prejudice to the right of the Congo to respect by France for the immunities of the President. The case has now been withdrawn from the Court's list at the request of the Government of the Republic of the Congo. Again, both these cases are considered in more detail in later parts of this book.

Immunity ratione materiae

This principle is reflected in the 2004 UN Convention on the Jurisdictional Immunities of States, where Article 1(b)(iv) defines the 'State' as including 'representatives of the State acting in that capacity'. It has also been referred to directly in a number of decisions by international courts and tribunals, most notably by the Appeals Chamber of the ICTY in *Prosecutor v Blaskic*, which acknowledged that the rule on the functional immunity of State officials was 'a well-established rule of customary international law going back to

[81] *Case Concerning Certain Questions of Mutual Assistance in Criminal Matters (Djibouti v France)* (2008) ICJ Rep 177 (see n 23 above).

[82] *Certain Criminal Proceedings in France (Congo v France)* (Provisional Measures) (2003) ICJ Rep 102.

the eighteenth and nineteenth centuries, restated many times since'.[83] More recently the ICJ, in a case dealing with the immunity of the State itself,[84] confirmed such immunity as a matter of customary international law at least insofar as civil cases are concerned where the State is directly or indirectly impleaded.

Endorsement of specific rules by national courts

Immunity ratione personae

(i) Heads of State, heads of Government, and Ministers for Foreign Affairs

The extensive immunity *ratione personae* of an incumbent foreign head of State in both criminal and civil proceedings has been the subject of clear, albeit relatively sparse, endorsement by national courts.[85] In the *Pinochet (No 3)* case, the House of Lords, in finding an exception to the immunity *ratione materiae* of a former head of State, acknowledged that the exception would not have applied in the case of a serving head of State.[86] In 2008, the Spanish *Audiencia Nacional* concluded that it did not have jurisdiction to prosecute Paul Kagame, the President of Rwanda, on the ground that as a sitting head of State he enjoyed full personal immunity.[87] It had earlier reached similar conclusions in criminal cases brought against the King of Morocco and the President of the Republic of Equatorial Guinea. In civil proceedings there have been several cases, most notably in the United States. In 2012, for example, the US Court of Appeals upheld the immunity of President Kagame following a civil claim against him.[88] More recently the Court of Appeals for the District of Columbia upheld the immunity of President Rajapaksa of Sri Lanka.[89] In each case the US courts followed a 'suggestion of immunity' put forward by the US State Department to the effect that the defendants were, as 'sitting heads of State', immune from suit under relevant principles of customary

[83] IT-95-14-AR108, (1997) 110 ILR 607, 707, para [38].

[84] See *Jurisdictional Immunities of the State (Germany v Italy)* (n 34 above).

[85] See eg *Re Honecker (Federal Republic of Germany)* (1984) 80 ILR 365; *Gadaffi* (2000)/(2002) 125 ILR 490 (France, Court of Appeal and Court of Cassation); *Lafontant v Aristide* (n 63 above) (US 1994); *Tachiona v Mugabe* 169 F.Supp 2d 259 (US 2001); *Wei Ye v Jiang Zemin* no 03-3989 F.38 (2004) WL 1984430 (US 2004); *Tatchell v Mugabe*, Judgment of 14 January 2004, reproduced in (2004) 53 ICLQ 769.

[86] See n 6 above. See in particular Lord Hope of Craighead, at 624; Lord Hutton, at 637–8; Lord Savile of Newdigate, at 642; Lord Millett, at 651; and implicitly Lord Phillips of Maltravers, at 660–1.

[87] *Re Kagame, Audiencia Nacional*, Auto del Juzgado Central de Instrucion No 4 (Spain 2008) 151–7.

[88] *Habyarimana v Kagame* (US 2011) WL 5170243.

[89] *Manoharan v Rajapaksa* (US 2013) US Ct of Appeals, DCC, 29 March 2013.

international law. The same principle has been upheld in a few cases involving foreign heads of Government in both criminal[90] and civil proceedings.[91]

The practice of domestic courts in regard to the immunities of Foreign Ministers and other officials of comparable rank is less developed. Where immunity has been conferred, it has often been on the ground that such an official is on a 'special mission' rather than on any specific recognition of an entitlement to immunity *ratione personae*. In an early case, *Chong Boon Kim v Kim Yong Shik and David Kim*,[92] a US court upheld the immunity of a Foreign Minister in civil proceedings while on US territory on an official visit. The court's emphasis on the fact that the Minister was in the United States on an official visit suggests, however, that the decision rests more on special missions immunity rather than on any notion of a free-standing personal immunity for such an individual.[93] Special missions immunity is capable of covering a broad range of State officials while travelling on official business but, unlike immunity *ratione personae*, would not extend to private visits. In *Tachiona v Mugabe*,[94] a US court upheld the immunity of the President of Zimbabwe while he was on official business in the United States and extended its finding of immunity to his Foreign Minister, Mudenge, 'travelling as Foreign Minister and as a member of Mugabe's official entourage' at the time he was served.

(ii) Other high-level officials

Following the decision of the ICJ in the *Arrest Warrant* case, there have been several cases in the United Kingdom in which magistrates' courts have accorded immunity *ratione personae* to a Minister other than a Minister of Foreign Affairs.[95] In *Mofaz*[96] it was alleged that the defendant in his capacity as Israeli Defence Minister had committed grave breaches of Article 147 of the

[90] See eg *Re Sharon and Yaron* (2003) 127 ILR 110, Belgium (Court of Cassation (Second Chamber) (2003) 42 ILM 596.

[91] See eg *Saltany v Reagan and Others*, 702 F. Supp 319 (US District Court for District of Columbia 1988); 87 ILR 680.

[92] (1963) 81 ILR 604 (US, CA 1st Circ), (1964) 58 AJIL 186.

[93] See also *Li Weixum v Bo Xilai* (US DCC Civ No 04-0649 (RJL)) where the court upheld the immunity of a Chinese Minister of Commerce and International Trade following a suggestion of immunity by the US government which asserted that foreign officials only temporarily in the United States on 'special diplomatic mission' are entitled to immunity from the jurisdiction (civil and criminal) of the US courts a claim against the Moroccan Foreign Minister on the basis that he was entitled to 'head of State' immunity. The Foreign Minister was not in the US at the time. See *Rhanime v Solomon* 01-1479 (DCD 15 May 2002).

[94] See n 85 above.

[95] See also *Evgeny Adamov v Federal Office of Justice*, Swiss Federal Tribunal, No 1 A.288/2005, Judgment of 22 December 2005, para 3.4.2, where it was suggested in an obiter dictum that a Minister for Atomic Energy could be entitled to immunity *ratione personae*.

[96] See *Application for Arrest Warrant Against General Shaul Mofaz* (decision of District Judge Pratt, Bow Street Magistrates Court, UK (2004) 12 February 2004;128 ILR 709.

Fourth Geneva Convention, contrary to section 1 of the Geneva Conventions Act 1957. The district judge held that he was entitled to 'state immunity in the same way as that pertaining to a Foreign Minister' and declined to issue an arrest warrant. In his ruling, he accepted, following *Pinochet (No 3)*, that the question of immunity was one for customary international law and noted that the decision of the ICJ in the *Arrest Warrant* case did not preclude the extension of such immunity to officials other than head of State, head of Government, and Foreign Minister. He concluded that the reasoning of the ICJ indicated that the reason for a Foreign Minister's entitlement to personal immunity was to enable him effectively to carry out his functions and, on this basis, determined that the role of a Defence Minister and a Foreign Minister were sufficiently similar for such immunity to extend to the former.[97] In 2009, the Westminster Magistrates' Court refused an application for an arrest warrant in respect of Ehud Barak, the Israeli Defence Minister and Deputy Prime-Minister on similar grounds.[98] In 2005, the Bow Street Magistrates' Court was faced with an application for the arrest of *Bo Xilai*, the Chinese Minister for Commerce, including international trade.[99] At the time of the application, he was on a visit to the United Kingdom and formed part of the official delegation for the State visit of the President of the People's Republic of China (PRC). As such, the district judge determined that he was entitled to immunity as a member of a special mission but also stated that his functions as Minister for International trade:

> were equivalent to those exercised by a Minister for Foreign Affairs and adopting the reasoning of the ICJ in the case of the *DRC v Belgium*, I reach the conclusion that under the Customary International Law Rules Mr Bo has immunity from prosecution as he would not be able to perform his functions unless he is able to travel freely.

None of these cases were appealed and the decisions are not binding on other courts. More recently in *Khurts Bat v Investigating Judge of the German Federal Court and others*[100] the claim of the Secretary of the Executive Office of the Mongolian National Security Office to be entitled to personal immunity as a high-ranking official was rejected by the Divisional Court. The court held

[97] District Judge Pratt stated: 'The function of various Ministers will vary enormously depending upon their sphere of responsibility. I would think it very unlikely that ministerial appointments such as Home Secretary, Employment Minister, Environment Minister, Culture, Media and Sports Minister would automatically acquire a label of State immunity. However, I do believe that the Defence Minister may be a different matter.

Although travel will not be on the same level as that of a Foreign Minister, it is a fact that many States maintain troops overseas and there are many UN missions to visit in which military issues do play a prominent role between certain States. It strikes me that the roles of defence and foreign policy are very much intertwined, in particular in the Middle East.'

[98] *Re Ehud Barak* (UK Westminster Magistrates Court 2009). Unreported.

[99] *Re Bo Xilai* (2005) 128 ILR 713.

[100] [2011] EWHC 2029 (Admin).

that he fell clearly outside the circle of high officials entitled to such immunity, describing him as an administrator far removed from the narrow circle of those who hold office which can be equated with the State they personify as identified by the ICJ. However, the scarcity of practice on this issue and the relatively low level at which most of the cases have been heard mean that this area of law remains uncertain.

Immunity ratione materiae

The practice of domestic courts with regard to the immunity *ratione materiae* to which all State officials, both serving and former, are entitled has been prolific and wide-ranging in the number of issues addressed. These issues and relevant *opinio iuris* will be discussed in later sections of this book. As a general principle, however, State officials enjoy immunity *ratione materiae* in respect of their official acts from the jurisdiction of the courts of other States, where the effect of the proceedings would be to undermine or nullify the immunity of the State itself.[101] This principle is reflected in the 2004 UN Convention on the Jurisdictional Immunities of States and Their Property.[102] As far as civil proceedings are concerned, the principle has received recent and unequivocal endorsement in a number of jurisdictions even where the proceedings related to allegations of serious crimes.[103]

There have been far fewer cases involving criminal proceedings. In *Italy v Lozano*,[104] the Italian Court of Cassation accepted that a US soldier enjoyed immunity *ratione materiae* in relation to a prosecution for acts performed by him in the discharge of his functions. The court expressed the view that a rule of customary international law was emerging which, in certain circumstances, may limit such immunity in relation to serious international crimes. However, as the soldier's acts did not, in its view, constitute such crimes, no exception to the general principle of immunity arose.[105]

The *Pinochet* case, in which the UK House of Lords allowed an extradition application by Spain in respect of the former Chilean President to proceed,

[101] See also Lord Browne-Wilkinson in *Pinochet (No 3)* (n 6 above) at 847F.

[102] See Art 1(b)(iv), which defines the 'State' as including 'representatives of the State acting in that capacity'.

[103] See *Jones v Ministry of the Interior of the Kingdom of Saudi Arabia and others* [2006] UKHL 26, [2007] 1 AC 270; NZ *Fang v Jiang* [2007] NZAR 420, HC NZ; *Belhas v Ya'alon*, US Court of Appeals (DC Circ) 515 F.3d 1279, 15 February 2008; *Matar v Dichter*, 563 F.3d.9 (2nd Circ, 2009).

[104] Case no 31171/2008; ILDC 1085 (IT 2008), 24 July 2008.

[105] But see *General Prosecutor at the Court of Appeals of Milan v Adler and others*, Final Appeal judgment, no 46340/2012; ILDC 1960 (Italy 2012) where the same court appeared to suggest that there was no general rule of customary international law conferring functional immunity on State officials in criminal matters.

remains the leading case on such an exception.[106] The case concerned allegations of widespread and systematic torture carried out in Chile and various crimes of murder and conspiracy to murder, including conspiracy to murder in Spain. The court confirmed that if he had been a serving head of State, Augusto Pinochet would have been entitled to an absolute personal immunity on all the charges and, as a former head of State, he would as a general rule continue to enjoy immunity *ratione materiae* in respect of acts carried out in his official capacity as head of State. Most of the judges took the view that Pinochet enjoyed immunity for the 'ordinary' crimes on the ground that the acts alleged, although criminal, had been governmental and must, therefore, give rise to immunity.[107] The court broke new ground, however, in deciding there could be an exception to immunity *ratione materiae* where the international crime of torture was involved. This case and other relevant decisions are discussed in more detail in later sections of this book.

[106] Note 21 above. And according to one commentator, 'the sole case in which a national court has denied functional immunity for human rights related reasons when immunity was clearly invoked by the State entitled to do so': see Wuerth, 'Pinochet's Legacy Reassessed' (2013) 106 AJIL 731.

[107] Lord Hope (at 881 and 887) found that the immunity *ratione materiae* of a former head of State could be relied upon in relation to charges of conspiracy to murder. See also Lords Browne-Wilkinson and Hutton at 848 and 888 respectively. But see Lord Millett who found that such immunity is not available in respect of an offence committed in the forum State (at 913). See also *Wei Ye v Jiang Zemin* 383F.3d 620. (n 85 above).

2

Heads of State

1. Constitutional Forms and Titles

It is a matter for each State to decide for itself its constitutional structure, including the type and title of the head of State it will have and the particular powers and functions to be assigned to that head of State.[1] In practice there has been and continues to be a wide variation between States both as to title and substance although it has been said that a very broad distinction can be drawn between monarchies on the one hand, usually headed by a king or queen, and republics on the other, usually led by a president.[2] In the case of monarchies, the titles of the head of State may vary considerably: emperor, king, queen, prince, grand duke, sultan, emir, and so on, although in republics he or she is most commonly known as a president. Even this may vary, however, as, for example, in the Islamic Republic of Iran where the President, although head of the Government, is not the highest-ranking official. This position is held by the '*rahbar*' or Supreme Leader who performs both religious and political functions and whose unique office is enshrined in the constitution.

Usually a single person is head of State but there can also be a joint or collective head of State as in Switzerland where the head of State is the seven-member Federal Council as a collective body.[3] Other examples are the two co-Princes of Andorra—the Bishop of Urgel and the President of France—and the two

[1] See *Western Sahara Case* (1975) ICJ Rep 6: 'no rule of international law, in the view of the Court, requires the structure of a State to follow any particular pattern, as is evident from the diversity of the forms of State found in the world today': 43–4.

[2] See A Watts, 'The Legal Position in International Law of Heads of States, Heads of Governments and Foreign Ministers' (1994) III 247 Recueil des Cours 21. But at times it seems the lines may be blurred, as shown by press speculation as to the possible return of the royal dynasty to Montenegro. Reports suggest that, despite the fact that Montenegro would remain a Republic, Crown Prince Nicholas could be appointed as a salaried representative of his country in dealings with other royals and international organizations. See also the case of King Simeon II of Bulgaria who returned to Bulgaria in 2001 after more than 50 years in exile. He had been Tsar of Bulgaria from 1943 to 1946 when the monarchy was overthrown. Following democratic elections, he served as Prime Minister from 2001 until August 2005.

[3] One member of the Council serves as President for one year in a *primus inter pares* capacity.

Captains Regent of San Marino.[4] Conversely, one person may be head of two or more States, as in the case of Andorra, referred to above, where the President of France is joint head of State. The most well-known example is Queen Elizabeth II, who is head of State of the UK and 15 other Commonwealth States. In those countries, she is usually represented by a Governor-General.

Some situations defy neat categorization as to title or structure, such as that of the Pope in his capacity as head of State of the Vatican City. The *sui generis* nature of the Pope's situation has occasionally prompted questions as to whether he can properly be regarded as a head of State. However, there can be no doubt that the Vatican City has a territory and a population, albeit tiny, and that there is a Government—the Holy See, headed by the Pope—which is in effective control of that territory. Moreover, it has independence or, more precisely, the capacity to enter into legal relations on the international plane. In these circumstances it would appear to possess all the criteria for statehood.[5] Even if that were not the case, it is probable that the Pope could claim similar privileges and immunities to those of a head of State simply in his capacity as head of the Holy See which has its own independent legal personality which predates that of the Vatican City itself. Such an analysis is in keeping with the practice of States which have consistently recognized the independence and statehood of the Vatican and the status of the Pope as its head.[6]

In the past, there have been 'States' which, while not fully independent (usually because of some form of treaty relations or relationship of protection with another State), have nevertheless enjoyed a degree of international personality as have their heads. An example of this was the position of the rulers of many of the former Indian Princely States, and of the States in the Malay peninsula, which formerly made up the Federated Malay States, and now Malaysia.

Another category which may give rise to ambiguity is a situation where the person who has seized the powers and functions of a head of State refrains from formally assuming that office or, having occupied that office, renounces it (even formally bestowing it on another) while retaining all essential powers.

[4] See also the three-member Presidency of Bosnia and Herzegovina, which consists of a chairman and two other members. Also British monarchs William III and Mary II who reigned as joint sovereigns from 1689 to 1694 when Mary died.

[5] See Crawford, *The Creation of States in International Law* (2nd edn, Oxford University Press, 2006) 225 where, following detailed analysis, it is concluded: 'it is clear that the Vatican City is a State in international law, despite its size and special circumstances.'

[6] See *O'Hair v Wotjyla* (1979) Digest US Practice in IL, 897, Civ No 79-2463. See also Suggestion of Immunity submitted by USA (19 September 2005) *Doe 1 v Archdiocese of Galveston-Houston*, Civ Action No H-05-1047 (SD Tex) where the US Department of Justice filed a brief stating that Pope Benedict XVI was immune, as the head of a foreign State, in a civil suit alleging that the Pope, then Cardinal Joseph Ratzinger, had participated in a conspiracy to shield a seminarian from sexual molestation charges involving three boys.

Such tactics may be designed to emphasize that the seizure of power is only temporary pending elections or that the individual in question intends to retire and relinquish power in the near future. In practice, however, the situation may last for some time and it may become necessary to determine whether the individual concerned may properly be regarded as a head of State (or head of Government).[7] The approach of national courts to such situations has varied considerably and appears to depend very much on the circumstances of the particular case. General Noriega of Panama claimed in a US court to be entitled to immunity as head of State but was denied that status on the basis that, although the effective ruler of Panama, he had not been formally recognized as its President. The US Government had continued to recognize another person as the legitimate President of Panama throughout the period Noriega was in power.[8] Applying similar principles, a court in the US upheld the immunity of President Aristide of Haiti despite the fact that he was in exile at the time of the proceedings and had not been able to return to Haiti for several years. It did so on the ground that the US government still recognized him as head of State.[9] The position of heads of State and other leaders in exile is examined in more detail below.

Another category which may give rise to uncertainty is that of heads of State who have been designated or elected as successor to an incumbent head of State but have yet to formally assume office. In a republic such a person is usually referred to as 'President-elect'. The question may arise as to what treatment such persons may be entitled to under international law. The question is not without some practical significance as the transition period concerned may last several months[10] or even longer during which the designated

[7] Two examples are: Muammar Gadaffi, the former Libyan leader, who in 1979 adopted the title 'Guide of the Revolution' and, while retaining absolute power, conferred his formal functions as a combined head of State/head of Government (known as Chairman of the Revolutionary Command Council) on the Secretary General of the General People's Congress and a Prime Minister, both controlled by him; and the former North Korean leader, Kim Jong-Il, who was officially styled 'Chairman of the National Defence Commission' while the formal role of head of State/head of Government was carried out by the Chairman of the Praesidium of the Supreme People's Assembly and a Premier respectively. To add further ambiguity to the situation, the leader's deceased father, Kim Il-sung, was designated 'Eternal President'.

[8] *United States v Noriega* 746 F.Supp 1506 (1990) 99 ILR 145 at 161–2. See also *Jimenez v Aristeguieta* (1962) 33 ILR 353 where a US Court of Appeals rejected a plea of 'act of State' raised by a former dictator of Venezuela who was facing extradition for various financial crimes he was alleged to have committed on the ground that he had not enjoyed the 'sovereign authority' necessary to bring his acts within the act of state docrine. The court stated: 'Even though characterized as a dictator, the appellant was not himself the sovereign—Government—of Venezuela within the "Act of State" doctrine. He was Chief Executive, a public officer, of the sovereign nation of Venezuela. It is only when officials having sovereign authority act in an official capacity that the Act of State doctrine applies.'

[9] *Lafontant v Aristide* 844 F.Supp 128 (1994) 103 ILR 581.

[10] In the United States, for example, the period lasts between election day in November and the inauguration of the new President on 20 January.

successor may undertake a round of visits to other States. Matters may become more uncertain if the incumbent head of State refuses to accept the successor or seeks to extend his or her term of office.[11] In practice, it would appear that such officials designate or elect are usually afforded the same protection, privileges, and courtesies as an incumbent head of State and that their statements may, in certain circumstances, be relied upon as evidence of their particular State's position on matters of international law and policy.[12] There is no clear authority as to whether or not such an individual would enjoy the extensive personal immunity of an incumbent head of State but, given his or her close proximity to power and designated character as successor to the incumbent head of State, some special treatment would appear to be justified by similar considerations of functional necessity and non-interference in the affairs of another State.

It could be argued that the position of such individuals is broadly similar to that of the heir apparent in a monarchy in that it is clearly established that he or she will succeed the incumbent head of State on the occurrence of a particular event—for example inauguration, ratification by Parliament, or, in the case of a monarchy, the death or abdication of the current ruler.[13] However, an heir apparent will often undertake official duties on behalf of the monarch and will, in some cases, effectively act in his or her place and, in this respect, it might be argued that the position of the latter is more akin to that of a Vice-President or other deputy head of State whose primary role is to replace the head of State in the event of his or her death, resignation, or incapacity but who may also assume certain formal and ceremonial duties on behalf of the head of State during his or her tenure of office.

A final category is that of regents, that is those who, in a monarchy, while not themselves head of State, temporarily exercise the powers and authority of the head of State while the latter is unable to do so.[14] This may be because the head of State is a minor, or is incapacitated through illness. A regent may

[11] A relatively recent example occurred in Cote d'Ivoire when President Alassane Ouattara won the presidential elections held in November 2010 but the incumbent President Laurent Gbagbo refused to give up power. The latter was eventually removed by force in April 2011.

[12] See *Case Concerning Application of the International Convention on the Elimination of All Forms of Racial Discrimnation CERD (Georgia v Russian Federation)* (2011) ICJ Rep 70 at para [77] where Georgia sought to rely, inter alia, on a statement given by President-elect Mikhail Saakashvili in a radio interview as evidence that it had made a claim of racial discrimination against the Russian Federation. In the event, the Court ruled that the statement in substance did not amount to such a claim but, if the substance had been there, it does not appear that the fact that it had been made by a President-elect would have caused any problems.

[13] The position of the family members of a head of State, including the heir apparent in a monarchy, is considered below at pp 102–9.

[14] As to the position in the UK, see the Regency Acts 1937–1953. One of the most unusual examples occurred in Belgium in 1990 when the late King Baudoin abdicated for a day rather than sign the country's new law legalising abortion.

also be appointed after a monarch has been deposed in order to demonstrate that the monarchy has not been abolished: this occurred after the overthrow of King Constantine of Greece in 1967, when a regent was appointed until, in 1973, the monarchy was abolished and Greece became a republic. Another example of a more complicated nature is that of General Franco of Spain, who assumed power as head of an authoritarian regime in the aftermath of the Spanish Civil War. He ruled Spain as 'Caudillo' and was the *de facto* head of State, head of Government, and chief of the armed forces until his death in 1975. However, in 1947 a law[15] was passed which proclaimed Spain to be a monarchy, with Franco as Regent for life with the power to designate the next king when he considered the time to be appropriate. Provision was also made for a Council of the Realm to assist Franco with the exercise of executive power and for a three-member Regency Council to be in charge during the transition period to the Caudillo's successor. There is no clear authority as to whether a regent is entitled to special treatment under international law. However, given that he or she is effectively exercising authority on behalf of the sovereign or head of State, similar considerations of functional necessity would appear to apply.[16]

The constitutional basis on which individuals become head of State or depart from that office may be as varied as the forms and titles of that office. The most common mechanisms applied are election or inheritance (whether in accordance with rules fixed in advance,[17] or by some other system of selection among members of a royal family).[18] These two common methods for selection correspond very broadly to republics and monarchies. But monarchies may be elective also and, in Malaysia, the king (the Yang di-Pertuan Agong) is elected for a five-year period by the Conference of Rulers, from among its

[15] Law of Succession.

[16] See *Apex Global Management Ltd v Fi Call Ltd and others* [2013] EWCA Civ 642, [2013] WLR D 228, where the UK Court of Appeal conceded obiter that a regent might properly be regarded as head of State but concluded, contrary to the ruling of the lower court, that there was no basis for regarding a regent per se as a member of a head of State's family forming part of his household within the terms of the relevant UK legislation.

[17] As to the UK, see *Halsbury's Laws of England*, vol 8 (4th edn), 845–51. A degree of precedence was given to male heirs which required a specific reservation by the UK when becoming a party to the Convention on the Elimination of All Forms of Discrimination Against Women 1979 (GA Res 34/180; UNTS, vol 1015, 243); see Multilateral Treaties deposited with the Secretary-General (status as at March 2011, UN Doc). However, under the Succession to the Crown Act 2013 this precedence has been removed. The new Act will come into force once it is approved by all 15 Commonwealth countries where the Queen is head of State. See also the position in Sweden where constitutional reforms have changed the law on succession allowing the Crown to pass to the eldest child of the monarch regardless of gender.

[18] In the Kingdom of Saudi Arabia, the next king is chosen from among the male descendants of the Founder of the monarchy, King Abdulaziz bin Abdulralunan Al Faisal Al-Saud. In practice, the selection process is carried out through the Allegiance Council, composed of those descendants, which operates by consensus.

members. The Conference is composed of the hereditary rulers of nine of the 13 states constituting the Malaysian Federation.[19] A similar system exists in the United Arab Emirates. It is also notable that not all republics have heads of State who are elected. Some have Presidents who hold office 'for life'[20] and, in some cases, even where some form of constitutional election or appointment is ostensibly applied, it is clear that there is a degree of *de facto* inheritance or dynastic continuity in the succession of one head of State to another.[21]

In general, questions of title and powers and the particular means by which a head of State may be elected or appointed are matters of domestic concern for each State. In some circumstances, however, the constitutional structure of a State and the dispositions made by it in regard to its head of State can raise issues of international law. One example of this would be where the nature of the office of head of State has been guaranteed by treaty by one or more other States.[22] In the past other cases have occurred when a State has placed itself under the protection of another State. By doing so, it would appear that it did not lose its international statehood altogether and that, therefore, its head of State might retain some international status. Such was the position, for example, of the rulers of some of the former Indian Princely States, and of the States which formerly made up the Federated Malay States and now Malaysia.[23] A third type of case can occur where events surrounding the election, succession, or continued occupation of office by a particular leader amounts to a threat to the maintenance of international peace and security, so as to justify action by the Security Council. In such circumstances,

[19] Malaysian Constitution, Art 32. See also Rawlings, 'The Malaysian Constitutional Crisis of 1983' (1986) 35 ICLQ 237 at 242 et seq.

[20] Marshal Tito of Yugoslavia became 'President for life' in 1963 and retained office until his death in 1980. For many others the title has proved to be more illusory. President Kwame Nkrumah of Ghana, who assumed the title in 1964, was deposed in 1966. The first President of Malawi (Dr Hastings Banda) was to hold office 'for his lifetime' under Art 9 of the Constitution but, in the event, constitutional reforms caused him to retire in 1994. Other examples are Idi Amin of Uganda, who was forced into exile in 1979 and, more recently, President Niyazov of Turkmenistan, who died in office in 2006.

[21] See eg the succession of Jean-Claude Duvalier to his father as President of Haiti in 1971 and of Kim Jong-un to his father Kim Jong-Il and grandfather Kim Il-Sung as President of the Democratic People's Republic of Korea in 2011. Another example can be found in the succession of Bashar al-Assad to his father Hafez al-Assad as President of Syria in 2000. For a general analysis, see Brownlee, 'Hereditary Succession in Modern Autocracies' (2007) 59(4) World Politics 595.

[22] See 1863 Guarantee given by UK, France, and Russia to Greece as a 'monarchical, independent and constitutional State': Martens, *Nouveau Recueil generale detraites*, 2nd series, 32 at 79; and the 1960 Treaty of Guarantee by which Greece,Turkey, and the UK guaranteed the position as established by the Basic Articles of the Cyprus Constitution.

[23] For a more modern example, see the special position of Bhutan which under a Treaty of 1949 agreed to be 'guided by the advice of the Government of India in regard to its external relations'. During that period and subsequently following the conclusion of a 2007 Treaty of Friendship between the two countries, no question has arisen as to the statehood of Bhutan nor as to the fact

action may include a call for the restoration of a deposed head of State or the appointment of some particular person to that office.[24]

In practice, it can be difficult to identify a particular feature which will always serve to distinguish a monarchy from a republic. In most cases the hereditary and elective bases for office will suffice but, in some situations, these may not be entirely adequate.[25] The traditional view suggests that the distinction may lie in the precise location of sovereignty within the State concerned.[26] If that sovereignty rests in a particular individual (or office) then that State is a monarchy and the individual (whatever the title of his or her office) is a sovereign. If sovereignty resides in its people, as a whole, rather than in any one individual, then that State is a republic. However, even this distinction, which rests largely on eighteenth- and nineteenth-century notions of sovereignty, cannot wholly account for the many varied forms of heads of State[27] and can certainly no longer be relied upon as a matter affecting the substantive treatment of heads of State.[28] It is clear that international law provides that all serving heads of sovereign independent States are entitled to extensive immunities *ratione personae* and are to be treated alike in this respect regardless of internal constitutional provisions affecting their title, appointment, and powers. The fact that the International Court of Justice (ICJ) has now clarified that heads of Government and Foreign Ministers are also entitled to such immunities[29] leaves little doubt on this question.

Whatever their titles, the powers allocated to heads of States differ greatly from one country to another. In the past, most held significant substantive authority within their own State so that relations between States were synonymous with relations between their heads. Today, however, a head of State may often fulfil only a formal, constitutional role while the real power is exercised

that its king is a head of State, although Bhutan's interaction with foreign States and international organizations remains at a fairly low level. See MPEPIL, vol 1 (Oxford University Press, 2012) 914.

[24] See eg SCR 841 of 6 June 1993, SCR 917 of 6 May 1994, and SCR 940 of 31 July 1994 calling for appointment of the elected President Aristide of Haiti; SCR 1132 of 8 October 1997, SCR 1270 of 22 October 1999, SCR 1289 of 7 February 2000 relating to Sierra Leone; and SCR 1975 of 2011 calling on President Laurent Gbagbo of Cote d'Ivoire to 'immediately step aside'.

[25] Watts (n 2 above) 23–4.

[26] See Jennings and Watts (eds), *Oppenheim's International Law* vol 1 (9th edn, Longman, 1992) 1035–36, paras 448, 449.

[27] See the 2010 report in *The Times* of legislation proposed in Montenegro (which abolished its monarchy when it was absorbed into Yugoslavia in 1918) which would retain its status as a republic but restore Crown Prince Nicholas as its formal representative in dealings with other royal heads of State and international organizations.

[28] See Jennings and Watts (n 27 above), para 450, n 1 for the obsolete view that a president's lack of sovereignty was a basis for denying him the same immunities as a monarch. But it was noted that there may still be some support for a distinction in relation to private visits (see Part 1, n 52).

[29] See *Arrest Warrant of 11 April 2000 (DRC v Belgium)* (2002) ICJ Rep 3.

by other organs of the State. Nevertheless, it is usual for certain acts to be performed in the name of the head of State even where in practice they have been performed on the advice of others (with which advice the head of State must, in effect, comply). In the UK, legislation and the power of judicature are still formally the expression of the Royal Pleasure, though for centuries such powers have had to be exercised in proper form, that is through the courts and with the advice and consent of Parliament. The distribution of powers between the various organs of State and the particular allocation to the head of State are, like matters of form and title, largely a matter of domestic concern. The office of head of State may, of course, be combined with that of head of Government.[30] There are, however, certain specific powers which are usually vested in a head of State and are directly relevant for international law.

2. Internationally Relevant Powers

The key practical consideration underlying the position of a head of State in international law is the presumption that he or she may act on behalf of the State in its international relations. Certain specific powers are almost always vested in heads of States. They are the power to make war and peace, to conclude international treaties on behalf of their State, and to appoint and receive ambassadors. In addition, powers to appoint a Minister for Foreign Affairs, acquire and cede territory, and accord recognition to foreign States and Governments are usually vested in heads of States. The scope of such powers and the particular procedures governing their exercise vary from one country to another. In the UK, the majority of powers relating to the control and conduct of international relations are conferred on the Queen, although the constitution requires that her function in this regard must be exercised on the advice of the responsible minister or ministers and, in matters to do with the treaty-making power, the power to make war, and the annexation or cession of territory, in concert with Parliament

Traditionally such powers fall within a category of acts which most national legal systems regard as not within their courts' power of review. In the UK such an act of the Crown in relation to foreign affairs is termed an act of State, which has been defined as an act of sovereign power which 'cannot be challenged, controlled or interfered with by the municipal courts'.[31] Where,

30 One of the most notable examples being the President of the US. For a list of States whose heads were then also heads of Governments and those in which the two offices were distinct, see HL Hansard, vol 388, cols 1405–6 (written answers, 14 February 1978).

31 *Salaman v Secretary of State for India* [1906] 1 KB 613, CA.

therefore, it is necessary for a court to have an authoritative determination on a matter within this sphere in order to decide the issue before it, it is common practice in many national systems for it to seek the views of its national Government. In many jurisdictions this has been formalized into evidential rules enabling the Court to take judicial notice of the facts as presented to it. Examples of such matters are: whether or not a state of war exists; whether a foreign State is recognized as such; or whether or not a particular individual has been received as a diplomat. In the UK, for example, a certificate from the Secretary of State may be conclusive of the matter in question.[32]

The power to make war and peace

In some States, the exercise of such a power must be done in strict compliance with certain procedures, although this is not the case in the UK where war may still be initiated by the Crown by formal proclamation, by an Order in Council for general reprisals, or informally without any declaration.[33] In some countries, questions have been raised as to whether strict adherence to constitutional procedures applies only in relation to a formally declared war or whether it also applies in relation to the commitment of the State's military forces to armed conflicts of a less defined type. There has, for example, been extensive debate in the US over the exercise of the 'war power' vested in the President. Under the US Constitution, only Congress has the power to actually 'declare war', with the President, as Commander in Chief, having the authority to direct that war. In practice, Congress has declared war on only five occasions but presidents have frequently engaged US troops in military conflicts over the years on the basis that they have authority to take such action in order to protect vital national interests and that congressional approval is not required unless the action concerned constitutes a fully fledged 'war'. In 1973, following debate on the issue, fuelled by concern about continued US involvement in the undeclared Vietnam war, Congress passed the War Powers Resolution. This authorized the President to respond with military action to 'a national emergency created by attack upon the United States, its territories or possessions or its armed forces' but, if the ensuing conflict lasted more than 60 days, the law required congressional approval. In practice, presidents have applied a very broad interpretation of 'national emergency' and have continued to exercise the power to deploy US troops where they

[32] For UK practice generally, see Wilmshurst, 'Executive Certificates in Foreign Affairs: the United Kingdom' (1986) 35 ICLQ 157–69.

[33] See *The Ionian Ships* (1855) 2 Ecc & Ad 212.

judge it to be in US interests to do so.[34] Essentially it is a matter for the constitutional laws of each State to determine how a constitutional power drawn up in terms of 'declaring war' should be applied in practice, although there is a more general and closely linked question as to whether the concept of a 'declaration of war' is still a relevant and significant concept in contemporary international law.

The treaty-making power

The traditional definition of the term 'treaty' refers to 'an international agreement concluded between States in written form and governed by international law, whether embodied in a single instrument or in two or more related instruments and whatever its particular designation'.[35] It is recognized that 'treaties' may also be concluded between States and international organizations or between international organizations themselves. Moreover, it is also established that, although the majority of treaties are recorded in writing there is no requirement in law or practice that this should be so.[36] States possess treaty-making capacity as an automatic aspect of their sovereignty and such capacity is usually reflected in internal constitutional provisions vesting the power to make treaties in the relevant head of State.

As in the power to make war, some constitutions may require the treaty-making power to be exercised in accordance with particular procedures, for example in the US the President must act with the advice and consent of the Senate. This requirement has led to the development of an elaborate practice whereby the term 'treaty' is reserved for certain kinds of very formal international agreements while the rest are characterized as 'executive agreements' so as to evade the restrictions imposed by the Constitution on the conclusion of 'treaties'. It has been noted that, while such matters are primarily of concern to the State in question, other States cannot be indifferent.[37] Article 46 of the Vienna Convention on the Law of Treaties 1969 provides that if a State's consent to be bound by a treaty has been expressed in violation of a provision of its internal law (which must include its Constitution) regarding its competence to conclude treaties, the State may invoke that violation as a ground for

[34] See President Reagan's interventions in Lebanon and Grenada, President George HW Bush's invasion of Panama, President Clinton's interventions in Somalia and Bosnia, President George W Bush's invasion of Iraq, and, most recently, President Obama's intervention in Libya.

[35] Article 2.1(a) of the Vienna Convention on the Law of Treaties, 1155 UNTS 331.

[36] See *Legal Status of Eastern Greenland case* (1933) PCIJ Series A/B, No 53, 71; and *Nuclear Tests cases (Australia v France, New Zealand v France)* (1974) ICJ Rep 267.

[37] Watts (n 2 above) 28.

invalidating its consent if the violation was manifest and concerned a rule of internal law of fundamental importance.[38]

The treaty-making power of a head of State does not mean that the head of State has to conclude every treaty in person and nowadays such personal participation is normally reserved for treaties of particular importance. Such treaties will be in a 'heads of States' form, indicating both in the opening recitals and in the final signatory provisions that the parties to the treaty are the heads of State. Such a treaty has been described as the 'clearest example of a treaty concluded for and binding upon the State'.[39] The 1957 Treaty of Rome establishing the European Economic Community and all the subsequent amending treaties are in 'heads of State' form. Where, as is now usual, treaties are not concluded by the heads of State personally but by representatives, such representatives will normally need to establish their authority to conclude the treaty. This is usually done by the production of a formal document known as 'Full Powers' which is signed by the head of State or someone to whom the necessary power has been delegated attesting to the representative's authority to perform the acts in question in connection with the conclusion of the treaty. Despite the general trend towards more informal treaty-making, full powers are still commonly required, although often dispensed with for bilateral treaties and almost never required for an exchange of notes.

As already noted, a head of State enjoys an inherent capacity to represent and act for the State, a capacity which is shared with heads of Government and Foreign Ministers. All three offices of State are considered as representing their State because of their particular functions and, because of this ostensible authority, are not required to produce full powers.[40] In the *Case Concerning the Application of the Genocide Convention*, the ICJ referred to this power to act on behalf of the State as 'universally recognised'[41] and noted, in particular, the provisions of Article 7(2) of the 1969 Vienna Convention on the Law of Treaties.

This automatic presumption of authority to bind their State raises the question whether, if a State's constitution requires treaties to be subject to parliamentary approval or some other constitutional process, the head of State (or head of Government or Foreign Minister) may nevertheless irrevocably commit the State to a treaty simply by signing it on the basis of his or her authority as head of State. This assumes, of course, that the treaty itself does not provide for ratification and that the head of State makes no reservation on that matter when signing. This issue was raised in proceedings before

[38] A violation is manifest if it would be objectively evident to any State conducting itself in the matter in accordance with normal practice and in good faith (Art 46.2).

[39] See Watts (n 2 above) 28.

[40] Article 7.2(a) of the Vienna Convention on the Law of Treaties 1969.

[41] Preliminary Objections (1996) ICJ Rep 4 at 31, para [44].

the ICJ in *Land and Maritime Boundary between Cameroon and Nigeria.*[42] Part of the dispute concerned the effect of what was termed the Maroua Declaration: a document signed in person by the then Presidents of the two States. Cameroon sought to rely on the Declaration as supporting its sovereignty over the disputed area; but Nigeria argued that the Declaration had no legal basis as it had not been ratified by the competent Nigerian legislative body. The ICJ rejected the argument that the Declaration was invalid under international law. While acknowledging that the rules concerning the authority to sign treaties for a State are constitutional rules of 'fundamental importance', it concluded that 'a limitation of a head of State's capacity in this respect is not manifest in the sense of Article 46, paragraph 2, unless at least properly publicized'. The Court added that this is particularly so because heads of State belong to the group of persons who, in accordance with Article 7, are considered as representing their State in virtue of their functions and without having to produce full powers.[43] In an earlier decision in the *Nuclear Tests Case*, the ICJ arguably went further in holding that statements made at a press conference by the President of France to the effect that a round of atmospheric tests was to be the last constituted a unilateral declaration binding the French State. It noted:

> Of the statements by the French government now before the Court, the most essential are clearly those made by the President of the Republic. There can be no doubt in view of his functions, that his public communications or statements, oral or written, as head of State, are in international relations acts of the French State. His statements and those of his French Government acting under his authority, up to the last statement made by the Minister of Defence... constitute a whole. Thus in whatever form these statements were expressed, they must be held to constitute an engagement of the State, having regard to their intention and the circumstances in which they were made.[44]

Appointment and reception of diplomatic representatives

The power to appoint and receive ambassadors is normally exercised by heads of State. This is done by means of letters of credence or credentials (as they are sometimes known). The sending State's head of State signs the letters

[42] (2002) ICJ Rep 89.

[43] For similar position of Foreign Minister, see *Maritime Delimitation and Territorial Questions between Qatar and Bahrain* (1994) ICJ Rep 112, (1994) 102 ILR 1 where Bahrain argued that Minutes signed by its Foreign Minister and his counterpart from Qatar could not be an international agreement as Bahrain's Constitution stipulated that treaties concerning the territory of the State could only come into effect after their enactment as law; and *Legal Status of Eastern Greenland (Denmark v Norway)* PCIJ Rep Series A/B No 53/71. See Part 3, at p 113 below.

[44] *Nuclear Tests Case (Australia v France/New Zealand v France)* (1974) ICJ Rep 253 at para [457].

of credence by which an ambassador is appointed, and it is to the receiving State's head of State that they are addressed and delivered by the ambassador in due course. Again, like the treaty-making power and power to make war, the exercise of this power may be subject to variations in detail designed to meet the constitutional requirements of different States.[45] However, the essence of any letter of credence is contained in the final phrase asking that credit may be given to all that the ambassador may say in the name of his sovereign or Government.[46] Usually the appointment and reception of diplomatic representatives are matters of protocol and ceremonial but they can have legal implications in the context of questions as to the legitimacy of a particular head of State: addressing letters of credence to, or accepting letters of credence from, a foreign head of State is clearly of relevance in the area of recognition.[47]

Ius repraesentationis omnimodae

In addition to the particular internationally relevant powers referred to above, a head of State usually possesses a more general quality which is seldom expressly conferred by constitutional provisions but is, nevertheless, an integral part of the international role played by that head of State. This is the general competence, as the highest organ of the State, to act for that State in all aspects of its international relations, and the corresponding attributability of such acts to the State concerned.[48] As we have seen, this quality has a particular relevance in the context of the treaty-making power and can produce unintended results. In essence, a head of State's acts or omissions when acting in an official capacity as an organ of the State are attributable to the State itself and, if they involve a breach of the State's international obligations, the State bears international responsibility for them.

This general competence, the so-called *ius repraesentationis omnimodae*, is an attribute of heads of State by virtue of international law rather than by

[45] Special procedures have developed in the UK with regard to representatives of the Commonwealth States of which the Queen is also head of State (who are known as high commissioners rather than ambassadors).

[46] See *Satow's Diplomatic Practice* (ed Sir Ivor Roberts) (6th edn, Oxford University Press, 2009) para 5.3.

[47] See Brownlie, *Principles of Public International Law* (7th edn, Oxford University Press, 2008) 93 where it is noted that the UK did not accord formal recognition of the statehood of Namibia but that it was implicit in the establishment of diplomatic relations in March 1990.

[48] See *Genocide Convention Case* (1951) ICJ Rep 15 at para [44]: 'According to international law, there is no doubt that every head of State is presumed to be able to act for it internationally, with all his legally relevant acts being attributable to the State.' See also *Armed Activities on the Territory of the Congo (DRC v Rwanda) (Jurisdiction and Admissability)* (2006) ICJ Rep 562 at para [46].

virtue of their own State's constitutional law. It is a competence which is exercised by heads of State on behalf of their States and not in their own personal capacity. In practice, this representative competence may be restricted by the provisions of a particular State's own constitution but this does not affect the international legal assumption which underlies many aspects of a head of State's role.

Closely linked with this general representative competence is the traditional notion of the head of State as the personal embodiment of that State.[49] While this identity of the head of State with the State itself originated with the position of sovereign monarchs, it is a notion which, to some extent, has also attached itself to presidents and other non-monarchical heads of State.[50] While it might be argued that this mystique of sovereignty as embodied in a head of State has diminished in recent decades, it has undoubtedly left its mark on the international legal rules relating to the position of heads of State and, in many places, may still exert a powerful influence.[51]

3. Recognition

General principles

The fact that heads of State possess a number of internationally relevant powers and are entitled under international law to special treatment by other States means that it is important that other States are clear as to whether or not a particular individual is accepted as head of a recognized State. In these days of virtually instant and worldwide communications there is seldom any difficulty in finding out who is held out as being a State's head. Nevertheless, States still often follow the practice—essential in former times—of formally notifying other States of the accession, election, or appointment of a new head of State: this is usually done by sending such notification through diplomatic channels, often coupled with an invitation to the recipient State to be represented at the relevant coronation or inauguration ceremonies. Even where this is not the case, the question of whether or not other States recognize the new head of

[49] See eg Art 1 of the Constitution of Japan: 'The Emperor shall be the symbol of the State and the unity of the people...'

[50] See Charles de Gaulle's description of the role of the French President in the French Constitution to the effect that he should embody 'the spirit of the nation' for the nation itself and the world. See also Watts (n 2 above) 32: 'it may be said generally that nowadays heads of States through their office manifest the spirit and grandeur of their nations as a whole.'

[51] See *Case Concerning Certain Criminal Proceedings in France* (*Republic of the Congo v France*) Provisional Measures Order (2003) ICJ Rep 102 where, in his dissenting judgment, Judge de Cara noted that 'in Africa, the head of State embodies the nation itself'.

State is a question which sooner or later poses itself in the context of practical dealings between the States concerned. Matters such as the appointment of ambassadors or the conclusion of treaties will, for example, involve, directly or indirectly, the powers and authority of the new head of State.

In the majority of cases this question does not give rise to any problems and is no more than a formality, particularly where the new head of State has assumed office in accordance with settled constitutional processes. The new head of State's position will usually be acknowledged expressly or implicitly by such means as the transmission through diplomatic channels of congratulatory messages, representation at formal inauguration ceremonies, or the eventual dispatch or acceptance of newly appointed ambassadors.

Problems can arise, however, where there is uncertainty as to the existence of the State concerned or in a situation where a leader has seized power and removed from office a previous head of State who may still lay claim to that title.[52] In practice, the recognition of someone as head of State raises two distinct questions. First, is there a State for anyone to be head of; and, second, if so, is the individual in question head of that State? If a State is unwilling to recognize a particular territory as a State it must equally decline to recognize an individual as head of that State. Thus there has been no general recognition of the Dalai Lama as a head of State because Tibet, although seen by many States as entitled to considerable autonomy is, nevertheless, perceived as existing under the suzerainty of China.[53] In *Kadic v Karadzic*,[54] a court in the US dismissed the claim of the defendant to 'head of State immunity' on the ground that the US Government did not recognize the 'State'—the self-proclaimed Republika Srpska—of which the defendant claimed to be head. This is not to say that a State must decline all dealings with such a person. The key factor is how that person is regarded in those dealings. Recognition of someone as leader of a particular community or *de facto* authority is one thing; recognition of someone as head of a foreign State is quite another.

There is, of course, a distinction in international law between the recognition of States and the recognition of Governments. At times they may be very closely related but the non-recognition of a particular regime does not necessarily mean that the State of which it purports to be the Government does

[52] See *Lafontant v Aristide* 844 F.Supp 128, 132–3 (EDNY 1994) where civil proceedings were brought against the exiled President of Haiti in the US. The court held he was entitled to immunity as he was still recognized by the US Government as head of State.

[53] See Hengtse Tu, 'The Legal Status of Tibet' [1970] 7 Annals of Chinese Society of International Law 1 at 28. See also, for example, the position which most States have adopted in relation to Dervis Eroglu, the elected leader of the Turkish Republic of Northern Cyprus (TRNC) and his predecessors who have usually been styled the 'Turkish Cypriot leader' rather than President.

[54] (1995) 34 ILM 1592.

not qualify for statehood. The latter question is most commonly regarded as a matter of law, dependent upon the existence of certain legal criteria and not upon recognition by other States. The position with regard to Governments is less settled and the practice of States has varied considerably over the years. Inevitably, the recognition or non-recognition of Governments can sometimes seem more political and primarily motivated by support for a particular cause or unwillingness to deal with the regime concerned rather than any objective judgment as to its effectiveness or degree of control.[55] In 1980, the UK Government announced a change in its policy[56] whereby it would no longer accord formal recognition to Governments but would leave its position to be inferred from the nature of the dealings it chose to have with any particular regime.[57]

The more usual recognition problems occur in relation to heads of State within a well-established and recognized State; this will, for example, be the case where there are political and constitutional upheavals and conflicts within a State or the existence of two competing Governments. In *United States v Noriega*, General Manuel Noriega, the *de facto* ruler of Panama, was arrested in Panama by US forces and brought to trial in the US on various criminal charges. He claimed immunity as a head of State but this was rejected by the US court on the ground that 'he had never been recognised as Panama's head of State neither under the Panamanian Constitution or by the United States'.[58] The case is unusual in that it provides a relatively rare example of a refusal to accord head-of-State immunity to an established *de facto* ruler of a recognized State. However, the court was able to rely on consistent US practice with regard to the continuing recognition of another individual as Panama's legitimate head of State.

The other side of the coin to the *Noriega* case is illustrated in *Lafontant v Aristide*.[59] President Aristide of Haiti was sued in the US for compensation

[55] The Taleban regime, even while in apparent control of Afghanistan, was recognized as a Government only by Pakistan, Saudi Arabia, and the United Arab Emirates. See *Satow's Diplomatic Practice* (6th edn, Oxford University Press, 2009) 75.

[56] See statement by Lord Carrington, Hansard, House of Lords, vol 408, cols 1121–2. *UK Materials on International Law* [1980] BYIL 367.

[57] But see 2011 statement by UK Foreign Secretary William Hague announcing that the UK recognized the Libyan Transitional Council as the sole governmental authority in Libya. For further analysis, see Warbrick, 'British Policy and the National Transitional Council of Libya' (2012) 61 ICLQ 247. See also announcement by UK Foreign Secretary on 20 November 2012 recognizing the newly united Syrian opposition forces as the sole legitimate representative of the Syrian people.

[58] See n 8 above. The Panamanian Constitution provided for an Executive Branch composed of a President and Ministers of State neither of which applied to Noriega who was officially designated Commandante of the Armed Forces. More significantly, the US Government had never accorded Noriega head-of-State status and had continued to recognize another individual as legitimate leader.

[59] 844 F.Supp 128, (1994) 103 ILR 581.

for the death of the plaintiff's husband, who was killed in January 1991 while in detention in Haiti, by soldiers who (as alleged) had acted on President Aristide's orders. Two days after the killing, there was a military coup in Haiti and Aristide was exiled to the US. He was in exile there when proceedings were brought against him. The court held that he was still recognized by the US Government as head of State, even though he had been in exile for nearly three years, and was, therefore, entitled to immunity from the court's jurisdiction.[60] In *Sierra Leone Telecommunications Ltd v Barclays Bank Plc*[61] a question arose as to the continuing authority of officials appointed by President Kabbah of Sierra Leone whose elected Government had had to move to a neighbouring State. In this connection the English court relied on public statements by the UK Government that, in its view, President Kabbah remained the legitimate head of State. The position of exiled heads of State is looked at in more detail below.[62]

Circumstances where a leader has deliberately refrained from formally assuming the office of head of State, or has renounced such office (even formally conferring it on others) while retaining power, may also be problematic. The former Libyan leader Muammar Gaddafi adopted the title 'Guide of the Revolution' in 1979, conferring all the formal functions of head of State and head of Government on the Secretary-General of the General People's Congress and a Prime Minister.[63] This did not, however, deter the French Court of Cassation from deciding that Gaddafi was entitled to head of State immunity with regard to criminal charges alleging his complicity in acts of terrorism resulting in the destruction of a French civil aircraft.[64] On this basis, it appears that where an individual is the effective ruler of a recognized State, the more important factor is whether or not he or she has been accepted and treated as *de facto* head of that State by other States and not the internal forms and titles he or she may choose to adopt.[65]

[60] See also *Republic of Somalia v Woodhouse Drake & Carey (Suisse) SA, The Mar* [1993] 1 QB 54 at para [382], where Hobhouse J noted that it 'would be contrary to public policy for the court not to recognise as a qualified representative of the head of State of a foreign State the diplomatic representative recognised by Her Majesty'.

[61] [1998] 2 All ER 821. See also note by Byers in [1998] BYIL 319.

[62] See pp 48–53 above.

[63] In 2011, *Al Jazeera* reported a statement from the Libyan Government put out in response to arrest warrants issued by the International Criminal Court (ICC), stating that 'the leader of the revolution and his son do not hold any official position in the Libyan Government, and, therefore, they have no connection to the claims of the ICC against them'.

[64] *Gaddafi* (2001) 125 ILR 490.

[65] See eg the observations submitted by the UK Government to the European Court of Human Rights in *Association SOS Attentats v France* regarding the immunity of the former Libyan leader Gadaffi, *UK Materials on International Law* [2006] BYIL 77.

Constituent territories of federal States

Questions sometimes arise in relation to the constituent territories of federal States and their heads; claims being made that, where such territories enjoy a high degree of autonomy, such persons are entitled to the same treatment accorded to heads of State (and heads of Government) under international law.[66] In *Italy v DM (Djukanovic)*,[67] a Naples tribunal refused a request of the Prosecutor's Office to issue an arrest warrant against Milo Djukanovic who was then serving as President of Montenegro which, at that time, was part of the Union of Serbia and Montenegro. Later in 2004, while Djukanovic was serving as Prime Minister of Montenegro, a new request for an arrest warrant was submitted but this was again rejected on the basis of the immunity enjoyed by Djukanovic as head of Government of Montenegro. On appeal to the Italian Court of Cassation, it was held that the international rules concerning the immunities of heads of State, heads of Government, and Foreign Ministers could not be applied by analogy to individuals who held similar offices within entities that do not have the status of a sovereign State. In order for an entity to be qualified as a State it must have the capacity to enter into international legal relations. In determining whether or not an entity had such international legal capacity, a number of factors may be relevant: the relevant constitution; the position taken by other States; agreements concluded between Montenegro and other States; and the views held by the Italian Ministry of Foreign Affairs. On the facts, it was clear that Montenegro's participation in international affairs was very limited and that it could not be characterized as a sovereign State. The Prime Minister of Montenegro was not, therefore, entitled to the immunity enjoyed by a head of State or head of Government.[68]

[66] Note that in the past UK courts have accorded immunity to semi-sovereign States dependent on the UK and to their rulers on the basis of certificates issued by the Foreign or Colonial Offices. See *Duff Development v Kelantan* [1924] AC 797; and *Sultan of Johore v Abubakar Tunku Aris Bendahar* [1952] AC 318 (FCO). See also the FCO certificate issued in *BCCI v Price Waterhouse* [1997] 4 All ER 108 which acknowledged that, even prior to 1971, the ruler of Abu Dhabi had been entitled to immunity notwithstanding the fact that the British Government had then been responsible for the conduct of its foreign relations.

[67] ILDC 74 (IT 2004).

[68] There can be little doubt that the approach of the Italian court was correct on the facts but it could be argued that its reasoning was too restrictive given the decision of the ICJ in the *Arrest Warrant* case (n 29 above) which appeared to leave open the possibility that very high-ranking officials other than a head of State, head of Government, or Foreign Minister might be entitled to immunity should their functions require it. However, see Second Report of ILC Special Rapporteur Concepcion Escobar Hernandez who has now proposed that personal immunities should be limited to the head of State, the head of Government, and the Minister for Foreign Affairs (UN Doc A/CN.4/661).

In the UK, section 14(5) of the State Immunity Act 1978 makes specific reference to 'Constituent territories of a federal State' providing that an Order in Council may provide for certain provisions of the Act to apply to a specified constituent territory as they apply to a State.[69] In *HRH Sultan of Pahang v SSHD*,[70] the Sultan claimed the immunities accorded to a head of State by virtue of section 20 of the 1978 Act or by common law, in particular freedom from the immigration control laws of the UK. Under the Constitution of Pahang, the Sultan was described as the 'Sovereign' of Pahang, one of nine Sultanates within the Federation of Malaysia. Under the Malaysian Constitution itself, the office of Supreme Head of the Federation of Malaysia rotates between the rulers of the nine Sultanates. The Sultan had been Supreme Head from 1979 to 1984 but had not served since then. Some years before the proceedings, the Sultan had requested the making of an Order under section 14 in relation to Pahang but the request had been declined. The Court of Appeal dismissed his appeal on the basis of a certificate submitted by the Foreign and Commonwealth Office (FCO) certifying that Pahang was 'a constituent territory of Malaysia' and that the Sultan was the head of that territory and 'not the head of State of Malaysia'.[71] In doing so, the court reaffirmed the conclusive nature of the FCO certificate as regards the recognition or non-recognition of States and the public policy need of the courts to follow that information.[72] The court also rejected the argument that a person could be regarded as a head of State at common law although not recognized as such for the purposes of Part I of the 1978 Act, reiterating its position that the question of whether or not a particular territory is a 'State' for the purposes of immunity must depend on whether it is recognized as such by Her Majesty's Government. The conclusive nature of FCO certificates has also been upheld by the Commercial Court in the *National Transitional Council of the State of Libya* case.[73]

[69] The concepts of 'constituent territory' and 'State' are, therefore, mutually exclusive for the purposes of the Act. See *Pocket Kings Ltd v Safenames* [2010] Ch 438.

[70] [2011] EWCA Civ 616.

[71] See also the certificate submitted in *BCCI (in liq) v Price Waterhouse et al* [1997] 4 All ER 108 in which liquidators of a bank proceeding against its former auditors sought to issue a third party notice against the Ruler of Abu Dhabi, a constituent territory of the United Arab Emirates. The court upheld the Ruler's immunity on the basis of the certificate, which stated that he was at the time regarded as 'head of State of the United Arab Emirates'.

[72] See judgment of Moore-Bick LJ quoting para [349] of the judgment in *Kuwait Airways Corpn v Iraqi Airways (Nos 4 & 5)* [2002] UKHL 19 and the quotation with approval by Maurice Kay LJ of Lord Atkin's statement in *The Arantzazu Mendi* [1939] AC 256 at 264: 'Our State cannot speak with two voices on such a matter [*viz* State sovereignty and matters deriving from it], the judiciary saying one thing, the executive another. Our Sovereign has to decide whom he will recognise as a fellow sovereign in the family of States; and the relations of the foreign State with ours in the matter of State immunities must flow from that decision alone.'

[73] *British Arab Commercial Bank Plc v The National Transitional Council of the State of Libya* [2011] EWHC 2274 (Comm) at paras [22]–[26].

In an earlier case, involving criminal charges against the Governor and Chief Executive of Bayelsa State, a constituent part of Nigeria,[74] the court had also emphasized the conclusive nature of the FCO certificate submitted[75] and held that the Governor was not entitled to immunity as a head of State. In reaching this conclusion, however, the court did enquire into the functions of the Governor as head of Bayelsa and, in particular, his involvement in international relations. This might suggest that, if it had been shown that Bayelsa was involved in such relations, there could have been a sustainable argument that it was entitled to a form of derivative State immunity which would enable its representative to claim head of State immunity or something analogous to it.[76] It is not clear how such an approach can be reconciled with the Court of Appeal's ruling on the conclusive nature of the FCO certificate and this aspect of the judgment was criticized in the later *Sultan of Pahang* case. One possibility is that, although the FCO certificate is conclusive as to the facts certified, namely that a particular individual is or is not to be regarded as head of State, such facts are not in themselves always determinative on the question of immunity.[77]

Deposition and exile

A challenge to a head of State's position may take the form of an ultimately unsuccessful rival claim but may go further and result in actual deposition by internal opposition forces. Alternatively, the State of which he or she is head may be invaded and occupied by foreign forces or may cease to exist as a result of its absorption into another State or unification with another State. In such circumstances, a head of State may voluntarily abdicate or resign thus removing any doubt as to whether or not he or she may still claim the special treatment accorded to a serving head of State. However, in some cases, a head of State, despite being exiled and/or having lost control of a part or the whole of the

[74] *R (on the application of Alamieyeseigha) v Crown Prosecution Service* [2005] All ER (D) 348.

[75] On 26 September 2005, a certificate was issued indicating that Bayelsa was a constituent territory of the republic of Nigeria, a federal State and that Alameiyeseigha was not to be regarded as head of State of the Republic of Nigeria.

[76] See paras [30], [53], and [55].

[77] Clearly, an individual will not be entitled to immunity as a head of State if the certificate indicates that he or she is not regarded as such, but the judgment of the ICJ in the *Arrest Warrant* case (n 29 above) left open a possibility that other high ranking officials who perform important international functions could be entitled to a similar immunity to that enjoyed by a head of State, head of Government, or Foreign Minister. But see draft articles adopted by the ILC on the topic of 'Immunity of State Officials from Foreign Criminal Jurisdiction', which provide that heads of State, heads of Government, and Foreign Ministers enjoy such immunity without mention of any other officials. See p 132 below.

territory forming his or her State, may still claim to be head of that State. It then becomes necessary for other States to decide whether the individual concerned can reasonably be considered to continue to hold that position.

This is an issue of considerable importance as only a legitimate head of State can be regarded as competent to bind his or her State, represent that State in international fora, and consent to armed intervention in its territory. Moreover, only a legitimate head of State can be entitled to the privileges and extensive personal immunity enjoyed by an incumbent head of State. State practice in this area has been uneven and sometimes difficult to reconcile with settled principle.[78]

The preliminary issue as to whether or not a particular individual is recognized as head of State was discussed above. As noted there, the acceptance of such an individual as a head of State by other States depends on the answer to two fundamental and distinct questions. First, is there a State for that individual to be head of? Secondly, if so, does the individual in question occupy the office of head of State? Where a State has clearly ceased to exist, other States cannot continue to accept the individual concerned as a serving head of State. As a result he or she can no longer claim the personal immunity to which such heads are entitled. It might be thought, however, that provided the individual had been accepted as the head of a previously existing State, he or she should continue to enjoy the immunity *ratione materiae* to which all State officials are entitled in respect of acts committed in an official capacity.[79] Recent indications that a forum State is obliged to confer such immunity only when it is invoked[80] might, however, cast some doubt on this given that there would be no State to claim immunity on behalf of its former head.

There may, of course, be many challenges to a head of State's position which do not affect the existence of the State itself. In these circumstances, the head of State may continue to be entitled to be treated by foreign States as a serving head of State.

During an armed conflict, for example, one State may occupy the territory of another. The belligerent occupation of territory does not extinguish the

[78] See MPEPIL (Oxford University Press, 2012) 570 referring in particular to treatment of Governments in exile by States.

[79] In this context, the criminal proceedings brought in 1992 and in 1995 in Germany against Erich Honecker and Egon Krenz are of interest. Both were former heads of State of the German Democratic Republic (which ceased to exist in 1990), and the proceedings were in respect of acts carried out during their terms of office and in the capacity of head of State. Honecker's trial was eventually discontinued because of his ill-health but Krenz was convicted and sentenced to six-and-a-half years in prison in 1997. Both cases were, however, complicated by the nature of the relationship between the German Democratic Republic and the Federal Republic of Germany.

[80] See ICJ in *Certain Questions of Mutual Assistance in Criminal Matters* (*Djibouti v France*) (2008) ICJ Rep 177.

sovereignty of the State under occupation. Thus during the Second World War, heads of States of those countries occupied by Germany did not, by virtue of that occupation, cease to be regarded as the head of their respective States.[81] A more recent example was the belligerent occupation of Kuwait by Iraqi forces in 1990 which led to the temporary exile of the Emir of Kuwait but did not affect his status as head of State.[82]

In such circumstances, State practice supports the view that the exiled leader remains entitled to some form of special treatment under international law. In 1914, President Poincare of France informed the exiled King Albert of the Belgians that he 'would immediately take the necessary measures in order to guarantee in France the stay of your Majesty and of his Ministers in full independence and sovereignty'. During the period of the Belgian Government's exile, a French court held that 'the rules of international law oppose any act of judicial sovereignty which is incompatible with the inviolability of their ministers and of the dignity of the State which they represent'.[83] During the Second World War, the British Government granted diplomatic privileges and immunities to all the members and some senior officials of the seven Allied Governments based in London.[84] In 1943 the Political Department of the Swiss Confederation confirmed (with regard to proceedings before the Higher Court of Zurich) that Queen Wilhelmina of the Netherlands continued to be covered by Article 296 of the Swiss Criminal Code providing for special protection of foreign heads of State against insults.[85] So long as a State continues to recognize an exiled leader as a head of State, it is, at least implicitly, acknowledging that the exile is only temporary, pending return to his or her rightful position. For the State which has accepted the leader into exile, he or she is, prima facie, a visiting head of State and entitled to be treated as such. In practice, however, where such exile is likely to be prolonged and or

[81] By the end of 1941, several heads of States, including King Haakon VII of Norway, Queen Wilhelmina of the Netherlands, the Grand Duchess of Luxembourg, King Peter II of Yugoslavia, and King George II of Greece had taken up residence with their Governments in the UK and continued to be regarded by all Allied States as the legitimate heads of their respective States.

[82] UNSC Resolution 662 (1990) stated that the Iraqi annexation had 'no legal validity, and is considered null and void'. It called on all States and other legal persons not to recognize the annexation and to refrain from any action or dealing that might be interpreted as a recognition of it, whether direct or indirect. See Art 41.2 of the ILC's articles on State Responsibility.

[83] *Charron v Evans et gouvernment Belge* (1915–16) 11–12 RDIP 208 at 213.

[84] Diplomatic Privileges (Extension) Act 1941. See also the grant of diplomatic status by Egypt to the members of the Greek Government when it transferred to Cairo on 24 March 1943.

[85] See Talmon, *Recognition of Governments in International Law* (Oxford University Press, 1998), 251. See also case of 1795 confirming exemption from militia service of William V of the Netherlands, who had fled to England following invasion of his country by France, on the grounds that he continued to be recognized as Netherlands head of State. BDIL, VII 106-108 and McNair, *International Law Opinions* (Cambridge University Press, 1956), i, 108–10.

complicated by the presence of accompanying family members and governmental officials, it is not uncommon for detailed special arrangements to be made between the host State and the exiled head of State.[86]

Given that an exiled leader, who is still recognized as a legitimate head of State, is entitled to special treatment, can it be said that there are any settled criteria determining when he or she should be accorded that recognition?

It is clear that the establishment of a 'puppet' ruler or Government in the territory under belligerent occupation will not, of itself, affect the position of an exiled head of State. Indeed, there will be a presumption that such a government is not independent and any previously existing government and head of State will not thereby lose their status. A similar presumption operates where a new Government has been installed by some form of illegal, outside intervention.[87] Over time, however, such a presumption may be rebuttable and, if subsequent events indicate that a new effective regime has emerged, States may choose to withdraw their recognition from an exiled head of State.[88] This is illustrated by the case of *Haile Selassie v Cable and Wireless Ltd*[89] where, following exile as a result of the Italian invasion of Ethiopia, the Emperor sued on a contract for moneys due to the public revenues of the State. The English court held that Haile Selassie, as the recognized sovereign of Ethiopia, had a right to sue for the money although Italy had *de facto* control of his country. The defendants appealed and, while the appeal was pending, Britain accorded *de iure* recognition to the regime established by Italy. As a result, the Court of Appeal allowed the appeal on the ground that Haile Selassie was no longer head of State.[90]

But what of the situation where the belligerent occupation does not lead to the ousting of the previous incumbent but to the purported continuation of the existing regime under the control of the occupying forces? A pre-existing regime which continues to function during occupation, such as the

[86] See, generally, *Oppenheim's International Law* (9th edn, Oxford University Press, 1992), 146 n4461 n 26; and de Kerchove, 'Quelques questions en droit international public relatives a la presence eta l'activite du gouvernement belge en exil a Londres' (1990) 23 Rev belge de droit int 93.

[87] See eg cases of Prince Norodom Sihanouk of Cambodia, who was ousted in a 1970 coup instigated by Vietnamese forces, and Archbishop Makarios of Cyprus, who was forced to flee in 1974 as a result of a Greek-inspired coup d'etat against his Government. Both succeeded in maintaining their position as heads of State while in exile and were later 're-instated' as such.

[88] See eg King Nicholas I of Montenegro, who was forced into exile by the Austro-Hungarian occupation of Montenegro during the First World War. In 1920, following elections for a new constituent assembly, which were interpreted as indicating that Montenegrins wanted to be included in the new Republic of Yugoslavia, allied Governments, including Britain, withdrew recognition from the previous regime. See Davies, *Vanished Kingdoms: The History of Half-Forgotten Europe* (Allen Lane, 2011) 602–16.

[89] (1939) Ch 182.

[90] He was later 're-recognized' and reinstalled as head of State.

Vichy Government in France, must be distinguished from a new 'puppet' Government established under belligerent occupation. In such circumstances, those who have opposed such occupation may seek refuge abroad and emerge as rival claimants to represent the occupied State. Here it is difficult to discern any consistent State practice. During the Second World War, General de Gaulle, although accepted by the Allies as leader of the Free French, was not regarded as head of State. This was partly due to the existence of the Vichy Government in France led by Marshall Petain but also to lack of unity among rival exiled French groups.[91] It would seem, therefore, that it is often more difficult for a leader appointed in exile to gain recognition as head of State from other States than it is for one who has already occupied that post prior to the belligerent occupation.[92]

The difficulty in identifying clear criteria by which States determine whether or not a particular exiled leader should continue to be regarded as head of State is even more acute in situations where the exile has occurred as a result of internal opposition rather than belligerent occupation. It could be argued that such a change of regime is always a domestic matter for the State concerned. Once a head of State has been ousted and replaced by another effective leader, he or she should cease to be regarded as 'head of State' and continued 'recognition' might, in certain circumstances, be construed as unlawful interference in the internal affairs of the State concerned. Since States have an obligation not to allow their territories to be used as a base for subversive activities against other States, the presence on a State's territory of another State's exiled leader can be problematic.[93]

In practice, however, there have been several examples where heads of State, ousted by internal opposition or by a mixture of internal opposition and outside intervention, have continued to be recognized by other States as the legitimate head of their State.[94] Where such recognition continues, the essence of the legal position adopted by such States is that, despite exile, the leader

[91] Several States continued to recognize the Vichy Government as the legitimate Government of France until August 1944.

[92] But not impossible: see example of the Provisional Czechoslovak Government and its President, Edvard Benes, who received the same privileges as the other allied Governments in exile in London.

[93] Not that this appears to have deterred States when opposition to the new order is sufficiently entrenched—see eg Britain's 'Glorious Revolution' in 1688 when King James II was overthrown and fled to France. France, led by Louis XIV, continued to recognize him as king and, on his death in 1701, recognized James' son as his successor.

[94] See eg President Delvalle of Panama (1988–89), President Aristide of Haiti (1991–94), and President Kabbah of Sierra Leone (1997–98). See statement to House of Commons by UK Foreign Secretary, Robin Cooke, on 13 May 1998 stating: 'President Kabbah, the democratically elected leader of Sierra Leone, was deposed in a military coup in 1997. Britain continues to recognise President Kabbah as the legitimate head of the Government of Sierra Leone...'

remains head of State and, as such, lawfully empowered to speak for and represent his or her State and promote the existence of developments conducive to his or her restoration, although any actions to this effect would have to be in compliance with the laws and regulations of the host State. In *Lafontant v Aristide*,[95] a US court acknowledged the immunity from jurisidiction of the President of Haiti on the ground that he was still recognized as the lawful head of State by the US Government despite the fact that he had been exiled for over three years. In such situations, an exiled leader may have been able to strengthen the position *vis-à-vis* a rival claimant by seeking some form of international endorsement of his or her claim to legitimacy and securing other Governments' support and assistance. The request made in July 1994 by President Aristide to the Secretary General of the United Nations is an example of this.[96]

Given the difficulty that can sometimes arise in determining who is to be regarded as the head of a particular foreign State and the lack of any settled criteria on this matter, it is not surprising that, in practice, national courts often seek the views of their respective Governments.

Role of the Executive: sitting heads of State

There is no internationally prescribed procedure for satisfying a domestic court on the question of whether or not a particular individual is regarded as a head of State (or occupies some other high office entitling the holder to special treatment). In practice, therefore, most national courts rely heavily on the opinions of their respective Governments but the extent to which each government may choose to intervene in a particular case and the extent to which each court is bound to comply with the terms of that intervention can vary. In many cases a formal certificate procedure is available whereby the courts must accept as conclusive certain statements of the Executive (at least as to fact) in determining a question of immunity. It is clear, however, that the way in which the Executive may choose to make its views known in a particular case may vary considerably, even within the same jurisdiction.[97]

In the *Djukanovic* case,[98] the Italian Court of Cassation proceeded on the basis that the view expressed by the Italian Ministry of Foreign Affairs was just one of the factors, albeit one to which considerable weight should be attached,

[95] See n 53 above.

[96] See n 24 above.

[97] See *Holy See v The Hon Eriberto U Rosario Jnr as Presiding Judge of Regional Trial Court of Makati, Branch 61 and Starbright Sales Enterprises Inc* (Philippines Supreme Court) cited by ILC Special Rapporteur Kolodkin in Third Report on *Immunity of State Officials from Foreign Criminal Jurisdiction* (A/CN.4/646 24) May 2011 at n 55.

[98] See n 67 above.

in determining whether or not a particular individual could be regarded as a head of State and thus entitled to special treatment under international law. In other jurisdictions, the Executive may play a more conclusive role.

The State Department in the US, for example, has a longstanding practice of affirmatively suggesting 'head-of-State immunity';[99] a practice which dates back to the mid-1960s, when suggestions were submitted with respect to the South Korean Foreign Minister and King Faisal of Saudi Arabia.[100] In *Habyarimana v Kagame*[101] it submitted a Suggestion of Immunity in a civil case brought against the President of Rwanda, the first paragraph of which stated:

> The United States has an interest in this action because the sole remaining Defendant, President Kagame, is the sitting head of State of a foreign State, thus raising the question of President Kagame's immunity from the Court's jurisdiction while in office. The Constitution assigns to the US President alone the responsibility to represent the nation in its foreign relations. As an incident of that power, the Executive branch has sole authority to determine the immunity from suit of sitting heads of State. The interest of the United States in this matter arises from a determination by the Executive Branch... in consideration of the relevant principles of customary international law, and in the implementation of its foreign policy and in the conduct of its international relations, to recognize President Kagame's immunity from this suit while in office... this determination is controlling and is not subject to judicial review. No court has ever subjected a sitting head of State to suit once the Executive Branch has suggested the head of State's immunity.

The submission went on to state that the fact that the Executive Branch has the constitutional power to suggest the immunity of a sitting head of State does not mean that it will do so in every case and that its decision on this would be guided by consideration of 'international norms and the implications of the litigation for the Nation's foreign relations'. As noted in the submission, the courts in the US have always complied with such suggestions in the context of determinations of head of State immunity even in a situation where it was clear that the head of State concerned had no effective control of his State.[102]

[99] See eg *Tachiona v Mugabe* 169 F.Supp 2d 259 (SDNY, 2001); *Wei Ye v Jiang Zemin* 383 F 3d 620 (7th Cir 2004); and *Manoharan v Rajapaksa* (US Ct of Appeals DC Cir, 29 March 2013). See Lyons, 'The Conclusiveness of the "Suggestion" and Certificate of the American State Department' (1947) 24 BYBIL 116 and Lyons, 'Conclusiveness of the Statements of the Executive: Continental and Latin-American Practice' (1948) 25 BYBIL 180; also Wuerth, 'Foreign Official Immunity Determinations in the US Courts: The Case Against the State Department' (2011) 51 Va J Int'l L 915.

[100] *Chong Boon Kim v Kim Yong Shik* (1964) 81 ILR 604; (1964) 58 AJIL 186 and *Kendall v Saudi Arabia* 65 Adm 885 (SDNY 1965).

[101] (2011) Civ No 10-437-W.

[102] See *Lafontant v Aristide* 844 F.Supp 128.

In the UK it has been the practice for the Executive to certify (usually on a request from the court) as to a person's status but not as to whether or not such status gives rise to immunity, it being left to the court to reach its own conclusions as to the law on the basis of the facts certified.[103] As noted above, the State Immunity Act 1978 contains an express provision that a certificate, by or on behalf of the Secretary of State, shall be conclusive evidence on, *inter alia*, any question 'as to the person or persons to be regarded for those purposes as the head or government of a State'.[104] However, the reference to 'those purposes' is a reference to the purposes of Part I of the Act, which is concerned with the immunity of a State. In practice, therefore, where head-of-State immunity is in question, any certificate is more likely to be issued under section 4 of the Diplomatic Privileges Act 1964, as brought into play by section 20(1) of the State Immunity Act 1978 (which applies to a head of State the provisions of the Diplomatic Privileges Act 1964 as they apply to the head of a diplomatic mission, 'subject to the necessary modifications'.[105]

Aside from these specific statutory provisions, and available if they are not relied upon, is a general power at common law to give a conclusive certificate as to facts peculiarly within the knowledge of the Secretary of State for Foreign and Commonwealth Affairs. An example of such facts in this context would be the period during which the UK Government had regarded a given person as the head of State of a foreign State.

Role of the Executive: former heads of State

The position of former heads of State is considered in Part 4 below but any question as to the immunity of a former head of State in regard to acts carried out while he or she was in office may potentially involve a complex analysis of exactly when such a person became head of State and exactly when that status elapsed. In the *Pinochet* case,[106] in which the UK courts were faced with a

[103] See Wilmshurst, 'Executive Certificates in Foreign Affairs: The United Kingdom (1986) 35 ICLQ 157. In *Apex Global Management Ltd v Fi Call Ltd et al* [2013] EWHC 587 (Ch) the court asked the FCO to certify whether two Saudi princes were members of the family forming part of the household of King Abdullah within the terms of s 20 of the State Immunity Act. As such they would have been entitled to an extensive immunity. The FCO declined on the basis that the question was one of mixed fact and law and that the role of the Executive was to certify only as to facts peculiarly within the knowledge of the FCO.

[104] See s 21(a) of the UK State Immunity Act 1978.

[105] Section 4 reads: 'If in any proceedings any question arises whether or not any person is entitled to any privilege or immunity under this Act a certificate issued by or under the authority of the Secretary of State stating any fact relating to that question shall be conclusive evidence of that fact.'

[106] *R v Bow Street Metropolitan Stipendiary Magistrate, ex parte Pinochet (No 1)* [2000] 1 AC 61 (HL, 25 November 1998); *R v Bow Street Stipendiary Magistrate, ex parte Pinochet (No 3)* [2000] AC 147, (2000) 119 ILR 49 and 135.

request from the Spanish authorities for the extradition of the former Chilean head of State, the defence argued that the criminal acts which Pinochet was alleged to have committed were committed by him in his official capacity as head of State. There was, therefore, a preliminary question as to whether and for what period Pinochet had been head of State of Chile. While it was clear from documents submitted to the court by the Chilean Government that General Pinochet had occupied the office of head of State for some time and had been regarded by the UK as doing so and treated accordingly, the precise date on which his term of office began was less clear.

In September 1973, Pinochet, who was then Commander-in-Chief of the army, had seized power by ousting the Government of President Allende. A new Constitution did not come into force until 11 March 1981, when Pinochet was designated President for a minimum period of eight years. It was clear that he ceased to be President following elections in 1990 when President Aylwin was installed.

In a document issued on 21 October 1998, the Chilean Ambassador in London distinguished between two periods, stating that General Pinochet was President of the Government Junta of Chile from 11 September 1973 until 26 June 1974 and then 'Head of State of the Republic of Chile' until 11 March 1990. On the totality of evidence, it was reasonably clear that he had been head of State from March 1981 until 1990 but there was some room for doubt regarding the period from 26 June 1974 to March 1981 and considerably more uncertainty regarding the period from the date of the military coup in 1973 to 26 June 1974.

In the first hearing before the House of Lords,[107] however, none of the judges enquired whether Pinochet had been the head of State at the time the alleged crimes were committed. They appear to have simply assumed that he had been. Two of them mentioned (without further comment) that there had been no certificate from the FCO on the matter.[108] The issue might have assumed more importance in the second substantive hearing when the Crown Prosecution Service extended the period during which the alleged crimes were said to have been committed, citing conspiracies to torture begun in 1972 at a time when Pinochet was clearly not head of State where immunity could not apply.[109] As a result, however, the defence renewed its focus on arguments

[107] *R v Bow Street Metropolitan Stipendiary Magistrate, ex parte Pinochet (No 1)* [2000] 1 AC 61 (HL, 25 November 1998).

[108] See Lord Nicholls at para [48]: 'There is no certificate from the Foreign and Commonwealth Office but the evidence shows that he was the ruler of Chile from 11 September 1973...until 11 March 1990.... I am prepared to assume that he was head of State throughout the period.' See also Lord Slynn (para [6]), Lord Lloyd (para [26]), Lord Steyn (para [57]).

[109] For this hearing counsel for both sides submitted specific questions to the FCO as to whether Pinochet had been recognized as head of State and, if so, from what date to which the FCO replied by letter. See *UK Materials on International Law* [2000] BYIL 584.

based on double criminality arguing that such charges, in particular those relating to torture and conspiracy to torture, were not 'extraditable crimes' because at the time the acts were committed they were not criminal under UK law. Any question relating to acts committed before 1973, therefore, became irrelevant as the court, ultimately, accepted that the charges of torture and conspiracy to torture relating to conduct before 29 September 1988 (the date on which section 134 of the Criminal Justice Act 1988 came into force creating a new crime of torture under UK law, whereby all torture, wherever committed worldwide as required by the Torture Convention,[110] was made criminal and triable in the UK) were not extraditable.

More recently in *Samantar v Yousef*[111] the role of the US Government in determining the entitlement to immunity of former heads of State and other foreign Government officials has received specific endorsement from the Supreme Court. The State Department filed a statement of interest indicating that Samantar, who had served as Defence Minister and then Prime Minister in the Siad Barre regime in Somalia and was being sued in respect of various alleged acts of torture committed during his period of office, 'enjoys no claim of official immunity from this civil suit'.[112] In doing so, it appeared to rely on the fact that Samantar was now resident in the US and the fact that there was, at the time, no currently recognized Government in Somalia to claim immunity on the former Prime Minister's behalf. It is not clear why the US Government's lack of recognition of the transitional Government of Somalia should have been determinative of the question of whether or not a former official of a previous regime was entitled to immunity, and the issue is discussed in more detail in Part 4 below.[113] In this context, the US Court of Appeals held that State Department determinations of functional or conduct-based immunity are entitled to substantial weight only. This is in contrast to determinations of status-based immunity, such as that enjoyed by a sitting head of State, which must receive absolute deference.[114]

[110] Convention Against Torture and Other Cruel, Inhuman or Degrading Treatment or Punishment 1984, 1465 UNTS 113.

[111] 130 S Ct 2278 (2010); see also Stewart, 'Samantar v Yousef: Foreign Official Immunity Under Common Law' ASIL INSIGHTS 14 June 2010, 15 February 2011 (FD Va).

[112] 15 February 2011 (FD Va).

[113] The decision of the ICJ in *Certain Questions of Mutual Assistance in Criminal Matters (Djibouti v France)* (2008) ICJ Rep 177, which suggested that a forum State is under no obligation to accord functional immunity unless invoked, may be a possible explanation. See also ILC Second Report, *Immunity of State Officials from Foreign Criminal Jurisdiction* UN Doc A/CN 4/631, para 216 and Third Report UN Doc A/CN 4/646, paras 16–19. In January 2013 the US formally recognized the new Government in Somalia, which has now requested immunity for its former Prime Minister.

[114] However, recent filings by the US Department of State in *Doe v Ernesto Zedillo Ponce de Leon* (Suggestion of Immunity of 7 September 2012 in respect of former President of Mexico); and

The case is primarily of interest, however, because it had prompted an earlier decision by the Supreme Court that the Foreign Sovereign Immunities Act (FSIA), which governs the immunity of States, does not apply to foreign Government officials. It had always been accepted that the Act did not apply as regards immunity for incumbent heads of State[115] but, in 1990, a US court ruled that it did apply to other foreign Government officials as 'agencies and instrumentalities'.[116] This was at odds with the view of the Executive Branch, which had always maintained that such immunity derived from federal common law as informed by international custom.[117] The Supreme Court confirmed this to be correct, noting '[w]e have been given no reason to believe that Congress saw as a problem, or wanted to eliminate, the State Department's role in determinations regarding individual official immunity'.

4. Protection, Privileges, and Immunities

Freedom of movement

It is perhaps obvious but still worth noting that, although heads of State are entitled to extensive privileges and immunities, they do not have the right to enter a foreign State without the consent, implied or otherwise, of that State. An official visit would, of course, always take place at the invitation of the receiving State, but heads of States frequently undertake private visits. It is, however, always open to a State to deny entry to a foreign head of State, thus avoiding the embarrassment of having to accord special treatment to a leader who may be considered politically undesirable.

In 1987, the US barred President Waldheim of Austria from entry into the US as a private citizen because of his activities during the Second World War.[118] In 1993, President Mobutu of Zaire was refused permission to enter France.[119] In 2012, the European Court of Justice (ECJ) held that Slovakia was entitled to refuse to allow the President of Hungary to enter its territory.[120]

Rosenberg v Lashkar-E- Taiba (Suggestion of Immunity of 17 December 2012 in respect of two former Directors-General of Pakistan's intelligence service) affirm the view of the US Government that the Executive branch retains sole authority to determine the immunity from suit of former foreign officials.

115 *First American Corpn v Al-Nahayan* 948 F. Supp 1107 (1996); (1996) 121 ILR 577.

116 *Chuidian v Philippine National Bank* 912 F 2d 1095 (1990).

117 See US Government Statement of Interest filed in *Matar v Dichter*, SDNY 05 Civ 10270 (WHP).

118 RGDIP, 91 (1987) 1315–16.

119 See press reports of 18 March 1993, referring to French Foreign Ministry statement on previous day.

120 Judgment in Case C-364/10 *Hungary v Slovakia*, 16 October 2012.

The President had wished to participate in a ceremony held to commemorate a sensitive event in recent Slovakian history. The ECJ held that, in view of the special status enjoyed by a head of State under international law which entails privileges and immunities, it was permissible for Slovakia to limit the President's freedom of movement in this way. This was in spite of the fact that, because of the enhanced freedom of movement conferred under the European Union (EU) Treaty, such a limitation could not have been imposed upon ordinary EU citizens.

Another example is the action taken by the UK Government in regard to the former Libyan leader Muammar Gadaffi and certain members of his family. Section 20(1) of the State Immunity Act 1978 stipulates that a sovereign or other head of State, members of his family forming part of his household, and his private servants, shall enjoy the same privileges and immunities as the head of a diplomatic mission, members of his family forming part of his household, and his private servants. In practice this means that heads of State are exempt from normal UK immigration controls and may enter the UK at any time without requiring leave to do so.[121] However, the exemption from control is subject to any direction to the contrary by the Secretary of State and, in 2011, such a direction was made effectively removing the exemption from Gadaffi, members of his family forming part of his household, and private servants. Such a direction did not, by itself, constitute any withdrawal of recognition of Gadaffi as Libya's head of State, nor did it deprive him or members of his family of any existing personal or functional immunities. It merely prevented him from entering the UK without specific permission.[122]

Nowadays such individual action by a State may be supplemented or preceded by collective measures by international organizations requiring Member States to take the necessary steps to prevent the entry into or transit through their territories of certain individuals, including heads of State and other members of a Government.[123]

The only exception to the general principle that a State remains free to refuse to permit entry to any foreign head of State may occur where that State is the host country for an international organization. In such circumstances, it

[121] Section 8(3) of the Immigration Act 1971.

[122] In 2013 the Government of Bolivia threatened to lodge a formal complaint with the UN over the alleged refusal by a number of European countries of overflight and/or permission to land for the Bolivian President's plane while he was returning from Moscow to Bolivia. However, the facts are disputed and it is unclear on what basis any such claim could be made.

[123] See para 15 of the UN Security Resolution 1970 (2011). See also 2012 EU travel ban on President Bashar Assad of Syria and members of the Assad family.

may be obliged to admit representatives from Member States, including heads of State, in accordance with its obligations under the host country agreement with the organization concerned. Such admission may take place subject to the normal procedures and conditions of the receiving State but, nonetheless, removes the right of the latter to refuse entry altogether. An example is the Agreement between the United Nations and the United States Regarding the Head Quarters of the United Nations 1947. Section 11 provides that the US Government shall not impose 'any impediments to transit to or from the Head Quarters District' for the representatives of member Governments accredited to the UN, the families of such representatives, and other persons invited by the UN on official business. Section 12 states that these provisions are applicable 'irrespective of the relations existing between the Government of the persons referred to [in section 11] and the Government of the United States'.[124] The Agreement does, however, confer a right on the US to require a representative of a member Government to leave its territory in the case of abuse of privileges in matters outside his or her official duties.

Freedom of communication

When visiting a foreign State, a head of State must be permitted to communicate freely with his or her home Government. Such freedom of communication is an essential guarantee of the functions of diplomatic missions, and is accordingly protected by Article 27 of the Vienna Convention on Diplomatic Relations 1961. Article 28 of the Convention on Special Missions 1969 contains equivalent provisions which apply to a head of State on a special mission.

There is, of course, a distinction between allowing a visiting head of State to keep in touch with his or her home State and other members of his or her Government wherever they may be and permitting such a head of State to actively participate in the conduct of State affairs while he or she is on the territory of another State. In the past, it was often difficult for a head of State to conduct affairs of State, other than those directly connected with the official visit to the receiving State: such matters usually had to await his or her return to the home State.[125] However, modern communications and the increasing frequency with which heads of States travel have changed this and it is now common for such business to be conducted while abroad. Strictly speaking,

[124] In 2012, for example, the US admitted the Iranian leader Ahmadinejad, together with an entourage of 140 Iranian officials.

[125] Although there were always exceptions—see Watts (n 2 above) 72 who gives the example of King Edward VII who appointed HH Asquith as Prime Minister of Britain, even though the king was at the time in Biarritz ((1908) RGDIP 442).

such action may involve the exercise by an organ of one State of sovereign powers in the territory of another.[126] In practice, however, it is almost always action which has no impact on the receiving State's territory and involves no encroachment upon or derogation from its territorial sovereignty; its effects are solely within the head of State's own State. In such circumstances, States seem content to permit visiting heads of State and other foreign Government officials to perform various acts associated with the conduct of governmental matters in their home States.[127]

The position may be different if the acts concerned take effect within the territory of the State being visited or have damaging consequences for the internal affairs or international relations of that State. It seems clear that a receiving State need not permit such acts. Watts gives the extreme example of a visiting head of State who seeks to condemn to death a member of his suite, and comments that it is clear that this would be regarded as an unacceptable exercise of authority.[128] A head of State, like an ambassador, is under a duty to respect local laws and regulations and must, similarly, avoid interfering in the host State's internal affairs. Conversely, that State is under no obligation to tolerate the continued presence of foreign heads of State who abuse their position in this regard.[129]

Dignity

Dignity is a quality often regarded as an inherent characteristic of sovereign States which other States are under a duty to respect. This dignity of the State was demonstrated particularly in the special regard with which a foreign head of State was to be held by other States. When visiting their territory, they were expected to ensure that such a head of State was not insulted or defamed and was accorded the appropriate treatment and protection. This would include strict observation of any formal title and form of address, acknowledgment of rank *vis-à-vis* other heads of State, and prevention of any attacks on the head of State's official symbols (such as the official coat of arms or national flag). Even the jurisdictional immunity enjoyed by States was attributed in part to

[126] In 1994, President Aristide of Haiti, who was still in the US, was reported to have ordered an extraordinary session of the Haitian Parliament to be held in order to consider an amnesty for those who had deposed him, *The Times*, 26 September 1994.

[127] Examples often given are the signing of decrees and appointment of officials: see MPEPIL vol 4 (Oxford University Press, 2012) *Governmental Activities on Foreign Territory* 557.

[128] Watts (n 2 above) 72.

[129] In 1967, the President of France, Charles de Gaulle, while on an official visit to Canada, made a speech supporting the secessionist movement in Quebec; this was regarded as an interference in Canada's internal affairs and the visit was brought to an end shortly thereafter—see (1967) 91 RGDIP 1315–16.

the impairment of their dignity, which it was thought would necessarily be involved were they to be subjected to the jurisdiction of the courts of another sovereign.[130]

It has been argued that the concept of States having a duty to protect the dignity of foreign sovereigns is an antiquated one in international law.[131] Dignity, whether of States or their heads, has also been described as an 'elusive notion'.[132] However, while it is true that many aspects of State practice in this regard survive, if they survive at all, as matters of protocol and ceremonial, there is still a residual element which survives as a matter of international law. A legal duty to protect the dignity of a State's representatives is expressly acknowledged in respect of diplomatic agents in Article 29 of the Vienna Convention on Diplomatic Relations 1961 (VCDR).[133] This duty is mirrored in Article 40 of the Vienna Convention on Consular Relations 1963 and it has been stated that the duty to respect the dignity of a head of State is an *a fortiori* case.[134] The Convention on Special Missions 1969, which includes special missions led by a head of State,[135] and the Convention on the Prevention and Punishment of Crimes against Internationally Protected Persons, including Diplomatic Agents 1973,[136] recognize a similar obligation. In 2001, at its meeting in Vancouver, the Institute of International Law adopted a resolution on the 'Immunities from Jurisdiction and Execution of Heads of State and Government in International Law', according to which States must take 'all reasonable steps to prevent any infringement' of a foreign head of State's 'person, liberty, or dignity'. Such general references, while showing a clear acceptance of the principle that States should protect a

[130] See *Schooner Exchange v McFaddon* (1812) 11 US 116 at 137 where Marshall CJ based the immunity of one sovereign from the jurisdiction of another in part on the former's obligation 'not to degrade the dignity of his nation' by submitting to the jurisdiction of another. And later, a sovereign in visiting another State is described thereby as 'not intending to subject himself to a jurisdiction incompatible with his dignity, and the dignity of his nation'.

[131] See Reisman, 'Sovereignty and Human Rights Law in Contemporary International Law' (1990) 84 Am J Int'l L 866.

[132] Watts (n 2 above) 41.

[133] In the UK, under the State Immunity Act 1978, those provisions of the VCDR which apply to the head of a diplomatic mission and have the force of law, shall also apply to a head of State with any 'necessary modifications'. Accordingly, the UK is obliged to treat a head of State with 'due respect and take all appropriate steps to prevent any attack on his person, freedom and dignity'.

[134] See Watts (n 2 above) 41. See also Memorandum of the Legal Bureau of the Canadian Ministry of Foreign Affairs, 31 January 1981, which notes 'even greater respect is owed to the visiting sovereign or head of State, since his own diplomatic envoys in the host State are clearly inferior to him': Canadian YBIL (1981) 325.

[135] Article 29 obliges the receiving State to treat State representatives on special mission 'with due respect and [to] take all appropriate steps to prevent any attack on their... dignity'.

[136] Article 2(3) recognizes the existence of an 'obligation... under international law to take all appropriate measures to prevent... attacks on the... dignity of an internationally protected person'.

foreign head of State's dignity, do not shed much light on precisely what this means in practice.

The respect owed to the dignity of a head of State is, of course, respect for the office of head of State rather than the personal dignity of the individual for the time being holding that office. This does not mean, however, that the protection afforded by customary international law does not apply to a head of State in his personal capacity. In practice it is clear that the obligation owed by a State is owed to a foreign head of State both in his public and private capacity.[137]

It is also clear that, in principle, violation of a foreign head of State's dignity may occur even when he or she is not present in the territory of the State where the acts prejudicial to dignity have occurred.[138] This is because the position as head of State is one which is held *erga omnes*, at all times.[139] It seems likely, however, that the standard of observance required may be more demanding when the head of State is present in the territory of the other State.[140] The wording of Article 29 suggests that the concept of an attack on 'dignity' is capable of being much wider than a purely physical attack and may include verbal abuse and the publication of insulting material. Indeed, in *JAMS v Public Prosecutor*, the Netherlands Supreme Court ruled that a scurrilous attack on a foreign head of State in the local press violated the obligation to prevent attacks on the dignity of such a person.[141]

It has been suggested that any such duty may be limited to dealings between friendly States 'since when relations have become strained, particularly where

[137] See *Harb v King Fahd Abdul Aziz* [2005] EWCA Civ 632 where it was assumed that Art 29 of the VCDR, which applies to heads of State in the UK through s 20 of the State Immunity Act 1978, was capable of applying to support an application for immunity in divorce proceedings against the King of Saudi Arabia to be heard in private; see also *Aziz v Aziz & Sultan of Brunei* [2007] EWCA Civ 712 at para [57].

[138] But see *Aziz v Aziz & Sultan of Brunei* [2007] EWCA Civ 712 at para [93] where Lawrence Collins LJ concluded that there was 'insufficient material to support... the existence of a rule of customary international law requiring States to take steps to prevent [*private*] individuals from insulting foreign heads of State abroad'.

[139] See Watts (n 2 above) 42. This may be contrasted with the position of an ambassador who has that quality only as regards the receiving State, and only in its territory with a limited extension when passing through a third State if travelling to or from the receiving State.

[140] See *Satow's Diplomatic Practice* (6th edn, Oxford University Press, 2009) 12.11. See also *JAM v Public Prosecutor* (1970) YBIL 222, (1970) 73 ILR 387, Netherlands Supreme Court, 21 January 1969, *Arrest Warrant* case *(Arrest Warrant of 11 April 2000 (DRC v Belgium)* (2002) ICJ Rep 3) where, in Joint Separate Opinion 88, Judges Higgins, Kooijmans, and Buergenthal indicated that the level of special protection owed to a foreign head of State might be a little less during private travel but would still exclude arrest and detention; and *Certain Matters of Mutual Assistance in Criminal Matters (Djibouti v France)* (2008) ICJ Rep 177 where the ICJ indicated that, if French authorities had passed confidential information relating to the Djiboutian head of State to the French press, *in the context of an official visit* by the latter, it would have constituted a violation of France's international obligations.

[141] See n 139 above.

they have degenerated into war or conflict, it is not unusual for States to make offensive observations about the heads of the other States concerned'.[142] There is a great deal of sense in this observation and, certainly, where all constructive contact between States has been abandoned, particularly where there is outright conflict, it would be difficult to argue that such a duty was still relevant given that one of the main purposes of the obligation is to preserve good relations between States. Relations between States may, however, become strained without necessarily breaking down completely, especially nowadays where it is more common than it once was for States to criticize the conduct of other States as regards internal matters such as their human rights record. In such circumstances, robust criticism of practice and policy is commonplace and it is unlikely that such criticism, even if directed at the head of State concerned, would contravene a State's international obligations.[143] However, unprovoked abuse of a more personal nature, particularly if committed by a State's own representatives or within the context of official contact between the two States such as an official visit, may be a different matter and could contravene the obligation to protect a head of State's dignity.

The duty to respect and take appropriate steps to prevent attacks on a head of State's dignity can be divided into two broad categories. The first is where the acts allegedly attacking such dignity are performed by the State itself through any of its organs or agents; and the second is where such acts are carried out by independent third parties such as private individuals, business, or a free press. As regards the first category, it is clear that States themselves have a duty under international law to refrain from offensive conduct against the head of another friendly State, and the only question is whether the acts concerned constitute such an attack on the dignity of the head of State. If they do so then the latter is entitled to complain and to request appropriate redress.

The second category requires a more complex analysis which must determine not only whether the acts concerned amount to an attack on dignity but also whether the respondent State has failed to take 'all appropriate' steps to prevent such attacks. This distinction was identified by the ICJ in the *Case Concerning Certain Questions of Mutual Assistance in Criminal Matters (Djibouti v France)*[144] when referring to Article 29 of the VCDR: 'This provision translates into

[142] See Watts (n 2 above) 42 where he notes that such practices are of longstanding and do not seem to have been the subject of protest by the other State concerned.

[143] See General Comment by Human Rights Committee on Art 19 of the ICCPR: '...all public figures, including those exercising the highest political authority such as heads of State and government, are legitimately subject to criticism and political opposition': CCPR/C/GC/34 (12 September 2011) para 38.

[144] (2008) ICJ Rep 177.

positive obligations for the receiving State as regards the actions of its own authorities, and into obligations of prevention as regards possible acts by individuals. In particular, it imposes on receiving States the obligation to protect the honour and dignity of heads of State, in connection with their inviolability.'

Turning first to a State's positive obligation in respect of actions by its own authorities. It is clear that service of legal process, even where such service is in respect of a third party, may violate a State's obligations in this regard. On a visit to the United States, the Chinese President was purportedly served with legal process in connection with a civil claim against him. The court held that the President was immune from suit and deferred to the view of the US Government that such service is often seen as an affront to foreign leaders and their States and is capable of damaging US foreign relations and impeding policy.[145] *Djibouti v France* is one of only two cases in which the ICJ has directly considered a State's obligation to prevent attacks on the dignity of a foreign head of State. Djibouti claimed that France, by sending two witness requests to the head of State of Djibouti, had violated its obligation to prevent attacks on the dignity of an internationally protected person.[146] It invoked the 1973 Convention on the Prevention and Punishment of Crimes against Internationally Protected Persons, including Diplomatic Agents in this regard and also relied on Article 29 of the VCDR. There were two witness requests; the first, which did not comply with the relevant French procedures, was sent to the Djiboutian head of State on 17 May 2005 while he was on an official visit to France; the second, which was issued on 14 February 2007 in accordance with normal procedures, was sent out when the Djiboutian President was in France for the 24th Conference of Heads of State of Africa and France.

The ICJ concluded that the 1973 Convention was not applicable to the facts but, referring to Article 29 of the VCDR, confirmed that there was a positive obligation on a receiving State to protect the honour and dignity of heads of State 'in connection with their inviolability'. However, despite

[145] *Wei Ye v Jiang Zemin* 383 F 3d 620 (7th Cir 2004). See also *Tachiona v United States* 386 F 3d 205, 2004 US App (2nd Cir, 6 October 2004) where the court held that service of process, irrespective of the identity of the defendant, on a person entitled to immunity from jurisdiction and personal inviolability under Art 29 'interferes with that person's representative functions and constitutes an affront to his or her dignity'. See also Memorandum of Law of 16 November 2001 submitted by US Government which stated that such service, even when directed at a third party, would give rise to 'vexatious and embarrassing assaults on the dignity of foreign leaders and diplomats'.

[146] Djibouti had also argued that the summonses constituted measures of constraint which, therefore, violated the head of State's inviolability and jurisdictional immunity. However, the ICJ rejected this argument on the ground that the summonses were merely invitations to testify which the head of State could freely accept or decline. For further discussion of this point see pp 76–80 below.

criticizing the incorrect procedure used to transmit the first witness request,[147] which it was stated had failed to comply with 'the courtesies due to a foreign head of State', the ICJ stopped short of ruling that such lack of courtesy amounted to a violation of France's obligation to protect the latter's dignity. It further held that the second request, which had been in the correct form prescribed by French law, did not constitute an attack on the dignity of the President merely because the invitation had been sent to him when he was in France to attend an international conference. It did, however, observe that if, as alleged by Djibouti, it could have been proved that the French authorities had passed confidential information relating to the investigation to the French media, such an act could, in the context of an official visit by the Djiboutian head of State, have constituted a violation by France of its international obligations.

A similar situation arose before the ICJ in *Certain Criminal Proceedings in France (Republic of Congo v France) (Provisional Measures)*.[148] The French authorities had issued criminal complaints against several Congolese Government officials and the terms of the complaints attributed responsibility for the crimes alleged to, among others, President Sassou Nguesso. During a State visit to France by President Nguesso, an investigating judge tried to obtain evidence from him under rules of procedure whereby evidence may be sought through the diplomatic channel. The Congo brought a claim before the ICJ alleging, among other matters, that France had violated the jurisdictional immunity of its head of State. The case was later withdrawn at the request of the Congo but, before that, the ICJ had considered the request of the Congo for provisional measures calling for the immediate suspension of the proceedings being conducted by the French investigating judge. In doing so, the Court was only required to examine the risk presented by the French proceedings and, in particular, whether they had caused or would cause 'irreparable prejudice' to the Congo's claimed rights. It was not required to determine whether or not those proceedings contravened those rights.

In seeking provisional measures, the Congo claimed that the criminal investigation in France was adversely affecting the Congo's international relations, especially in relation to the functions of the head of State, whose honour and reputation had thus been publicly impugned. It further stated that without provisional measures there would be a 'continuation and exacerbation of the prejudice already caused to the honour and reputation of the highest authorities of the Congo, and to internal peace in the Congo, to the international

[147] Instead of being sent through the Ministry of Foreign Affairs (MFA) as required by French law, it had been transmitted by fax to the Djiboutian Embassy inviting the President to attend as a witness the next day.

[148] (2003) ICJ Rep 102.

standing of the Congo and to Franco-Congolese friendship'. The Congo's claim was based on an allegation that France had failed to respect the jurisdictional immunity of a head of State. French law made it clear, however, that the President could only have been approached to give evidence with the express agreement of the Congo. Moreover, France was able to show that its laws clearly embodied the principle of head of State immunity and stated that it 'in no way denies that President Sassou Nguesso enjoys as a foreign head of State, immunities from jurisdiction both civil and criminal'. On this basis the ICJ denied provisional measures.

It is not entirely clear but the reasoning of the majority suggests that, even if the original claim had been pleaded specifically on the issue of France's obligation to protect the President's dignity, provisional measures would still have been denied, and that the continuing investigation of a foreign head of State, without the application of any measures of constraint, would not have been considered sufficient to cause 'irreparable prejudice' to the Congo's claimed rights. The absence of any formal measures of constraint seems to be the key factor, although presumably the presence of such measures would also have breached the President's inviolability. It is worth noting that three of the judges took a different view. Even on a claim based solely on violation of jurisdictional immunity, they considered that provisional measures would have been justified. The separate opinion of Judge de Cara focused in particular on the potential interference with the head of State's ability to carry out his duties but also on the damage to the *dignity* of the Congo as personified by its President.[149]

The approach taken by the ICJ, or at least the majority, was robust in the sense that a modern head of State is clearly expected to tolerate investigative and evidence-seeking activities by the relevant authorities of other States, provided they are bona fide, conducted in accordance with settled procedures, and do not involve measures of constraint or elements of gratuitous insult or offensive behaviour. In 2010, the French Court of Cassation ruled that an investigation into allegations of corruption against Presidents Sassou Nguesso of the Republic of Congo, Teodoro Obiang Nguema Mbasogo of Equatorial Guinea, and Ali Bongo of Gabon could proceed. The ruling followed the compilation by French police of an extensive list of properties, including houses, bank accounts, and luxury motor cars, owned by the three Presidents and their families. It is clear that, if the investigation were to result in criminal proceedings, the three rulers would be immune from prosecution as sitting

[149] He stressed that the position of a head of State in Africa was, in his view, unique because 'he symbolizes the existence of a nation'. As such, any attack on his honour or reputation is essentially an attack on the State he represents.

heads of State. However, the position with regard to their family members and associates may be less straightforward.[150]

Generally speaking, States and their representatives are mindful of the usual international courtesies due to a foreign head of State and cautious in their dealings with such persons, but private individuals can be less restrained. It is evident, however, that the modern trend in such cases is to strike a balance between the respect due to a foreign head of State and the interests of justice and the rights of individuals.

This aspect has been demonstrated in two cases involving private litigants before the English courts. In proceedings between a former wife of the Sultan of Brunei and a fortune-teller, the Sultan intervened to seek directions to redact and anonymize all references to himself and the intimacies of his married life.[151] He did so on the basis that, as a serving head of State, he was entitled under UK law to the same respect as an ambassador[152] and that the UK was, therefore, obliged to treat him with 'due respect...and take all appropriate steps to prevent any attack on his dignity'. The court held there to be 'no supervening right in a foreign sovereign to complete protection irrespective of the interests of justice but the courts will do all that can be done consonantly with the interests of justice to protect any third party, a foreign sovereign included, from the fallout of other people's litigation'. In an earlier case, the English Court of Appeal had held that the obligation to prevent attacks on a head of State's dignity did not entitle the King of Saudi Arabia to a private hearing of his preliminary plea of immunity in connection with proceedings brought against him for ancillary relief under the Matrimonial Causes Act 1973.[153]

It seems likely, therefore, that where settled legal procedures (such as the collection of evidence in a criminal investigation or the proper conduct of litigation) are involved, a foreign head of State is entitled to no more protection than any ordinary citizen, provided inviolability or immunity from jurisdiction are not compromised.[154] Such procedures may, of course, embarrass

[150] See *The Times*, 10 November 2010. But see ICJ press report of 26 September 2012 (*Equatorial Guinea v France*) reporting that Equatorial Guinea is seeking to institute proceedings against France alleging that the investigation of the President and arrest warrant issued against the second Vice-President of Equatorial Guinea violates principles of equality between states, non-intervention, sovereignty, and respect for immunity from criminal jurisdiction.

[151] *Aziz v Aziz & Sultan of Brunei* [2007] EWCA Civ 712 at para. [172], per Sedley LJ.

[152] See s 20(1) of the State Immunity Act 1978.

[153] *Harb v His Majesty King Fahd Bin Abdul Aziz (No 2)* [2006] 1 WLR 578 (CA (Civ)). See Thorpe LJ: 'In my judgment a claim to state immunity is essentially a public claim that demands open litigation.'

[154] It has been argued that the applicant's argument in the *Harb* case '...was simply specious. Article 29 deals with the inviolability of the person of a diplomat and, for present purposes, of a head

a head of State and give rise to some criticism and adverse publicity, but unless an element of gratuitous and or deliberately insulting conduct is involved they will not amount to an attack on the dignity of that foreign head of State.

It is unclear to what extent international law imposes a positive obligation on States to prevent offensive conduct by private individuals in other contexts. In the past, States were often prepared to take a fairly hard line in suppressing material and conduct which they considered offensive to a friendly foreign head of State and frequently proffered apologies. It was not always clear, however, whether such States saw themselves as acting because they were under an international obligation to do so or because local law required them to do so. Similarly, it is not always clear whether a particular apology was intended as anything more than a diplomatic courtesy rather than a recognition of legal fault. Some States, but by no means all, have enacted legislation prohibiting offensive conduct towards foreign heads of States: thus Article 118 of the Criminal Code of the Netherlands makes it an offence to 'intentionally insult' the head (or head of Government or other member of government) of a friendly State. Similar general provisions still exist in some other European countries and other States around the world. In others there is more limited provision in regard to intimidatory or harassing language or behaviour within a certain distance of a visiting foreign head of State.[155]

It is clear, however, that international law does not make the creation of special offences or penalties for offensive conduct by private individuals against foreign heads of State compulsory.[156] Some States, including the UK, do not have special offences in this regard and, generally speaking, offensive comments have been punishable only if they are obscene or constitute a criminal libel.[157] Where the offensive conduct directed against a foreign head of State satisfies the requirements for a criminal prosecution under a particular State's law, it has been suggested that the State is probably under an international obligation to ensure respect for the dignity of the head of State by instituting

of State; and an attack on a diplomat or head of State's person, freedom or dignity, for the purposes of the provision, involves more concrete and immediate acts, such as manhandling, jostling and direct verbal assault': O'Keefe (2005) 76 BYIL 575. See also Denza, *Diplomatic Law* (3rd edn, Oxford University Press, 2008) 264 referring to the conclusion in *Aziz v Aziz* that 'There was no authority from custom or precedent for the proposition that respect for dignity required confidentiality of court proceedings'.

155 See US Act for the Protection of Foreign Officials and Official Guests of the United States 1972 (1973) 67 AJIL 622.

156 See *Oppenheim's International Law* (9th edn, Oxford University Press, 1992) 380; *Satow's Diplomatic Practice* (5th edn, Oxford University Press, 1979) para 15.4.

157 The offence of criminal libel has now been abolished in the UK. See s 73 of the Coroners and Justice Act 2009.

criminal proceedings against those concerned.[158] Apart from that, an injured party, including a head of State, may, if they choose, pursue civil law remedies under the law of defamation or libel.[159]

Even where special offences do exist they are nowadays rarely invoked and it has been argued that such offences may be inconsistent with modern notions of freedom of expression. In *Colombani and others v France*,[160] the European Court of Human Rights held that a French law of 1881, which made it an offence 'publicly to insult a foreign head of State', contravened Article 10 of the European Convention.[161] The case was brought by two French journalists who had been convicted under the law for insulting the King of Morocco. In an article on drug manufacture and trafficking in Morocco published in the newspaper *Le Monde*, it had been stated that Morocco was a serious contender for the title of 'the world's leading hashish exporter' and that a confidential report had cast doubt on King Hassan II's entourage. It went on to question the avowed determination of the king and other Moroccan authorities to combat the increase in drug-trafficking on Moroccan territory. The European Court took the view, at least in the context of Article 10, that special protection for heads of State cannot be justified, stating:

> The Court notes that the effect of a prosecution under section 36 of the Act of 29 July 1881 is to confer a special legal status on heads of State, shielding them from criticism solely on account of their function or status, irrespective of whether the criticism is warranted. That in its view, amounts to conferring on foreign heads of State a special privilege that cannot be reconciled with modern practice and political conceptions. Whatever the obvious interest every State has in maintaining friendly relations based on trust with the leaders of other States, such a privilege exceeds what is necessary for that objective to be attained.[162]

The judgment made no direct reference to the duty imposed on all States by international law to treat foreign heads of State with due respect and take all appropriate steps to protect their dignity. Nevertheless, it does not seem likely that it would have been prepared to accept that such a duty requires an entirely uncritical approach. It is notable that, where cases have arisen in the past, there has been a tendency to distinguish between reasoned, albeit fairly robust criticism (which is permissible), and conduct which is gratuitously

[158] Watts (n 2 above) 46.

[159] See eg *Haile Selassie v Evening Standard Co Ltd*, *The Times*, 28 July 1938, 4; and *Zog, King of the Albanians v Sunday Pictorial Newspapers (1920) Ltd*, *The Times*, 28 May 1943, 8.

[160] ECHR App No 51279/99, Judgment of 25 June 2002.

[161] France subsequently abolished the provision. In 2005 Belgium repealed a similar law with respect to the punishment of insults to foreign heads of State.

[162] At para [68].

offensive or which, even if associated with political criticism, oversteps reasonable limits and becomes deliberately insulting, alarming, or offensive (which is not).[163]

There is little modern State practice with regard to the precise meaning of a State's duty to 'take all appropriate steps to prevent any attack' on a foreign head of State's dignity, although it is clear that it confers a wide discretion on States in determining what may be appropriate in a particular case. A useful analogy in this regard can be found in Article 22.2 of the Vienna Convention on Diplomatic Relations which imposes a duty on States parties to 'take all appropriate steps' to protect the premises of a foreign mission on its territory against intrusion or damage and 'to prevent any disturbance of the peace of the mission or impairment of its dignity'. In practice, most receiving States determine the measures necessary to protect foreign missions in the light of the particular circumstances prevailing at the time. In 1984 in the UK, the shooting of a woman police constable from the Libyan People's Bureau during a demonstration outside its premises by Libyan dissidents prompted the House of Commons Foreign Affairs Committee to look closely at the nature of the Government's powers and duties in respect of such demonstrations. The Libyan mission had requested that the demonstration be prevented. In its *Report on the Abuse of Diplomatic Immunities and Privileges*, the Committee concluded that the duty to prevent:

> cannot be given so wide an interpretation as to require the mission to be insulated from expressions of public opinion within the receiving State. Provided always that work at the mission can continue normally, that there is untrammelled access and egress, and that those within the mission are never in fear that their mission might be damaged or the staff injured, the requirements of article 22 are met.

It also noted the unreported case of *R v Roques* where a magistrates' court had refused to uphold the right of the police to move demonstrators from the pavement outside the South African Embassy, on the basis that impairment of the dignity of the mission would require 'abusive or insulting' behaviour and that political demonstrations did not in themselves amount to such.[164]

The meaning of the requirement to 'take all appropriate steps' to prevent the impairment of a mission's dignity was considered in detail by the Australian Federal Court in *Minister for Foreign Affairs and Trade and others v Magno and another*.[165] A hundred small white crosses had been placed outside the

[163] See Watts (n 2 above) 44–5.

[164] For further comment, see Higgins, 'The Abuse of Diplomatic Privileges and Immunities: Recent United Kingdom Experience' (1985) 79 AJIL 641 at 651.

[165] (1992) 101 ILR 202.

Indonesian Embassy in Australia by demonstrators protesting against the killing of people in East Timor by Indonesian military forces. Acting under regulations enacted to give effect to Australia's obligations under the Vienna Convention, the Minister had certified that removal of the crosses was an 'appropriate step' within the meaning of Article 22 (and Article 29) as their presence could lead to the 'impairment of the dignity, or the disturbance of the peace, of the mission or of the head, or other diplomatic agent of the mission'. By a majority, the court upheld the validity of the regulations but was not required to consider whether removal of the crosses had been a proper exercise of the powers conferred. Nevertheless, it went on to make a number of observations on the nature of the duty under Article 22. Judge French (who was in the majority which upheld the regulations) noted that disturbance of the peace of the mission and impairment of its dignity may overlap but are separate notions in that 'the dignity of the mission may be impaired by activity that would not amount to a disturbance of its peace'.[166] He went on to give some examples of what might constitute such activity. Offensive or insulting behaviour in the vicinity of and directed to the mission may fall into this category. The burning of the flag of the sending State or the mock execution of its leader in effigy if committed in the immediate vicinity of the mission could well be construed as attacks upon its dignity. So too might the depositing of some offensive substance and perhaps also the dumping of farm commodities outside mission premises in protest against subsidy practices of the sending State.[167]

He emphasized that any such incident would need to be assessed in the light of the surrounding circumstances and that notions of peace and dignity are 'not amenable to clear rules of definition'. The need to strike a balance between a receiving State's duties in this regard and fundamental freedoms of speech and assembly was also stressed. In this connection it was observed that 'the sending State takes the receiving State as it finds it. If it finds it with a well established tradition of free expression, including public comment on matters of domestic and international politics, it cannot invoke either Article 22(2) or Article 29 against manifestations of that tradition'.

Judge Einfield (dissenting) supported a very narrow interpretation of the term 'impairment of dignity' and of the duty to protect under Article 22, considering that in order to qualify such conduct must be linked to a disruption of the mission's essential functions. In his view any obligation to 'take appropriate steps' could only arise when an activity is occurring or is threatened 'which is so undignified and ungracious to visiting foreign diplomats

[166] (1992) 101 ILR 202 at 231. [167] (1992) 101 ILR 202 at 232.

as to bear down on their capacity to carry out the particular tasks they are in Australia to perform'. He added that any action taken to prevent impairment had to be consistent with freedom of expression and must, therefore, meet the test of proportionality. On this analysis, he found the regulations to be too broad and hence invalid.[168] This dissent carries echoes of the decision of the US Supreme Court in *Boos v Barry*.[169] The court held, by a majority, that a provision of the District of Columbia Code prohibiting the display of any sign within 500 feet of a foreign mission, if it tended to bring the foreign government concerned into 'public odium' or 'public disrepute', was a violation of the First Amendment. The US Government had urged that the legislation be upheld on the ground that there was a compelling Government interest in protecting the dignity of foreign diplomatic personnel in order for it to give effect to its obligations under the Vienna Convention. The court did not address the question whether a 'dignity interest' existed under international law but, on the assumption that it did, took the view that the prohibition was too broad and was 'not narrowly tailored to serve a compelling State interest'.

The practice relating to foreign missions suggests that, while States enjoy a wide margin of discretion in deciding what action, if any, may be appropriate in order to comply with their duty to prevent attacks on a head of State's dignity, they need to be careful in doing so to strike a balance between that obligation and traditional freedoms of expression and assembly. In 1999, the UK police removed banners and flags from Free Tibet protesters while the Chinese President Jiang Zemin was on a state visit. They also used police vans to mask the President's view of demonstrators during his visit to Buckingham Palace and the Chinese Embassy. Proceedings for judicial review were brought challenging the lawfulness of the police action.[170] The action was settled on the basis of a consent order under which the court granted declarations that it was unlawful for the police to remove banners and flags from demonstrators just because they were protesting against Chinese Government policy and that it was unlawful to place police vans in front of such demonstrators if the purpose was to suppress free speech.

[168] In 2002, the Australian Minister for Foreign Affairs signed certificates under the same powers entitling police to stop demonstrations by Falun Gong outside the Chinese Embassy on the basis that noise amplifiers and large staked banners used by the protesters impaired the dignity of the mission; see (2002) 23 AYIL 351 (Australian Practice in International Law).

[169] [1988] 485 US 312. See also extracts in *Digest of US Practice 1981–1988*, vol 1, 954–60.

[170] *R v Commissioner of Police for the Metropolis* CO/129/2000, unreported; *The Times*, 20 October 1999. See account also in Denza, *Diplomatic Law* (3rd edn, Oxford University Press, 2008) 174.

Protection

The rules of customary international law regarding the protection of foreign heads of State are clearer than those relating to dignity largely because the concept of physical protection does not change over time and is much less susceptible to varying interpretation. It has long been accepted that a State is under an obligation to protect a visiting head of State from physical attack and to take all appropriate steps to ensure that protection and to punish anyone who attempts such attack or, despite the steps taken, succeeds in causing injury or damage to a head of State. Some States have laws dealing specifically with the matter[171] while in others, like the UK, there is no specific offence or special penalty. The obligation to protect extends, not only to the safety of a head of State's person but also to the premises in which he or she resides while in the receiving State's territory, personal baggage, and other property accompanying the head of State and any means of transport used by the head of State in entering, leaving, and travelling within the territory of the receiving State.

When considering the extent of the obligation to protect a visiting foreign head of State, Article 29 of the Vienna Convention on Diplomatic Relations again provides a useful analogy. As in the case of 'dignity', the duty to prevent any attack on the person or freedom of a diplomatic agent is not cast in absolute terms. Instead, a State must 'take all appropriate steps to prevent' any such attack. In the late 1960s and early 1970s a series of kidnappings of diplomats took place mainly in South America with the object of extorting political concessions and money from the receiving State. In one of the cases, involving the kidnap of the West German ambassador to Guatemala, the Guatemalan Government refused to release prisoners or pay the ransom demanded by the kidnappers on the grounds that such action would endanger national security and violate its Constitution. Following the murder of the ambassador, the German Government protested that Guatemala should have done more to secure his release and had violated its obligations under Article 29.[172] In some other cases, receiving States had capitulated to the hostage-takers' demands. However, as incidents increased, State practice hardened and it became apparent that for most States a policy of giving in to kidnappers when the safety of diplomatic personnel was threatened could not be regarded as an inherent

[171] Watts refers in this context to an early practice of including in extradition treaties a so-called *attentat* clause by which crimes against foreign heads of State were not to be considered as political offences for which extradition could be declined: (n 2 above) 49.

[172] See Denza, *Diplomatic Law* (3rd edn, Oxford University Press, 2008) 259.

requirement of Article 29. There were limits to the duty to protect and it seems likely that similar considerations would apply in regard to a visiting head of State.

As in the case of foreign diplomats, international law allows receiving States a wide margin of discretion in determining the 'appropriate steps' to be taken to protect the person of a visiting head of State. Nevertheless, the initial duty to prevent such attacks, particularly in the case of a visiting head of State, is an onerous one. In practice, measures are determined in the light of the relevant circumstances and any particular threats or dangers. Arrangements for any visit, including relevant security precautions, are settled in advance by consultation between sending and receiving States. Heads of State frequently take with them their own official means of transport and their own personal protection staff who work with local security authorities, including the police, in carrying out their task. However, whatever the arrangements, it is the receiving State not the head of State's own security personnel that has the international obligation to protect the head of State concerned.

In 1973, following the series of kidnappings and attacks on senior State representatives, the UN General Assembly adopted, by consensus, a Convention on the Prevention and Punishment of Crimes Against Internationally Protected Persons, including Diplomatic Agents. The definition of an 'internationally protected person' includes a head of State and 'any member of a collegial body performing the functions of a head of State under the Constitution of the State concerned'. In adopting the Convention, the Assembly emphasized the importance of:

> the rules of international law concerning the inviolability of and special protection to be afforded to internationally protected persons and the obligations of States in relation thereto

thereby acknowledging that international law requires States to give heads of State special protection.

A key element of the Convention is the distinction made between heads of State and other senior State representatives falling within the category of 'internationally protected person'. While the former qualifies as such a person 'whenever' he or she is in a foreign State, other representatives fall within the definition only 'when... entitled pursuant to international law to special protection' from any attack on person, freedom, or dignity. This may suggest that there are times when such persons are not so entitled, for example in the case of private visits to foreign States. The Convention also contains a specific provision stating that the fact that certain serious offences against internationally protected persons are expressly listed does not derogate from the obligation of States Parties under international law to take all appropriate measures to prevent other attacks on the person, freedom, or dignity of such persons.[173]

The main provisions of the Convention require that persons alleged to have committed any one of the specified offences should either be extradited or prosecuted. The offences include murder, kidnapping, or other attacks on the person; attacks on official premises, the private accommodation, and means of transport of an internationally protected person likely to endanger his person or liberty; and threats or attempts to commit any such attack or participation as an accomplice in any such attack. The Convention requires that a State Party make these offences crimes under its internal law, punishable by appropriate penalties which reflect their grave nature. It does not require that the penalty should be greater because of the fact that the victim was an internationally protected person.

Inviolability

The personal inviolability of serving heads of State is one of the oldest established rules of international law relating to their treatment. The positive obligations imposed on a receiving State to protect visiting foreign heads of State and to take all appropriate steps to prevent attacks on their person, freedom, and dignity is just one aspect of this inviolability. The key element is, however, the receiving State's obligation to refrain from exercising sovereign powers and, in particular, those relating to the enforcement of its laws in any way which might infringe that inviolability. Unlike jurisdictional immunity, it is not just a procedural bar but an absolute physical privilege. Accordingly, the police or other authorities of a State may not arrest or physically detain a foreign head of State without his or her consent. Moreover, in the *Arrest Warrant* case,[174] the ICJ held that the 'mere issue' of an arrest warrant violated the inviolability which an incumbent Foreign Minister enjoyed. The same must *a fortiori* be true in relation to a head of State.[175] This aspect of the judgment has been criticized by some on the basis that only an attempt to actually enforce the arrest warrant would have infringed Mr Yerodia's immunity[176] and that holding that mere issue and circulation was sufficient, particularly in regard to a subject who was not visiting the forum State, represented a significant extension of the customary international law rule in this regard.

The inviolability extends to the residence, personal baggage, and other accompanying property and means of transport of the visiting head of State. In this context, it should be noted that inviolability attaches to premises in

[173] Article 2(3).

[174] *Arrest Warrant of 11 April 2000 (DRC v Belgium)* (2002) ICJ Rep 3 at paras 70–1.

[175] See *Case Concerning Certain Questions of Mutual Assistance in Criminal Matters (Djibouti v France)* (2008) ICJ Rep 177 at paras [170], [174].

[176] See dissenting opinion of Judge Oda (para [51]).

which a head of State resides by virtue of that residence and not by virtue of any ownership or title which he or she may have; thus, inviolability may attach to even a temporary residence such as a hotel suite. If, however, a head of State owns a house or apartment in a foreign State, it will not be inviolable except when he or she is in residence.

In those cases where the visit of a head of State falls within the scope of the 1969 Convention on Special Missions, its provisions broadly reflect the inviolability of the person, premises, and property of a visiting head of State. A head of State, as part of a special mission, has personal inviolability and is not liable to any form of arrest or detention.[177] The Convention also provides for the inviolability of the premises of the special mission so that agents of the receiving State may not enter them without permission; and those premises, their furnishings, and other property used in the operation of the mission and its means of transport are immune from search, requisition, attachment, or execution;[178] the archives and documents of the special mission are inviolable at all times and wherever they may be, as is the official correspondence of the mission.[179] Provision is also made for the inviolability of any private accommodation of the head of State as a member of the special mission, as well as his papers, correspondence, and (with limitations matching those applying to immunity from suit) private property.[180]

In practice there have been very few cases on the inviolability enjoyed by a foreign head of State, and it is, therefore, difficult to draw firm conclusions as to its precise limits. Again, however, the inviolability conferred on a diplomatic agent under the Vienna Convention provides a useful analogy.[181] Article 29 provides that 'the person of a diplomatic agent shall be inviolable'. Like Article 22, which provides for the inviolability of the mission premises, the provision is unqualified although it seems likely that a very limited exception to the otherwise absolute prohibition on detention or other forms of restraint may be implied on the basis of self-defence or of an overriding duty to protect life. This exception has been generally acknowledged by writers in relation to diplomatic agents,[182] but circumstances justifying such exceptional measures are, of course, less likely to arise in the case of a visiting head of

[177] Article 29. [178] Article 25. [179] Article 28. [180] See pp 89–96 below.

[181] In the UK, the link is made explicit with s 20 of the State Immunity Act 1978 providing that the Diplomatic Privileges Act 1964 (which gives the force of law to certain provisions of the Vienna Convention, including Art 29) shall apply to a sovereign or other head of State 'as it applies to the head of a diplomatic mission'.

[182] See Denza, *Diplomatic Law* (3rd edn, Oxford University Press, 2008) 267–8 in which it is concluded that the risk to the public must be of an 'extreme and continuing character' to justify any restraint on an inviolable diplomat.

State who, unlike a diplomat, is rarely in the territory of the receiving State for much time.

It is clear that personal inviolability would preclude personal service of legal process on a head of State.[183] However, questions have arisen as to whether inviolability would preclude such service where the legal process concerned does not involve any direct assertion of compulsory jurisdiction over the head of State as such. This could occur, for example, where the service of process is in respect of a complaint against a non-immune third party or involves a request to appear as a witness in proceedings against another.

In *Tachiona v United States*[184] suit was filed against President Mugabe of Zimbabwe while he was visiting the US for the UN Millenium Summit. The complaint also named Foreign Minister Robert Mudenge and the ruling Zimbabwe African National Unions-Patriotic Front (ZANU-PF). Mugabe and Mudenge were served both in their individual capacities and in their capacities as representatives of ZANU-PF. The US Government filed a 'suggestion of immunity' asserting that both Mugabe and Mudenge were entitled to absolute personal immunity under the customary international law doctrine of head of State immunity and, as representatives of the Government of Zimbabwe to the United Nations Millenium Summit, were also entitled to 'diplomatic immunity' under the Convention on Privileges and Immunities of the United Nations ('the UN Convention'). Under both the doctrine and the UN Convention they enjoyed personal inviolability and could not be the subject of service of process in any capacity, including on behalf of ZANU-PF. The US district court refused to give effect to the assertions of inviolability in respect of the claims against ZANU-PF, reasoning that service of process on behalf of a third party did not involve any form of legal compulsion. In a strongly worded Memorandum, the US Government challenged this ruling stating that it would give rise to:

> vexatious and embarrassing assaults on the dignity of foreign leaders and diplomats, as individuals who wish to protest or humiliate such individuals will be able through simple artifice to plead a complaint against a non-governmental entity with which an official allegedly is affiliated and then to publicise and stage a highly visible service of process on the visiting dignitary.

On appeal, the Second Circuit reversed the ruling of the lower court finding that both Mugabe and Mudenge, as persons entitled to immunity from jurisdiction

[183] There is a question as to whether service of legal process relating to a narrow range of purely private professional and/or commercial acts performed by the head of State would be prohibited under international law particularly in the context of a private visit to the forum State, but this matter is discussed later under the section dealing with private acts.

[184] 386 F 3d 205, 2004 US App.

and personal inviolability as set out in Article 29 of the Vienna Convention, were protected from service not only in their own right but also as agents for ZANU-PF. It did so, however, by reference to the UN Convention only and did not address head of State immunity, concluding that service of process on an individual entitled to personal inviolability (irrespective of the identity of the defendant) 'interferes with that person's representative functions and constitutes an affront to his or her dignity'.

The same issue arose in *Wei Ye v Jiang Zemin*[185] where a US district court again rejected the US Government's argument that the personal inviolability enjoyed by a foreign head of State must protect him against service of process even where such process was ultimately directed at a non-immune third party (the Falun Gong Control Office). Citing the decision of the district court in the *Mugabe* case, it held that 'service of process cannot be seen under all circumstances to be an affront to a head of State's inviolability'. Nevertheless, it went on to dismiss the complaint against the third party, holding that President Jiang Zemin had not been an agent of the Office and that there was no basis for jurisdiction over the latter. On appeal, the Seventh Circuit ruled that the district court had erred in rejecting the US Government's contention as to a head of State's inviolability from legal process, even in the case of service directed at a third party. It noted that such questions pertain to the effective conduct of foreign affairs and diplomatic relations and a court should accept the Government's assertion in this regard as conclusive and binding upon it.

In the *Mutual Assistance* case[186] the ICJ examined alleged attacks on the inviolability and immunity from jurisdiction of the Djiboutian head of State involving two witness 'summons' issued by a French investigating judge. The usual form of such summons included a warning that failure or refusal to attend could result in the witness being compelled to do so and was punishable by a fine. This warning was omitted from both requests sent to the Djiboutian head of State. The Court referred to its statement in the *Arrest Warrant* case in which it had noted that the immunity and inviolability enjoyed by a head of State and certain other very high-ranking officials was designed to protect him or her 'against any act of authority of another State which would hinder him or her in the performance of his or her duties'. The key consideration was whether the head of State had been subjected to any 'constraining act of authority'.[187] In this connection it found that the first 'summons' (which had

[185] 383 F 3d 620, 2004 US App (7th Cir 8 Sept 2004).

[186] *Case Concerning Certain Questions of Mutual Assistance in Criminal Matters (Djibouti v France)* (2008) ICJ Rep 177.

[187] See also Dissenting Opinion of Judge Al-Khasawneh in the *Arrest Warrant* case *(Arrest Warrant of 11 April 2000 (DRC v Belgium)* (2002) ICJ Rep 3) where he expressed the view that the mere opening of an investigation could not, in itself, amount to an infringement of an incumbent Foreign Minister's immunity.

not been issued in the correct form) had not been associated with any measures of constraint and 'was in fact merely an invitation to testify which the head of State could freely accept or decline'. The second 'summons', which was in the form prescribed by law, was again a mere request. As such, they did not infringe his inviolability or immunity from jurisdiction.

This case, together with *Certain Criminal Proceedings in France (Republic of Congo v France)*[188] is important in establishing that national courts may investigate alleged crimes committed abroad and, in the course of those investigations, seek testimony from an incumbent foreign head of State without necessarily infringing the latter's immunity from jurisdiction or inviolability.[189] It is worth noting that in the *Mutual Assistance* case, the subject of the investigation concerned international crimes allegedly committed by third parties, whereas in *Republic of Congo v France* the alleged crimes concerned acts for which responsibility was attributed, among others to the incumbent President himself. It is, however, difficult to draw any firm conclusions from the latter case as it was withdrawn from the Court's list at the request of the Government of the Republic of Congo, following the decision to deny the latter's request for provisional measures.[190]

Immunity from suit before foreign courts

In considering a head of State's immunity from the jurisdiction of foreign courts, it is necessary to distinguish carefully between the extensive personal immunity enjoyed by incumbent heads of State and the separate functional immunity or immunity *ratione materiae* enjoyed by all State officials in

[188] *Certain Criminal Proceedings in France (Republic of Congo v France) (Provisional Measures)* (2003) ICJ Rep 102.

[189] See O'Donnell, 'Certain Criminal Proceedings in France (Republic of Congo v France) and Head of State Immunity: How Impenetrable Should the Immunity Veil Remain?' (2008) 26 Boston University International LJ 375 where it is concluded that, although an incumbent head of State enjoys absolute personal immunity, the ICJ's decision to reject the Congo's request for provisional measures (which would have stopped the French investigation entirely) indicates that it will not allow that 'veil of absolute immunity' to 'blindfold the Court or human rights litigants from international law violations. An incumbent head of State's decisions, while cloaked in an impenetrable veil during his tenure, are not invisible. Rather they are carried out on an international stage'.

[190] In 2010, the French Court of Cassation upheld a call by Transparency International for an investigation into corruption charges involving Presidents Denis Sassou Nguesso of the Republic of the Congo, Teodoro Obiang Nguema Mbasogo of Equatorial Guinea, and Ali Bongo of Gabon (Re Investigation of Assets 'Bien Mal Acquis' Case, Court of Cassation, No 6042 9 November 2010). As sitting heads of State the three rulers will be able to claim immunity from any resulting prosecution but investigation could lead to proceedings against their relatives and associates and to their own prosecution following departure from office. See *The Times*, 10 November 2010 and the *Sunday Times*, 10 April 2011. However, on 26 September 2012, the Republic of Equatorial Guinea instituted proceedings against France (including a request for provisional measures) before the ICJ seeking the annulment of the proceedings and investigative measures against President Mbasogo and its Vice-President (against whom an arrest warrant has also been issued) on the ground that such actions violate 'the principles of equality between States, non-intervention, sovereignty and respect for immunity from criminal jurisdiction'. See Press Release <http://www.icj-cij.org>.

respect of official acts carried out while they were in office. A former head of State continues to be entitled to the latter after he has left office but it is far less extensive than the personal immunity enjoyed by an incumbent head of State. The differences between these two types of immunity are discussed in section 1 above.

Personal immunity of incumbent head of State

(a) Criminal proceedings

It has long been accepted that, under customary international law, a serving head of State enjoys absolute immunity from the criminal jurisdiction of foreign courts.[191] Moreover, the ICJ has held that this type of immunity applies not only in relation to official acts but also in relation to private acts and regardless of whether the head of State is on official business or on a private visit.[192] Similarly, the immunity will apply whether the act concerned was carried out before the head of State assumed office or during the period of office.[193] The extensive nature of a sitting head of State's personal immunity in this regard has long been acknowledged by national courts. In 1989 the Swiss Supreme Court agreed with the following proposition:

> Heads of State are absolutely exempt *ratione personae* from all measures of constraint and exercise of jurisdiction on the part of a foreign State for acts committed by them, anywhere in the world, in the exercise of their official functions. By contrast with immunity from civil jurisdiction...immunity from criminal jurisdiction of heads of State is absolute...This immunity would appear to cover, without reservation, to private acts.[194]

The ICJ's conclusion in *Arrest Warrant of 11 April 2000 (DRC v Belgium)* was based upon the view that such full immunity is necessary to protect the head of State against any act of authority of another State which would hinder that individual in the performance of his or her duties. Before that decision, it had been argued that an exception to this rule of absolute inviolability and immunity from criminal jurisdiction should be accepted in the case of serious crimes under international law. However, the relatively sparse State practice that existed did not support such a contention and, even in the *Pinochet* case, where an exception was admitted to the functional immunity enjoyed by a former head of State in relation to the crime of torture, the Court emphasized that the personal immunity to which an incumbent head of State was

[191] See eg *Re Honecker* (1984) 80 ILR 365.

[192] This is in contrast to the type of personal immunity enjoyed by a person on special mission which applies only when the individual concerned is on official business and for the duration of the special mission.

[193] See *Arrest Warrant of 11 April 2000 (DRC v Belgium)* (2002) ICJ Rep 3 at para [55].

[194] See *Marcos v Federal Department of Police* (1989) 102 ILR 53 at 57.

entitled remained unaffected by any such exception.[195] The 2001 Resolution of the Institut de droit international provides:

In criminal matters the head of State shall enjoy immunity from jurisdiction before the courts of a foreign State for any crime he or she may have committed, regardless of its gravity.[196]

In 2013, the International Law Commission (ILC) adopted three draft articles within the context of its work on the topic 'Immunity of State Officials from Foreign Criminal Jurisdiction', draft Article 3 of which declares that serving heads of State, heads of Government, and Ministers for Foreign Affairs enjoy immunity *ratione personae*.[197]

The full immunity of a serving head of State in this respect is widely supported in State practice. In 1999, a Spanish court ruled that, for as long as he was in office, the Cuban leader Fidel Castro could not be prosecuted in Spain for international crimes[198] and in 2001 the French Court de cassation confirmed that, under customary international law, sitting foreign heads of State enjoyed full immunity from criminal proceedings before French courts regardless of the gravity of the crime charged, which in that case involved the alleged shooting down of a civil aircraft.[199] It stated that international custom must preclude such proceedings in the absence of specific international provisions to the contrary binding on the parties concerned.[200] More recently, the Spanish Audiencia Nacional upheld the immunity of President Kagame of Rwanda on charges of genocide, crimes against humanity, war crimes, and terrorist acts.[201]

[195] See Lord Browne-Wilkinson: 'immunity enjoyed by a head of State in power and an ambassador in post is a complete immunity attached to the person of the head of State or ambassador and rendering him immune from all actions and prosecutions...'. See also statement by UK Attorney-General that Saddam Hussein was immune from criminal proceedings in the UK while a serving head of State in Iraq, HL Deb, 27 January 2003, vol 643, cols 910–12, (2003) 74 BYIL 670; and *Mugabe*, Senior District Judge at Bow Street Magistrates, 14 January 2004, (2004) 53 ICLQ 769 where the judge refused to issue an arrest warrant against Robert Mugabe in regard to allegations of torture on the grounds that, as the serving head of State of Zimbabwe, he was entitled to immunity from the criminal jurisdiction of the UK courts.

[196] Article 2 of 2001 Vancouver Resolution on the Immunities from Jurisdiction and Execution of Heads of State and of Governments in International Law.

[197] See Second Report of ILC Drafting Committee A/CN.4/L.184.

[198] See Order (auto) of 4 March 1999 (no 1999/2723) Audiencia Nacional.

[199] *Ghadaffi* (2001) 125 ILR 456 (France Court of Cassation). Although some commentators have interpreted the judgment as suggesting implicitly that international law may recognize some exceptions to the personal immunity of incumbent heads of State for certain crimes. See Zappala, 'Do heads of State in Office Enjoy Immunity from Jurisdiction for International Crimes?: The Ghadaffi Case Before the French Court of Cassation' (2001) 12 EJIL 595.

[200] See the original French version which reads as follows: 'la coutume internationale s'oppose a ce que les chefs d'Etats en exercice puissent, en l'absence de dispositions internationales contraires s'imposant aux parties concernees, faire l'objet de poursuites penales d'un Etat etranger.'

[201] *Audiencia Nacional, Auto del Juzgado Central de Instruccion* No 4, 6 February 2008. See Art 3.1 VCDR. See also case filed against the King of Morocco (*Auto de la Sala Penal de la Audiencia Nacional*, 23 December 1998). See *US v Al Nashiri, Suggestion of Immunity* 6 February 2012 (Motion filed 31 January 2012).

It is clear that a diplomatic agent is not obliged to give evidence in criminal (or civil) proceedings.[202] Under customary international law it seems that the personal immunity enjoyed by a sitting head of State would, at least, preclude his or her compulsion in regard to appearing or giving evidence as a witness.[203]

(b) Civil and administrative proceedings

(i) Scope of immunity It is clear that, under customary international law, a serving head of State is entitled to an extensive immunity from the civil and administrative jurisdiction of foreign courts. However, from time to time, questions have arisen as to whether such immunity is quite as comprehensive as in the case of criminal proceedings and, in particular, whether a head of State may be sued in relation to his private acts or even acts carried out in an official capacity if they are of a commercial or purely private law character. The development of the restrictive theory of State immunity might suggest that it should be possible to sue a head of State in contexts where exceptions to immunity for a State have been clearly established. Against this, however, a comparison with the immunity enjoyed by the head of a diplomatic mission would suggest that immunity from civil jurisdiction should be granted for all acts, including those of a private law nature with the possible exception only of the narrow categories set out in Article 31 of the Vienna Convention on Diplomatic Relations. These would, by analogy, relate to matters of inheritance, real property, and commercial or professional activities in the forum State involving the head of State in his non-official capacity.

Any uncertainty as to an incumbent head of State's immunity from the civil jurisdiction of foreign courts can, of course, be avoided if the view is taken that he or she is entitled to an absolute personal immunity along the lines of that enjoyed in respect of criminal proceedings. In modern times this has been the approach in some jurisdictions. In 1964 the Austrian Supreme Court held that the *acta iure imperii/acta iure gestionis* distinction did not apply to cases involving foreign heads of State and dismissed the claim of an Austrian national against the Prince of Liechtenstein who had been regarded as responsible for a road accident in Austria.[204] More recently, it held that a serving head of State was immune from a paternity suit.[205] In *Lafontant v Aristide*, a US district court held the President of Haiti to be 'absolutely immune

[202] See Article 31.2 VCDR

[203] See *US v Al Nashiri*, Suggestion of Immunity February 6 2012 (Motion filed January 31 2012 Case before Military Commission) where defendant tried to depose President Saleh of Yemen (US Digest (2012) 347.

[204] *Prince of X Road Accident Case* (1964) 65 ILR 13 (Austria, Supreme Court).

[205] *AW v J(H)F v L (Head of State)*, Austria Supreme Court, 15 February 2001. Also reported as *W v Prince of Liechtenstein and others* Oxford Reports on International Law (ILDC) 1 (see p 91 below).

from personal jurisdiction in United States courts' in respect of an unlawful killing in Haiti. In doing so, the court considered it to be irrelevant whether the conduct alleged was official or private, because his immunity as head of State barred the exercise of all personal jurisdiction over him. This broad approach has continued to be reflected in the current practice of the US, both as regards judicial decisions and the practice of the Executive in submitting 'suggestions' of immunity with regard to incumbent heads of State.[206] Following the collapse of the Bank for Credit and Commerce International (BCCI) as a result of fraud, the trustees of a US bank owned by BCCI brought a civil suit in the US courts against, among others, the ruler of Abu Dhabi, who owned a substantial percentage of BCCI. A suggestion of immunity was filed with the court on behalf of the ruler as a foreign head of State. This was accepted by the court as conclusive.[207]

The approach in other jurisdictions has not always been as clear cut. In some civil law jurisdictions practice has been particularly variable. It is useful, therefore, to examine a head of State's personal immunity (immunity *ratione personae*) from civil proceedings under three separate headings relating to different categories of acts. Such distinctions are, of course, more important when the functional immunity (*immunity ratione materiae*) of a former head of State is in question but, even in the context of personal immunity, they can serve to illuminate the different considerations and rationales applicable to such cases.

Before doing so, one general question remains as to whether a head of State's immunity from civil or administrative jurisdiction would preclude a State from holding an inquest into his or her death. Such a question is, perhaps, unlikely to arise very often but, given the modern tendency for foreign leaders to seek medical treatment abroad it is not without some practical relevance. The matter is not entirely free from doubt but, by analogy with the position of a diplomat, it seems unlikely that such an inquest would take place without the consent of the State concerned. Under Article 39(2) of the Vienna Convention on Diplomatic Relations, a diplomat's immunities subsist for a 'reasonable period' after his or

[206] See *Kendall and others v Kingdom of Saudi Arabia and others* (1966) 60 AJIL 100; *Alicog and others v Kingdom of Saudi Arabia and others* 860 F Supp 379 (District Court for the Southern District of Texas, 1994) (dismissal of complaint against King Fahd for false imprisonment and abuse); *Anonymous v Anonymous* (1992) 581 NYS 2d 776 (divorce proceedings dismissed against head of State); *Daventree Ltd v Republic of Azerbaijan* No 09-01106 (No 02-6356 SDNY, 10 March 2003) claims alleging fraud against Azerbaijani President dismissed (unreported); *Al Hassan v Al Nahyan* (No 09-01106 CD Cal, 17 September 2010) claim against UAE President dismissed (unreported); *Habyarimana v Kagame* (US Ct of Appeals 10th Circ, 2012) (civil suit against President Kagame of Rwanda alleging his involvement in the shooting down of aeroplane carrying the then Presidents of Rwanda and Burundi); *Tawfik v Al Sabah* 2012 WL 3542209 (SDNY) (claim against the Emir and sitting head of State of Kuwait dismissed); *Fotso v Cameroon et al.* (No 12-01415 D.Ore 2012) claim against President Biya of Cameroon; and *Manoharan v Rajapaksa* (US Ct of Appeals DDC) 29 March 2013 (civil claim against President of Sri Lanka alleging torture). See also *Digest of US Practice in International Law* (2012) Ch 10 Immunity of Foreign Officials 323–48.

[207] *First American Corpn and others v Sheikh Zayed Bin Sultan Al-Nahyan and others* (US 1996) 1119.

her functions have come to an end and, although the Convention contains no express provision on inquests, it appears to be general practice that such inquiries do not take place unless the sending State agrees.[208]

(ii) Official and sovereign acts It has long been accepted that a head of State has immunity at least in respect of conduct involving matters of sovereign, governmental, or public authority. Indeed, this principle was established long before any clear rules on the personal immunity of foreign sovereigns had emerged. In *Duke of Brunswick v King of Hanover*,[209] an English court held that a foreign sovereign could not be made responsible 'for an act done in his sovereign character in his own country whether it be an act right or wrong…'. It went on to rule that:

> the courts of this country cannot sit in judgment upon an act of a sovereign effected by virtue of his sovereign authority abroad, an act done not as British subject, but supposed to be done in the exercise of his authority vested in him as sovereign.

Similarly, in *De Haber v Queen of Portugal*[210] the court confirmed that:

> an action cannot be maintained in an English court against a foreign potentate for anything done or omitted to be done by him in his public capacity as representative of the nation of which he is the head.

It went on to note that such proceedings would be contrary to the law of nations and an insult which a foreign sovereign would be entitled to resent. In an 1870 case a French businessman sued the Russian Tsar for damages suffered from alleged illegal arrests and seizures committed by the Russian police on Russian territory. The French court dismissed the claim on the grounds that the operation of a State's justice system within its own territory was clearly an attribute of State sovereignty for which no foreign State or its head could be sued before the French courts.[211] However, the reasoning applied in these early cases indicates that they were decided on immunity *ratione materiae* grounds rather than on any clear concept of the personal immunity of a foreign head of State.

The functional immunity to which all State officials, including heads of State, are entitled would cover sovereign acts. Where civil proceedings are brought in regard to an act carried out in the exercise of sovereign and official authority, it could be said, therefore, that such proceedings are instituted against a head of State impersonally, in his official capacity as an organ of that State. As such, they could be characterized as proceedings against the State

[208] See Denza, *Diplomatic Law* (3rd edn, Oxford University Press, 2008) 284.

[209] (1848) 2 HLC 1 (UK, HL).

[210] (1851) 17 QB 171 (UK Court of Queen's Bench).

[211] *Ministere Public v Dlle Masset*, in Kiss, *Repertoire de la pratique francaise en matiere de droit international public* (1965) III, 269 (France, Cour de Paris, 1870). See also *Emperor of Austria v Lemaitre* 1874 1 JDI 32, A-C Kiss (1965) iii 269 (France Cour de Paris 1872).

itself which would be barred on general grounds of state immunity. Practice, therefore, generally treats the State as the true defendant and nowadays this is reflected in the UN Convention on the Jurisdictional Immunities of States and Their Property 2004, which includes, in the definition of 'State', 'its various organs of government' and 'representatives of the State acting in that capacity'.[212] In this way it confers upon a serving head of State acting in a public capacity the same immunity in respect of civil proceedings as the State enjoys.

In practice, many national courts have accepted a similar definition in the operation of their own state immunity legislation.[213] The overlapping aspect of the two different types of immunity in this context has sometimes made it difficult to tell on what basis exactly national courts have upheld a foreign head of State's immunity in regard to official and sovereign acts. However, immunity in such circumstances has almost always been recognized.[214]

One way of looking at the matter would be to conclude that the immunity *ratione materiae* of a head of State becomes relevant only after he has left office. Before then, it is effectively masked by the more extensive 'head of State' personal immunity which it is generally accepted covers private acts (at least in respect of criminal proceedings) as well as those which are of an official and sovereign nature. Alternatively, one could take the view that an incumbent head of State's immunity *ratione personae* is not brought into play by proceedings brought in regard to acts carried out in an official and sovereign capacity which are covered by the immunity of the State itself and the ancillary immunity *ratione materiae* to which all State officials are entitled. However, such an approach could give rise to difficulty in relation to acts of a non-sovereign but official character in respect of which a State's immunity is now usually limited.

Where sovereign acts are concerned there may, of course, be an additional obstacle for any claimant in that those acts may fall within a category on which the courts of a foreign State lack competence to adjudicate. That is, they may be 'acts of State' (as this term is understood in the US) or acts which in other jurisdictions are regarded as 'non-justiciable' or require 'judicial restraint'. This categorization is essentially based upon the notion that such cases involve issues which cannot be properly resolved by the exercise of judicial functions. In *Buttes Gas and Oil v Hammer*[215] Lord Wilberforce, having considered the *Duke of Brunswick* case referred to above, stated:

> I find the principle clearly stated that the courts in England will not adjudicate on acts done abroad by virtue of sovereign authority.

[212] See Art 2.1(b)(i) and (iv).

[213] See UK courts in respect of State Immunity Act 1978.

[214] See eg *O'Hair v Wojtyla and Andrus* US Digest 1979, 897 (immunity of the Pope as head of State of the Vatican City upheld in civil proceedings brought against him in connection with the celebration of a public mass).

[215] [1982] AC 888; *Guinto v Marcos* (1986) 654 F.Supp, 276.

Such lack of competence cannot, unlike jurisdictional immunity, be cured by any waiver[216] and, if established, would effectively preclude any claim in relation to a defendant head of State. 'Non-justiciability' is, however, a substantive defence which goes to the merits of a case and it would, therefore, usually be addressed after any preliminary issues of jurisdiction, including immunity had been decided. In practice, therefore, any case involving a head of State is likely to focus first on the issue of immunity.

(iii) Official, but non-sovereign, acts Official but non-sovereign acts are often acts of a commercial nature although the term can cover acts of a private law nature which go beyond the strictly commercial. The relevant considerations of principle are conflicting.[217] Like sovereign acts, acts of an official but commercial character involve a head of State acting in an official capacity as an organ of the State. However, if reliance is placed solely on immunity *ratione materiae*, it could be argued that they should attract immunity only to the extent enjoyed by the State itself. The restrictive theory of State immunity would deny a State immunity in respect of its commercial activities and, on this basis, heads of State could also be regarded as enjoying no immunity in respect of official but commercial conduct. As we have seen, the UN Convention on the Jurisdictional Immunities of States and Their Property makes it clear that a head of State in his public capacity as a principal organ and representative of the State is included within the definition of a 'State' for the purposes of the Convention. In that sense he or she is entitled to immunity to the same extent as the State itself.

In practice, there have been few cases where heads of State have been personally sued for acts of a commercial or private law nature carried out in their public or official capacity. The fact that in the past the legal identity of a State was often equated with that of its sovereign ruler is, however, still capable of generating uncertainty and raising questions as to whether it is the State or its ruler which is the proper defendant.[218] In *Village Holdings Sdn Bhd v HM The Queen in Right of Canada*[219] a Malaysian court upheld the immunity of a foreign monarch in respect of the sale of immoveable property used for diplomatic purposes in the forum State. The transaction was commercial but was also clearly carried out by the head of State in her official and public

[216] See *Mbasogo, President of the State of Equatorial Guinea and another v Logo Ltd and others* [2005] EWHC 2034 (QB); [2006] EWCA Civ 1370; and *Occidental v Ecuador* (2005)EWCA Civ 1116 where Mance LJ noted: 'we accept the English principle of non-justiciability cannot, if it applies, be ousted by consent'.

[217] See Watts (n 2 above) 60.

[218] See *BCCI v Price Waterhouse (No 4)* [1997] 4 All ER 108 (Laddie J).

[219] (1987) 87 ILR 223.

capacity. It was, however, unclear whether the court reached its decision as a result of that factor or simply on the application of a rule of absolute personal immunity. The fact that the property had been used for diplomatic purposes may also have been a factor.

A refusal to grant immunity to a head of State for a commercial or other act of a private law nature carried out in an official capacity would, arguably, be inconsistent with the position in respect of diplomatic agents who are clearly entitled under the terms of the Vienna Convention to immunity in respect of commercial acts carried out in their official capacity even where the sending State is not.[220] Article 3 of the UN Convention makes it clear that its provisions are without prejudice to the privileges and immunities accorded under international law to heads of State *ratione personae*. Uncertainty on this issue can give rise to considerable controversy, as illustrated by the litigation begun in the early 1990s in the US in connection with the collapse of BCCI.[221] The proceedings were brought against Sheikh Zayed bin Sultan Al Nahyan, the then President of the United Arab Emirates (who owned over 70 per cent of the Bank) and other defendants who were alleged to have conspired to defraud the US banking system. Sheikh Zayed asserted 'head of State' immunity and sought a 'suggestion' of immunity from the Executive. This prompted the House of Representatives' Committee on Banking, Finance and Urban Affairs to conduct hearings into the question of head of State immunity.[222] The case appeared to settle[223] but then proceeded, prompting the State Department to file a suggestion of immunity which the court accepted as conclusive.

Before the development of the restrictive doctrine of State immunity, distinctions between *acta iure imperii* and acts of a commercial or private law nature were much less important. In upholding the immunity of foreign heads of State, national courts, therefore, often failed to make any distinction between the personal immunity to which such a head of State was entitled and the immunity of the State itself.

A head of State's immunity *ratione personae*, although linked closely with State immunity, is now recognized as a distinct type of immunity and has

[220] See Art 31 of the VCDR (albeit only in regard to the receiving State).

[221] *First American Corpn and others v Sheikh Zayed Bin Sultan Al-Nahyan and others* (US 1996) 1119.

[222] 'Head of State Immunity': Hearing before the Committee on Banking, Finance and Urban Affairs; House of Representatives, 103rd Congress, 9 December 1993: Serial No 103–4. The Chairman, Henry Gonzalez, had called for a hearing 'because giving Zayed immunity "would be a mockery of our US banking statutes and a terrible precedent"'. See Sharon Walsh, 'BCCI Suit becomes a diplomatic battle: Rep Gonzalez disputes Abu Dhabi Ruler's immunity claim in case', *Washington Post*, 9 December 1993, B14.

[223] See 'Abu Dhabi's Ruling Family must forfeit $104million', *Washington Post*, 31 July 1992, A10.

been so since modern States developed identities distinct from their heads of State. As such, there is no logical imperative for it to be affected by changes to the rules applying to the State itself and no indication in the State practice that exists that it has been affected by restrictive approaches to State immunity itself. It is submitted, therefore, that the better view is that it continues to shield an incumbent head of State from any suit based upon commercial or other private law acts carried out in an official capacity. In the majority of cases involving such proceedings there will, of course, be a question as to whether it is the State itself which is the proper defendant and, in practice, according immunity to the head of State should cause no hardship to the plaintiff, who will be able to sue the State under the restrictive doctrine of State immunity.

(iv) Non-official or private acts State practice has been most variable with regard to the private acts of heads of State. There are indications in case law from a variety of jurisdictions that the decision by a head of State to enter into commercial or other private law activities, particularly where such transactions are closely linked with the forum State, may effectively constitute a 'waiver' of immunity.[224] This is most notably expressed in the celebrated dictum of Marshall CJ in *The Schooner Exchange v McFaddon*[225]:

> A prince by acquiring private property in a foreign country, may possibly be considered as subjecting that property to territorial jurisdiction; he may be considered as so far laying down the prince, and assuming the character of a private individual.

There are several early cases in which it was suggested that immunity should be denied to incumbent heads of State in respect of their private activities.[226] Even in *Duke of Brunswick v King of Hanover*[227] and *De Haber v Queen of Portugal*,[228] where the courts upheld the immunity of heads of State in regard to acts carried out in their sovereign and public capacity, they emphasized the fact that the foreign sovereign concerned had not been sued in his or her private capacity with the implication that, had this been so, immunity

[224] But see Art 32 of the VCDR 1961 and Art 41 of the Convention on Special Missions 1969, which suggest that any waiver of immunity should always be express.

[225] (1812) 11 US 116 at 137.

[226] See *Isabelle de Bourbon v Mellerio* (1874) 1 JDI 32 (France, Cour de Paris, 1872), in Kiss, *Repertoire de la pratique francaise en matiere de droit international* (1965) III, 270, where immunity was refused to the former Queen of Spain in a dispute concerning the purchase of jewellery for personal use; also *Wiercinski v Seyyid Ali Ben Hamond* (1917) 44 JDI 1465 (France, Tribunal civil de la Seine, 1916); A-C Kiss vol III (1965) 270 where the court rejected the argument of the former Sultan of Zanzibar that he was entitled to immunity in respect of a claim that he had failed to pay fees owing to a private masseur; and *Nobili v Charles II of Austria, Ann Digest*, I (1919–22) No 90 where the Italian Court of Cassation held that the claim before it related to a private contract made in Italy and not to an act done by the emperor as head of State.

[227] See n 208 above. [228] See n 209 above.

might not have been available. In Italy, the Rome Court of Cassation allowed proceedings to continue against the Emperor of Austria. The proceedings had been commenced before he became head of State and had their origin in 'contracts and acts of a private nature which arose in Italy'.[229] These decisions have led some commentators to conclude that early case law on heads of State does not support a rule of personal immunity from civil jurisdiction for private acts.[230]

However, as heads of State began to travel abroad more frequently, for both official and private purposes, courts in some countries began to accord such immunity. Such a practice became particularly notable in common law countries and, as early as 1894, an English court granted the Sultan of Johore immunity in respect of a claim for breach of promise.[231] It is fair to say, however, that it is not clear whether the decision was founded on the recognition of a sovereign's personal immunity in respect of private acts or simply on the fact that, at that time, the courts often made no distinction between the immunity of a State and that of its head and that as the former enjoyed absolute immunity there could be no question of allowing suit against the Sultan.[232] In later cases, however, the separate personal immunity enjoyed by a head of State has been acknowledged as potentially applicable to private, non-official acts.[233]

Modern practice in some civil law jurisdictions has been more uneven. In 1994, a French court rejected a claim to head of State immunity from President Mobutu of Zaire in respect of a claim by a French company on a contract for services supplied. In doing so it emphasized the private character of the transaction concerned.[234] The President had ordered tents for the celebration of his sixtieth birthday and allegedly had failed to pay for them. It was argued unsuccessfully on his behalf that the order related to 'the organisation of a public celebration which is a matter of national sovereignty involving the exercise of sovereign powers' and should, as such, attract immunity. This may

[229] See *Nobili v Charles I of Austria* (1921) 48 JDI 626, (1921) 1 ILR 136.

[230] See van Alebeek, *The Immunity of States and Their Officials in International Criminal Law and International Human Rights Law* (Oxford University Press, 2008) 169.

[231] *Mighell v Sultan of Johore* (1894) 1 QB 149 (at the time he had contracted the engagement, the Sultan had been living incognito in the UK under the name of 'Albert Baker'). See also *Statham v Statham and the Gaekwar of Baroda* [1912] P 92 (where head of State named as co-respondent in divorce proceedings); *Sayce v Ameer Ruler of Bahawalpur State* [1952] 2 QB 390 (private contract); and *Anonymous v Anonymous* (1992) 581 NYS 2d 776 (divorce proceedings against head of State).

[232] The case was cited by Scrutton LJ in *The Porto Alexandre* [1920] P 30 at 36–7, who stated: 'I think it has been well settled first of all as to the sovereign that there are no limits to the immunity which he enjoys. His private character is equally free as his public character.'

[233] See eg *Lafontant v Aristide* 844 F.Supp 128.

[234] *Mobutu and Republic of Zaire v Societe Logrine* (1994) 113 ILR 481 (France Court of Appeal of Paris).

be contrasted with a much earlier case in which a French court upheld the immunity of the incumbent Emperor Maximilian of Mexico who had been sued in respect of contracts for the purchase of furniture.[235]

There is some practice to suggest that a distinction should be made between the position of a head of State who is outside the forum State and one who is on an official visit (or perhaps even a private visit). The Swiss Federal Department for Foreign Affairs has stated that its authorities would grant immunity for a head of State's private acts if he or she were sued while visiting Switzerland but not if the head of State was no longer in the country.[236] In 2001, the Institute of International Law adopted a resolution in which it was declared that a head of State does not enjoy any immunity from jurisdiction before the courts of a foreign State in civil and administrative matters, unless that suit relates to acts performed in the exercise of his or her official functions and that even in such a case there should be no immunity in respect of a counterclaim.[237] The resolution went on to state that, nonetheless, no action may be taken by way of legal proceedings in regard to a head of State while he or she is in the territory of the forum State, in the exercise of official functions.

Nevertheless, many national court decisions suggest a broader immunity from civil proceedings for incumbent heads of State. In 1964 the Austrian Supreme Court dismissed a claim regarding a road accident against a foreign head of State on the basis of the latter's immunity.[238] In a later case, the incumbent head of State of Liechtenstein, Prince Hans-Adam II, was sued in an Austrian court by a woman claiming to be his sister.[239] She sought a declaratory judgment regarding affiliation to the Prince's father and had joined the latter's legal successors, including the Prince and his younger siblings as parties. The court held that matters of absolute personal immunity must be strictly construed and that questions of personal and family (including marital) status belong exclusively to the private life of a head of State, particularly in the present case where the question of family status related to the head of State's father rather than directly to the head of State himself and did not affect the latter's public and constitutional position. It held, however, that the Prince, as an incumbent foreign head of State, enjoyed immunity even in respect of his private functions. There have also been a number of French cases in which the

[235] *Heritiers de L'Empereur Maximilien de Mexique v Lemaitre*, French Court of Appeal, Dalloz II (1873) 24, 15, 4, 1872; Clunet I (1974) 32.

[236] *Ann.suisse de droit int*, 1984, 184.

[237] Article 3 of the Resolution of L'Institut de Droit International on Immunities from Jurisdiction and Execution of Heads of State and of Government in International Law, Thirteenth Commission, 26 August 2001.

[238] See n 202 above.

[239] *W v Prince of Liechtenstein and others*, Oxford Reports on International Law, ILDC 1 (AT 2001).

courts, although determining that a former head of State does not enjoy immunity in respect of private acts, nevertheless appeared to acknowledge that such immunity would be applicable for heads of State in office.[240] In 1988, a Belgian court took the view that President Mobutu of Zaire could rely on head of State immunity *ratione personae* when sued by a company from whom the President had expropriated property for his own personal use, although the case was in fact decided on other grounds.[241]

More recently, an Australian court upheld the immunity of the Amir of Qatar in proceedings brought *in rem* against a private vessel owned by the head of State.[242] Australia, like the UK, is one of the States in which some narrow exceptions to a head of State's immunity in civil proceedings has been expressly admitted. It was common ground between the parties that the action and any claim to immunity by the Amir related to commercial conduct performed in a private capacity. Under Australian legislation, the relevant provisions of the Diplomatic Privileges and Immunities Act 1967 (which largely incorporates into domestic law the terms of the Vienna Convention on Diplomatic Relations 1961) had been applied 'with such modifications as are necessary' to foreign heads of State.[243] Accordingly, the judge had to consider whether any of the 'diplomatic' exceptions to immunity contained in the 1967 Act could be applied. He concluded that only Article 31(1)(c) of the Vienna Convention might be of relevance. This removes immunity for 'an action relating to any professional or commercial activity exercised by the diplomatic agent in the receiving State outside his official functions'. However, there was no evidence that the Amir had engaged in any professional or commercial activity within the jurisdiction of the forum or, indeed, had ever entered Australia. In these circumstances, he found that, as head of State, the Amir enjoyed immunity from criminal, civil, and administrative jurisdiction, including immunity from execution.

In the UK, the State Immunity Act 1978 confers the same immunity on a foreign head of State 'subject to any necessary modifications' as that enjoyed by an ambassador. Article 31(1) of the Vienna Convention on Diplomatic Relations makes the immunity of an ambassador in regard to civil proceedings for private acts subject to only three exceptions: real actions relating to private immovable property in the receiving State which the ambassador holds otherwise than on behalf of his State for the purposes of the mission; actions relating

[240] See *Ex King Farouk of Egypt v SARL Christian Dior* (1957) 84 JDI 716 (Cour d' Appel de Paris, 1957); A-C Kiss vol III (1965) 271, no 459; and *Jean Desses v Prince Farouk et Dame Sadek* (1964) 91 JDI 285, (1964) 65 ILR 37 (Tribunal de la Seine, 1963).

[241] *Mobutu v SA Cotoni* (1988) 91 ILR 259 (Civil Court of Brussels).

[242] *Thor Shipping A/S v The Ship 'Al Duhail* [2008] FCA 1842 (Dowsett J). See also (2009) 58 ICLQ 702–11.

[243] See Art 36(1) of the Foreign States Immunity Act 1985 (Australia).

to matters of succession and inheritance in which the ambassador is involved as a private person; and actions relating to any professional or commercial activity exercised by the ambassador in the receiving State outside his official functions.[244] All three exceptions concern conduct of a private non-official nature and involve or are likely to involve a direct connection with the territory of the receiving State. The Convention on Special Missions 1969 contains a similar list of exceptions[245] to the immunity enjoyed by members of a special mission.

However, although there is an argument that similar exceptions should apply to a head of State,[246] it is by no means clear that customary international law would support such an approach[247] and practice is not sufficiently widespread to be conclusive. As we have seen, the UK is not the only State to have applied the three 'diplomatic' exceptions to heads of State. Australia has adopted a very similar approach in its legislation on State immunity.[248] However, in other States, most notably the US, its equivalent statute—the Foreign Sovereign Immunities Act 1976—does not refer to the position of heads of State and it has been held that the Act has left untouched earlier customary international law regarding their immunities.[249]

Even in the UK, the precise extent to which the 'diplomatic' exceptions may apply to a foreign head of State is not free from doubt. The 1978 Act brings into play the provisions of the Diplomatic Privileges Act 1964 as they apply to the head of a diplomatic mission but this is 'subject to any necessary modifications'. The Act does not provide any further guidance as to what this may mean in practice. The House of Lords wrestled with this problem in the *Pinochet* cases in the context of the functional immunity of a former head of State. As was explained by Lord Nicholls in the first *Pinochet* case:

> Transferring to a former head of State in this way the continuing protection afforded to a former head of a diplomatic mission is not an altogether neat exercise, as their functions are dissimilar. Their positions are not in all respects analogous.[250]

[244] See also Art 42 which precludes an ambassador from practising in the receiving State any professional or commercial activity for profit. It is not clear what implications, if any, this may have as regards the position of a head of State.

[245] There is also a fourth exception in respect of actions for damages arising out of an accident caused by a vehicle used outside the official functions of the person concerned.

[246] See eg *Maharaj Indrajitsinghji Vijaysinghji v HH Maharaja Rajendrasinghji Vijaysinghji* (1955) 22 ILR 244 in which immunity was denied in probate proceedings on the ground that such proceedings were not a 'suit' in which immunity could apply.

[247] See eg *Mandalsa Kumari v M Ramnarin Private Ltd* (1958) 27 ILR 109 in which immunity was upheld in relation to a ruler who was a partner in a commercial firm, although his immunity did not prevent proceedings against the other partners.

[248] Section 36(1) of the Foreign States Immunities Act 1985.

[249] See eg *Lafontant v Aristide* 844 F.Supp 128; *United States v Noriega* 746 F.Supp 1506, (1990) 99 ILR 145; and *Tachiona v Mugabe* 169 F.Supp 2d 259, 290–1 (SDNY 2001).

[250] *R v Bow Street Magistrates Court ex parte Pinochet Ugarte (Pinochet (No 1))* [2000] AC 61 (HL); 119 ILR 49.

The question has also been considered in a more closely related context in *Apex Global Management Ltd and others v Fi Cal Ltd and others.* The case concerned civil proceedings brought against two princes of the Saudi royal house in respect of various private shareholdings. The princes claimed immunity on the basis of section 20 of the 1978 Act which provides that the members of a head of State's family 'forming part of his household' shall enjoy the same immunity as the members of an ambassador's family forming part of his household. Immunity was refused on the ground that neither qualified as a family member of the king's household within the terms of the legislation.[251]

However, in the case before the lower court Mr Justice Vos did consider whether, if the princes had enjoyed immunity, it would have covered private commercial activities conducted outside the UK.[252] The only relevant exception for the head of a diplomatic mission and family members of his household relates to activities carried on within the receiving State. It was argued, however, by the petitioner that a 'necessary modification' was required when this was applied to heads of State and their families so as to remove this restrictive territorial requirement. Not surprisingly, this was opposed by the princes' counsel who argued that no such modification was necessary and that, if any modification was necessary, it should require the removal of any exception altogether so as to 'restore' the absolute immunity of a head of State from civil proceedings in relation to private acts. In this context, counsel referred to *BCCI International (Overseas) Ltd (in liquidation) v Price Waterhouse*[253] in which an English court upheld the immunity of the President of the United Arab Emirates in regard to claims brought against him in his private capacity. In that case, however, there had been no suggestion that the ruler had been carrying on any business activity within the UK.

The judge concluded that a modification to remove the territorial limitation on the exception was indeed necessary and ruled that, if the princes had enjoyed immunity under section 20, 'such immunity would not have extended to any commercial activity exercised by them outside their official functions anywhere in the world'. In reaching this conclusion, he was influenced by two main factors: first, the different position of diplomats and their families from that of heads of State and their families; and, secondly, the prevailing thinking, just before the enactment of the 1978 Act, that customary international law had developed so as to prevent States and their emanations from claiming immunity for their commercial activities.[254] On the first point it was

[251] See [2013] EWCA Civ 642, [2013] WLR (D) 228.

[252] See [2013] EWHC 587 (Ch).

[253] [1997] 4 All ER 108; 111 ILR 604.

[254] In this connection, Mr Justice Vos referred to the majority judgments in *Trendtex Trading Corpn v Central Bank of Nigeria* [1977] 1 QB 529.

noted that diplomats may enjoy a broader protection than heads of State in this respect but only *vis-à-vis* the receiving State and for the duration of their mission so as to enable them to carry out their duties untroubled by vexatious litigation. By contrast, a head of State who could expect to be in a foreign country only for brief visits would enjoy such immunity worldwide. On the second point, such a wide personal immunity was seen as anomalous and out of keeping with the commercial exception which had been applied to sovereigns acting in their public capacity. The judge stated:

> It would, in my judgment, be remarkable if Parliament could have intended no limitation, vis a vis commercial acts, on the personal immunity of the sovereign, his family and private servants.[255] One of the big changes introduced by the State Immunity Act, even if it was a codification of existing principles, was the commercial exception—an exception of that kind was expressly applied to States and sovereigns exercising public functions and to sovereigns acting in their private capacities. The complete abrogation of the uncertain extent of the exception to personal immunity as it existed at the time in 1978 seems a most improbable parliamentary intention.[256]

In the ensuing appeal, the UK Court of Appeal indicated that, if it had been necessary to determine the issue, it too would have ruled that the princes were not entitled to personal immunity in regard to private commercial activity carried on outside the UK. It added, however, that any binding decision on the matter should await an occasion when further argument could be deployed.

The 'diplomatic' exceptions, as applied to heads of State, have been the subject of criticism and have, in particular, been characterized as too narrow in relation to private commercial conduct. In such cases, as we have seen, immunity is ostensibly restricted only in relation to activity engaged in within the forum State thus conferring greater immunity on a head of State in relation to his or her private commercial dealings than that afforded to a State in respect of its commercial transactions. In its original form, the relevant UK legislation which equates the position of a foreign head of State with that of an ambassador[257] did so only in regard to a visiting head of State. Later the wording was broadened to cover heads of State who were not physically present in the UK 'subject to any necessary modifications'. It has been argued that this is, in fact, an extension of the immunity enjoyed by heads of State in respect of private commercial activities and is inappropriate in that it confers an immunity designed to protect individuals required to reside for long periods in the forum State. It is interesting that the initial draft of the International

[255] Note that members of the family of a diplomat forming part of his household enjoy substantially the same immunities as the diplomat but private servants enjoy only very limited exemptions. See Art 37 of the VCDR.

[256] [2013] EWHC 587 (Ch), para [140].

[257] s 20(1) UK SIA 1978.

Law Commission's Draft Articles on the Jurisdictional Immunities of States and Their Property included a provision which acknowledged an exception to immunity in relation to any commercial transactions conducted by the head of State 'outside of his or her official functions'.[258] However, due to the debate which ensued, the relevant provision was eventually dropped and replaced with a general savings clause.

The decision of the ICJ in the *Arrest Warrant* case was concerned with the inviolability and immunity of Foreign Ministers (and heads of State and Governments) from criminal prosecution and not with immunity from civil proceedings. The rationale behind the decision emphasized the need to ensure that those entitled to personal immunity should be able to travel freely and not be inhibited from exercising their important diplomatic functions by the threat of arrest or criminal prosecution. In the case of civil proceedings such an argument is not quite so compelling. Where civil proceedings are brought against a head of State in respect of acts carried out in his public capacity where the State is immune, there is, of course, a further justification based upon the argument that such action would infringe his or her functional immunity and circumvent the immunity of the State itself. It could also be argued that such proceedings, insofar as they relate to the conduct of a foreign State's public affairs, would constitute an interference with the internal affairs of that State. Such arguments do not apply in regard to the private activities of a head of State.

Nevertheless, where a head of State is travelling on official business, an argument from functional necessity might still be applied on the grounds that the possibility of civil suit could constitute a disincentive for the conduct of diplomatic functions and would be inconsistent with the dignity of States.[259] It is, however, likely that, in such circumstances, any service of legal process would be effectively precluded by the application of special missions immunity Where the head of State is outside the forum State, such arguments of functional necessity carry much less weight.

In conclusion, most State practice appears to support a fairly broad immunity from civil proceedings for incumbent foreign heads of State in respect of private acts, particularly when he or she is in the forum State. It remains questionable, however, as to whether that immunity is absolute.

[258] ILC Jurisdictional Immunities of States and Their Property (1986) YBILC 1(1)5, para 10.

[259] This latter consideration would apply even in the case of a private visit and, in this connection, the statement of the Swiss Federal Department for Foreign Affairs that it would accord immunity for a head of State's private acts if he or she were sued while visiting Switzerland but not if the head of State was no longer in the country, is worth noting—see n 234 above.

Waiver of immunity

Immunity operates as a procedural bar, not a substantive incapacity or defence. As such, it can be waived and consent given to the exercise of jurisdiction (although if the immunity is accorded by statute without any provision for waiver by the defendant, an alleged waiver may be disregarded).[260] There is a question, however, as to who has the authority to waive the immunity of a head of State. Under Article 32(1) of the Vienna Convention on Diplomatic Relations, the immunity of diplomatic agents (including the head of Mission) can only be waived by the sending State. Article 41 of the Convention on Special Missions also provides for waiver to be by the sending State. Yet the fact that a head of State is generally regarded as the ultimate authority within the State might suggest that the he or she ought to be able to waive his or her own immunity. The UN Convention on the Jurisdictional Immunities of States does not offer any specific guidance on this matter although Articles 7, 8, and 9 acknowledge the possibility of waiver where proceedings are brought against a State.

Such proceedings may, of course, include proceedings against a head of State in his or her public capacity. They do not, however, specify which particular organ of State has the power to waive its immunity. Since both the head of State (as an organ of Government) and the Government itself are comprised within the definition of 'State' in Article 2(1)(b), it seems likely that a waiver by either would be regarded as effective for the purposes of the Convention.[261] In principle, this would seem correct, since where a head of State is sued on some matter involving his public capacity or official functions, the proceedings are, in reality, against the State and any waiver is a matter for that State's normal organs of Government, but equally, given the head of State's position as the highest organ of the State, his or her waiver should also be accepted as valid.

Where proceedings are brought against a head of State in a private and personal capacity, it is clearer that the head of State, himself or herself, can effectively waive immunity.[262] Since, however, that immunity is not a personal

[260] See *Gaekwar of Baroda State Railways v Hafiz Habib-ul-Haq*, Ann Digest 9 (1938–40) no 78; and *Thakore Saheb Khanji Kashari Khanji v Gulam Rasul Chandbhal* (1955) 22 ILR 253.

[261] Under Art 7(2)(a) of the Vienna Convention on the Law of Treaties, heads of State and of Governments and Ministers of Foreign Affairs are considered by virtue of their functions to represent their State for the purposes of performing all acts relating to the conclusion of a treaty. A logical extension of this provision would imply that they would also have the authority to waive their State's immunity before foreign courts. See Fox, *The Law of State Immunity* (2nd edn, Oxford University Press, 2008) 480.

[262] See *Prince of X Road Accident* case (1964) 65 ILR 13 (Austria, Supreme Court).

attribute but one enjoyed by a head of State in acknowledgment of his or her special status and functions in relation to the State, a waiver by that State is also capable of being effective.

In the event of a dispute between the head of State and his or her Government where, for example, the former wishes to waive immunity but the Government is unwilling, or vice versa, the position is a little less clear. However, by analogy with the immunity of a diplomatic agent, it could be assumed that as the immunity does not belong to the head of State as an individual[263] the question is ultimately one for his or her State to decide in accordance with its constitution. Such an approach is also consistent with the modern functional justifications usually advanced in support of such immunity.

A further question is whether a waiver has to be express, or may, in certain circumstances, be implied. In *Mighell v Sultan of Johore*[264] a claim for breach of promise of marriage was brought against the Sultan who at the time of the contract had been living *incognito* in England under the name 'Albert Baker'. It was submitted that, in coming to England and living under a false name, he had waived his immunity. The English Court of Appeal rejected this argument and held that, in this respect, there could be no enquiry into the conduct of the Sultan prior to his court appearance. In the absence of any express waiver and submission to the jurisdiction, he was entitled to immunity.

In cases involving a foreign head of State, it is highly unlikely that any court would lightly imply a waiver[265] and an express waiver will obviously be preferred. The analogy with Article 32 of the Vienna Convention on Diplomatic Relations 1961 suggests that waiver should be express, as does Article 41 of the 1969 Convention on Special Missions. In relation to a head of State sued in a public capacity, Article 7 of the UN Convention on the Jurisdictional Immunities of States requires that consent to the exercise of jurisdiction be express. The only exception which is common in all three texts is where the head of State himself or herself initiates proceedings. The initiation of such proceedings also precludes any assertion of immunity in relation to a directly connected counter-claim. Moreover, the UN Convention includes an additional exception where a head of State, acting in a public capacity, intervenes in proceedings or takes any other step relating to the merits.[266]

Immunity of property

Where a head of State owns property in a foreign State in an official capacity and for the purposes of his or her State, it is likely to be treated in accordance

[263] See Denza, *Diplomatic Law* (3rd edn, Oxford University Press, 2008) 331.
[264] See n 229 above. [265] See Watts (n 2 above) 68. [266] Article 8.

with the rules relating to State immunity. Generally speaking, those rules do not allow for immunity in respect of immovable property situated in the forum State[267] although there are some exceptions, most notably in relation to property used for diplomatic or consular purposes.[268] The position is less clear with regard to immovable property privately owned by a head of State. In some older cases it has been suggested that, in such circumstances, a head of State would not enjoy immunity.[269] This view has been supported by a number of commentators, including *Satow* where, in the fifth edition, it was noted that 'If the foreign sovereign owns real property in a personal capacity, his immunity cannot prevent the hearing of an action to establish the title or the right to possession of that property, since otherwise no forum would exist competent to hear such an action'.[270] Such an approach is also consistent with the position in regard to heads of foreign missions under the Vienna Convention on Diplomatic Relations.[271] This exception has been reflected in legislation in the UK and Australia which equates, in this respect, the position of ambassadors with that of foreign heads of State.[272] However, practice has not always been consistent in this regard and, in 1988, a Belgian court granted immunity in respect of such property.[273]

As regards proceedings brought against a head of State in respect of movable property in the forum State, it is probable that, in accordance with generally recognized rules on State immunity, a head of State would enjoy immunity if

[267] See Art 13 of the UN Convention on the Jurisdictional Immunities of States and their Property.

[268] See Art 3 of the UN Convention on the Jurisdictional Immunities of States, and their Property.

[269] See *The Schooner Exchange v McFaddon* (1812) 11 US 116 at 145 where Marshall CJ left open the possibility that a head of State, by acquiring property in a foreign State, had thereby subjected that property to the territorial jurisdiction and divested himself to that extent of his sovereign character and assumed the character of a private individual. See also *The Charkieh* (1873) LR 4 A&E 59 at 97; and *Sultan of Johore v Abubakar* [1952] AC 318 where the point was argued (at 322–31) but left undecided (at 343–4).

[270] Satow, *A Guide to Diplomatic Practice* (ed Gore-Booth) (5th edn, Longman,1979) 10. See also Rivier, *Principes de droit des gens*, vol 1 (Paris, Rousseau, 1896) 417; Hall, *A Treatise on International Law* (ed Pearce Higgins) (8th edn, Clarendon Press, 1924); and Salmon, *Manual de droit diplomatique* (Bruylant, 1986).

[271] See Art 31(1)(a) which provides that a diplomatic agent shall not enjoy immunity from the civil and administrative jurisdiction of the receiving State in the case of 'a real action relating to private immoveable property situated in the territory of the receiving State unless he holds it on behalf of the sending State for the purposes of the mission'.

[272] See s 20 of the UK State Immunity Act 1978 and s 36(1) of Australia's Foreign States Immunities Act 1985. In the UK, measures of execution cannot be taken against the property of a diplomatic agent except in relation to the three exceptions listed in Art 31 of the VCDR: proceedings relating to immovable property in the receiving State held in a private capacity; proceedings relating to succession in which he or she is involved in a private capacity; and proceedings relating to professional or commercial activities in the receiving State undertaken in a private capacity. However, such measures must not infringe the inviolability of the diplomatic agent or of his or her residence.

[273] See *Mobutu v SA Cotoni* (1988) ILR 259; also *Rewa Shankar v Narasinghji Maharaj* (1957) 24 ILR 229.

sued in respect of such property owned by him or her in an official capacity and held for sovereign purposes. If held in an official capacity but for non-sovereign purposes, entitlement to immunity may be more uncertain: proceedings relating to rights or interests in such property are not among the generally accepted specific exceptions to the general rule on immunity for States, except insofar as they concern rights or interests arising by way of succession, gift, or *bona vacantia*, or in relation to the administration of property such as trust property, the estate of a bankrupt, or the property of a company being wound up.[274] There are some further specific exceptions with regard to proceedings relating to rights in intellectual and industrial property[275] and proceedings relating to the operation of ships used for other than government non-commercial purposes.[276]

As regards privately owned movable property, the position should, logically, be consistent with the immunity to which a head of State is entitled in respect of proceedings relating to his private conduct. As noted earlier, the modern trend has been to accord a serving head of State a fairly extensive immunity in this regard although practice has not always been consistent particularly in civil law countries.[277]

Questions have arisen as to whether collective measures, for example within the EU context, to freeze the assets of certain foreign heads of State would violate the immunity to which they and their property are entitled. Leaving aside arguments that, in some circumstances, such measures may be justified as legitimate counter-measures carried out in response to a legal injury, it seems clear that such action is capable of infringing that immunity. Whether such action is regarded as a measure of execution or an assertion of administrative jurisdiction, it would be difficult to argue that it was not a measure of constraint. Given, however, that the modern rationale for immunity stresses its functional aspect, it might be argued that the simple freeze of a foreign head of State's personal bank account does not necessarily impede the performance of official functions. It is, however, notable that the Institut de Droit International rejected this argument in preparing its 2001 resolution on the 'Immunities from Jurisdiction and Execution of heads of State and heads of Government in International Law'. Article 4(1) of the Resolution provides:

> Property belonging personally to a head of State and located in the territory of a foreign State may not be subject to any measure of execution except to give effect to a final judgement, rendered against such head of State.

[274] See Art 13 of the UN Convention on the Jurisdictional Immunities of States and their Property.

[275] See Art 14 of the UN Convention on the Jurisdictional Immunities of States and their Property.

[276] See Art 16 of the UN Convention on the Jurisdictional Immunities of States and their Property.

[277] See press reports regarding the seizure in France of various assets, including luxury cars registered to President Teodoro Obiang Nguema Mbasogo of Equatorial Guinea in connection with a corruption investigation (1 October 2011 <http://www.dailymail.co.uk/news/article-2043836>).

However, in time of war, States have been prepared to be more ruthless as regards the private assets of the head of an enemy State, treating those assets as enemy property, as happened during the Second World War with the property in the UK of King Victor Emmanuel III of Italy.[278]

Finally, it is worth noting that all immovable and movable property in the ownership or possession of a foreign head of State may benefit from the protection and inviolability which flows from the presence of a visiting head of State during the course of an official visit to the forum State.[279]

Exemption from dues and taxes, and customs duties

It is generally accepted that a head of State is exempt from national and local taxation levied by foreign States, at least where they are levied in respect of his or her presence in that State on an official visit. Not surprisingly, there is little case law on the subject although Watts refers to a number of Indian cases in his 1994 monograph on the legal position of heads of State in international law.[280] Such exemption is broadly in line with the treatment of diplomatic agents under the Vienna Convention on Diplomatic Relations and is also consistent with the provisions of the Convention on Special Missions as it applies to a special mission led by a head of State. Article 34 of the former and Article 33 of the latter confer exemption from all dues and taxes, personal or real, national, regional, or municipal, subject to certain specific exceptions: these are indirect taxes of a kind normally incorporated in the price of goods and services, dues, and taxes on private immovable property in the receiving State (unless held on behalf of the sending State for the purposes of a diplomatic or special mission); estate, succession, or inheritance duties levied by the receiving State (subject to certain exceptions[281]); dues and taxes on private income having its source in the receiving State; and capital taxes on investments made in commercial undertakings in the receiving State, charges levied for specific services rendered, and registration, court, or record fees, mortgage dues, and stamp duty (with an exception for mission premises).

A visiting head of State is also exempt from customs duties and taxes, and from customs inspection, of goods and personal baggage. Articles 36 and 35 respectively of the two Conventions referred to above make equivalent provision in regard to diplomatic and special missions and it seems logical

[278] *Republic of Italy v Hambros Bank Ltd* [1950] 1 Ch 314.

[279] See Convention on Special Missions 1969.

[280] Watts (n 2 above) 70.

[281] State or public property held by a foreign head of State is immune from inheritance tax. His or her private property is also immune provided it passes to his or her successor as head of State.

that heads of State should be entitled to no lesser degree of exemption.[282] It is likely, however, that such exemption is limited to articles for the head of State's official and personal use, as it is in the equivalent Convention provisions. Similarly, the exemption from inspection may, in theory, exclude situations where there are serious grounds for suspecting that the head of State's baggage contains articles, the import of which is prohibited by the receiving State's laws or controlled by its quarantine regulations. In practice, however, it is likely that the customs authorities of the State being visited would be very reluctant to seek such inspection unless they had very strong grounds indeed to suspect a serious violation.

It has now become standard practice for diplomatic agents and others entitled to exemption from customs inspection to, nevertheless, submit to security screening of their baggage as a condition of carriage even in the absence of any particular reason for suspicion. These checks are not usually carried out by customs authorities but by or on behalf of the air carrier.[283] In practice, such considerations are less likely to affect heads of States, who often travel by private or military aircraft rather than commercial carriers.

Families and Members of the Entourage

The treatment of members of a head of State's family and entourage has been closely linked with that accorded to the head of State and, in practice, such persons have often been accorded the same protection, privileges, and courtesies as the head of State. However, there is a question as to whether or not such persons are entitled to special treatment under customary international law. Where they have received such treatment, it has often been unclear on what basis it has been granted.

The entitlement of family members to special treatment is often seen as part and parcel of the privileges and immunities accorded to members of the entourage of a head of State. They are, however, distinct categories although there may sometimes be some overlap between the two both in fact and principle. State practice is scant but what there is suggests that accompanying members of a head of State's family during an official visit would be entitled to the same immunities and privileges as those enjoyed by the head of State.

[282] See Watts (n 2 above) 70.

[283] See Denza, *Diplomatic Law* (3rd edn, Oxford University Press, 2008) 388 where she quotes section 16 of the *US Handbook for Foreign Diplomatic and Career Consular Personnel in the United States,* which says that: 'The United States does not regard the exemption from inspection as preventing an airline from refusing to carry any individual who does not voluntarily submit to personal or technical inspection of his or her person and personal baggage for security reasons.'

In this connection, it is worth noting that Article 39(1) of the Convention on Special Missions 1969 confers on the accompanying family members of a head of State, who leads a special mission, the same privileges and immunities as those enjoyed by the head of State. A Swiss Federal Tribunal has, in one respect, gone further, stating:

> customary international law has always granted to heads of State, as well as to members of their family and their household visiting a foreign State, the privileges of personal inviolability and immunity from criminal jurisdiction... This jurisdictional immunity is also granted to a head of State who is visiting a foreign State in a private capacity and also extends, in such circumstances, to the closest accompanying family members as well as to the senior members of his household staff.[284]

On this basis a family member travelling with the head of State will be entitled to the same treatment as the head of State at least as regards inviolability and immunity from criminal jurisdiction but, when outside the forum State or travelling alone, any entitlement may become more questionable.

There have, however, been some cases where States have accorded immunity to family members even when unaccompanied by the head of State or even where the family member is outside the forum State. Such treatment has been accorded simply on the basis of their family relationship with the head of State.

Such an approach is most commonly taken with regard to the spouse of a head of State, whose status is seen as entirely assimilated to that of the head of State.[285] In 1945, an Indian court held that the wife of the ruler of one of India's former vassal States was not entitled to immunity but nevertheless seems to have taken the view that the wife of a fully sovereign head of State would have enjoyed the same immunity as her husband.[286] In 2009, a criminal complaint of assault was made against Grace Mugabe, the wife of the President of Zimbabwe. The assault had allegedly occurred while she was visiting Hong Kong on a private visit unaccompanied by her husband. The Department of Justice in Hong Kong issued a public statement stating that she was 'not liable to arrest or detention and enjoys immunity from prosecution'.[287] Inevitably

[284] *Marcos and Marcos v Federal Department of Police* (1989) 102 ILR 198 (Swiss Federal Tribunal).

[285] See eg the view expressed by the Swiss Federal Department for Foreign Affairs: *Ann.suisse de droit int*, 1984, 184. See also *Oppenheim's International Law* (9th edn, Oxford University Press, 1988) vol 1, para 453 where it is noted that, except insofar as they may be regarded as part of the head of State's retinue, a family member's entitlement to immunities is questionable '*except in the case of the head of State's spouse*' (my emphasis).

[286] *Rani Amrit Kunwar v Commissioner of Income Tax* (1955) 22 ILR 73.

[287] See *Times* report online, 22 March 2009 (it was explained that her right to immunity arose from Chinese regulations on diplomatic privileges and immunities). Under the Basic Law governing the Hong Kong Special Administrative Region (HKSAR), it is stipulated that the Central People's Government is responsible for foreign affairs and defence.

the question arises as to whether other family members may benefit from the same immunity.

The entitlement of a head of State's family to some kind of special treatment in their own right finds some support in the analogy with the family of an ambassador: under Article 37(1) of the Vienna Convention on Diplomatic Relations 1961 the members of an ambassador's family forming part of his household also enjoy the main immunities and privileges conferred on the ambassador. Similarly, as noted above, Article 39(1) of the Convention on Special Missions 1969 confers on the accompanying family members of a head of State who leads a special mission the same privileges and immunities as those enjoyed by the head of State himself or herself.[288] These entitlements arise under specific Conventions and apply, of course, only in the particular circumstances envisaged by those Conventions. Under the 1969 Special Missions Convention it is necessary that the family member accompanies the head of State on the special mission in order to qualify for the special treatment. Under the 1961 Convention the family member must form part of the ambassador's 'household' in the receiving State. This latter term is not defined in the Convention, and although, at the time of its negotiation, most delegations were in favour of adding a definition, differing concepts of the family made it impossible to draft a generally acceptable formula.[289] Most States have not given any formal indication as to who will be accepted as a member of a diplomat's family forming part of his or her household but some, including the US and the UK, have published statements of practice. The latter usually include the spouse, civil partner, and minor children who reside with the diplomat but the list is not exhaustive and other persons may be included in certain circumstances, for example a child between 18 and 25 resident with and financially dependent on the diplomat and in full-time education, and dependent parents normally resident with the diplomat.

State practice on this matter is scant and uneven. In the UK, section 20(1) of the State Immunity Act 1978 provides that members of the foreign head of State's family forming part of his or her 'household' and his or her 'private servants' shall enjoy the same immunities as apply to the family members and private servants of the head of a diplomatic mission. Section 36(1) of the

[288] See also the 1973 Convention on the Prevention and Punishment of Crimes Against Internationally Protected Persons, including Diplomatic Agents, which, in Art 1(1)(a), includes in the definition of 'internationally protected person' members of a head of State's family accompanying the head of State.

[289] See Denza, *Diplomatic Law* (3rd edn, Oxford University Press, 2008) 392.

Australian Foreign States Immunities Act takes a more restrictive approach and limits immunity to the 'spouse of the head of a foreign State'.[290] No distinction is made between official or private visits. Nor indeed does it appear to be necessary for the head of State or family member to be present in the territory of the forum State in order to benefit. In the UK, therefore, a head of State's spouse and minor children forming part of his or her 'household' would be entitled to the same privileges and immunities as the head of State regardless of whether or not they were accompanying the latter.

The position with regard to other family members, for example adult children not falling within that narrow formulation, is more problematic. It has been suggested that the term 'household' may not always bear the same meaning in the context of a head of State's family as it does in relation to the members of an ambassador's family. In the circumstances of a diplomatic mission, membership of an ambassador's household could reasonably be thought to require an element of dependence and residence under the same roof. But it has been pointed out that a head of State's circumstances may be very different, particularly within the context of a hereditary monarchy.[291] It is not, for example, uncommon for adult members of a monarch's family to share in and support the head of State in the performance of his or her official and representative functions even though they may reside in separate households. Such considerations may be particularly relevant in respect of an heir to the throne.[292]

In 1978, in *Kilroy v Windsor, Prince of Wales*, Prince Charles, the heir to the throne of the UK, was granted immunity in the US when sued there during a visit to address a university audience in Cleveland, Ohio. The State Department filed a 'suggestion of immunity' stating that it regarded the visit of Prince Charles as a 'special diplomatic mission and considers the Prince to have been an official diplomatic envoy while present in the United States on that special mission…'. It was on this basis, therefore, rather than an immunity linked to that of the head of State herself, on which immunity was granted.[293] However, in commenting on the rationale behind the grant of such immunity the court

[290] Both provisions are based on an extension, with any necessary modifications, of the immunities accorded to the head of a diplomatic mission. Article 37(1) of the 1961 Vienna Convention on Diplomatic Relations provides that the 'members of the family of a diplomatic agent, forming part of his household shall, if they are not nationals of the receiving State, enjoy the privileges and immunities' granted to the latter, including inviolability and immunity from criminal jurisdiction.

[291] Watts (n 2 above) 78.

[292] In 1994, Norway declined to allow Princess Martha Louise (who was second in line to the throne of Norway) to give evidence in divorce proceedings in which she had been cited as co-respondent. The court did not, apparently, press the matter: *The Times* (London), April 1994.

[293] 81 ILR 605 (District Court for Northern District of Ohio, 1978). See also *HRH Prince Turki Bin Abdulaziz v Metropolitan Dade County* (1984) 741 F.2d 1328 where a member of the ruling family of Saudi Arabia was similarly considered to be a special diplomatic envoy.

also appeared to place some weight on the Prince's particular constitutional role, stating: 'When the person sued is not just a foreign minister or special envoy, but the Heir Apparent to the throne of the possibly offended nation, the foreign policy ramifications are extraordinary.' It is notable, however, that in a later incident the Swiss authorities applied their normal investigative procedures in regard to a skiing accident in which the Prince of Wales had been involved while on a private visit. No question of immunity was raised.[294]

In this context, it is interesting to consider the position of a sovereign who chooses to abdicate. In such circumstances, he or she may continue to carry out constitutional and ceremonial functions on behalf of the new king or queen and may thus, as a member of the royal household, continue to qualify for special treatment. It is more likely, however, that abdication has occurred in order to secure a more retired lifestyle. In these circumstances, it must be doubtful that international law would require States to accord special treatment in the event of a private visit. However, given the fact that such individuals, especially if long-serving, may still inspire strong feelings of loyalty and be regarded by their people as the embodiment of the State, it is probable that many States would be prepared to grant some privileges.[295]

Another area in which there is some uncertainty relates to civil claims against family members who are not present in the territory of the forum State. In *Mobutu v SA Cotoni*,[296] a Belgian court, in considering a civil claim against the absent Zairean President and his wife and children, held that the family members, in contrast to the head of State himself, could not rely on a rule of immunity from jurisdiction. By contrast, the Austrian Supreme Court has indicated that close family members of a head of State forming part of his or her household enjoy the same immunity as the head of State in both criminal and civil matters.[297] The head of State of Liechtenstein, his sister, and two brothers were the subject of a civil claim in the Austrian courts.

[294] See *The Times* (London), 11–12 March 1988; *Sunday Times* (London), 13 March 1988; *The Times* (London), 14–16 March, 28 June, and 6 November 1988. See also arrest in Switzerland in July 2008 of Hannibal Gadaffi, the son of the then Libyan leader on charges relating to the abuse of his servants at a Geneva hotel.

[295] Up to now such cases have been relatively rare but, in April 2013, Queen Beatrix of the Netherlands abdicated in favour of her eldest son, the Prince of Orange, who succeeded her as King Willem-Alexander. Under the Netherlands Royal House Act, which narrowly defines the members of the royal family qualifying as members of the royal house, she will, following abdication, continue to be so regarded; see also the abdication of Albert II, King of Belgium in favour of his son, Crown Prince Philippe, who assumed the throne on 21 July 2013 (*Sunday Times*, 7 July 2013); see also the example of Pope Benedict XVI whose resignation in 2013 prompted speculation as to his legal position in regard to various claims made against him during his papacy. See n 6 above.

[296] (1988) 91 ILR 259 (Civil Court of Brussels).

[297] *W v Prince of Liechtenstein and others* Oxford Reports on International Law ILDC 1. (Austria 2001). See also pp 83 and 91 above.

On the facts, the Supreme Court held that Prince Hans-Adam II enjoyed immunity but that, as his siblings could not be regarded as 'the closest family members of the head of State forming part of his household', they could not benefit from such immunity. More recently, an English court held that two Princes who were members of the ruling royal house in Saudi Arabia, namely a brother and nephew of king Abdullah, could not be regarded as members of the king's family 'forming part of his household' within the terms of the UK legislation. As such, they were not entitled to any immunity.[298] The judge in the lower court noted that it might be possible for an adult member of a sovereign's family, who regularly exercised royal or constitutional duties on behalf of the sovereign, to satisfy that criteria even if he or she lived apart from the sovereign, but concluded that neither respondent was sufficiently instrumental in the performance of such functions on a full-time basis to qualify in this regard. The Court of Appeal, although agreeing that the princes did not qualify as members of the king's household, took a more restrictive view, holding that there was no basis for giving the term 'members of his family forming part of his household' a wider meaning in relation to heads of State than in relation to heads of diplomatic missions.

US courts (which rely heavily on suggestions of immunity from the Executive) have accepted that the spouses of foreign heads of State enjoy a broad immunity from civil jurisdiction even when not present on the territory of the US.[299] In *Leutwyler v Queen Rania Al- Abdullah*,[300] following an Executive suggestion of 'head of State immunity', a US court dismissed a suit for breach of copyright against the wife of the King of Jordan. It is not clear to what extent they would be prepared to accord such immunity to other family members.[301]

Watts, in his study on this matter, concluded that it must be 'doubtful' whether family members making a private visit abroad, not in the company of the head of State, enjoy any particular entitlement under international law

[298] *Apex Global Management Ltd v Fi Cal Ltd and others* [2013] EWHC 587 (Ch); [2013] EWCA Civ 642, [2013] WLR (D) 228. In the context of criminal proceedings, see also the prosecution and conviction for murder in a UK court of Prince Saud Abdulaziz bin Nasir al Saud, a grandson of King Abdullah of Saudi Arabia. It is not reported whether immunity was raised at any stage in the proceedings. See 'Saudi prince guilty of servant's murder' <http://www.guardian.co.uk>.

[299] See *Estate of Silme G Domingo v Ferdinand Marcos* (1983) 77 AJIL 305 (suggestion of immunity issued in respect of Imelda Marcos, wife of the President of the Philippines); *Kline v Kaneko* (1988) 535 NYS 2d 303 and *Kline v Cordera de la Madrid* (1989) 546 NYS 2d 506 (suggestion of immunity issued in respect of the wife of the President of Mexico, although Watts points out this may have been based as much on grounds of sovereign activity as on her immunity as the wife of a head of State: Watts (n 2 above) 77).

[300] 184 F.Supp.2d 277, 280 (SDNY 2001).

[301] See *Junquist et al v Sheikh Sultan Bin Khalifa Al Nayhan et al* 940 F.Supp 312 (US 1996) where the State Department did not issue any suggestion of immunity in respect of the grandson of the ruler of Abu Dhabi and the court refused immunity.

to immunities and privileges.[302] Clearly, States are often prepared to grant special treatment in such circumstances but, despite the analogy with the family of an ambassador, the view has been expressed that family members' enjoyment of immunities and privileges is derived from international comity rather than established rules of international law.[303] Other authorities have stated less categorically that such immunity (together with that enjoyed by members of the retinue of a head of State) 'remains an uncertain matter' or one where State practice has remained 'limited and uneven'.[304]

It remains doubtful, therefore, whether family members travelling on private visits without the head of State or outside the forum State are entitled to special treatment, although the forum state may often choose to accord it. There is some practice which supports an entitlement on the part of spouses and minor children in such circumstances but it remains relatively sparse and uneven. When accompanying the head of State on official visits, however, practice would seem to support an entitlement to the same or similar privileges and immunities as the head of State. In such circumstances, family members may also benefit from the customary international law on special missions. Where they accompany the head of State on a private visit the position is a little less developed. While it may be arguable that they benefit from general rules relating to members of a head of State's entourage, the precise application of such rules is obscure and, again, often regarded as derived more from comity than established rules of international law. As a matter of practice, however, it is likely that most States would, as a minimum, be prepared to accord close family, within the category of 'household' members, inviolability and immunity from criminal jurisdiction.

Spouses and other family members may, of course, undertake official functions in their own right. Nowadays they frequently travel abroad to represent their State (or, indeed, the head of State himself). In such circumstances,

302 See (1994) 247 III Recueil des Cours 80.

303 See Special Rapporteur on Jurisdictional Immunities of States and Their Property: YBILC, 1989, vol II, Pt 2, paras 446, 450 (102–3). See also Art 5 of the Institute of International Law 2001 Resolution on Immunities from Jurisdiction of Heads of State and Government, which provides: 'Neither family members nor members of the suite of the head of State benefit from immunity before the authorities of a foreign State, unless afforded as a matter of comity. This is without prejudice to any other immunities they may enjoy in another capacity, in particular as a member of a special mission, while accompanying a head of State abroad.'

304 See International Law Commission, Memorandum by the Secretetariat, Immunity of State Officials from Foreign Criminal Jurisdiction, 76–7, para 114. See also Van Alebeek, *The Immunity of States and Their Officials in International Criminal Law and International Human Rights Law* (Oxford University Press, 2008): 'It is highly questionable whether the rule of head of State immunity extends its protection to the family members of a foreign head of State.'

they may benefit from the rules of customary international law which apply to persons on special mission. They may also benefit from the provisions of the 1973 Convention on the Prevention and Punishment of Crimes Against Internationally Protected Persons, including Diplomatic Agents.[305]

Section 20(1) of the UK State Immunity Act 1978, in addition to its provision on family members forming part of the head of State's household, provides for a head of State's 'private servants' to enjoy the same special treatment as that enjoyed by the private servants of an ambassador. In practice, however, such treatment is usually limited to various fiscal privileges (for those who are not nationals of the receiving State) and does not require any grant of immunity. The receiving State is, however, obliged to exercise its jurisdiction over those persons in such a manner as not to interfere unduly with the performance of the functions of the mission.[306] Section 20 is silent as regards other possible members of the entourage. A Swiss Federal Tribunal has stated that customary international law would grant personal inviolability and immunity from criminal jurisdiction to 'senior' members of a head of State's 'household staff' as well as close family members accompanying the head of State.[307] However, given the scant State practice available and the modern emphasis on functional necessity which is now accepted as the primary justification for immunity, it must be doubtful whether such treatment has been accorded on the basis of anything more than prevailing notions of comity rather than international law.

[305] The Convention includes in its scope not just heads of State but 'any representative . . . of a State . . . who . . . is entitled pursuant to international law to special protection . . .' (Art 1(1)(b)).

[306] See Art 37.4 of the VCDR.

[307] See n 282 above.

3

Heads of Governments, Foreign Ministers, and Other Senior State Representatives

(A) Heads of Governments and Foreign Ministers

1. Internal Forms and Titles

A State enjoys legal personality as a subject of international law and, on the international plane, it is, formally, the State which acts. The supreme organ of the State is the head of State. He or she represents the international persona of the State and is often seen as symbolic of that State. The Government, on the other hand, is the organ which exercises the executive authority of the State and it is usually the Government through which the State acts on a day-to-day basis and which determines how it acts. A Government is essentially a collectivity of senior persons in the State, each with individual responsibility for a particular aspect of State activity. Together they constitute the executive authority which governs the State.

Head of Government

The head of Government is a separate role from that of head of State although the same person may occupy both offices or the two roles may be combined into one office, as with the Presidency of the US. Where it is a separate office, the head of Government is most commonly referred to as the Prime Minister. He or she is the head of the executive authority governing the State rather than being an embodiment of the State itself or representative of its international persona. Although the distinction between the two offices may sometimes be somewhat blurred in popular attitudes and reporting, it is usually maintained in formal State practice—for example, in the titles given to meetings at which representatives of both type attend, such as the Meetings of Heads of States and Government of the Member States of the European Union.

The head of State may play only a formal or 'constitutional' role and the head of Government may exercise the real power and authority within the State. The titles and relative balance between the two offices are internal matters for each State to determine in accordance with its own constitutional structure and traditions. In most cases these matters are set out clearly in the internal laws of the States concerned but, as we have seen, a State's constitution may not necessarily reflect the realities of power as exercised in that State.[1] There have been instances where the offices of head of State or Prime Minister have been occupied by relatively subordinate officials, with another individual exercising the real power in the land. Such circumstances were frequent, for example, in former Communist States, where the General Secretary of the Communist Party was often the most powerful official, although not formally holding either of the two principal offices of State as head of State or head of Government. There are other examples, particularly where the armed forces occupy a prominent role in Government and where a so-called 'strong man' (usually a senior military officer) has featured. The political importance of such individuals is a matter which other States must necessarily take into account in their dealings with the State concerned, but such political factors may not in themselves confer a standing in international law entitling the individual to the kind of treatment required for heads of State and heads of Government. Thus, General Noriega of Panama, while undoubtedly the effective leader of Panama, was formally neither head of State nor head of Government. As a consequence, his claim to immunity as head of State was rejected by a US court.[2]

Minister for Foreign Affairs

The Foreign Minister is the member of Government with responsibility for the conduct of a State's international relations; and that responsibility is generally carried out through the Foreign Ministry of which he or she is head. The titles of the Minister and Ministry vary from State to State. In many States, particularly the larger ones, there may be more than one Minister in the Foreign Ministry Such junior, deputy, or assistant ministers do not themselves rank as the Foreign Minister. Again, the title and internal organization of the Foreign Ministry are essentially matters for each State to determine for itself. But whatever structure or titles are adopted, the Foreign Minister's position, like that of head of State and head of Government, has a special significance in international law. It is an office specifically dedicated to the conduct of a State's international relations. The Foreign Minister and the Foreign Ministry are the recognized channels of communication for the conduct of diplomatic business, and other States are entitled to look to the Foreign Minister if they want to know the State's position on any international matter, or to make

[1] See Part 2 at pp 30–31.

[2] See *United States v Noriega* 746 F Supp 1506 (1990), 99 ILR 145.

their views on any such matter known to that State. This aspect of a Foreign Minister's responsibility is expressly provided for in Article 41(2) of the Vienna Convention on Diplomatic Relations 1961:

> All official business with the receiving State entrusted to [the sending State's diplomatic] mission by the sending State shall be conducted with or through the Ministry of Foreign Affairs of the receiving State or such other ministry as may be agreed.[3]

Thus, although titles may not matter, it is important for a State to have a designated Government department which is primarily responsible for the conduct of its international relations. Without such a department, practical difficulties may arise for that State[4] and it may even find it difficult to fulfil its international obligations if it is a party to a treaty which, expressly or by necessary implication, requires the existence of a Foreign Ministry.

2. Internationally Relevant Powers

The international representative capacity possessed by heads of Government and Foreign Ministers may not be as all-encompassing as that possessed by heads of State. It is, always prudent, therefore, to consider their powers in the light of the particular constitutional provisions governing their position. Nevertheless, at the international level their powers usually cover the full range of their State's international activities. In the *Arrest Warrant* case, the International Court of Justice (ICJ) observed that:

> a Minister for Foreign Affairs, responsible for the conduct of his or her State's relations with all other States, occupies a position such that like the head of State or the head of Government, he or she is recognized under international law as representative of the State solely by virtue of his or her office. He or she does not have to present letters of credence.[5]

A good example of this is the treaty-making power of the State which usually ultimately resides in the head of State as the principal organ of the State. Important treaties are, however, often concluded personally by the head of Government or Foreign Minister and when this happens it is not necessary, unlike other

[3] The last eight words were particularly important for the UK where, until 1968, there was a separate ministry—the Commonwealth Relations Office—to handle relations with independent Commonwealth States.

[4] The absence of any foreign ministry in a State is rare but not unknown. In 1979, as a result of political changes in Libya, the various offices of State were restructured in such a way as to create considerable uncertainty and difficulty for other States especially as regards their compatibility with the requirements of the Vienna Convention on Diplomatic Relations. See Jennings and Watts (eds), *Oppenheim's International Law* vol 1 (9th edn, Longman, 1992) 469, n 2 (para 2 at 1060).

[5] See *Arrest Warrant of 11 April 2000 (DRC v Belgium)* (2002) ICJ Rep 3 at para [53].

State officials, for them to establish their authority to act for their States by the production of Full Powers.[6] Just as with heads of State, Article 7(2) of the Vienna Convention on the Law of Treaties 1969 provides that, simply in virtue of their functions and without having to produce Full Powers, they are considered as representing their State for the purpose of all acts relating to the conclusion of a treaty. The special position of heads of Government and Foreign Ministers is also recognized in Article 21 of the Convention on Special Missions 1969.

The acknowledged capacity of the head of Government and Foreign Minister to act internationally in the name of their State has important legal consequences in the sense that oral statements made by them to diplomatic representatives of other States may be held to be legally binding on their State.[7] Similarly, a Foreign Minister has been held entitled to alienate State property merely by executing an assignment in his own name.[8] As with heads of State, the question has been raised as to whether they can commit their State to a treaty even when some internal requirement regarding the conclusion of such a treaty has not been complied with. In *Aegean Sea Continental Shelf Case (Greece v Turkey)*[9] the ICJ admitted the possibility for a communiqué between two heads of Government to bind their respective States, although in the particular circumstances it found that the wording of the communiqué did not have this effect. Similarly, in the *Maritime Delimitation and Territorial Questions Between Qatar and Bahrain* case,[10] the Court found that minutes signed by Bahrain's Foreign Minister and his counterpart from Qatar could bind his State, notwithstanding the fact that Bahrain's constitution stipulated that treaties concerning the territory of the State could only come into effect after enactment as law.

3. Recognition

As in the case of heads of State, any dealings with heads of Government and Foreign Ministers as representatives of their States, and, in particular,

[6] Full Powers are written evidence that the person named in them is authorized to represent the State in performing certain acts in relation to a treaty, most commonly its signature. These are usually issued through a State's foreign ministry and will often be signed by the Foreign Minister or someone acting on his or her instructions (such persons themselves acting pursuant to an authority conferred by the head of State in whom the treaty-making power of the State ultimately resides). Although there is a growing tendency to dispense with such formalities in the case of many bilateral treaties, particularly with less formal exchanges of notes, such Full Powers must be produced for the signature of treaties for which the UN Secretary General is depositary.

[7] See *Legal Status of Eastern Greenland* PCIJ, Ser A/B, No 53 (1933).

[8] See *State of Russia v National City Bank of New York, Ann Digest*, 7 (1933–34), No 26.

[9] [1978] ICJ Rep 3 at para [96].

[10] (1994) ICJ Rep 112, 102 ILR 1. See also Part 2, pp 38–40.

acknowledgment of their special status, will involve questions of recognition. Such questions may involve considerations relating to recognition of the Government of which they are head or Foreign Minister, or of the State of which that Government purports to be the Government, or both.

In most cases no problem arises but, as we have seen, issues may arise particularly where there is some kind of struggle for power within a State to the extent that alternative 'Governments' may claim to exist. Such situations are not infrequent. In the 1990s there were rival Prime Ministers in Haiti, one appointed by President Aristide who had been forced into exile in the US) and the other appointed by General Cedras (who had seized power in the country). In 2011, uncertainty arose when a new 'Prime Minister' was appointed by the Parliament in Papua New Guinea in place of the incumbent Sir Michael Somare who was absent in Singapore receiving medical treatment. The new 'Prime Minister' took control and refused to give up power despite the fact that the Supreme Court had ruled that his appointment was unconstitutional and that Somare remained the legitimate Prime Minister.[11]

In such situations other States may have to consider their dealings with the members of those 'Governments' carefully, so as to ensure that they do not inadvertently 'recognize' them as the Government of the State in question. In the past the practice in many countries was to issue some form of general declaration or policy statement indicating the position with regard to recognition of new foreign Governments.

More recently, however, the prevailing tendency has been to leave the matter to be judged by the nature of the dealings that take place with a new Government. Despite this trend there still appear to be situations involving competing claims by rival groups where a State may judge it to be necessary to make some form of declaration.[12]

4. Protection, Privileges, and Immunities

Comparison with heads of State

State practice in regard to the treatment of heads of Government and Foreign Ministers is less well developed than for heads of State. Other States have, however, almost always been prepared to accord such persons special respect and protection, although it has not always been clear whether such treatment was required by rules of customary international law or derived merely from comity or diplomatic courtesy. Heads of Government and Foreign Ministers are very

[11] See <http://www.telegraph.co.uk> report 22 October 2012.

[12] See Part 2 at 42–58.

senior and important figures but do not symbolize or personify their States in the way that heads of States do. This suggests that they cannot enjoy, in international law, any entitlement to special treatment by virtue of qualities of sovereignty or majesty attaching to them personally[13] and that any entitlement must, therefore, be based upon considerations of functional necessity derived from their international role.

In this respect, the two offices, unlike other senior Government offices, have traditionally been linked with that of head of State. As we have seen, Article 7.2 of the Vienna Convention on the Law of Treaties 1969 recognizes that all three, by virtue of their functions and without having to produce Full Powers, are considered as representing their State for the performance of all acts relating to a treaty. Moreover, the Convention on Special Missions 1969 has a provision which carries the clear implication that heads of Government and Foreign Ministers are entitled to special treatment under customary international law which may exceed that provided for in the Convention.[14] However, although the Convention acknowledges that the two offices, like that of head of State, enjoy special protection under international law, it does refer to them in a separate paragraph, using slightly different wording from that used in respect of heads of State. It is not clear whether this was prompted by a belief that such protection may differ in certain respects from that accorded to heads of State but the distinction is one that has been made in other contexts as well.

The UN Convention on the Jurisdictional Immunities of States and Their Property 2004, for example, contains a savings clause in respect of the immunities *ratione personae* enjoyed by heads of State but is silent on heads of Government and Foreign Ministers. The ILC's Commentary on the relevant draft Article explains, however, that it does not 'prejudge the extent of immunities granted by States to heads of Government and ministers for foreign affairs'. The Commentary also notes that the decision not to include such persons expressly within the scope of the savings clause was because 'it would be difficult to prepare an exhaustive list, and any enumeration of such persons would moreover raise the issue of the basis and of the extent of the jurisdictional immunity [enjoyed] by such persons'.[15] The point was also picked up by the Chairman of the Ad Hoc Committee on Jurisdictional Immunities of States and their Property in his statement to the Sixth Committee, where he explained that the general approach of the Convention was that it did

[13] See Watts, 'The Legal Position in International Law of Heads of States, Heads of Governments and Foreign Ministers' (1994) 247 III Recueil des Cours 102–3.

[14] Article 21(2) provides that: 'The head of Government, the Minister for Foreign Affairs and other persons of high rank, shall enjoy in the receiving State or in a third State, in addition to what is granted by the present Convention, the facilities, privileges and immunities accorded by international law.'

[15] ILC Commentary, draft Art 3, para 7 UN Doc A/46/10 YBILC 1991 vol II(2).

not apply where there was a special immunity regime, including immunities *ratione personae*. He specifically noted:

> Sometimes that was expressly stated in the text, sometimes not. Thus, for example, the express mention of heads of State in Article 3 should not be read as suggesting that the immunity *ratione personae* of other State officials was affected by the Convention.[16]

What then is the basis for this special treatment? The role and functions of a head of Government and of a Foreign Minister have changed in many respects over the last 60 years. In former times, it was the almost exclusive role of the resident ambassador and his diplomatic mission to conduct international negotiations in the receiving State. The position of such officials was generally recognized to call for special treatment (particularly in the form of protection, inviolability, and immunity from legal proceedings). Without such special treatment it was argued that such diplomatic officials would be unable to perform their functions effectively. Nowadays, however, the conduct of international relations is as much a matter for ad hoc talks, both bilateral and multilateral, in the form of brief visits to other States by heads of Government, Foreign Ministers, and, indeed, other State representatives, as it is for resident diplomatic missions. It would seem, therefore, that the special treatment accorded to heads of Government and Foreign Ministers must be based on functional considerations similar to those which apply to resident diplomatic missions. When heads of Government and Foreign Ministers are abroad on official business they will normally be leading, or senior, members of a special mission and, as such, their position falls within the scope of the Convention on Special Missions 1969. Its provisions are a guide to the level of treatment to which they may be entitled on such missions but, as we have seen, those provisions are only a minimum, since Article 21(2) appears to implicitly accept that international law may call for further facilities, privileges, and immunities to be accorded.[17]

In the UK there is no specific legal provision conferring privileges and immunities on heads of Government or Foreign Ministers and the matter is governed by customary international law. This is in contrast to the position on heads of State where, as we have seen, section 20 of the State Immunity Act 1978 provides expressly that a sovereign or other head of State shall, subject to 'any necessary modifications', enjoy the same privileges and immunities as the head of a diplomatic mission.

[16] Statement by Gerhard Hafner, Chairman of Ad Hoc Committee, para 37. See also the endorsement of this position in declarations made by Norway and Sweden on ratification, both States declaring that the express mention of heads of State in Art 3 should not be read as suggesting that the immunity *ratione personae* of other State officials is affected by the Convention.

[17] See n 14 above.

The following pages set out the position with regard to heads of Government and Foreign Ministers under headings roughly corresponding to those used for heads of State in Chapter 2. In some cases their position appears to be identical or substantially similar to that of heads of State and can be dealt with very briefly with reference to the earlier sections on heads of State. In others, the position is less clear and a fuller treatment is required.

Freedom of movement

In this context there is no reason to regard the position of heads of Government and Foreign Ministers as any different from that of heads of State.[18] It is normally a matter for each State to decide the persons it chooses to receive. An official visit can only take place by invitation. Once an official visit has been agreed it is for the host State to ensure that the visitor may enter and travel, as necessary, within its territory. Article 27 of the Convention on Special Missions 1969 confers, subject to certain conditions, freedom of movement and travel so far as is necessary for the performance of the functions of the special mission.

It is generally open to a State to refuse entry to a foreign head of Government or Foreign Minister, just as it can in respect of any other foreign individual. Indeed, in certain cases it may be obliged to do so pursuant to international obligations imposing travel bans on State officials and others from particular countries.

The only exception to this principle is where a State is the host country for an international organization where it may be obliged to admit representatives from member States, including heads of Government and Foreign Ministers, in accordance with its obligations under the host country agreement with the organization concerned. Such admission may take place in accordance with the normal procedures and visa requirements of the receiving State but, nonetheless, reduces the flexibility of the latter to refuse entry altogether.

Freedom of communication

Again, as in the case of heads of State, heads of Government and Foreign Ministers appear to be free to communicate with their home State and missions abroad even when such communication may involve the performance of official acts in a foreign State. The performance of such acts, which are generally of an internal administrative nature affecting their home States, do not, in principle, involve any breach of international law on the part of those performing them. The fact that most heads of Government and other State officials now travel

[18] See Part 2 at 58–60.

more frequently than they used to means that, in practice, the performance of such acts while they are abroad has become something of a necessity. It is accepted practice that they must routinely keep in close touch with affairs in their home State even when on visits to other States and must perform there such acts of internal administration as may be required; host States do not normally object to such a practice on the part of high-level visitors, although, as we have seen, they may do so if the acts are such as to affect the host State itself or are otherwise controversial.[19] In this context Article 28 of the Convention on Special Missions 1969 states that the receiving State shall 'permit and protect free communication' of a special mission and goes on to provide detailed provisions on inviolability of correspondence, and use of bags and couriers analogous to those of diplomatic missions.

Protection of dignity, person, and property

It has long been accepted that, as with heads of State, there is, in general customary international law, an obligation on States to protect heads of Government and Foreign Ministers, when visiting other States on official business, from attacks on their persons, freedom, or dignity. There remains some uncertainty, however, whether such a duty applies only in the context of official visits or might also apply, as it does for heads of State, to private visits and, if so, whether its content is the same in both circumstances. As regards dignity there is a further question as to whether a violation of a State's obligation in this regard can take place even when the foreign head of Government or Foreign Minister is not present in the territory of that State.[20]

Under Article 29 of the Vienna Convention on Diplomatic Relations 1961 a receiving State is under a duty to take all appropriate steps to prevent any attack on the person, freedom, or dignity of a diplomatic agent. As with heads of State, it could be argued that such a duty in regard to heads of Government and Foreign Ministers is an *a fortiori* case. Moreover, Article 29 of the Convention on Special Missions 1969 requires that the receiving State shall treat such representatives on special mission with 'due respect and shall take all appropriate steps to prevent any attack on their persons, freedom or dignity'.

Considerations of respect and dignity are thus acknowledged to be elements in the protection to which a head of Government or Foreign Minister is entitled at least while he or she is on special mission to the receiving State. Although the Convention does not enjoy a particularly wide participation, its

[19] See Part 2 at 60–61.

[20] It is clear that violation of a foreign head of State's dignity may occur in such circumstances. See Part 2 at 63.

provisions can reasonably be accepted as reflecting customary international law in this regard.

The Convention also provides that any premises of a special mission are entitled to protection. Article 25(2) imposes a 'special duty' on the receiving State to take all appropriate steps to protect the premises against any intrusion or damage and to prevent any disturbance of the peace of the mission or impairment of its dignity; Article 30 applies the same obligation to the private accommodation of the representatives on special mission.

The entitlement of heads of Government and Foreign Ministers to special protection is also recognized by the Convention on the Prevention and Punishment of Crimes Against Internationally Protected Persons, including Diplomatic Agents 1973. The preamble acknowledges that there are rules of customary international law requiring States to afford special protection to 'internationally protected persons'—a term which is expressly defined to include heads of governments and foreign ministers.[21] The Convention specifies various acts of a grave nature against such persons which must be made criminal and punished but provides expressly that the list of acts specified is not exhaustive and does not derogate from any general obligation under international law to take all appropriate measures to prevent other attacks on the person, freedom, or dignity of the person concerned.

Where such a duty does apply it is reasonable to assume that similar considerations come into play as for heads of State, for example:[22] a State is itself under a duty to refrain from such attacks; but as regards the actions of independent third parties its duty is not an absolute one and it is merely required to take 'all appropriate steps' to prevent such attacks; customary international law does not make the creation of special offences or penalties in States' domestic law compulsory in relation to attacks on dignity; States enjoy a wide margin of discretion in determining what may be the appropriate steps in any particular case but need to be careful in doing so to strike a reasonable balance between the interests of justice and the rights of individuals.

A head of Government or Foreign Minister, although often charged with the exercise of similar international functions and powers as a head of State, is not symbolic of the State itself nor representative of its majesty and international persona. There is, therefore, some uncertainty as to whether he or she should be entitled to the same treatment as heads of State when on a private visit to another State. It has been suggested, for example, that, although in practice, a head of Government or Foreign Minister may be accorded special treatment, this is more likely to be a matter of courtesy and respect for the importance of the visitor, than a

[21] See Art 1(1)(a). [22] See Part 2 at 61–73.

reflection of any belief by the host State that such treatment is required by international law.[23]

It may also be significant that the Convention on the Prevention and Punishment of Crimes against Internationally Protected Persons, including Diplomatic Agents 1973, distinguishes in this connection between heads of State and other senior State representatives. While the former is an internationally protected person 'whenever' he or she is in a foreign State, the latter falls within the definition only when 'entitled pursuant to international law to special protection from any attack on his [or her] person, freedom or dignity'; this suggests that there may be times when such persons are not so entitled, and private visits may be one of them. As far as attacks on dignity are concerned, it must also be doubtful whether States are under any legal duty to prevent such attacks when the head of Government or Foreign Minister concerned is not within their territory.

Inviolability

Again, it has long been accepted that a head of Government or Foreign Minister enjoys personal inviolability when visiting a foreign State on official business. This means that the host State must not itself, through its officials and agents, hinder that person in the exercise of his or her functions, or otherwise interfere with the security of his or her person, property, or place of residence. This is reflected in Article 29 of the Convention on Special Missions 1969, which provides that a head of Government or Foreign Minister on special mission enjoys personal inviolability and is not liable to any form of arrest or detention; similarly his or her papers, correspondence, and, with some exceptions, property are also inviolable.[24]

In 2002 it became clear, however, that the inviolability enjoyed by a head of Government and Foreign Minister went further than that envisaged under the Special Missions Convention and was effectively co-extensive with that of a head of State. In that year, the ICJ delivered its judgment in a case involving the issue by a Belgian investigating judge of an international arrest warrant against Yerodia Ndombasi, who was at the time Minister for Foreign Affairs of the Democratic Republic of the Congo.[25] According to the Court, a Minister for Foreign Affairs occupies a position comparable to that of a head of State or

[23] See Watts (n 14 above) 109–10.

[24] Article 25 provides that the premises of the special mission are also inviolable so that the agents of the receiving State may not enter them except with consent; and those premises, its furnishings, other property used in its operations, and means of transport are immune from search, requisition, attachment, or execution. Under Arts 26 and 28(2) the archives, documents, and official correspondence of the mission are inviolable.

[25] See *Arrest Warrant* case *(Arrest Warrant of 11 April 2000 (DEC v Belgium)* (2002) ICJ Rep 3).

a head of Government and the functions of the office are such that, throughout the duration of that office, the Minister must enjoy personal inviolability and immunity from criminal jurisdiction for all acts whether performed in a private or official capacity. The inviolability and immunity applies regardless of whether he or she is visiting in an official or private capacity or, indeed, is present in the territory of the arresting State at all.

The Court adopted a purely functional analysis of the rationale for such inviolability, stating that it must protect the individual concerned 'against any act of authority of another State which would hinder him or her in the performance of his or her duties'.[26] The facts of the case concerned the issue and circulation of an arrest warrant and on this matter the Court held more precisely that '... given the nature and purpose of the warrant, its mere issue violated the immunity which Mr Yerodia enjoyed as the Congo's incumbent Minister for Foreign Affairs'.[27] It further held that the 'circulation of the warrant, whether or not it significantly interfered with Mr Yerodia's diplomatic activity,... infringed the immunity from criminal jurisdiction and inviolability then enjoyed by him under international law'.

The fact that the necessary steps to enforce the warrant in third countries had not been taken by the Belgian authorities suggests that the mere risk that a Foreign Minister may be hindered in carrying out his or her official functions may be sufficient to violate inviolability or immunity; proof of actual impediment is not required.

Judges Higgins, Kooijmans, and Buergenthal indicated in their joint separate opinion that, although the precise scope of the immunities during private travel was not clear, it is certain that a Minister for Foreign Affairs may not be subjected to any measures which would prevent the effective performance of his functions.[28] In this connection, they added, however, that the mere commencement of an investigation would not infringe the inviolability or immunities of the individual concerned.[29] Judge Al-Khasawneh also picked up this point in his dissenting opinion:

> A Minister for Foreign Affairs is entitled to immunity from enforcement when on official mission... but the mere opening of criminal investigations against him can hardly be said by any objective criteria to constitute interference with the conduct of diplomacy. A faint-hearted or ultra-sensitive Minister may restrict his private travels or feel discomfort but this is a subjective element that must be discarded.[30]

[26] *Arrest Warrant* case, para [54].

[27] *Arrest Warrant* case, para [70]. The warrant issued contained express language to the effect that it was not to be enforced if Mr Yerodia was on Belgian territory on an official mission.

[28] *Arrest Warrant* case, Joint Opinion, para [84].

[29] *Arrest Warrant* case, Joint Opinion, para [59].

[30] *Arrest Warrant* case, Dissenting Opinion of Judge Al-Khasawneh, para [4].

Later this issue was considered in more detail by the Court in the *Mutual Assistance* case[31] where the key consideration was whether the person had been subjected to any 'constraining act of authority'. The Court concluded that both of the witness 'summons' issued by the investigating authorities had not been associated with any such measures of constraint and had in fact constituted mere invitations to testify, which the head of State had been free to accept or decline. As such they did not infringe his inviolability or immunity from jurisdiction.[32]

Immunity from suit before foreign courts

It has long been accepted that a head of Government or Foreign Minister, while visiting another State on official business, should not be subject to legal proceedings there. If faced with such proceedings, they would be likely to find their ability to carry out their functions seriously impaired. Even the risk that, by visiting another State, they could be opening the way for the institution of such proceedings could deter them from the visit to the prejudice of their conduct of their State's international relations. Such reasoning led Watts in his study on this subject to conclude that:

> Principle thus suggests that a head of government or Foreign Minister who visits another State for official purposes is immune from legal process while there, and that that applies both in respect of matters arising during the visit as well as those arising previously; furthermore, it applies as regards both criminal and civil proceedings.[33]

Article 31 of the Convention on Special Missions 1969 contains provisions in this sense. Under that Article, representatives of the sending State on a special mission enjoy full immunity from the criminal jurisdiction of the receiving State. They also enjoy immunity from the its civil or administrative jurisdiction but subject to four exceptions, concerning private immovable property in the receiving State, private involvement in actions relating to succession, private professional or commercial activities in the host State, and private motor vehicle accidents.

As far as heads of Government were concerned there was also some evidence of a more far-reaching general acceptance that a head of Government should enjoy immunities similar to those of a head of State.[34] Such immunities would apply whether the head of Government was on an official or private visit or, indeed, outside the forum State altogether. This assimilated position

[31] *Certain Questions of Mutual Assistance in Criminal Matters (Djibouti v France)* (2008) ICJ Rep 177.

[32] For fuller discussion of implications of this case and current litigation involving criminal investigations of heads of States, heads of Governments etc, see Part 2 at 64–8.

[33] See Watts (n 13 above) 106.

[34] See *Satow's Diplomatic Practice* (6th edn, Oxford University Press, 2009) 184, para 12.17.

is reflected in the 2001 Resolution adopted by the Institute of International Law on Immunities from Jurisdiction and Execution of Heads of State and of Government in International Law. Article 15(1) states that a head of Government 'shall enjoy the same inviolability, and immunity from jurisdiction recognised, in this Resolution, to the Head of State'.

In *Saltany v Reagan*,[35] a number of Libyan nationals brought a civil action in the US against the Government of that country and numerous additional defendants including President Reagan and Margaret Thatcher who was then head of Government in the UK. The Court dismissed the complaint against Margaret Thatcher, accepting the State Department's 'suggestion' that she was immune from the jurisdiction as 'the sitting head of Government of a friendly foreign State'. The UK Prime Minister was not present in the US at the time so the decision acknowledged the immunity from jurisdiction of an incumbent head of Government even when not on an official visit at least where the proceedings clearly involved the exercise of governmental authority.[36]

The position of Foreign Ministers was less defined. The 2001 Resolution of the Institute of International Law[37] does not refer to them.[38] However, the scant State practice that existed tended to support the view that, while travelling abroad on official business, they were regarded as entitled to immunity from the jurisdiction of the host State. In 1963 a US court, following a 'suggestion' by the State Department,[39] dismissed proceedings brought against the Foreign Minister of the Republic of Korea while he was on an official visit to the US.[40]

Criminal proceedings

The decision of the ICJ in the *Arrest Warrant* case has now removed any uncertainty as to whether the position of a Foreign Minister in this respect may be different from that of a head of Government, and confirmed that both

[35] (1989) 87 ILR 679.

[36] See also *Doe I v State of Israel* 400 F.Supp 2d 86 (DDC 2005); and *Daventree Ltd v Republic of Azerbaijan* No 2-6356 (SDNY, 15 October 2003) where US courts dismissed claims against the Israeli Prime Minister Sharon and the Azerbaijani Prime Minister Ilham Aliyev based on the Executive Branch's suggestions of 'head of State' immunity.

[37] See also the view of the International Law Commission's Special Rapporteur on Jurisdictional Immunities of States and Their Property that privileges and immunities enjoyed by Foreign Ministers are granted on the basis of comity rather than on the basis of established rules of international law: YBILC 1989, vol II, Part 2, 102–3, paras 446, 450.

[38] But note that the draft Resolution did include them and effectively assimilated their position to that of heads of State and heads of Government but this reference does not appear in the final text. See Fox, 'The Resolution of the Institute of International Law on the Immunities of Heads of State and Government' (2002) 51 ICLQ 119 at 120.

[39] *Chong Boon Kim v Kim Yong Shik* (1964) 58 AJIL186.

[40] See also *Ali Ali Reza v Grimpel* (1961) 47 ILR 275 where a French court denied a claim to immunity by a Minister of State of Saudi Arabia but did so in terms which, although *obiter*, suggested that, had he been Foreign Minister, he would have enjoyed immunity.

enjoy the same extensive personal immunity from the criminal jurisdiction of foreign courts as heads of States. Such immunity applies to both private acts and those performed in an official capacity and regardless of whether they are present in the territory of the forum State at all or, if they are, whether they are there on an official or private visit. The Court also confirmed that the extensive personal immunity enjoyed by Foreign Ministers (and, by implication, heads of State and Government) was unaffected by the gravity of the crime alleged, thus firmly rebutting any suggestion that an exception existed where international crimes were concerned. In keeping with this approach, in 2003, the Belgian Court of Cassation dismissed criminal proceedings against Prime Minister Ariel Sharon of Israel concerning alleged war crimes.[41] It did so on the grounds that, as a sitting head of Government, he was entitled to personal 'head of State' immunity under customary international law.

The decision in the *Arrest Warrant* case has been the subject of some criticism particularly as regards its assimilation of the position of incumbent Ministers for Foreign Affairs with that of heads of State and Government. Some commentators have argued that there is simply no support in State practice for the application of such an extensive personal immunity to such persons as regards their private travel and acts committed in their private capacity.[42]

Civil and administrative proceedings

The *Arrest Warrant* case was concerned with criminal proceedings for which it is now clear that heads of State and of Government and Foreign Ministers are entitled to full immunity. The position with regard to civil proceedings (at least as regards private visits or circumstances where the individual concerned is outside the forum State) is less straightforward. There have been several cases involving claims in respect of acts carried out in an official capacity in which, as one might expect, immunity has been upheld. In *Saltany v Reagan*[43] a US court dismissed a claim against the Prime Minister of the UK on the ground that she was the sitting head of Government of a friendly foreign State. This was despite the fact that she was not visiting the US at the time. In *Tachiona v United States*,[44] a civil claim, the US Government filed a suggestion

[41] *Re Sharon and Yaron* (2003) 42 ILM 596.

[42] See eg Akande and Shah, 'Immunities of State Officials, International Crimes, and Foreign Domestic Courts (2010) 21(4) EJIL 815; and Wouters and De Smet, 'The ICJ's Judgment in the Case Concerning the Arrest Warrant of 11 April 2000: Some Critical Observations', Institute for International Law, WP No 27—January 2003. It has been argued that, while removing immunity from a head of State or head of Government goes to the root of the principle of the equality of States, a refusal to accord such full personal immunity to other senior officials on private visits would not have the same dramatic effect.

[43] See n 36 above.

[44] 386 F3d 205, 2004 US App. See Part 2 at 140–1.

of immunity asserting that both the President of Zimbabwe and his Foreign Minister Mudenge were entitled to personal immunity under the customary international law doctrine of 'head of State' immunity. Both were visiting the US at the time on official business. However, a US court has, subsequently, dismissed a suit against the Moroccan Foreign Minister, Benaissa, who was not in the US at the time. The dismissal was based upon an Executive Branch suggestion of 'head of State' immunity.[45]

There remains a question, however, as to whether, under customary international law, their immunity for private acts is absolute or may be subject to certain exceptions. While the functional rationale adopted by the ICJ in the *Arrest Warrant* case could be extensively applied, as it is in criminal proceedings, to cover private visits or circumstances where the persons concerned are outside the forum State, the arguments are less compelling. As we have seen, it remains questionable whether a head of State's immunity is absolute in this context[46] and, in a number of jurisdictions, legislation has imposed specific limitations in this regard.[47] Such limitations would apply even where the head of State is in the forum State on official business. It is also notable that the Convention on Special Missions 1969 expressly provides that the immunity from civil jurisdiction enjoyed by representatives of the sending State shall be subject to four exceptions,[48] although it is not clear to what extent these would also apply to heads of State, heads of Government, and Foreign Ministers given the provisions of Article 21. In any event, no measure may be taken by the receiving State in regard to these exceptions if its effect would be to infringe the inviolability of the representative or his or her accommodation.

Other exemptions and privileges

Aside from the above, it is difficult to identify any other immunities, privileges, or special treatment which could reasonably be said to be necessary in order to enable a head of Government or Foreign Minister to perform his or her functions effectively. Where an official visit is concerned it is certainly the normal practice of States to facilitate entry and departure and to dispense with many of the formalities to which other visitors are subject. The Convention on Special Missions 1969 makes provision for the grant of certain privileges and exemptions to be enjoyed by a head of Government or a Foreign Minister

[45] *Rhanime v Solomon* 01-1479 (DCD, 15 May 2002).

[46] See Part 2 at 89–96.

[47] See eg s 20(1) of UK State Immunity Act 1978 which has been interpreted so as to apply the so-called 'diplomatic exceptions' to a head of State. See also *Apex Global Management Ltd v Fi Cal Ltd and others* [2013] EWHC 587(Ch) 19 March 2013.

[48] See Art 31. The exceptions relate to: private immovable property situated in the territory of the receiving State; actions relating to succession in which the representative is involved as a private person; actions relating to any professional or commercial activity exercised by the person concerned in the receiving State; and actions for damages arising from a vehicle accident used outside official functions.

when on a special mission. These include exemption from social security legislation (Article 32), exemption from dues and taxes (Article 33), exemption from personal services (Article 34), and exemption from customs duties and inspection (Article 35). Apart from the latter, it is unlikely that such matters would be of much practical application in the case of temporary official visits of the kind carried out by such foreign dignitaries. In addition, it is usual for States to facilitate the entry and departure of heads of Government and Foreign Ministers even in the case of private visits, including transit visits. Such facilitation arrangements may include exemption from customs, immigration, and quarantine procedures as well as aviation security screening, although it is usually made clear that commercial airlines have their own policy on carriage of unscreened passengers and that such policies cannot be overridden by any exemptions offered by Governments.[49]

It would be difficult to argue that a head of Government or Foreign Minister had been impeded in the exercise of his or her functions by reasonable and efficiently administered immigration and customs inspection or, indeed, by a requirement to pay normal and reasonable duties on arrival, particularly when on a private visit. For this reason, it seems likely that such special treatment is essentially a matter of courtesy rather than derived from obligations under customary international law.[50]

5. Families

The position under customary international law of members of the families of heads of Government and Foreign Ministers, when accompanying them on visits to other States, is uncertain. The most likely possibility is that close family members, such as a spouse or minor children who are included in any official invitation, would enjoy the same privileges and immunities as the heads of Government and Foreign Ministers themselves.

As far as their physical protection is concerned, this is recognized by the Convention on the Prevention and Punishment of Crimes Against Internationally Protected Persons, including Diplomatic Agents 1973. Article 1(1)(b) includes members of the family of senior State representatives who form part of their households in the definition of 'internationally protected person'. Similarly, Article 39 of the Convention on Special Missions 1969 provides that the main privileges and immunities conferred on heads of Government and

[49] When an airline insists on screening, matters can usually be resolved by some private arrangement for doing so but, in any event, many world leaders now choose to travel in private or Government aircraft.

[50] See Watts (n 13 above) 109: 'a State which agrees to accept a visit by a foreign head of Government or Foreign Minister is most unlikely then to jeopardise the effectiveness of the visit by acting less than generously in these matters.'

Foreign Ministers on a special mission shall be enjoyed also by members of their families accompanying them so long as they are not nationals of or permanently resident in the receiving State. These provisions are modelled closely on equivalent provisions in the Vienna Convention on Diplomatic Relations 1961 which cover the family members of a diplomatic agent forming part of his or her household.[51]

The existence of the provisions relating to diplomats' families is strongly supportive of a rule of customary international law which would entitle the family members of senior State representatives accompanying them on special mission to similar special treatment. However, the provisions of the 1969 and 1973 Conventions are, of course, limited to situations where the State representative is travelling abroad in his or her official capacity.

The position when family members accompany a head of Government or Foreign Minister on private visits or make unaccompanied private visits on their own account is unclear. The ICJ has confirmed in the *Arrest Warrant* case that incumbent Foreign Ministers and, by implication, heads of Government enjoy the same extensive personal inviolability and immunity from foreign criminal jurisdiction as heads of State. Such immunity applies wherever the individual may be and, if abroad, whether he or she is visiting in an official or private capacity. The question arises, therefore, whether it could reasonably be argued that a family member forming part of the head of Government's or Foreign Minister's household should enjoy the same immunity. Certainly the argument from functional necessity is much less compelling. It is not obvious how a head of Government or Foreign Minister could be impeded in the exercise of his or her functions merely by the fact that family members were not entitled to privileges and immunities when making private visits to other States.

Moreover, a head of Government or Foreign Minister cannot claim to be regarded as a personal embodiment of the State itself in the way that many heads of State are. Unlike heads of State, it is rare for their family members to have an official or constitutional role. Even in the case of the families of heads of State, the position as we have seen, is far from certain and there are some who would argue that the special treatment they receive is more a matter of courtesy than legal obligation. In these circumstances it is unlikely that the families of heads of Government or Foreign Ministers are entitled, as a matter of international law, to special treatmentment except when they accompany the latter on official business at the invitation of the host State.[52]

[51] See Art 37(1). [52] See Watts (n 13 above) 111.

(B) Other Senior State Representatives

1. Personal Immunities

The judgment of the ICJ in the *Arrest Warrant* case left open the question whether there were any other categories of high-ranking State representative (apart from heads of Government and Foreign Ministers) who may be entitled to the same wide-ranging personal immunity as a head of State. The Court made it clear that it was only considering the inviolability and immunity from criminal jurisdiction of an incumbent Minister for Foreign Affairs, but the language used in the judgment, with its reference to 'certain holders of high-ranking office in a state, such as the head of State, the head of Government and Minister for Foreign Affairs',[53] suggested that there could be other holders of high office entitled to such immunities.

The Court emphasized that such immunities are not for the personal benefit of the individual concerned but designed to enable the effective performance of his or her functions on behalf of the State. Such functions include frequent travel on diplomatic missions on behalf of the State and the need to communicate at any time with representatives of other States. In addition to the travel aspect, the Court also noted that a Foreign Minister has full powers to act on behalf of the State, observing that this is a position similar to a head of State or head of Government in that 'he or she is recognized under international law as representative of the State solely by virtue of his or her office'.

Unfortunately, neither criteria provides any clear basis for determining which offices of State should benefit from such extensive personal immunity. In modern times, international functions have been extended to a much wider range of officials than before. Many Government ministers and even senior officials of non-ministerial rank exercise such functions and are required to travel frequently in order to do so. It is now common for ministers, other than those designated as responsible for Foreign Affairs, to represent their State internationally. In the *Case Concerning Armed Activities on the Territory of the Congo* (*Democratic Republic of the Congo v Rwanda*),[54] the ICJ noted:

> that with increasing frequency in modern international relations other persons representing a State in specific fields may be authorized by that State to bind it by their statements in respect of matters falling within their purview. This may be true, for example, of holders of technical ministerial portfolios exercising powers in their field of competence in the area of foreign relations, and even of certain officials.

[53] *Arrest Warrant* case, para 51.

[54] (2006) ICJ Rep 6.

It concluded that 'the possibility cannot be ruled out in principle that a Minister of Justice may, under certain circumstances, bind the State he or she represents by his or her statements'.

There is, as yet, little guidance in State practice or in the jurisprudence of the ICJ itself as to which other offices of State, if any, may be covered by personal immunity. There are a number of international treaties which specifically affirm the special position of the three office holders mentioned so far—heads of State and Government and Ministers of Foreign Affairs—but no specific reference in any of them to other office holders.[55] The limited case law that exists suggests that officials at an administrative level, as opposed to those of ministerial rank, would not be regarded as entitled to such immunity particularly where their functions are primarily internal. In the *Case Concerning Certain Questions of Mutual Judicial Assistance in Criminal Matters (Djibouti v France)*,[56] the ICJ did not suggest that the Djiboutian Head of National Security or its Procureur de la Republique[57] would enjoy personal immunity.[58] France had stated earlier that, in its view, they would not, 'given the essentially internal nature of their functions'.[59]

In 2011, a UK court held that the Secretary of the Executive Office of the National Security Council of Mongolia fell clearly outside the circle of high-ranking officials entitled to such immunity. In doing so it described him as an administrator far removed from the narrow circle of those who hold such high office that they can be equated with the State they personify.[60]

Where ministers have been involved, however, some courts appear more willing to accord personal immunity. In 2005, a Swiss court suggested in an obiter dictum that a Minister for Atomic Energy may be entitled to immunity *ratione personae*.[61] A Belgian court has also extended such immunity to

[55] See eg Art 7 of the Vienna Convention on the Law of Treaties; Art 21 of the Convention on Special Missions.

[56] (2008) ICJ Rep 177.

[57] Public Prosecutor.

[58] The ICJ held at para [194] of the judgment that 'there are no grounds in international law upon which it could be said that the officials concerned were entitled to personal immunities, not being diplomats within the meaning of the Vienna Convention on Diplomatic Relations of 1961, and the Convention on Special Missions of 1969 not being applicable in this case'.

[59] See 241–2, para [186] of the judgment. See also *Case Concerning Criminal Proceedings (Republic of the Congo v France) (Provisional Measures)* (2003) ICJ Rep 102 where the ICJ refused provisional measures in a case where the French authorities had issued a warrant for the appearance as a suspect and witness of the Inspector General of the Congolese Armed Forces.

[60] *Khurts Bat v Investigating Judge of the German Federal Court and others* [2011] EWHC 2029 (Admin).

[61] *Evgeny Adamov v Federal Office of Justice*, Swiss Federal Tribunal, No 1A.288/2005, Judgment of 22 December 2005, para 3.4.2.

a Vice-President of the Democratic Republic of the Congo (DRC).[62] Courts in the UK have (albeit only at magistrates' court level)[63] accorded personal immunity from criminal jurisdiction to a Defence Minister[64] and a Minister for Commerce and International Trade.[65] In the *Mofaz* case, an application was made for a warrant for the arrest of General Shaul Mofaz, who was then the incumbent Israeli Defence Minister and was believed to be visiting the UK. The application alleged that the general, in his capacity as Defence Minister, had committed grave breaches of Article 147 of the Fourth Geneva Convention, contrary to section 1 of the Geneva Convention Act 1957. The Senior District Judge, noting that the basis for a Foreign Minister's entitlement to immunity in the *Arrest Warrant* case had been to enable him to effectively carry out his functions, stated:

> The functions of various Ministers will vary enormously depending upon their sphere of responsibility. I would think it very unlikely that Ministerial appointments such as Home Secretary, Employment Minister, Environment Minister, Culture, Media and Sports Minister would automatically acquire a label of state immunity.[66] However, I do believe that the Defence Minister may be a different matter.

He went on to note that, although a Defence Minister may not be required to travel to quite the same extent as a Foreign Minister, a defence portfolio may, nevertheless, require frequent travel and that 'the roles of defence and foreign policy are very much intertwined...'. The case was decided without any reference to the nature of General Mofaz's visit to the UK.

In 2009, a Deputy Senior District Judge refused an application for the arrest of Ehud Barak, the Israeli Defence Minister and Deputy Prime Minister on similar grounds.[67] Before doing so, however, the judge had, reportedly,

[62] See D'Argent, *Jurisprudence belge relative au droit international public (*2004–07), RBDI, 2007-1, n 51, 185. But see issue of arrest warrant by French authorities in respect of a Vice President of Equatorial Guinea (see Part 2, n 190 above).

[63] The decision of a magistrates' court is not a binding precedent under UK law.

[64] See *Re Mofaz* (2004) 128 ILR 709; and *Re Ehud Barak*, unreported; but see Franey, *Immunity, Individuals and International Law* (Lambert Academic Publishing, 2011) 146–7.

[65] See *Re Bo Xilai* (2005) 129 ILR 713.

[66] The judge's use of the term 'state immunity' in this context was misleading in that the term is usually taken to refer to the immunity *ratione materiae* (or subject-matter immunity) which applies to serving and former State officials in respect of acts performed by them in an official capacity. The immunity recognized in the *Arrest Warrant* case and applied to General Mofaz was, however, like diplomatic or head of State immunity, an absolute personal (or status) immunity applicable only for the duration of the holder's term of office but regardless of whether the acts concerned were performed in a private or official capacity.

[67] See n 65 above. See also decision of 25 July 2012 of Swiss Federal Criminal Court in *Khaled Nezzar* which denied immunity *ratione materiae* to a former Defence Minister but confirmed that he would have been entitled to personal immunity during his period of office. Note, however, that

made enquiries of the Foreign and Commonwealth Office as to the nature of the Defence Minister's visit and, on receiving confirmation that the visit was for official purposes, had also concluded that he was entitled to immunity under customary international law as a member of a special mission as well as personal immunity as Defence Minister.

In the earlier case of *Re Bo Xilai*[68] an application was made for the arrest of the Chinese Minister for Commerce, including international trade, in respect of allegations of conspiracy to torture. Again the Senior District Judge concluded, adopting the reasoning of the ICJ in the *Arrest Warrant* case, that 'his functions are equivalent to those exercised by a Minister for Foreign Affairs' and that he was entitled to personal immunity from prosecution 'as he would not be able to perform his functions unless he is able to travel freely'. The Senior District Judge also decided that the Minister was entitled, under customary international law, to immunity as a member of a special mission as he had formed part of the official delegation for a state visit of the Chinese President.

As we have seen, international law has accorded a special position to heads of State, heads of Government, and Ministers for Foreign Affairs. This special position has been expressly recognized in a number of international treaties and reflected (certainly as far as heads of State and Government are concerned) in State practice. The same cannot be said of other offices of State. It has to be said, therefore, that the reasoning applied in the three cases referred to above is thin and not entirely satisfactory. If the need to travel frequently on official business is the key criterion, then it is hard to see why, for example, a Home Department Minister or Environment Minister should be ruled out as such offices can nowadays require frequent travel. Clearly this criterion does not in itself provide an adequate reason for distinguishing between different Government ministers or, indeed, a wide variety of senior government officials. It could be argued that the need to travel must also be connected with the exercise by the official concerned of a traditional aspect or aspects of the State's foreign relations. In this way one could include a Defence Minister and perhaps one dealing with matters of international trade.[69] Such a test could, however, prove difficult to apply in practice and, given the differences in titles and distribution of ministerial portfolios in different States, is unlikely to result in the production of an exhaustive list. Also it would not resolve

he had also served as a member of the five-man High Council of State which had replaced the office of President.

[68] See n 66 above.

[69] Norway and Switzerland have expressed the view that immunity *ratione personae* should be granted to Ministers of Defence and Trade, with Norway also suggesting that Finance Ministers should also be so entitled in the light of the current international financial/banking crisis.

current uncertainty as to the level of seniority required in order to qualify. Is the category limited to those at 'Cabinet' level, that is those equal in rank to a Minister for Foreign Affairs, or could deputy ministers or more junior ministers and officials be included?

In view of these difficulties, some States have indicated that they are disinclined to accord immunity *ratione personae* to foreign officials outside the 'troika' expressly identified by the ICJ in the *Arrest Warrant* case.[70] Others, although prepared to consider such a grant, have indicated that they would see it as constituting progressive development. The ILC Special Rapporteur, Concepcion Escobar Hernandez,[71] has also proposed that the scope of such immunity from foreign criminal jurisdiction should be limited to heads of State, heads of Government, and Ministers for Foreign Affairs.[72] The justification for this proposal was stated as:

> the fact that their functions include representing the State in international relations, a function that, it should be borne in mind, is based on international law and performed automatically, without the need for any express authorization by the State that they represent [...] It is a representational function which international law attributes to these offices, independently of a State's domestic law, the sole function of which is to establish a homogeneous hierarchical model for representation of the State within the international community as a whole, and which promotes and facilitates the maintenance of international relations. It is precisely this automatic representational nature, based on international law, which explains the status that is granted to these three State officials within the framework of international law as a whole (for example, in treaty law and the law of State responsibility) and which is also recognized in the context of immunity from foreign criminal jurisdiction, whereby the regime that applies to such officials (immunity ratione personae) differs from the regime that applies to other State officials.[73]

The Commission has adopted three draft Articles, draft Article 3 of which confirms that these three office-holders enjoy immunity *ratione personae* only during their term of office.[74] No other office-holders are mentioned. It is clear, however, that opinions within the Commission remain divided on the issue.[75] The fact remains that the judgment of the ICJ in the *Arrest Warrant* case contained no such limitation and some members have taken the view that this, together with the existence of some State practice, suggests that such immunity must now extend beyond the three traditional offices to other representatives of States for whom foreign travel is essential. Those who support this view

[70] See eg Statement by Belgium in UN Sixth Committee.

[71] Appointed on 22 May 2012 to replace Mr Roman Kolodkin, who is no longer a member of the Commission.

[72] See Second Report UN Doc A/CN.4/661, 4 April 2013, para 67.

[73] See Second Report UN Doc A/CN.4/661, 4 April 2013, para 60.

[74] See Second Report of the Drafting Committee A/CN.4/L 184.

[75] See Statement of the Chairman of the Drafting Committee, ILC 65th Session, 7 June 2013.

argue that such immunity is necessary so as to protect the right of States to be represented abroad at a political level by persons of their choice. Such an approach would, of course, involve taking on the difficult task, referred to above, of identifying clear criteria for the selection of such offices. At the other end of the spectrum, others within the Commission have taken the view that, despite the *Arrest Warrant* case, even Ministers for Foreign Affairs should not enjoy immunity *ratione personae* under customary international law as there has been no clear State practice in this regard.

The formula adopted by the ILC in the draft article appears, therefore, to represent something of a compromise on the question and avoids the difficulty of identifying settled criteria for the selection of additional offices. It is, however, difficult to predict how matters may develop in the future. Whatever approach is finally adopted, it is unlikely that the ICJ intended to expand the category of high State representatives entitled to personal immunity far beyond the three officials specifically mentioned in its judgment. Such persons would need to be of similar political and or constitutional prominence, with the need to travel and represent their State, sometimes at short notice, being an essential part of their functions. This would probably rule out officials of less than senior ministerial rank but could conceivably encompass certain high State offices of an important constitutional character such as a Vice-President or parliamentary leader or, in a monarchy, an heir apparent regularly carrying out official functions on behalf of the sovereign. Such an approach would be consistent with the view of the ILC's former Special Rapporteur, Roman Kolodkin, in his Second Report,[76] where it is stated that such immunity should be confined to 'a narrow circle of high-ranking State officials'.

2. Special Missions

If the need to ensure and facilitiate official travel is the main concern, it is probable that this could be adequately addressed in the majority of cases by the application of special missions immunity.[77] In provisionally adopting draft Article 3, the ILC recognized explicitly that other high-ranking

[76] Roman Kolodkin, Second Report UN Doc A/CN.4/631,10 June 2010, para 94(i).

[77] See eg *Kilroy v Windsor (Prince of Wales)* 1978 Digest of US Practice in International Law 641, (1978) 81 ILR 605; *Li Weixum v Bo Xilai*, US District Court for District of Columbia, 24 July 2006 Civ No 04-0649. See also refusal by UK Director of Public Prosecutions of private application for warrant to arrest Ms Tzipi Livni, the Israeli opposition leader who was visiting London, on grounds that the FCO had consented to her visit as a 'special mission' and she had been received as such (CPS News Brief 06/10/2011); and *Re Gorbachev* (unreported) 30 March 2011 where a district judge accepted that the former Russian President was entitled to special missions immunity based on information provided by the FCO that he was in the UK for a meeting with the Prime Minister and for a fund-raising event.

officials of the State may benefit from immunity under rules of international law relating to special missions. While there is still some uncertainty as to the precise content of the privileges and immunities, under customary international law, to which persons on special mission are entitled, it is generally accepted that inviolability and immunity from criminal jurisdiction for the duration of the special mission are included. It is also generally accepted that, in order to qualify as such, a special mission must take place with the consent of the receiving State. Following the *Khurts Bat* case,[78] the UK Government announced the introduction of 'a new pilot process by which the Government will be informed of inward visits which may qualify for special mission immunity status'.[79] On the same date, the Foreign and Commonwealth Office issued a Note to all diplomatic missions and international organizations in London which drew attention to this new procedure and was designed to clarify where the UK consents to an official visit as a special mission.[80] The Note stated:

> Under customary international law, a special mission is a temporary mission representing a State which is sent by one State to another State with the consent of the latter, in order to carry out official business. In this context, 'official business' will normally involve official contacts with the authorities of the United Kingdom, such as a meeting [with] officials of her Majesty's Government, or attendance at a ceremonial occasion, for example a Royal Wedding.

It is clear that under UK practice a certificate as to facts relevant to the question of immunity, for example, as to whether or not the UK has consented to a particular visit as a special mission will be conclusive.[81] The UK Government has already applied the procedure in two cases involving visits by the Chief of Staff of the Israeli Army, Benny Gantz and a former Israeli Major-General, Doron Almog.[82]

Practice in other States also tends to support the existence of customary rules regarding the immunity of high-ranking members of special missions and the fact that special mission immunity depends on the consent and recognition of the receiving State.[83] The US Restatement of 1987 provides, for example, that:

[78] See n 82 below.

[79] Written Ministerial Statement (William Hague) House of Commons, 4 March 2013.

[80] Missions may seek in advance clarification of whether or not the UK consents to a particular visit as a special mission. It is clear from the Note that missions are not expected to avail themselves of this process in relation to every official visit but only in potentially sensitive cases where they judge such clarification to be desirable. In such cases they are invited to submit: the visitor's full name and title; the visitor's role or function; full details of any accompanying delegation; the duration of the visit; and the reason for the visit, including an explanation of any official element.

[81] *Khurts Bat* (n 61 above) *at* paras [37]–[8] (Moses LJ).

[82] The visit by Major-General Almog was, in fact, cancelled.

[83] See Wood, 'The Immunity of Official Visitors' (2012) 16 Max Planck Year Book of United Nations Law 35.

High officials of a foreign State and their staffs on an official visit or in transit, including those attending international conferences as official representatives of their country, enjoy immunities like those of diplomatic agents when the effect of exercising jurisdiction against the official would be to violate the immunity of the foreign State. Many such officials would enjoy immunity equivalent in all instances to that enjoyed by diplomatic agents under the Convention on Special Missions...[84]

On this basis, the US Department of State has put forward several 'Suggestions of Immunity' in regard to persons visiting the US, including the Prince of Wales and a Chinese Minister of Commerce.[85] Such suggestions have always been followed by the US courts concerned. In 2007 criminal proceedings in France against the Director-General of Police of the Republic of Congo were halted following a note from the French Ministry of Foreign Affairs confirming that the Director-General was on an official mission and 'In this capacity, and by virtue of customary international law, he benefits from immunity from jurisdiction and execution'.[86] More recently, the Government of the Netherlands in a response to an advisory report issued by its Advisory Committee on Issues of Public International Law (CAVV) confirmed its agreement that:

under customary international law members of official missions enjoy immunity. This applies both to members of foreign official missions visiting the Netherlands and to members of Dutch official missions visiting other countries. Members of official missions can be regarded as 'temporary diplomats'.[87]

[84] Restatement (Third) of Foreign Relations Law of the United States, 1987, vol 1, para 464. In a Reporter's Note 13 it is stated: '...the Convention on Special Missions reflects what is increasingly practiced and in many respects may emerge as customary international law.'

[85] See n 78 above.

[86] See *Jean Francois N'Dengue,* judgment of 20 June 2007 of Cour d'appel de Versailles,Chambre de l'instruction, 10eme chamber-section A.

[87] Letter of 26 April 2012 from the Ministry of Foreign Affairs and the State Secretary for Security and Justice to the Senate and the House of Representatives on the immunity of members of foreign official missions.

4

Position After Loss of Office

1. General Principles

Once a head of State, head of Government, or Foreign Minister has left office, they are no longer entitled to the extensive personal immunity enjoyed by an incumbent of those offices. This was made clear by the ICJ in the *Arrest Warrant* case when it observed that a former Minister for Foreign Affairs could be brought before the courts of another State for 'acts committed prior or subsequent to his or her period of office, as well as in respect of acts committed during that period of office in a private capacity'.[1]

The legal position of a former head of State under international law is, therefore, very different from that of an incumbent. He or she no longer enjoys the benefit of what has been described as an 'absolute and possibly irrefutable' presumption of immunity for virtually all acts. Instead, any question of immunity will depend upon whether the acts in question were carried out in an official capacity. This is a matter which will need to be assessed by the relevant authorities or courts of the forum State and decided on the basis of the particular elements of each case.[2]

It is generally accepted that all State officials are entitled to immunity from the jurisdiction of other States in relation to acts performed in their official capacity. It is also recognized that functional immunity applies to State officials regardless of their position in the State hierarchy. This immunity attaches to the official act, not to the office of the individual concerned, and can, therefore, be relied upon by all former officials, including former heads of State, heads of Government, and Foreign Ministers, as well as incumbent officials. It may also be relied upon by non-State individuals or entities who have acted on behalf of a State. In principle, therefore, the legal position of

[1] *Arrest Warrant of 11 April 2000 (DRC v Belgium)* (2002) ICJ Rep 3. See also ILC Immunity of State officials from foreign criminal jurisdiction, A/CN.4/L.814 draft Art 4(1), which states: 'Heads of State, Heads of Government and Ministers for Foreign Affairs enjoy immunity ratione personae only during their term of office.'

[2] See *Case Concerning Certain Questions of Mutual Assistance in Criminal Matters (Djibouti v France)*, Pellet, Oral Proceedings, CR 2008/5, 25 January 2008, 51, para [77].

a former head of State, head of Government, or other high official, who had been entitled to personal immunities while in office, is no different from that of any other State official. In practice, of course, the treatment they receive may be different based upon perceptions of their continuing importance and the potential impact on relations with their home State if any action is taken against them. In the UK and Australia the position of a former head of State is expressly assimilated to that of a former diplomat who continues to enjoy immunity with respect to 'acts performed in the exercise of his functions as a member of the mission'.[3]

Relationship with State immunity

Functional immunity can cover only official acts[4] and a key issue is therefore the nature of its relationship with the immunity of the State itself. Traditionally, functional immunity has been characterized as an aspect of State immunity. In *Holland v Lampen-Wolffe*,[5] the UK House of Lords emphasized the fact that State immunity, of which the immunity *ratione materiae* of officials is an integral part, 'is a subject-matter immunity' which 'operates to prevent the official and governmental acts of one State from being called into question in proceedings before the courts of another'.[6] In the *Pinochet* case, the same judge, Lord Millett, made a similar point adding that immunity *ratione materiae* 'only incidentally confers immunity on the individual' and that 'it is closely similar to and may be indistinguishable from aspects of the Anglo-American Act of State doctrine'.

Another purpose of such immunity is to ensure that an individual official is not held responsible for acts which are, in reality, those of the State and to prevent litigants from seeking to circumvent the rules on State immunity by taking action against the individuals carrying out the business of the State.[7] The first part of this rationale was summarized by the Appeals Chamber of the International Criminal Tribunal for the Former Yugoslavia in *Prosecutor v Blaskic*:

> State officials are mere instruments of a State and their official action can only be attributed to the State. They cannot be the subject of sanctions or penalties for conduct that is not private but undertaken on behalf of the State. In other words, State officials cannot suffer the consequences of wrongful acts which are not attributable to them

[3] See Art 39.2 of the Vienna Convention on Diplomatic Relations (VCDR) which is given the force of law in the UK by the Diplomatic Privileges Act 1964.

[4] See *Case Concerning Certain Questions of Mutual Assistance in Criminal Matters (Djibouti v France)* (2008) ICJ Rep 177 where the ICJ referred in this context to 'acts within the scope of duties [of State officials] as organs of the State'.

[5] See p 146 below.

[6] [2000] 1 WLR 1571 at 1584 (per Lord Millett).

[7] See Part 1 at pp 7–10.

personally but to the State on whose behalf they act: they enjoy so-called 'functional immunity'. This is a well established rule of customary international law going back to the eighteenth and nineteenth centuries, restated many times since.[8]

An early example of this principle being applied in practice is the *McLeod* or *Caroline* case. During the Canadian rebellion of 1837, British forces captured a US vessel *The Caroline* while it was on the US side of the border. They set fire to it and set it adrift which led to the death of two American citizens. Later in 1840, McLeod, allegedly one of the British officials involved in the seizure, was arrested while visiting New York and charged with murder and arson. The British Government argued that Mcleod could not bear individual responsibility for acts which had been performed on the orders of and under the authority of the British State. The US Government eventually accepted this, stating its position in internal correspondence as follows:

> That an individual forming part of a public force and acting under the authority of his Government, is not to be held answerable, as a private trespasser or malefactor, is a principle of public international law sanctioned by the usages of all civilised nation, and which the Government of the United States has no inclination to dispute.[9]

There are some features of the *McLeod* case which might raise a question, nowadays, as to whether functional immunity should apply,[10] although in this context it is important to note that the dispute arose in the context of an armed conflict. It remains, however, an early and very clear statement of one of the underlying purposes of immunity *ratione materiae*.[11]

The second part of the rationale was acknowledged by the UK Court of Appeal in *Propend Finance Pty Ltd v Sing* when it stated that the protection afforded by the State Immunity Act 1978 would be:

> undermined if employees, officers, (or as one authority puts it, 'functionaries') could be sued as individuals for matters of state conduct in respect of which the State they were serving had immunity. Section 14(1) must be read as affording to individual employees or officers of the foreign State protection under the same cloak as protects the State itself.[12]

[8] *Prosecutor v Blaskic* (Objection to the Issue of *Subpoena duces Tecume*) IT-95-14-AR108, (1997) 110 ILR 607, 707, para [38].

[9] Letter, Webster, 15 March 1841, 29 British and Foreign State Papers, 1139. See also Jennings, 'The Caroline and McLeod Cases' (1938) 32 AJIL 82.

[10] See pp 160–5 below.

[11] See also UK Law Officers Reports (1854) FO 83.2209 in which it is stated: 'The principle of International Law that an individual doing a hostile act authorised and ratified by the government of which he is a member cannot be held individually answerable as a private trespasser or Malefactor, but that act becomes one for which the State to which he belongs is in such case alone responsible, is a principle too well established to be now controverted.'

[12] (1977) 111 ILR 611 at 669.

On this analysis functional immunity is, again, linked directly with the immunity of the State itself and, while the latter has been limited in modern times by the development of the restrictive doctrine in relation to acts of a private law nature (*acta iure gestionis*), the continued applicability of State immunity to activities *iure imperii* remains the accepted rule.[13]

The traditional view of functional immunity as an integral part of the immunity of the State itself is reflected in the 2004 UN Convention on the Jurisdictional Immunities of States and Their Property, which explicitly includes representatives of the State acting in their official capacity.[14] The term 'State' is defined very broadly and under Article 2(1)(b) includes all its organs of Government as well as the constituent units of a federal state or the political subdivisions of the state if 'entitled to perform acts in the exercise of sovereign authority, and... acting in that capacity'.[15] Also included are the 'agencies and instrumentalities of the State or other entities to the extent that they are entitled to perform and are actually performing acts in the exercise of sovereign authority of the State'. By explicitly including individuals who represent the State, the Convention clearly endorses the principle of immunity *ratione materiae* for acts performed in an official capacity. This approach has also been reflected in the national legislation on State immunity adopted in some countries or, at least, in the way in which courts in those countries have chosen to interpret and apply that legislation. It is notable, however, that a slightly different approach has developed in the US where the functional immunity of officials has been separated from that of the State itself.[16]

State immunity and State responsibility

In *Jones v Kingdom of Saudi Arabia*,[17] the UK House of Lords linked the law of State immunity directly with the law of State responsibility, stating that:

> the circumstances in which a State will be liable for the act of an official in international law mirror the circumstances in which the official will be immune in foreign domestic law.[18]

[13] See ICJ, *Jurisdictional Immunities of the State (Germany v Italy); Greece Intervening* (Judgment) ICJ, 3 February 2012.

[14] Article 2(1)(b)(iv). See also s 14(1) of the UK State Immunity Act 1978, which has been construed by the UK courts to include individuals in the definition of a foreign State.

[15] See *Summary Records of the 2602nd Meeting* [1999] 1 YBILC 254, 255–7, UN Doc A/CN.4SER.A/1999.j

[16] See *Samantar v Yousef* 130 S Ct 2278 (2010) at 2287 where the US Supreme Court held that the US Foreign Sovereign Immunities Act (FSIA) does not apply to suits against foreign officials. It did, however, indicate that a suit against a foreign official might nonetheless be precluded by principles of 'foreign sovereign immunity under the common law'. See pp 173–4 below.

[17] (2006) 129 ILR 713, HL.

[18] Per Lord Hoffmann. See also Arts 4 and 5 of the ILC Articles on State Responsibility.

Under this approach the only question is whether the act concerned was an official one for which responsibility may be attributed to the State or a purely private act for which the individual official alone bears responsibility. Functional immunity will attach to the former but not to the latter.[19] Such an analysis might suggest that an official should be immune in respect of all official acts which are regarded as acts of the State and attributable to the State. On this basis it has been argued that functional immunity must apply not only to sovereign acts (or acts *iure imperii*) in respect of which the State itself has immunity but also to non-sovereign acts provided they were carried out in an official capacity. So, for example, an individual official should not be held responsible for a commercial act or transaction which he or she has entered into on behalf of the State. Such an approach would be consistent with the position of a former diplomat *vis-à-vis* the courts of the receiving State.[20] As we have seen, however, there is a question as to whether it is immunity that protects the official in such circumstances or rather the fact that the act in question cannot, as a matter of law, be properly attributed to the individual.[21] In such circumstances, one of the underlying purposes of functional immunity would not be applicable because proceedings against the individual could not risk circumventing the State's immunity as it would have none. The notion that functional immunity can apply to an official even when the State itself is not immune is also somewhat at odds with the orthodox theory that it is merely an aspect of the immunity of the State itself and exists to benefit the State not the individual.[22]

Whatever analysis or justification is adopted in regard to immunity *ratione materiae*, it is clear that the idea that an individual official, including heads of State and other very high-ranking officials, should not be held responsible for what are essentially acts of the State has played a significant part in its development. In modern times, however, it has become generally accepted that international law does permit responsibility for certain serious crimes to be

[19] The same point was made by Denza in relation to the specialized functional immunity provided under Art 39.2 of the VCDR when she wrote that the 'correct test to be applied... is one of imputability. If the conduct in question is imputable or attributable to the sending State—even if it did not expressly order or sanction it—then continuing immunity *ratione materiae* should apply. The diplomat remains immune because his own sending State is really responsible'. See 'Ex Parte Pinochet: Lacuna or Leap?' (1999) 48 ICLQ 949 at 951.

[20] See Art 39 of the VCDR.

[21] It would usually be open to the forum court to strike out the action against the individual official and consider whether it had jurisdiction over the State as the proper defendant in the case.

[22] See *Guevara v Peru and others* 468 F 3d 1289 (11th Circ 2006) ILDC 804 (US 2006) where the court held that the foreign sovereign immunity of State officials acting in their official capacity is derivative and does not apply where the sovereign itself is not entitled to immunity.

attributed to individual officials as well as to the State they serve.[23] The official nature of an act is no longer a substantive defence to a charge of having committed an international crime.[24] These developments have prompted some to question whether it is appropriate for State officials to be able to invoke functional immunity for such crimes. It has also been suggested that, as international law does not recognize the concept of State criminal responsibility,[25] criminal proceedings against an individual official do not directly implead the State in the same way as civil proceedings do.[26]

Comparison between criminal responsibility and civil liability

The 2004 UN Convention does not apply to criminal proceedings,[27] which remain subject to rules of customary international law. In practice, the application of immunity *ratione materiae* to State officials has been far more common in civil than criminal cases and it is, therefore, in that context that the rules have been most analysed and developed. This is not surprising given that the criminal jurisdiction of States is primarily territorial and State officials (other than diplomatic or consular agents who are covered by separate regimes) do not normally exercise their official functions in the territory of other States.

Within the context of functional immunity, a number of significant distinctions between criminal responsibility and civil liability can be made. In a criminal prosecution, the proceedings are primarily concerned with the responsibility and punishment of the individual official. They are not concerned with the liability or punishment of the State. It is, therefore, arguable that such proceedings constitute less of a threat to sovereign immunity. There is also the fact that the prosecution of crimes is generally in the hands of the forum State's authorities who usually retain the power to halt proceedings in appropriate cases. By contrast, civil suits may have the effect of imposing liability on a State or calling into question its acts. They may, indeed, be deliberately designed to do so. Even when the State itself is not joined as a party, it may, in practice, be the only

[23] See Principle IV: 'The fact that a person acted pursuant to order of his Government or of a superior does not relieve him from responsibility under international law provided a moral choice was in fact possible to him': Principles of International Law Recognized in the Charter of the Nuremberg Tribunal and in the Judgment of the Tribunal [1950] YBILC vol II, 191.

[24] See Art 33 of the Statute of the International Criminal Court (ICC) 17 July 1998.

[25] Draft Art 19 of the ILC's Draft Articles on State Responsibility which referred to international crimes of a State was eventually removed following some disagreement among States as to whether a State could commit an international crime. As a result, Art 12 of the Articles does not distinguish between civil and criminal responsibility and simply refers to breach of an international obligation.

[26] *Bouzari v Islamic Republic of Iran* (2004) 124 ILR 427, Canada. See also *Jones v Saudi Arabia* (2006) 129 ILR 713, HL.

[27] See ILC Commentary, draft Art 2, para 2. Statement Chairman Ad Hoc Committee 6, para 32 and GA Res 59/38, 2 December 2004.

source from which any award of damages can be satisfied. Such proceedings are usually instigated and largely controlled by private individuals and groups who may be undeterred by considerations relating to the damaging impact of such proceedings on international relations. In many countries criminal proceedings cannot take place without the physical presence of the accused in the forum State. Civil cases, by contrast, do not depend upon the physical presence of the defendant official and may proceed (particularly where former officials are involved) without the official's home State even being aware of the proceedings.

2. Acts Performed in an Official Capacity

It has long been accepted (even before settled principles of personal immunity had evolved) that incumbent heads of State and Government and other senior officials are entitled to immunity in respect of conduct involving matters of sovereign, governmental, or public authority.[28] Such immunity applies in both criminal and civil proceedings and subsists even after the official has left office. It is not, however, always easy to distinguish between acts performed in a former head of State's or head of Government's official capacity and those performed in his or her personal capacity. This difficulty is compounded by the fact that such high State officials are often charged with a very wide range of responsibilities and, unlike more junior officials, are less likely to be acting under orders.[29] There is also an expectation that they are to be on duty at all times.[30]

What is an official act?

The existing case law, both civil and criminal, shows that it is entirely possible for a head of State or other official to engage in conduct, in the course of his or her public functions, which is unlawful or even criminal. Such criminality does not in itself destroy the official or sovereign character of the act. The key test would seem to be whether the conduct was engaged in under colour of

[28] See eg *Duke of Brunswick v King of Hanover* (1848) 2 HLC 1 (UKHL 1848) and *De Haber v Queen of Portugal* (1851) 17 QB 171.

[29] See *Doe v Zedillo Ponce de Leon* (2013) No 3: 11-cv-01433 (US District Court in Connecticut) where Suggestion of Immunity submitted by the US Government in respect of a former President of Mexico noted: 'In determining whether certain acts were taken in an official capacity, the Department of State, generally presumes that allegations relating to the official's exercise of the powers of his or her office fall into that category. This preliminary assessment is particularly apt for former heads of State, who typically, have wide-ranging responsibilities', filed 7 September 2012. (2012) US Digest 345.

[30] See letter of State department legal adviser Koh of 7 December 2012.

or in ostensible exercise of the public authority of the head of State, head of Government, or other senior official.[31] The International Law Commission has indicated that, for the purpose of attributing an act to the State, it is irrelevant that the official concerned may have had an ulterior or improper motive or may have been abusing his or her power, and has warned that a case of purely private misconduct should not be confused with that of an official, acting as such, but acting *ultra vires* or in breach of particular rules.[32] In a domestic law context the US Supreme Court has held that the phrase 'acting under color of state law' requires merely that a defendant has exercised powers 'possessed by virtue of state law and made possible only because the wrongdoer is clothed with the authority of state law'.[33] In this connection, it has been held that there is no material difference between the notion of 'acting in an official capacity' for the purposes of the definition of torture set out in the 1984 Torture Convention and the concept of 'acting under color of law'.[34] As such it would appear to be irrelevant that the wrongdoer may have exceeded his instructions or acted *ultra vires* provided that the conduct in question can properly be attributed to the State.[35] For this reason it has been suggested that the term 'official act', which carries connotations of legality, is misleading and that the phrase 'act of public power', as derived from the French, would be a better description.

Some analogy has been made with Article 39.2 of the Vienna Convention on Diplomatic Relations 1961 which provides that the immunity of a former diplomat shall continue to subsist 'with respect to acts performed by such a person in the exercise of his functions as a member of the mission'. On a narrow interpretation, such 'functions' could be limited to those listed in Article 3, together, perhaps, with other duties of a clearly diplomatic nature. In practice, however, national courts have applied a more extensive interpretation where the fact that the former diplomat was acting under the authority of the sending State with consequent attribution to that State appears to be

[31] See Watts, 'The Legal Position in International Law of Heads of States, Heads of Governments and Foreign Ministers' (1994) 247 III Recueil des Cours 56. See also Art 7 of the ILC's Articles on State Responsibility which states: 'The conduct of an organ of a State or person or entity empowered to exercise elements of the governmental authority shall be considered an act of the State under international law if the organ, person or entity acts in that capacity: even if it exceeds its authority or contravenes instructions.' See also *Mallen v United States* (1927) IVRIAA 173 where a US deputy constable, after showing his badge, stopped, assaulted, and detained the Mexican consul in the county jail. These acts were committed in pursuit of a private grudge, but an international arbitration tribunal held that the US was liable because the deputy constable had acted under colour of public authority. See also *Caire* (1929) 5 Reports of International Arbitral Awards 516 at 531.

[32] Paragraph 13 of ILC commentary Art 4,YBIL 2001 vol II (Part Two) 42, para 77.

[33] See *United States v Classic* 313 US 299, 326 (1941); quoted in *West v Atkins* 487 US 49 (1988). See also *Kadic v Karadzic* 70 F 3d 232, 245 (2nd Circ 1995).

[34] *United States v Roy M Belfast aka Chuckie Taylor*, US Ct of Appeals (11th Circ, 15 July 2010).

[35] See n 32 above.

the determining factor. In the *Former Syrian Ambassador* case,[36] for example, the German Federal Constitutional Court accepted that the former Syrian Ambassador to East Germany had been acting in the exercise of his functions when, on instructions from his government, he temporarily stored explosives later used in a terrorist attack in West Berlin.[37]

The issue of how to distinguish between acts of a sovereign or governmental nature and those of a private character for which there is no immunity is of equal relevance in civil and criminal cases. In *Pinochet (No 3)*[38] the majority accepted that the crime of torture within the meaning of the Torture Convention was capable of being carried out in the exercise of official or government functions.[39] However, criminal cases have been rare so that, in practice, it is in civil proceedings that the question has been most frequently addressed. In *Herbage v Meese*, a British national brought proceedings in a US court against several British government officials and agents, including the Home Secretary, the Director of Public Prosecutions, and a senior police officer. It was alleged that serious irregularities in his extradition to the US had taken place and that immunity could not apply as the defendants had been acting illegally. The court rejected this argument, holding that the acts concerned were sovereign or governmental in nature and could only have been performed by the defendants in their official capacity as law enforcement officers. As such they were covered, so far as the State was concerned, by State immunity and that immunity must extend to the officials also 'for a government does not act but through its agents'.[40] Where the acts concerned fall squarely within traditional fields of sovereign or governmental activity, such as policing and law enforcement, it seems likely, therefore, that most courts would have little difficulty in holding that they had been carried out in an official capacity even where elements of malice or criminality are alleged to have been involved.

Where the conduct concerned is of a more personal nature, however, it can be more difficult to draw the line between official acts and the personal activities of the individual concerned. As noted above, the wide-ranging

[36] Case No 2 BvR 1516/96, 115 ILR 595, (1998) AJIL 74.

[37] But see Denza, *Diplomatic Law* (3rd edn, Oxford University Press, 2008) 448 where it is suggested that although a test as to whether the act was carried out under instructions from the sending State may be relevant to State immunity, it is incorrect for the purpose of determining whether a former diplomat acted 'in the exercise of his functions as a member of the mission' where a test based upon Art 3 should be applied.

[38] *R v Bow Street Metropolitan Stipendiary Magistrate ex parte Pinochet Ugarte (No 3)* [2000] AC 147, 119 ILR 135.

[39] See pp 150–2 below.

[40] (1990) 98 ILR 101. See also *Jaffe v Miller* (1994) 95 ILR 446 where the court made it clear that motive was not, in itself, determinative and that the key consideration is the apparent authority under which the individual acts, stating that the 'illegal and malicious nature of the acts alleged do not of themselves move the action outside the scope of the official duties of the responding defendants'.

responsibilities of a head of State and the expectation that he or she is on duty at all times may make this especially difficult. This aspect was considered indirectly by the Supreme Court of Austria in the context of distinguishing between an ambassador's exercise of the functions of the mission and his private conduct. The Austrian Ambassador to Yugoslavia was invited by the President of Yugoslavia to a hunt, where he accidentally shot and killed the French Ambassador. In proceedings for damages by the family of the French Ambassador, the court held that the function of representing the sending State in the receiving State and protecting its interests included participating in social activities of the kind involved. It stated: 'The fostering of such contacts is a condition for the exercise of the office of ambassador and forms part of the fulfillment of his official duties.' The court concluded, therefore, that the Austrian State was liable to pay compensation.

In this context financial misconduct can also be problematic. *Jimenez v Ariteguieta*,[41] which was a criminal case, illustrates this point. A US appeals court was faced with a request for the extradition of the former dictator of Venezuela on various charges, mostly involving financial misconduct carried out during his period in office. The court rejected his argument that the acts in question had been performed in his official capacity as head of State and were, therefore, beyond the power of the court to review, holding that they were just 'common crimes committed by the Chief of State done in violation of his position and not in pursuance of it'. Leaving aside the question of whether the decision to refuse immunity was correct on the facts, it is clear that the reasoning in support does not go far enough. As we have seen, criminality does not, in itself, destroy the official or sovereign character of the act and the key test must focus on the nature of the act and whether it was engaged in under colour of or in ostensible exercise of the head of State's or other official's public authority.[42] In a Suggestion of Immunity submitted by the US government, it was indicated that the executive branch would generally determine that a former head of State was entitled to functional immunity unless a claimant provided it with a basis for questioning that initial presumption. It was further stated that 'such a base might arise, for example, in a suit challenging a former official's personal financial dealings which generally would not be considered to constitute acts taken in an official capacity'.[43] The issue of alleged

[41] 311 F 2d 547 (Court of Appeals 5th Cir 1962).

[42] See Art 7 of ILC Articles on State Responsibility; and *Mallen v United* States (1927) IVRIAA 173 where a US deputy constable, after showing his badge, assaulted and detained the Mexican Consul in the county jail. He was acting in pursuit of a private grudge but an international arbitration tribunal held that the US was responsible because the deputy had acted under colour of public authority.

[43] *Doe v Zedillo Ponce De Leon* (see n 29 above).

financial misconduct is considered in more detail below under the heading of private acts.

It is clear that the concept of an act carried out in an official or governmental capacity so as to attract immunity *ratione materiae* is capable of embracing a wide range of ancillary conduct provided it is directly related to sovereign activity. In *Holland v Lampen-Wolfe*[44] the House of Lords upheld the immunity of a US civilian employed as an educational services officer by the US government at a US military base in the UK. He was sued for defamation by a US university professor in connection with a letter written to the latter's university reporting criticisms of the professor by his students and requesting his replacement. The court emphasized that each case must depend upon a careful assessment of the relevant facts and that the key consideration in determining that the act concerned was *iure imperii* was the fact that it formed part of services provided exclusively to US personnel at US military bases and was thus closely related to US military programmes.[45]

It is for national courts (and, sometimes, the executive branch of the forum State) to determine the issue of whether a particular act constitutes an official act capable of attracting functional immunity. In this context, it has been noted that the rule of functional immunity does not oblige courts to 'blindly accept' any claim of a foreign State that an official has acted under its authority.[46] In *US v Noriega*[47] the court did not, for example, accept that drug-trafficking for personal benefit could be a sovereign activity[48] although the case was decided primarily on the ground that Noriega had not been recognized by the US Government as a head of State. Nevertheless, the views of a former official's home State are bound to carry considerable weight. In *Re P (No 2)*[49] a US diplomat, whose term of appointment at the US embassy in London had ended, returned to the US with his children. His German wife, who had started divorce proceedings in Germany and had sought unsuccessfully to obtain restraining orders to prevent the removal of the children from

[44] [2000] 1 WLR 1573.

[45] See also *Littrell v USA (No 2)* [1995] 1 WLR 82 which related to a claim for damages in connection with medical care received at a US military hospital in the UK.

[46] See Van Alebeek, *The Immunity of States and Their Officials in International Criminal Law and International Human Rights Law* (Oxford University Press, 2008) 115. In the US, the Executive branch has recently confirmed its view that it retains the power to determine this issue and, in doing so, will consider a foreign Government's request that immunity should be accorded but, notwithstanding such a request, could determine that a foreign official is not entitled to immunity. See *Rosenberg v Lashkar-E-Taiba*, Statement of Interest and Suggestion of Immunity,17 December 2012.

[47] (1990) 746 F.Supp 1506.

[48] See also *Tabatabai* (1983) 80 ILR 389 where a German court held that the import of illegal drugs could not be classified as one of the official functions of a special envoy.

[49] [1998]1 FLR 1026, (1998) 114 ILR 485.

the UK, brought proceedings in the UK seeking a declaration that the father had wrongfully removed the children from the jurisdiction. The father and the US Government, which had intervened in the proceedings, argued that the UK courts lacked jurisdiction on the ground that the father had returnd to the US with the children on the orders of the US Government. It was claimed that his act was, therefore, one performed 'in the exercise of his functions as a member of the US diplomatic mission' and that, on this basis, he was entitled to diplomatic immunity under Article 39 of the VCDR 1961. It was further claimd that, as the US Government had ordered the removal of the children, that act, following the completion of the father's mission, was 'an act of a governmental nature and is, as such, subject to State immunity from legal process'. The court rejected the claim of immunity under Article 39 of the VCDR but accepted the plea of functional immunity and dismissed the mother's application. The court's acceptance of the plea of immunity *ratione materiae* has been criticized as excessively deferential to the foreign State's view as to the nature of the act.[50] The act of a father in removing his children from a foreign jurisdiction when in dispute with the mother who wishes them to remain is not, on the face of it, a governmental matter. Can the simple fact that the employer State has ordered such action make it so? It is difficult to reconcile such an approach with the principle that it is the nature of the act that counts and it is probably best to regard *Re P (No 2)* as decided on its particular facts, most especially the fact that the act concerned was performed in the context of the management of a diplomatic mission and the deployment of staff abroad and the fact that States have a legitimate interest in preventing such staff from becoming embroiled in foreign litigation in cases of family breakdown and estrangement.[51]

Criminal proceedings

Criminal prosecutions of foreign State officials are rare and, where they do occur, are usually concerned with relatively low ranking officials. In 1997, however, a German court convicted the former head of State of the German Democratic Republic (GDR), Egon Krenz, of manslaughter in connection with decisions he had taken in an official capacity on the GDR border

[50] See eg Barker, 'State Immunity, Diplomatic Immunity and Act of State: A Triple Protection Against Legal Action?' (1998) ICLQ 950 at 957.

[51] Before the Court of Appeal, which dismissed the mother's appeal on the issue of jurisdiction, the respondent father and the US had submitted that: 'If the Court were to hold that the defendant's act of returning to the United States with the minors, as ordered by his government, was a wrongful act, that would amount to an interference with the right of the US government to determine the manner of its representation in the UK and would have serious repercussions for the conduct of diplomatic relations in general.'

policing regime which resulted in the deaths of certain individuals attempting to escape across the border to the then Federal Republic of Germany.[52] The issue of immunity did not arise given that by then the GDR had ceased to exist and, more significantly, had become part of a reunified Germany. As such, the situation was, arguably, little different from a case where the leader of a previous regime is prosecuted by the authorities of his or her own State for crimes committed while in office.

In *Pinochet*, the majority were of the view that the former Chilean leader was entitled to functional immunity for the alleged ordinary crimes carried out in his official capacity.[53]

In *Lozano v Italy*[54] a US soldier, who was manning a US army checkpoint in Iraq, shot and killed an Italian citizen. He was prosecuted *in absentia* before the Italian courts for homicide and for a crime defined as 'an indiscriminate or excessive attack against civilians during war'. The soldier maintained that the car in which the victim was travelling had approached the checkpoint at speed and that the use of force had been justified. On this basis, the US authorities had taken no further action. The Italian Court of Cassation held that, reasonably or not, the soldier had acted at all times in the ostensible discharge of his functions and that the Italian courts' jurisdiction in relation to such *acta iure imperii* was clearly precluded by immunity.

By contrast, in 2012 the Indian Supreme Court rejected a plea of functional immunity by the Italian Government on behalf of two Italian marines who had shot and killed two Indian fishermen. The marines had been deployed by the Italian Government on the Italian oil tanker *Enrica Lexie* as part of a naval military protection squad in response to the threat from Somali pirates. The marines had been arrested and charged with murder. It was undisputed that they had been operating under the direct control of the Italian military and, after an initial dispute, it was accepted by both India and Italy that the incident had taken place in international waters. It is difficult, however, to draw any firm conclusions from this as the plea of immunity was rejected without

[52] See Part 2 n 79 above. Criminal proceedings were also brought against a former GDR head of State, Erich Honecker, and former Prime Minister Willi Stoph in respect of conduct which had been carried out in their official capacity. Both trials were discontinued in the light of the defendants' ill-health.

[53] See *Pinochet (No 3)* [2000] AC 147, (2000) 119 ILR 135. All except Lord Millett seemed to agree that Pinochet would enjoy immunity for alleged offences of murder and conspiracy to murder provided such offences were committed in his official capacity as head of State. This was in spite of the fact that the offences had been allegedly committed on Spanish territory. See p 150 below.

[54] Case No 31171/2008, ILDC 1085 (IT2008) 24 July 2008. But see *General Prosecutor at the Court of Appeals of Milan v Adler and others*, ILDC 1960 (IT 2012) where the court's decision seems to run counter to the opinion expressed in the *Lozano* judgment that State officials are generally entitled to functional immunity in criminal proceedings for *acta imperii.* It is possible, however, that the decision can be distinguished on the basis that the crimes for which the US officials were convicted were committed on Italian territory. See pp 160–5 below.

detailed deliberation, the court merely noting the absence of any Status of Forces agreement between the two States.[55]

It is clear that, in criminal cases, State practice, while extremely scant, has not always been consistent. As a general principle, however, it seems that a former head of State or other former high-level official is entitled to immunity *ratione materiae* in criminal proceedings for acts carried out in an official capacity. This is consistent with the view expressed by the International Criminal Tribunal for the Former Yugoslavia that it is a well established rule of customary international law that State officials acting in their official capacity enjoy immunity from foreign jurisdiction.[56] It is also consistent with the obiter dictum of the ICJ in the *Arrest Warrant* case, which suggested that, as a general rule, immunity would continue to bar proceedings against a former Foreign Minister for acts committed during his period of office except for acts committed in a 'private capacity'. In recent years, however, there has been some speculation as to the emergence of possible exceptions to this general rule.

International crimes

In the *Lozano* case the Italian Court of Cassation noted that a customary international rule was emerging that crimes under international law (as opposed to ordinary crimes prohibited under national laws) are not protected by immunity *ratione materiae*. A similar point had been made by Judges Higgins, Kooijmans, and Buergenthal in their Joint Separate Opinion in the *Arrest Warrant* case where they indicated that the existence of any rule applying immunity *ratione materiae* to serious international crimes was, at least, doubtful and that a trend in State practice pointing to the absence of such immunity may exist.

The idea that such an exception may exist is not new. At least since the Nuremberg trial in 1945, it has been accepted that, where the acts of a State official can be characterized as international crimes such as war crimes or genocide, they cannot be attributed solely to the State. The individual official bears responsibility also under international law and must be susceptible to trial before an international court. Some have gone further and argued that, in such circumstances, the individual has no right to claim functional immunity before foreign domestic courts. In the *Eichmann* case,[57] a former official of the Nazi regime was prosecuted in Israel on allegations of crimes against humanity committed in Europe during the Second World War. The defence argued that the alleged acts were acts of the German State for which

[55] See also indictments issued by a Turkish court in respect of four senior Israeli military commanders in connection with the Israeli action on the 2010 Gaza flotilla.

[56] *Prosecutor v Blaskic*, ICTY Subpoena decision, 29 October 1997, para 38.

[57] *Attorney General of Israel v Eichmann* (1961) 36 ILR 5 (District Court of Jerusalem).

Eichmann, as an organ of that State, could not be held responsible. This was firmly rejected by the Israeli Supreme Court which held that:

> there is no basis for the doctrine when the matter pertains to acts prohibited by the law of nations, especially when they are international crimes of the class of 'crimes against humanity'... Of such odious acts it must be said that in point of international law they are completely outside the sovereign jurisdiction of the State that ordered or ratified their commission, and, therefore, those who participated in such acts must personally account for them and cannot shelter behind the official character of their task or mission...

The question of functional immunity was not addressed by the court, which focused on the issue of individual criminal responsibility. Clearly, however, it did not consider such immunity to be an obstacle to Eichmann's prosecution and conviction. It would be wrong to place any great weight on this, however, given that the *Eichmann* trial is often seen as particularly linked with the Nuremberg International Military Tribunal, the circumstances of Germany's defeat, and the effective dismantling of its State apparatus. In practice, it was not followed by other cases and the principle that State officials are generally entitled to immunity from the jurisdiction of other States in relation to acts performed in their official capacity remained largely undisturbed.

The *Pinochet*[58] case, in which the UK House of Lords allowed an extradition application by Spain in respect of the former Chilean President to proceed, is the leading case on the emergence of an exception to immunity for acts *iure imperii.* The case concerned allegations of widespread and systematic torture carried out in Chile together with various ordinary crimes of murder and conspiracy to murder. The court confirmed that if Pinochet had been a serving head of State he would have been entitled to personal immunity on all the charges and that, as a former head of State, he would, as a general rule, continue to enjoy functional immunity in respect of acts carried out in his official capacity as head of State. The majority took the view that Pinochet enjoyed immunity for the so-called 'ordinary crimes' on the grounds that the acts alleged, although criminal, had been governmental. According to the established rules of State immunity, such acts must attract immunity *ratione materiae* and no arguments had been advanced as to why those established rules should be displaced.[59] The court broke new ground, however, in deciding that there was an exception where the international crime of torture was involved.

The United Nations Convention Against Torture (UNCAT),[60] to which Chile, the UK, and Spain were all parties at the material time, lies at the heart

[58] *R v Bow Street Magistrates' Court, ex parte Pinochet (No 3)* [2000] AC 147, (2000) 119 ILR 135.

[59] See per Lord Browne-Wilkinson at 205: 'No one has advanced any reason why the ordinary rules of immunity should not apply and Senator Pinochet is entitled to such immunity.'

[60] Convention Against Torture and Other Cruel, Inhuman or Degrading Treatment or Punishment 1984 (adopted 10 December 1984, entered into force 26 June 1987) 1465 UNTS 85.

of the decision in *Pinochet.* The Convention makes no reference to the international law rules on immunity but does set up a system of extraterritorial criminal jurisdiction for torture, which is defined in Article 1 as an act which must be 'inflicted by or at the instigation of or with the consent or acquiescence of a *public official or other person acting in an official capacity*'. As a consequence it is likely that any defendants prosecuted under the national legislation giving effect to the UNCAT will be State officials or former State officials or other persons who have carried out the acts which are alleged to be torture as official acts for which they will claim immunity.[61] In *Pinochet,* it seems that the tension between this fact and the object and purpose of the UNCAT was the main factor in prompting the majority to conclude that there could be no functional immunity for the international crimes of torture and conspiracy to torture.

The detailed reasoning applied by each judge in reaching this conclusion varied considerably, with two referring to the theory that an act that constitutes an international crime cannot, of itself, be an official act.[62] In 2000, in the *Bouterse* case[63] (where the then former military leader of Suriname was accused of torture and murder), the Amsterdam Court of Appeal noted that 'the commission of very grave criminal offences of this kind can never be regarded as part of the official duties of a head of State'.[64] Such an analysis is, however, problematic given the well-established principle that the illegality, or even criminality, of an act does not destroy its official character provided it has been performed under colour of or in ostensible exercise of the official's authority. The problem is compounded in the context of allegations of torture, the very definition of which relies upon its official character. Accordingly, this approach has been the subject of some criticism[65] and specifically rejected by the UK House of Lords in a civil case where it was noted that it would produce an asymmetry between the rules of liability and immunity.[66]

[61] See Lord Millett at 273: 'The very official or governmental character of the acts, which is necessary to found a claim to immunity *ratione materiae* and which still operates as a bar to the civil jurisdiction of national courts, was now to be the essential element which made the acts an international crime.'

[62] See Lords Browne-Wilkinson and Hutton.

[63] R 97/163/12 Sv & R 97/176/12 Sv (Netherlands, Gerechtshof Amsterdam 2000).

[64] See Zegfeld, 'The Bouterse Case' (2001) 32 Netherlands Yearbook of International Law 97. See also *In re Estate of Ferdinand Marcos* 25 F.3d 1469 (9th Cir 1994) where plaintiffs brought a claim against the former Philippine leader alleging acts of torture and extra judicial killing. The US Government did not file a suggestion of immunity and the Court ruled that the claim could proceed on the basis that violations of human rights norms could not constitute legitimate official acts (at p 1472).

[65] See eg Akande and Shah, 'International Crimes, Human Rights Violations and Foreign Domestic Courts' (2010) 21 EJIL 815.

[66] See *Jones v Kingdom of Saudi Arabia* [2006] UKHL 26, [2007] 1 AC 270; 129 ILR 713 per Lord Hoffmann at paras [78]–[9]: 'Furthermore in the case of torture, there would be an even more striking asymmetry between the Torture Convention and the rules of immunity if it were to be held that the same act was official for the purposes of the definition of torture but not for the purpose of immunity.'

Some of the judges in *Pinochet* referred to the *ius cogens*[67] status of the prohibition against torture, suggesting that such a prohibition, by reason of its peremptory and supreme nature, must override any immunity. This was a theory later espoused by the Italian Court of Cassation in *Ferrini v Germany*[68] where it held that Germany was not entitled to immunity for serious violations of human rights carried out by German occupying forces. This analysis has not been well received by many writers on international law.[69] It has been pointed out that rules on state immunity which are purely procedural in character cannot conflict with substantive *ius cogens* norms prohibiting international crimes.[70] Moreover, in the case brought by Germany against Italy before the ICJ, following the *Ferrini* judgment, the ICJ ruled that Italy had failed to respect Germany's jurisdictional immunity as a sovereign State.[71] In doing so it specifically held that 'customary international law does not treat a State's entitlement to immunity as dependent upon the gravity of the act of which it is accused or the peremptory nature of the rule which it is alleged to have violated'.[72] The Court also emphasized the essentially procedural nature of the law on State immunity which is 'thus entirely distinct from the substantive law which determines whether that conduct is lawful or unlawful'.

To what extent, therefore, can the *Pinochet* case be regarded as evidence of a significant shift in State practice on this issue? The key surviving rationale underlying the judgments of the majority seems to be the fact that it would be absurd and inconsistent with UNCAT to allow an immunity that was virtually co-extensive with the offence created by that Convention.[73] The

[67] See Art 53 of the VCLT.

[68] (2004) 128 ILR 659.

[69] See eg Cassese, 'When May Senior State Officials Be Tried for International Crimes? Some Comments on the Congo v Belgium case' (2002) 13 EJIL 853 at 869 where he describes the theory as 'unsound and even preposterous'.

[70] See Fox, *The Law of State Immunity* (2nd edn, Oxford University Press, 2002) 528: 'State immunity is a procedural rule going to the jurisdiction of a national court. It does not go to substantive law; it does not contradict a prohibition contained in a *ius cogens* norm but merely diverts any breach of it to a different method of settlement.' See also *Jones v Kingdom of Saudi Arabia* (2006) 129 ILR 713, UK (HL) where this passage was quoted with approval.

[71] *Jurisdictional Immunities of the State (Germany v Italy)* [2012] ICJ Rep although it was made clear in the judgment that it was not addressing the functional immunity of officials and was concerned solely with the immunity of the State itself.

[72] The ICJ decision in *Arrest Warrant of 11 April 2000 (DRC v Belgium)* (2000) ICJ Rep 3 also undermines any argument that *ius cogens* norms are hierarchically superior to rules on immunity for, if they were, then logically the personal immunity of a sitting head of State, head of Government, or Foreign Minister would be affected.

[73] See in particular Lord Millett at 227A–278B. The case was also explained in this way by Lord Bingham in the subsequent judgment of the House of Lords in *Jones v Kingdom of Saudi Arabia* (n 68 above): 'The essential ratio of the decision, as I understand it, was that international law could not without absurdity require criminal jurisdiction to be assumed and exercised where the Torture Convention conditions were satisfied and, at the same time, require immunity to be granted to those properly charged. The Torture Convention was the mainspring of the decision.'

same argument against immunity could be applied to an official charged with the international crime of 'enforced disappearance' under the Convention for the Protection of All Persons from Enforced Disappearance,[74] which, like torture, must be committed by or with the acquiescence of a public official.

However, in *Pinochet*, Lord Phillips went further in stating that functional immunity cannot coexist with international crimes where a system of extra-territorial jurisdiction has been established, as the latter must necessarily override the principle on which functional immunity is based—namely that one State should not interfere with the internal affairs of another. On this basis it has been suggested that the true rationale for an exception to immunity *ratione materiae* in the case of certain international crimes lies in the development of international Conventions providing for the exercise by States Parties of extra-territorial jurisdiction over such crimes, showing that international law now accepts that States may exercise jurisdiction over certain official acts of foreign States in the context of assigning individual criminal responsibility for such acts.[75] Such an analysis would expand the list of possible crimes for which an exception may apply beyond torture and enforced disappearance to genocide, war crimes, and crimes against humanity.

Against this, however, is the general approach of the ICJ in the *Arrest Warrant* case, which suggested that treaty-based extensions of jurisdiction and obligations to prosecute or extradite should not override immunities under customary international law. It was, for example, stated that 'jurisdiction does not imply absence of immunity, while absence of immunity does not imply jurisdiction'. The ICJ was, of course, concerned with the immunity *ratione personae* of a serving Foreign Minister in that case, but the reasoning is, nonetheless, at odds with such an analysis. Moreover, in an obiter dictum the ICJ listed the circumstances in which immunity would not apply to a former Foreign Minister, mentioning 'acts committed prior to or subsequent to his or her period of office, as well as in respect of acts commited during that period of office in a private capacity'.[76]

This has been interpreted by some as implying that functional immunity continues to bar the prosecution of State officials and former State officials for international crimes committed in their official capacity and that immunity will cease to apply only in relation to conduct which can be characterized

[74] See Art 2, which defines 'enforced disappearance' as a crime which must be carried out by 'agents of the State' or 'persons or groups of persons acting with the authorisation, support or acquiescence of the State'.

[75] See Akande and Shah, 'International Crimes, Human Rights Violations and Foreign Domestic Courts '(2010) 21 EJILl 815.

[76] *Arrest Warrant case* (n 72 above), at para 61.

as 'private'. The judgment does not, however, directly address international crimes in the context of functional immunity and it must be doubtful that such a reference was intended to provide a conclusive determination on this issue.[77] It is also worth noting that, in their Joint Separate Opinion, Judges Higgins, Kooijmans, and Buergenthal indicated that the 'current trend' of State practice suggested that the continued existence of immunity *ratione materiae* for serious international crimes was at least open to doubt.[78]

Since *Pinochet*, there has been considerable debate as to whether a fully fledged exception to functional immunity in the case of international crimes can be said to have emerged. Many commentators have argued for the existence of such an exception and, in 2009, the Institute of International Law, in its Resolution on the Immunity from Jurisdiction of the State and of Persons Who Act on Behalf of the State, provided, in Article III, paragraph 1, that:

> [N]o immunity from jurisdiction other than personal immunity in accordance with international law applies with regard to international crimes.

The rules governing the immunity of heads of State, heads of Government, and other high-ranking State officials are largely contained in customary international law. As such, the conduct of States in practice and their recognition that such custom is accepted as law is the key factor in determining the existence and detail of such an exception. The views of Governments on such matters are not always easily accessible. Sometimes these views can be derived from international and national case law but such cases, particularly those involving high-level former officials, are comparatively rare and inevitably somewhat adventitious. In addition, national case law has to be viewed against the particular features of the forum State's legal system and the prevailing political situation; all of which may have far more bearing on the outcome of a particular prosecution than any considerations of immunity.

It is fair to say that State practice on this issue has been mixed. There have been several prosecutions and attempted prosecutions of foreign State officials and former State officials in national courts for a range of international crimes. These proceedings have taken place in a number of different countries, although the majority have been within Europe. In most cases, it has been reasonably clear that the crimes alleged were carried out in pursuance of State policy and that the

[77] It is also notable that in *Jurisdictional Immunities of the State (Germany v Italy)* (2012) ICJ Rep where the ICJ was concerned with the immunity of the State itself in relation to 'serious violations of international human rights law or the international law of armed conflict' it took pains to emphasize that the question of the immunity of officials in criminal proceedings was not in issue.

[78] See also view of ICTY Appeals Chamber in *Prosecutor v Blaskic* Case No IT-95-14-A, para 41.

officials concerned were acting in an official capacity. However, in most of the cases, particularly those involving lower-ranking officials, the issue of immunity was not raised directly. Only a few of the cases have involved former heads of State, heads of Government, or other high-level officials.

In 2000, a Senegalese court indicted the former President of Chad, Hissene Habre, on charges of torture and crimes against humanity. However, following some pressure from the Senegalese Government, the appellate court dismissed the case on the grounds that the Senegalese courts had no jurisdiction to try crimes committed abroad. A Belgian court filed a further complaint against the former President in Belgium and, in 2005, he was indicted by a judge there. The Belgian Government then requested his extradition from Senegal. The case does not provide further guidance as to the circumstances in which immunity *ratione personae* may cease to apply to a former head of State because the Chadian Government waived any immunity to which Habre may have been entitled in order to facilitate his trial in Belgium. The ICJ has now ruled in *Questions Relating to the Obligation to Prosecute or Extradite (Belgium v Senegal)*[79] that Senegal must, without further delay, pursuant to its obligations under the Torture Convention, submit the case to its competent authorities for prosecution or extradite Hissene Habre to Belgium.

German, Italian, and Spanish courts have issued arrest warrants for torture, genocide, and other serious human rights violations in respect of a number of former foreign military heads of State, although in all the cases so far jurisdictional factors unrelated to immunity have prevented matters from progressing further.[80] In Belgium a private criminal complaint was brought against Ariel Sharon and Amos Yaron relating to various international crimes allegedly committed while they were serving as senior officers in the Israeli Army. The case against Sharon, who was then the incumbent Prime Minister, was dismissed on the ground of his personal immunity. The case against Yaron was, however, allowed to proceed and was only subsequently dropped on the basis of jurisdictional factors unrelated to immunity.[81] In the Netherlands, the former military leader of Suriname, Desi Bouterse,[82] was indicted following

[79] See ICJ Rep 20 July 2012. On 2 July 2013 Hissene Habre was charged with crimes against humanity, torture, and war crimes and is to be tried by the Extraordinary African Chambers in the Senegalese courts (see p 196 below).

[80] See Lutz and Reiger, *Prosecuting Heads of State* (Cambridge University Press, 2009) which refers in the Appendix to indictments in Germany, Italy, and Spain relating to former military heads of State in Argentina and Guatemala.

[81] *Re Sharon & Yaron, HSA v SA* (2003) 42 ILM 596, Cour de Cassation. See also *Wakim v Ya'alon* (Distict Court, Auckland, Civ-2006-004, 27 November 2006) where an arrest warrant issued against former Israeli General Moshe Ya'alon was eventually extinguished and proceedings permanently stayed following the NZ Attorney-General's refusal of consent for prosecution on the ground that the evidence was insufficient.

[82] See *In Re Bouterse* (Gereschtshof Amsterdam, 20 November 2000), NJ 2001, 51; (2001) Netherlands YBIL 266, 277; and L Zegveld, 'The Bouterse Case' (2001) Netherlands YBIL 97.

allegations of torture and murder of political opponents but proceedings were abandoned on the grounds that an accused could not be tried *in absentia* and that the prohibition against torture contained in the Torture Convention could not be applied retrospectively to acts committed before it came into force. In 2008, Dutch prosecutorial authorities concluded that an Israeli Minister and former Director of Shin Bet, the security service, would not enjoy immunity before the Dutch courts in relation to charges of torture.[83] Following these cases, the Dutch Minister of Foreign Affairs asked its Advisory Committee on Issues of Public International Law[84] to report on the relationship between the trial of international crimes in the Netherlands and the obstacle imposed by the immunity of foreign State officials. After confirming that, during their period of office, heads of State, heads of Government, and Ministers of Foreign Affairs generally enjoy full personal immunity for all their acts whether performed in an official or private capacity, the Committee concluded that they were also entitled to functional immunity after their term of office for acts performed in an official capacity but that this immunity does not extend to international crimes.[85]

In 2012, a Swiss Federal Criminal Court refused immunity to a former Algerian Defence Minister, Khaled Nezzar, in respect of war crimes and torture allegedly committed during that country's period of civil conflict between 1992 and 2000.[86] Nezzar had also been a member of the five-man High Council of State which had been established in 1992 to replace the office of President. The court concluded that it was 'undeniable that there is an explicit trend at the international level to restrict the immunity of (former) heads of State *vis-à-vis* crimes contrary to rules of *ius cogens*'.[87] This can be contrasted, however, with a reported statement from a spokesman for the Swiss Justice Ministry which indicated that the former US President, George W Bush, would be immune from prosecution for torture.[88]

[83] See *Ami Ayalon*, Press release, Palestinian Centre for Human Rights (PCHR). 'Torture Victim Seeks Prosecution of Former Head of of Israeli General Security Services', 6 October 2008 which indicates that Ayalon had already left the Netherlands by the time this conclusion was reached.

[84] See Advisory Report No 20, The Hague, May 2011.

[85] See Advisory Report No 20, The Hague, May 2011, para 5.1. The Netherlands Government accepted this conclusion. See Statement of Netherlands 2013 UNGA 68th Session, Sixth Committee, Report of the ILC, Immunity of State Officials.

[86] See Judgment of 25 July 2012.

[87] See also criminal complaint made in Switzerland in 2003 against the former Tunisian Minister of the Interior, General Habib Ammar, alleging acts of torture carried out between 1987 and 1988 by security and police forces under his command. The complaint was declared admissible but did not proceed on the ground that the general benefited from immunity as a member of the official Tunisian delegation to the International Telecommunications Union.

[88] See <http://www.guardian.co.uk/law/2011/Feb/06/George-Bush-trip-to-switzerland> ('Folco Galli, a spokesman for the Swiss Justice Ministry told the Associated Press that the department's

In practice, many States, citing reasons of immunity, remain reluctant to prosecute former high-level foreign officials. In 2007, a criminal complaint alleging torture was filed in France against Donald Rumsfeld, the former US Secretary of Defence. The district prosecutor dismissed the claim on the ground of immunity. In doing so the Office of the Prosecutor, which was apparently relying on views expressed by the French Ministry of Foreign Affairs, referred specifically to the dicta in the *Arrest Warrant* case which could suggest that former officials retain their immunity for all acts carried out while in office except those which can be characterized as private.[89] German prosecuting authorities have also declined to proceed against former Chinese President Jiang Zemin on the ground of his immunity and against former Uzbek Interior Minister, Zokirjon Almatov, although in the latter case the reasons advanced were evidential and the fact that the likelihood of a successful prosecution was thought to be 'non-existent'.

Since *Pinochet*, there have been no further prosecutions of former heads of State or other high-level officials in the UK although, in 2011, a private application for an arrest warrant was made in respect of the former Russian President, Mikhail Gorbachev. The application alleged torture but was dismissed by the district judge on grounds that the elements of the offence had not been made out and that, in any event, Mr Gorbachev would have been entitled to immunity under customary international law as a member of a special mission. According to information received by the court from the Foreign and Commonwealth Office, one of the purposes for which he was visiting the UK was to attend an official meeting with the Prime Minister.[90] The issue of functional immunity was not addressed by the court. In an earlier case, apparently undeterred by any considerations of functional immunity, a UK Court had issued a warrant for the arrest of Tzipi Livni, a former Israeli Foreign Minister and Leader of the Opposition for war crimes. The warrant was withdrawn when it emerged that

initial assessment was that Bush would have enjoyed immunity from prosecution for any actions taken while in office'). In the event no complaint was filed against the former President but he did cancel his trip, although the reason given was his concern about protests rather than fear of arrest.

[89] German prosecuting authorities have also declined to proceed against the former US Secretary for Defence although reasons other than immunity were invoked. See Decision of German Federal Prosecutor at Federal Court of Justice: *Centre for Constitutional Rights et al v Donald Rumsfeld et al* (2006) 45 ILM 119.

[90] Note that the former position in the UK by which a private citizen could initiate proceedings in relation to international crimes by applying directly to a judge for the issue of an arrest warrant in respect of a specific individual known to be visiting the country has now been amended by s 153 of the Police Reform and Social Responsibility Act 2011 (c 13), which provides that where a person who is not a public prosecutor lays an information before a justice of the peace in respect of certain offences (including grave breaches of the Geneva Conventions and Torture) alleged to have been committed outside the UK, no warrant shall be issued without the consent of the Director of Prosecutions.

she was not in the UK and had no immediate plans to visit. Later when she did visit the UK, the Director of Public Prosecutions refused consent to a private prosecutor for the issue of an arrest warrant on the ground that she was on a special mission.[91] In 2006, a New Zealand District Court judge issued an arrest warrant against Moshe Ya'alon, a former Israeli General who was visiting New Zealand.[92] The proceedings were, however, stayed by the Attorney General on advice that the evidence was insufficient to warrant pursuing a prosecution.[93]

In practice, prosecuting authorities appear more willing to take action against lower-ranking foreign officials particularly where their home State seems unlikely to object. There have been a number of successful prosecutions involving more junior officials. In Spain, a former Argentinian naval officer, Adolfo Scilingo, was prosecuted for torture, crimes against humanity, and other offences. In 2007, the Spanish Supreme Court upheld his conviction for crimes against humanity but dismissed the torture charge on the grounds that the acts concerned had all taken place before torture had become a crime under Spanish law.[94] The French courts have convicted a Mauretanian General, Ely Ould Dah,[95] and a former Tunisian Police Chief, Khaled Ben Said,[96] for torture committed in their own States. Both officials were convicted *in absentia*. In the Netherlands, there have been several successful prosecutions of former State officials for torture, including two Afghan intelligence officers and a former Commander of the Zaire (now Democratic Republic of the Congo) Garde Civile.[97] In 2000, a Swiss military tribunal convicted a former Rwandan local government official of war crimes in connection with massacres committed in his municipality during the 1994 genocide.[98] In 2010, the son of the former Liberian President Charles Taylor was convicted by a US court of torture committed abroad in his capacity as commander of a special security

[91] The UK Foreign and Commonwealth Office had issued a certificate to this effect.

[92] *Ex Parte Application for issue of warrant to arrest Lieutenant General Moshe Ya'alon* (District Court, Auckland, Civ-2006-004, 27 November 2006).

[93] n 92 above.

[94] A second Argentinian naval officer, Ricardo Cavallo, was extradited to Spain from Mexico to face similar charges. However, following the decision of the Argentine Supreme Court in 2005 that jurisdiction over crimes committed during the country's so-called 'dirty war' lay in that country, he was extradited back to Argentina for trial.

[95] See also ECHR Decision on Admissability, *Ould Dah v France (13113/03)* (2009) 48 ILM 869.

[96] See Langer, 'The Diplomacy of Universal Jurisdiction: The Political Branches and the Transnational Prosecution of International Crimes' (2011) 105 AJIL 1 at 22.

[97] See *HH and HJ* and *Sebastien Nzapali* (Netherlands, Judgment of 7 April 2004 (District Court of Rotterdam)).

[98] '*The FN case*' ruling of Military Court of Appeal 1A of 26 May 2000 and decision of Military Court of Cassation on 27 April 2001.

unit meant to protect his father during his presidency from 1999 to 2003.[99] The defendant was a US citizen and was prosecuted under a 1994 US law allowing the prosecution of US citizens and any other individual on US soil for torture committed abroad. The issue of immunity was not raised.

These developments, although often inconclusive on the question of immunity, are indicative of an increasing willingness on the part of national courts and prosecutorial authorities in many States to bring criminal proceedings against foreign officials in regard to alleged international crimes committed in their official capacity. They may suggest an initial assumption, explicit or implicit, that immunity *ratione materiae* should not necessarily bar the prosecution of such crimes. It is difficult, however, to draw firm conclusions in this regard as the reasons underlying national decisions to proceed or not to proceed with a particular prosecution are often unclear. The role of the home State can be similarly ambiguous. In some cases, proceedings have been abandoned or suspended because of difficulties concerning the evidence, the death or absence of the accused, or simply because the home State has decided to investigate or prosecute the matter on its own account. Where cases have proceeded, the home State may have waived any immunity or simply failed to raise the issue at all; internal disorder may have meant that it was not in a position to assert immunity or to object to the proceedings on those grounds. This could be significant given the approach of the ICJ in *Certain Questions of Mutual Judicial Assistance in Criminal Matters (Djibouti v France)*,[100] which suggests that functional immunity has to be claimed actively by the official's home State.[101]

Where the official's home State objects or is likely to object to the proceedings, practice suggests a continuing reluctance on the part of many national authorities to prosecute foreign State officials particularly when they have occupied a prominent or high-ranking position. In 2006, the issue of arrest warrants by France and Spain[102] against various high-ranking Rwandan Government officials, including the former Chief of Protocol, Rose Kabuye, provoked strong protests from Rwanda and led to a severance of diplomatic relations between France and Rwanda. The prosecutions were eventually discontinued although not before Kabuye had been arrested in Germany and extradited to France pursuant to the French warrant.[103] On an earlier occasion

[99] *United States v Roy M Belfast aka Chuckie Taylor*, US Court of Appeals (11th Cir 15 July 2010).

[100] (2008) ICJ Rep 177.

[101] See pp 172–5 below.

[102] See eg *Sala v Kabarebe*, Indictment, IDLC 1198 (Spain 2008).

[103] Rwanda refused to cooperate with the Spanish and French authorities and complained to the African Union about the prosecutions. In response, the African Union criticized the practice by some European States of seeking to prosecute African nationals on the basis of very wide jurisdictional claims. See Assembly of the African Union, Decision on the Report of the Commission on the Abuse of the Principle of Universal Jurisdiction, Doc.Assembly/AU/Dec.199(XI) (1 July 2008); see also 'The Spanish Indictment of High-Ranking Rwandan Officials' (2008) 6 J Int'l Crim Just 1003.

the German authorities had declined to arrest her on the ground that she had immunity since she was accompanying the Rwandan President on an official visit. In 2008, however, they took the view that she was on a private visit and did not, therefore, enjoy immunity.[104]

This reluctance on the part of many States and the general uncertainty as to the precise contours of any exception has prompted the ILC Special Rapporteur, Roman Kolodkin, to conclude that, as regards international crimes, it is 'difficult to talk of exceptions to immunity as having developed into a norm of customary international law'.[105]

Crimes committed in the forum State

The focus on State practice in the area of prosecution of foreign State officials has highlighted another possible 'exception' to functional immunity or, as the International Law Commission's Special Rapporteur would have it, an 'absence of immunity'.[106] This is the situation where an individual acting in an official capacity commits a crime in the territory of the State seeking to exercise jurisdiction. It is not necessary for the act to be a grave international crime and ordinary crimes may be covered. If, however, immunity *ratione materiae* is not to apply, it would appear to be crucial that the territorial State did not consent to the discharge in its territory of the official functions in question. There is a further possibility that the question of whether or not it consented to the presence of the foreign official as such in its territory may also be of importance.

In the oral pleadings before the ICJ in *Certain Questions of Mutual Judicial Assistance in Criminal Matters (Djibouti v France)*,[107] counsel for Djibouti made the point (which was not directly relevant to the case) that exceptions to the principle of immunity existed in the event of war crimes and acts of espionage and sabotage carried out in the territory of the forum State. However, this area of State practice has not received much attention until comparatively recently.

In the *Pinochet* case, Lord Millet, when dealing with the charge of conspiracy to murder allegedly committed in the territory of the State requesting extradition, remarked that 'the plea of immunity *ratione*

[104] Thalmann, 'French Justice's Endeavours to Substitute for the ICTR' (2008) 6 J Int'l Crim Justice 995.

[105] See Roman Kolodkin, Second Report of the ILC Special Rapporteur, 56 and ILC Report 2011, Ch VII UN Doc A/66/10.

[106] Second Report on Immunity of State Officials from Foreign Criminal Jurisdiction, A/CN. 4/ 631, para 94(p).

[107] See n 100 above.

materiae is not available in respect of an offence committed in the forum State'. He did not elaborate further and it seems that the majority were of the view that Pinochet *was* entitled to immunity for the 'ordinary' crimes carried out in his official capacity even if committed on Spanish territory. A closer study of State practice does suggest, however, that where such crimes are discovered, States are often prepared to arrest and prosecute the perpetrators even when it is clear that the acts concerned were performed in an official capacity. Conversely, the home States of the officials involved do not claim immunity on their behalf.

Following the sinking of the Greenpeace vessel *Rainbow Warrior* in New Zealand, a court there convicted two French agents of manslaughter and wilful damage.[108] The judge noted that the defendants had acted under French military orders but stated that this was not a matter on which he would place any great weight. The French Government did not raise any issue of immunity at the trial stage but later argued that the defendants' detention in a New Zealand prison was inappropriate 'taking into account, in particular, that they acted under military orders and that France [was] ready to give an apology and to pay compensation to New Zealand for the damage suffered'.[109] It is also notable that, in the memorandum submitted by France to the UN Secretary General, it emphasized the issue of responsibility but did not refer to immunity.

In the *Lockerbie* case, a member of the Libyan Intelligence Service and another Libyan national were prosecuted on charges of conspiracy to murder, murder, and breaches of the UK Aircraft Security Act 1982 in connection with the blowing up of an aircraft over the Scottish village of Lockerbie. It was alleged that both men were acting on behalf of the Libyan Intelligence Service and that their actions were officially sanctioned and in furtherance of Libyan State policy. The two men were eventually tried in a Scottish court convened under special arrangements in the Netherlands.[110] Libya did not claim State immunity for its agents and the men did not raise the plea on their own behalf. On 31 January 2001, one of the defendants, Mr Al-Megrahi, was convicted and sentenced to life imprisonment while the other was acquitted and released.

In *R v Lambeth Justices, ex parte Yusufu*,[111] a Nigerian national was charged with the kidnapping of the former Nigerian Transport Minister, Umaro Dikko,

[108] *R v Mafart and Prieur* 74 ILR 241.

[109] See Ruling of UN Secretary General of 6 July 1986, UN Reports of International Arbitration Awards vol XIX, 213; Also Rainbow Warrior (NZ v France) (1986) 74 ILR 241.

[110] *Her Majesty's Advocate v Abdelbaset Ali Mohamed Al Megrahi and Ali Amin Khalifa Phimah*, High Court of Justiciary, Camp Zeist Case No 1475/99.

[111] [1985] Crim LR 510.

in London. The court was aware that the kidnapping had been arranged and paid for by the Nigerian High Commissioner in his official capacity and that the crate, in which it had been planned to smuggle Mr Dikko out of the UK, had been addressed to the Nigerian Ministry of External Affairs and accompanied to the airport by several Nigerian diplomats. The defendant, Mr Yusufu, claimed to be a diplomat but, although he was travelling on a Nigerian diplomatic passport, he had not been notified as a member of the staff of the Nigerian High Commission. The court found that he was not, therefore, entitled to diplomatic immunity. Nigeria did not assert immunity *ratione materiae* on his behalf.

In 2009, an Italian court convicted 22 agents of the US Central Intelligence Agency, one US military official, and two Italian secret service agents on charges of kidnapping for their alleged participation in the 'extraordinary rendition' of a suspected terrorist, Abu Omar, who had been abducted in Milan and flown to Cairo where he was allegedly tortured. Among the US defendants, who were all tried *in absentia*, were two consular officers. These two had claimed immunity from criminal proceedings under the Vienna Convention on Consular Relations and had also claimed immunity *ratione materiae* on the basis that they had been acting at all times in an official capacity. All the defendants appealed to the Court of Cassation which held that the two former consular agents were not entitled to consular immunity as the kidnapping could not be regarded as performed in the exercise of consular functions because the act had been unlawful under Italian law. It further held, apparently contrary to its decision in *Lozano*, that there was no customary international law rule which recognized functional immunity from criminal proceedings for all State officials in regard to their official acts.[112] The rationale of the decision is not entirely clear but it is probable that the fact that the crime alleged was of a covert nature and committed on the territory of the forum State played a significant role.[113]

More recently a court in the UK has directly addressed the issue of crimes committed in the forum State in an official capacity. In *Khurts Bat v Investigating Judge of the German Federal Court and others*[114] the Secretary of the Executive

[112] *General Prosecutor at the Court of Appeals of Milan v Adler and others*, Final Appeal Judgment, No 46340/2012; ILDC 1960 (IT 2012). See also *Lozano* (n 53 above).

[113] See also *Prosecutor v Blaskic*, ICTY Appeals Chamber, which alluded briefly to the view that spies, although acting as organs of a State, could be held personally accountable for their wrongdoing. See also *Staschynskij*, Case 18 FRG Bundesgerichtshof 1962 where a former KGB agent was prosecuted and convicted by a German court of the murder of two political exiles in Munich in 1959; a 2004 decision by the Qatar Court of Appeal convicting two Russian agents for the murder of a former Chechen leader in Qatar; and a 2004 decision of the Argentinian Supreme Court (24-08-2004, Case A.533.XXXVIII) confirming the conviction of a former Chilean secret agent for the murders of Chile's former Army Commander-in-Chief and Vice-President in Buenos Aires in 1974.

[114] [2011] EWHC 2029 (Admin).

Office of the Mongolian National Security Office was arrested in London pursuant to a European arrest warrant issued by a German Federal court. He was charged with the kidnapping of a Mongolian national in France who was then forcibly transported to Berlin, ill-treated, drugged, and flown abroad using a diplomatic passport. The crimes were alleged to be part of a plan by the Mongolian Secret Service. At the time they were committed, the defendant had been a member of the staff of the Mongolian Embassy in Budapest. His claim to immunity *ratione personae* as member of a special mission and as a high-ranking State official was rejected by the judge at first instance. He then appealed on both issues to the Divisional Court, adding a further claim for functional immunity based upon the ground that his acts had been official acts of Mongolia. The Divisional Court affirmed the judgment of the lower court on the claim for personal immunity. It also rejected the additional claim for immunity *ratione materiae*, holding that customary international law does not afford such immunity in relation to official acts performed in the territory of the forum State in circumstances where that State has not given its consent to the presence of the foreign official and his presence is unknown.[115]

The sparse national case law on this issue[116] means that it is difficult to identify with any certainty the precise criteria necessary in order to establish this exception or 'absence of immunity'. However, in his Second Report on the topic of the 'Immunity of State Officials from Foreign Criminal Jurisdiction', the ILC's Special Rapporteur has concluded:

> If a State did not give its consent to the presence of a foreign official and his activity which led to the commission of a criminally punishable act in its territory, there would appear to be sufficient grounds for assuming that the official does not enjoy immunity *ratione materiae* from the jurisdiction of that State.

The classic examples given are acts of terrorism, espionage, and sabotage but, if the Special Rapporteur is correct in his conclusion, there would appear to be no reason why other criminal activities could not fall within this exception. The examples of State practice referred to above involve the prosecution of relatively junior State officials who were directly and actively involved in

[115] [2011] EWHC 2029 (Admin). Following his extradition to Germany in August 2011, prosecutors dropped the charges against Mr Khurts and he was allowed to return to Mongolia (see 'A Murky Mongolian Saga', *The Economist*, 30 September 2011).

[116] For a further account of some of the above cases and other examples of State practice in this area, see Franey, *Immunity, Individuals and International Law* (Lambert Academic Publishing, 2011) 244–85 where the author goes further in concluding that State officials do not have immunity *ratione materiae* in criminal proceedings for acts committed on the territory of the forum State or the territory of a third State, unless that immunity is accorded by a special regime such as that afforded to diplomats, consular agents, or persons on special mission or by ad hoc agreement.

the commission of the crimes alleged and often apprehended in the territory of the forum State. It is not clear whether the 'absence of immunity' in their case would also apply to former heads of State or other high-level officials who had instigated the actions concerned. The view of the majority in *Pinochet* regarding the 'ordinary' crimes allegedly committed on Spanish territory might suggest otherwise but the identification of such an 'absence' of immunity does, at least, raise the question as to why more senior officials should not be prosecuted provided it could be shown that the acts in question were directly ordered or sanctioned by them.

In this context, it is worth recalling that Article 12 of the 2004 UN Convention on the Jurisdictional Immunities of States and Their Property provides that the State itself is not immune from foreign proceedings in which pecuniary compensation is claimed for death or personal injury or damage to or loss of tangible property caused by the State's act or omission if:

> the act or omission occurred in whole or in part in the territory of that other State and if the author of the act or omission was present in that territory at the time of the act or omission.[117]

The Article 12 exception is the only one capable of applying to acts *iure imperii* as all the other exceptions are based, at least in part, on the non-sovereign nature of the activity concerned. By contrast, Article 12 is justified solely by reference to the place where the act took place, namely in the territory of the forum State. The exception was initially recognized in some States in the context of proceedings concerning road traffic accidents where the driving of a motor vehicle, even for governmental purposes, was regarded as an act *iure gestionis*. It developed more generally, however, and, in those States which have legislation on State immunity, the terms of the exception are not limited to such unintentional, insurable torts and can, in principle, encompass intentional harm such as acts of sabotage or assassination even when carried out in the exercise of sovereign authority. Indeed the courts of two such legislating States have expressly held that the exception as embodied in their respective statutes is without regard to the *iure imperii/iure gestionis* distinction.[118]

In some States, however, the courts have declined to extend the exception to acts *iure imperii* committed in the forum State[119] and it remains questionable to what extent the broader approach taken in some States reflects customary

[117] See O'Keefe and Tams (eds), *The United Nations Convention on Jurisdictional Immunities of States and Their Property: A Commentary* (Oxford University Press, 2013) 210–24.

[118] See *Letelier v Republic of Chile* (1980) 63 ILR 378 at 386–7 (US (DDC)); and *Schreiber v Canada (Attorney General)* 2002 SCC 62, paras [32] and [35]–[6] (Can SC, 2002).

[119] See *McElhinney v Williams and Her Majesty's Secretary of State for Northern Ireland* (1995) 104 ILR 691 at 703 (Ireland (SC)).

international law. The European Court of Human Rights has noted that recognition of the territorial tort exception is 'by no means universal' and concluded that the present state of the development of international law did not enable it to conclude that a State which accorded another State immunity in proceedings in respect of personal injury caused by an act *iure imperii* carried out in the territory of the forum State fell 'outside any currently accepted standards'.[120] This conclusion was reached three years before the adoption of the UN Convention, although the final adoption of the ILC Draft Articles which contained the territorial tort exception in its unlimited form had taken place ten years before.

Since then the ICJ has held that:

> customary international law continues to require that a State be accorded immunity in proceedings for torts allegedly committed on the territory of another State by its armed forces and other organs of State in the course of conducting an armed conflict.[121]

The ICJ did not address the wider question as to whether there was a territorial tort exception applicable to *acta iure imperii* in general but did suggest that, notwithstanding the absence of any armed conflict, a State would be entitled to immunity in respect of *acta iure imperii* committed by its armed forces on the territory of another State.[122] It is not entirely clear whether the UN Convention itself applies to proceedings in respect of the activities of a foreign State's armed forces, particularly when such activities are carried out in the territory of the forum State. Such proceedings are not expressly excluded from the Convention's scope, which is in contrast to Article 31 of the European Convention on State Immunity 1972 and to several national legislative provisions.[123] However, when introducing the draft Convention to the Sixth Committee, the Chairman of the Ad Hoc Committee indicated that 'the general understanding had always prevailed' that military activities were not covered. In this context he also referred to the ILC Commentary on Article 12 stating that it did not apply to 'situations involving armed conflict'.[124]

[120] *McElhinney v Ireland* (2001) 123 ILR 73 at 85, para [38] (ECHR (Grand Chamber)).

[121] *Jurisdictional Immunities of the State (Germany v Italy)* (n 75 above), para [78].

[122] *Jurisdictional Immunities of the State (Germany v Italy)* (n 75 above), para [72].

[123] See eg s 16(2) of the State Immunity Act 1978 (UK); s 6 of Foreign States Immunities Act (Australia); and s 19(2)(a) of the State Immunity Act (Singapore).

[124] In declarations attached to their respective instruments of ratification, Norway and Sweden have expressed their understanding that the Convention 'does not apply to military activities, including the activities of armed forces during an armed conflict, as those terms are understood in international humanitarian law, and activities undertaken by military forces of a State in exercise of their official duties'.

Civil proceedings

The rules relating to the functional immunity of State officials have developed mainly in the context of civil proceedings. States cannot be prosecuted but they can be sued so that, in this context, the liability of both State and individual official may be in question in the same case.

Hatch v Baez[125] is an early case involving a civil suit against a former head of State. It concerned a former President of the Dominican Republic who had been granted asylum in the US. He was sued in respect of injuries sustained by the plaintiff in Santo Domingo allegedly as a result of the defendant's conduct. The exact circumstances in which these injuries were inflicted is not clear. The judgment of the US court states simply that the complaint alleges that they were inflicted by the Dominican Government and consisted of 'acts done by the defendant in his official capacity of President of that republic'. It had been argued that Baez was not entitled to immunity as he was no longer President of the Dominican Republic but this was firmly rejected by the court, which noted that the acts for which he was being sued had been 'done by him in the exercise of that part of the sovereignty of St Domingo which belongs to the executive department of that government…'. The fact that he was no longer President could not affect his immunity in respect of such acts as it sprang from 'the capacity in which the acts were done, and protects the individual who did them because they emanated from a foreign and friendly government'. It was also argued that the US court should have jurisdiction because the acts had been done in violation of the law but again the court rejected this approach on the basis that it was a well-established rule of international law that the courts of one State should not judge the acts of another State done within its own territory.[126]

In applying functional immunity to protect State officials in civil cases, national courts have justified their approach by invoking the two basic rationales referred to in the first part of this section.[127] In the *Church of Scientology* case,[128] for example, the Church sought an injunction in a German court to restrain the Commissioner of the Metropolitan Police in London from making allegations against it in an official report. The German Supreme Court held that, in issuing the report, the Commissioner was acting as the agent of the British State. As such, his acts were acts of the State and could 'not

[125] 7 Hun 596 (1876).

[126] See also *Underhill v Hernandez* 168 US 250 (US SCt, 1897).

[127] See pp 137–9 above.

[128] (1978) 65 ILR 193, Supreme Court of the Federal Republic of Germany.

be attributed as private activities' to the person authorized to perform them. The court added that:

> Any attempt to subject state conduct to German jurisdiction by targeting the foreign agent performing the act would undermine the absolute immunity of sovereign states in respect of sovereign activity.[129]

In *Propend Finance Pty and others v Sing and others*,[130] proceedings for contempt of court were brought in the UK courts against a police superintendant who was an accredited diplomat at the Australian High Commission in London and against the Commissioner of the Australian Federal Police Force. The proceedings concerned the breach of an undertaking given by the police superintendant on behalf of the Australian Government that certain documents seized in the UK in connection with a criminal investigation in Australia would not be removed from the UK or used in the Australian investigation until the legality of their seizure had been settled. Despite the undertaking, the superintendant faxed parts of the documents to Australia where they were copied and distributed. The Divisional Court held that the superintendant was entitled to diplomatic immunity as an accredited member of the diplomatic staff of the Australian High Commission but that the Commissioner had no immunity. On appeal, the Court of Appeal found that both the superintendant and the Commissioner were immune. Both enjoyed State immunity within the terms of section 14(1) of the State Immunity Act 1978 as the acts impugned had been performed in the exercise of their police functions, which were sovereign activities. In addition, the superintendant had diplomatic immunity. The key finding of the court was that the protection afforded by the 1978 Act would be undermined if State officials could be 'sued as individuals for matters of State conduct in respect of which the State they were serving had immunity'.[131]

As we have seen, the UN Convention[132] specifically endorses the principle of functional immunity for State officials and former State officials in civil proceedings by including within its definition of the 'State' its various organs of government and 'representatives of the State acting in that capacity'. The same principle is often reflected in national legislation in those countries

[129] See also *Church of Scientology in the Netherlands Foundation and others v Herold and Heinrich Bauer Verlag* 65 ILR 380 where a Dutch court held in a similar case against the Chief of the German Federal Police that his act in compiling a report 'can only be regarded as an act done in his official capacity and not as a private person'. See also *Zoernsch v Waldock and another* (n 37) (1964) 41 ILR 438 (UK CA).

[130] (1997) 111 ILR 611 (CA).

[131] (1977) 111 ILR 611 at 669 (UK CA).

[132] See Art 2(1)(b)(i) and (iv) of the 2004 UN Convention on the Jurisdictional Immunities of States and Their Property.

which have legislation on State immunity and, even when not explicit, is reflected in the approach adopted by national courts in applying that legislation. In the past, most US federal courts interpreted the Foreign Sovereign Immunities Act (FSIA) as covering foreign officials as 'agencies or instrumentalities' of the foreign State based upon a view that, in enacting the legislation, Congress had intended to fully codify the common law of sovereign immunity. However, in *Samantar v Yousef*,[133] the Supreme Court accepted the US Government's position that the FSIA does not govern the immunity of foreign officials when they are sued in their personal capacity. The court held that it will apply only where the foreign State is the real party in interest in the case. Foreign officials and former officials, including former heads of State and heads of Government, cannot, therefore, invoke the FSIA as a shield unless it is clear that it is the foreign Government itself which will be responsible for paying any damages, as would be the case if an official is sued in his or her official capacity.[134] The court made it clear, however, that a foreign official sued in his or her personal capacity may still enjoy immunity as common law immunity derived from customary international law still exists and may apply to such a case. The implications of this decision are not yet clear and, in practice, the separation of the immunity of foreign officials from that of the State itself may not lead to significantly different results from those where the courts applied the FSIA, particularly when the official's Government is prepared to claim immunity on his or her behalf.[135] The continued practice of the Executive in intervening in such cases and the deference of the US courts to its suggestions are also important factors. Nevertheless, the decision has opened up the possibility of a divergence between the immunity of an official and that of the State he or she served as it could suggest that a lawsuit against a foreign official will not necessarily be regarded as a suit against the foreign State itself merely because it involves passing judgment on the conduct of an official acting on its behalf. The court noted expressly that the immunity of the State and that of its officials might not always be co-extensive and that there could be lawsuits in which the State would be entitled to immunity but the foreign official would not unless he or she were entitled to some form of personal immunity, such as diplomatic immunity or 'head of State immunity'.

[133] (2010) 130 S .ct 2278

[134] See Justice Stevens, who explained that lawsuits directed at foreign officials would be covered by the FSIA only if they are 'in all respects other than name, to be treated as a suit against the entity. It is not a suit against the official personally, for the real party in interest is the entity'.

[135] See eg Doe v Zedillo No 3:11-cv-01433 2013 (US District Court in Connecticut) where court dismissed claim against former President of Mexico based upon a suggestion of immunity filed by the Executive branch on 7 September 2012.

Civil liability for international crimes

As we have seen, there is now some debate as to whether foreign officials, including former heads of State, heads of Government, and Foreign Ministers, should be entitled to functional immunity in respect of certain international crimes. The issue has achieved most prominence in the context of criminal proceedings but has also been raised in civil cases.

In *Jones v Kingdom of Saudi Arabia*,[136] the claimants brought proceedings in the English High Court against Saudi Arabia and a number of Saudi officials—two police officers, the deputy-governor of a Saudi prison, and the head of the Ministry of the Interior. They claimed aggravated damages for assault and negligence on the grounds that they had been tortured in Saudi Arabia by the two police officers which the deputy-governor and head of the Ministry had caused, permitted, or negligently failed to prevent. The claimants relied on the clear international law prohibition on torture contained in the 1984 United Nations Convention Against Torture and Other Cruel, Inhuman or Degrading Treatment or Punishment (UNCAT), to which both the UK and Saudi Arabia were parties. Article 14 of the Convention provided that each State party was to ensure in its legal system that the victim of an act of torture could obtain redress and had an enforceable right to fair and adequate compensation. The claimants argued that these facts, inter alia, meant that States and their officials could no longer claim immunity *ratione materiae* for acts of torture, which could not be regarded as governmental acts covered by such immunity. The Court of Appeal, confirming the decision of the lower court, dismissed the proceedings against the Kingdom of Saudi Arabia on the grounds of State immunity but, unexpectedly, allowed the appeal in respect of the four individual defendants. The claimants then appealed against the dismissal of their claims against the State and the Kingdom appealed against the refusal of immunity for the individual defendants.

The House of Lords rejected the claimants' appeal, holding that both Kingdom and officials were protected by State immunity. In doing so, Lord Bingham noted that the Court of Appeal had without 'principled reason' departed from the principle laid down in *Propend Finance Pty Ltd v Sing*[137] stating:

> A State can only act through servants and agents; their official acts are the acts of the State; and the State's immunity in respect of them is fundamental to the principle of State immunity. [The Court of Appeal's] error had the effect that while the Kingdom was held to be immune, and the Ministry of Interior, as a department of the government, was held to be immune, the Minister of Interior (the fourth defendant in the second action) was not, a very striking anomaly.

[136] [2006]UKHL 26;[2007]1 AC 270;129 ILR 713.

[137] (UKCA 1977) 111 ILR 611.

The court distinguished clearly between criminal and civil proceedings in this context, noting that it was erroneous to assume that a civil claim against an individual torturer did not directly implead the State in any more objectionable respect than a criminal prosecution. A civil action in such a case must indirectly implead the State since the actions of the individual torturer are attributable to it. By contrast a State is not criminally responsible in international or English law. Moreover, Article 14 of the Convention merely requires a private right of action for damages for acts of torture committed in territory under the jurisdiction of the forum State, not in respect of torture committed elsewhere.

The same conclusion was reached by the New Zealand High Court in *Fang and others v Jiang Zemin*[138] where several New Zealand residents brought proceedings against the former Chinese President and other high officials in the Chinese Government alleging that they had been tortured by State authorities while living in China as part of a systematic persecution of the Falun Gong movement and its followers. The court substantially adopted the reasoning of the House of Lords in *Jones v Kingdom of Saudi Arabia* holding that no proper distinction between the immunity of the State and its officials could be made in the context of civil proceedings.

The ICJ has noted that there is a substantial body of State practice[139] which demonstrates that:

> customary international law does not treat a State's entitlement to immunity as dependent upon the gravity of the act of which it is accused or the peremptory nature of the rule which it is alleged to have violated.[140]

In the same case it also drew a very clear distinction between the immunity of officials in criminal cases and that of the State in civil proceedings. Referring specifically to *Pinochet (No 3)*, the ICJ made the point that several of the judges in that case had themselves emphasized this distinction and noted Lord Bingham's remarks in *Jones v Saudi Arabia* where he described the distinction between criminal and civil proceedings as fundamental to the decision in *Pinochet*.[141]

In the US, there has been a line of cases decided under the Alien Tort Statute (ATS) which is at odds with this approach. The ATS, passed in 1789, confers jurisdiction upon US Federal courts in all 'causes where an alien sues

[138] See 21 December 2006 (NZ High Court) HCAKCIV 2004-404-5843.

[139] See eg *Bouzari v Islamic Republic of Iran* (2004) 128 ILR 586 (Canada); *Margellos* (2005) 129 ILR 525 (Greece); and *Kalegoropoulou and others v Greece and Germany*, App No 59021/00, (2002) 129 ILR 537.

[140] *Jurisdictional Immunities of the State (Germany v Italy)* (n 75 above) para [84].

[141] *Jurisdictional Immunities of the State (Germany v Italy)* (n 75 above) para [87].

for a tort only [committed] in violation of... the law of nations'. Under this legislation there have been a number of lower court cases which reflect the view that torture (and possibly other international crimes) cannot be official acts for the purposes of State immunity or the act of State doctrine.[142] These ATS cases have, however, been described by the ICJ Judges Higgins, Kooijmans, and Buergenthal in their Joint Separate Opinion in the *Arrest Warrant* case as a 'unilateral exercise of the function of guardian of international values' unsupported by any general State practice.[143]

It is also notable that, in recent years, the higher US courts have taken a more cautious approach to civil suits brought against foreign State officials and former officials based on allegations of international crimes.[144] In 2008, for example, the US Court of Appeals upheld the immunity of a former Israeli Head of Army Intelligence in proceedings relating to alleged war crimes.[145] The court accepted that the defendant had been acting in his official capacity which, in its view, made him 'an agency or instrumentality' of the State of Israel within the meaning of the FSIA. Similarly, in *Matar v Dichter*,[146] it was held that a former Director of the Israeli General Security Service was entitled to immunity in regard to claims for alleged war crimes, crimes against humanity, 'extrajudicial killing', and 'cruel, inhuman, or degrading treatment or punishment' within the meaning of the Torture Victim Protection Act (TVPA).[147] The claims were brought under the ATS and related to Dichter's participation in a military attack against an alleged Hamas leader which also killed a number of civilians. It was accepted that Dichter's actions had been undertaken in his official capacity and that the

[142] See *Filartiga v Pena-Irala* (1980) 630 F.2d 876; *Re Estate of Ferdinand Marcos, Hilao v Estate of Ferdinand Marcos* (1994) 25 F.3d 1467; and *Xuncax v Gramajo* (1995) 886 F.Supp 162. In a recent decision of the US Supreme Court, however, it has been held that ATS claims will not generally be allowed if they concern conduct occurring in the territory of a foreign State: see *Kiobel v Royal Dutch Petroleum Co* 133 S Ct 1659 (2013). This is likely to lead to a significant reduction of human rights litigation in the US.

[143] See also Lord Hoffmann in *Jones v Kingdom of Saudi Arabia* [2006] UKHL 26 at [99].

[144] *In Mamani and others v Sanchez de Lozada and Sanchez Berzain* (US Ct of Appeals 11th Cir) 29 August 2011, a civil claim was brought against the former President of Bolivia and the former Minister of Defence alleging their involvement in numerous extra-judicial killings in Bolivia during their term of office. The Bolivian Government waived any immunity but the US court dismissed the case on the ground that the complaint had not been made out, stating 'we know and worry about the foreign policy implications of civil actions in federal courts against the leaders (even the former ones) of nations. And we accept that we must exercise particular caution when considering a claim that a former head of State acted unlawfully in governing his country's own citizens'.

[145] *Belhas v Moshe Ya'alon* (2008) 515 F.3d 127.

[146] 500 F Supp 2d 284 (SDNY 2007).

[147] Pub Law 102-256 (1992), *codified* at 28 USC 1350. The TVPA was enacted in 1992 as a note to the ATS and provides a cause of action for US nationals and aliens for extra-judicial killing and torture carried out by foreign nationals 'under actual or apparent authority, or color of law'.

fact that his conduct may have been unlawful or violated *ius cogens* rules of international law did not alter that fact. The court also recognized that, under customary international law, there is no exception to the immunity of foreign officials based purely on alleged violations of *ius cogens* norms. In reaching this conclusion, the court relied on the views expressed in the US Government's Statement of Interest. It also held that there was no need to decide whether or not the defendant, as a former official, was covered by the FSIA since he was entitled to functional immunity under common law and the US legislation had left untouched the common law on sovereign immunity (as derived from customary international law) as it applied to former foreign officials.[148]

The uncertainty as to whether the US FSIA covered foreign officials as 'agencies or instrumentalities' of the foreign State has now been resolved by the decision of the Supreme Court in *Samantar v Yousef* and it is clear that the position of foreign officials sued in their personal capacity is governed by the common law on sovereign immunity as derived from customary international law.[149]

Necessity for functional immunity to be invoked

The role of an official's home State in asserting the official character of a particular act has already been touched upon in the context of the means by which the forum court is to draw the line between official and private conduct. Such a distinction is ultimately one for the court to make and it need not always accept an assertion by the foreign State that an official has acted under its authority. In practice, however, its views will usually carry substantial weight. It is also well settled that any immunity asserted belongs to the foreign State not the individual official and that only the State can waive that immunity. But what of the situation where the foreign State plays no role in the proceedings? There is no waiver but also no intervention in support of the official concerned and, therefore, no invocation of immunity. In such cases can it be concluded that the forum State is under no obligation to accord immunity *ratione materiae*?

[148] See also *Balcero Giraldo v Drummond Co*, 10-mc-00764 (JDB) 2011 WL3926372 (DDC 8 September 2011 where the State Department filed a pleading stating that the former Colombian President, Alvaro Uribe, who had been served with a subpoena to appear as a witness in a TVPA/ATS suit 'enjoys residual immunity from this Court's jurisdiction insofar as the plaintiffs seek information (i) relating to acts taken in his official capacity as a government official; or (ii) obtained in his official capacity as a government official'. The court ruled that the former President could not be forced to testify.

[149] 130 S Ct 2278 (2010). See also Stewart, 'Samantar v Yousef: Foreign Official Immunity Under Common Law', ASIL INSIGHTS, 14 June 2010, 15 February 2011 (FD Va).

In *Certain Questions of Mutual Assistance in Criminal Matters (Djibouti v France)*, France argued that functional immunity must be invoked and, in holding that Djibouti's head of national security was not entitled to functional immunity before the French courts, the ICJ relied in part on the fact that Djibouti had never invoked immunity on his behalf, stating:

> The State which seeks to claim immunity for one of its State organs is expected to notify the authorities of the other State concerned.

It concluded that, if it failed to do so, the forum State is not obliged to consider the issue of its own motion and may proceed with the prosecution. The ILC Special Rapporteur has referred to this case in reaching the same conclusion, adding that such an approach is 'logical' given that individuals entitled to functional immunity are former officials or often relatively junior incumbents and that the forum State may, therefore, have no reason to know that such persons acted in an official capacity.[150] These conclusions were reached in the context of criminal proceedings but the Special Rapporteur also referred, by way of illustration, to the US civil cases of *Matar v Dichter*[151] and *Belhas v Ya'alon*[152] where the functional immunity of the defendants was upheld following active assertions as to the official character of their conduct by the Israeli Government.

The US State Department has suggested that the absence of any recognized Government to claim immunity on behalf of a former official could be a legitimate reason for refusing functional immunity in a civil case. In *Yousef v Samantar*[153] two US citizens (formerly Somali nationals) brought proceedings against Mohamed Ali Samantar, who had served as First Vice President, Prime Minister, and Minister of Defence of Somalia under the Siad Barre regime in the 1980s before seeking refuge in the US. The claims alleged Samantar's responsibility for widespread and systematic acts of torture, arbitrary detention, and extra-judicial killings carried out in Somalia during his terms of office. After ruling that the FSIA did not apply to individual officials, the Supreme Court remanded the case back to the trial court to consider whether Samantar might be entitled to common law immunities derived from customary international law. It declined to offer any guidance as to the scope of those immunities. The trial court asked the State Department for its views on the matter and, in response, the latter submitted a statement of interest indicating that the defendant was not entitled to immunity. Two factors seem to have been been particularly important to the State Department's

[150] Third Report on Immunity of Foreign State Officials from Criminal Jurisdiction UN Doc A/CN.464/6 (24 May 2011), paras 16–19.

[151] 500 F. Supp 2d 284 (SDNY 2007).

[152] 515 F.3d 1279, 1282 (DC Cir 2008).

[153] No 11–1479 US Court of Appeals, 2 November 2012.

determination on this question. First, it concluded that any immunity claim was undermined by the fact that Samantar is 'a former official of a State with no currently recognized Government to request immunity on his behalf' or to take a position as to 'whether the acts in question were taken in an official capacity'. Second, the defendant's status as a permanent legal resident of the US was important because 'US residents like Samantar who enjoy the protections of US law ordinarily should be subject to the jurisdiction of our courts, particularly when sued by US residents'.[154]

Samantar had claimed two different types of immunity: 'head of State immunity' and immunity *ratione materiae* based upon the assertion that the allegations related to conduct carried out in his official capacity. So far as 'head of State immunity' was concerned, denial of immunity was not surprising. Samantar was no longer a serving official and, in this context, the court confirmed that it felt bound to give absolute deference to the State Department's position on status-based immunity doctrines. It indicated, however, that the latter's determinations on conduct-based immunity, although carrying substantial weight, were not conclusive in the same way.[155] It acknowledged, however, that both factors advanced by the State Department added substantial weight in favour of denying immunity *ratione materiae*.[156]

Practice on this issue has again been very mixed. There are numerous examples of immunity being accorded by the forum State following formal invocation by the foreign State. It is also clear that States may be prepared to accord immunity in the absence of any such invocation.[157] In such cases it is not always possible, however, to be sure that some diplomatic exchanges have not occurred between the States concerned. In cases where immunity has been refused the role of the official's home State has often been unclear. It is possible that in some cases the Government concerned was simply unaware of the case[158] or, as in *Samantar*, not in a position to assert such immunity on behalf of its former official.[159] In other cases, States have refused to cooperate or even objected to

[154] See also Statement of Interest of the United States—Order *Ahmed*, No 2:10-cv-34 (SD Ohio 6 Dec 2010), 1–2, 7; *Ahmed v Magan*, No 2:10-cv-34 (SD Ohio 15 Mar 2011) (US District Court for Southern District of Ohio)).

[155] But see the contrary view of the Executive that it retains the sole authority to determine the immunity from suit of former foreign officials. See Part 2 n 114 above.

[156] The court went further in applying the somewhat discredited argument that 'ius cogens violations are not legitimate official acts and, therefore, do not merit foreign official immunity'.

[157] See *Rumsfeld* case at p 157 above.

[158] See Wuerth, 'Pinochet's Legacy Reassessed' (2012) 106 AJIL 751 where it is suggested that such lack of awareness 'seems likely in some civil cases in the United States'.

[159] In January 2013 the US formally recognized the new Government in Somalia. Somalia has now written to the State Department requesting immunity for its former Prime Minister Samantar whose lawyers are reportedly preparing his appeal to the Supreme Court. See Associated Press Report, 1 March 2013.

the proceedings but have not formally invoked functional immunity. Where immunity has been specifically pleaded, it has sometimes been raised by the individual official himself rather than his State of nationality.

It is likely, that, where the home State is aware of proceedings, its reasons for deciding whether or not to claim functional immunity on behalf of its officials may vary considerably. In some cases it may judge such intervention to be unnecessary given the presence of other jurisdictional factors likely to prevent matters from proceeding. Invocation of immunity may not always be a particularly attractive option since it could be interpreted as tantamount to a declaration by the State that it is responsible for the conduct which is the subject of the proceedings.[160] In the case of former officials where there has been a regime change, the new Government may be reluctant to protect such individuals particularly when doing so could associate it with criminal acts carried out by a previous Government. In some cases the new Government may itself be seeking to prosecute the former official concerned. Such decisions are not, therefore, necessarily based upon any considered legal assessment of the conduct in question and may be prompted by other unrelated factors.

If, therefore, it is correct that there is no obligation on the forum State to accord functional immunity unless it is invoked, what are the implications for former heads of State, heads of Government, and other high-level officials? It is likely that those who have represented powerful States with relatively well-organized and stable regimes are most likely to have functional immunity asserted on their behalf and to benefit from the continuing support of their national Governments.[161] By contrast the position of those from less stable regions of the world may be more precarious.

3. Private Acts

In principle, it is clear that a State official or former State official, including a former head of State, head of Government, or Foreign Minister, is not entitled to functional immunity in respect of private acts whether carried out

[160] See *Case Concerning Certain Questions of Mutual Assistance in Criminal Matters (Djibouti v France)* (2008) ICJ Rep 177.

[161] It has been suggested that 'the most significant conferrals of immunity *ratione materiae* in criminal cases involve defendants from China and the United States'. See Wuerth, 'Pinochet's Legacy Reassessed' (2012) 106 AJIL 731, 766.

before, during, or after their period of office.[162] As we have seen, such important officials enjoy an extensive personal immunity while in office but, in the case of private acts and, by analogy with the position of ambassadors, there is some support for the argument that their immunity may not be absolute so far as immunity from civil jurisdiction is concerned. For a former head of State who enjoys only functional immunity, the position is clear and immunity cannot apply, whether in civil or criminal proceedings, unless the conduct in question was carried out in an official capacity. Thus, for example, a former head of State has been held to have no immunity from legal proceedings in respect of purchases by him of clothes for his wife while she was queen.[163]

Some acts are of such an inherently personal nature or so obviously unconnected with the performance of official functions that no one could reasonably assert that they were performed under the authority of the State. In *United States v Noriega*, for example, a US court had little difficulty in concluding that trading in illegal narcotics for personal benefit could not be properly regarded as a function carried out in the exercise of Noriega's official position as *de facto* leader of Panama.[164] But as we have seen the mere fact that conduct is illegal, malicious, or even criminal does not in itself destroy its official character.[165]

Financial misdeeds carried out while in office can be problematic, especially when they form part of an official's duties in managing and investing State assets or handling government contracts. There is some practice, however, which suggests that national courts are often willing to treat financial misconduct carried out for personal benefit as prima facie not entitled to immunity. As we have seen in *Jimenez v Ariseguieta*,[166] a US court rejected the former Venezuelan dictator's argument that his financial misdeeds had been committed in an official capacity and held that they were just 'common crimes committed by the Chief of State done in violation of his position and not in pursuance of it'. In *Jean-Juste v Duvalier*[167] proceedings were brought in a US court against the former President of Haiti and his wife, alleging that they had misappropriated public funds for their own personal use. The defendants did

[162] See the *Arrest Warrant* case where the ICJ noted that a former Foreign Minister would not enjoy immunity 'in respect of acts committed prior or subsequent to his or her period of office, as well as in respect of acts committed during that period of office in a private capacity'.

[163] *Ex-King Farouk of Egypt v Christian Dior* (1957) 24 ILR 228; *Societe Jean Desses v Prince Farouk and Mrs Sadek* (1963) ILR 37.

[164] 746 F.Supp 1506 (1990); 99 ILR 145 but note that the case was primarily decided on the ground that 'head of State' immunity was not applicable as Noriega had not been recognized as a head of State.

[165] *Jaffe v Miller and others* (Canada 1993) see n 40 above.

[166] See (1962) 33 ILR 353.

[167] (1988) No-86-0459 Civ (US District Court), SD Fla, noted in (1988) 82 AJIL 594.

not appear and the court entered a default judgment awarding the plaintiffs over half a billion dollars.[168] In 2003 a Swiss court convicted the former Prime Minister of Pakistan, Benazir Bhutto, and her husband on charges relating to the deposit in Swiss banks of US$10 million given to them by a Swiss company in exchange for a contract in Pakistan.[169] The issue of functional immunity was not raised. In 2005, Evgeny Adamov, a former Minister for Atomic Energy of the Russian Federation and former head of the Russian Institute for Nuclear Research, was indicted in the US on criminal charges of conspiracy to transfer stolen money and securities, conspiracy to defraud, money laundering, and tax evasion. All the acts alleged related to funds obtained from US sources while Adamov was in office. The former minister was visiting Switzerland when the US requested his extradition. Adamov was arrested but while the Swiss authorities were preparing for his extadition to the US, Russia also requested his extradition on charges of embezzling US$17 million in Russian State funds while serving as a minister. In the meantime, the Swiss Justice ministry ruled that Adamov should be extradited to the US but an appeal was then made to the Swiss Federal Supreme court. The ensuing proceedings were primarily concerned with the issue of how to assign priority in cases of multiple extradition requests. The court did, however, note that a former minister's functional immunity is derived from the principle that no State shall extend its domestic jurisdiction to the sovereign acts of other States and their organs. As such it should not grant impunity to officials for crimes such as corruption or common crimes committed in a purely private capacity.[170]

In many of these cases it is, of course, the home State of the former official that is pursuing the matter and seeking recovery of any misappropriated assets. In such circumstances it is not unreasonable to assume that, if immunity applies to the conduct in question, it has been effectively waived. In Switzerland, the Philippines Government obtained an order freezing various deposits made by the former President Marcos in Swiss banks. The court rejected a claim to 'head of State' immunity as Marcos was no longer head of State. It did not appear to consider it necessary to address the question as to whether functional immunity could apply.[171] Similarly, in the US, the Philippines Government obtained injunctions restraining its former President from

[168] But see comment in Watts (n 31 above) 127 that the Court's judgment hardly touched on the difficult legal issues raised by the case.

[169] See *New York Times* report, 6 August 2003.

[170] *Adamov v Federal Office of Justice*, Appeal Judgment, No 1A 288/2005; ILDC 339 (Switzerland 2005). It was concluded by the court that the closer link to the Russian legal system justified giving priority to the Russian extradition request.

[171] See *Marcos and Associates v Chambre d'accusation, Geneva* (1987) 82 ILR 53.

transferring properties (including some outside the US) pending the resolution of disputes concerning their ownership.[172]

It could be argued, however, that some of the acts and transactions concerned in cases of alleged financial misconduct, are carried out under colour of or in ostensible exercise of governmental functions. In such circumstances, national courts can be reluctant, even where the former official's home State is involved in the proceedings, to assume jurisdiction. In 1986, Haiti started proceedings in the French courts against its former President, Jean-Claude Duvalier, his wife, and mother for the recovery of large sums of money which they had allegedly embezzled from State funds during Duvalier's term of office. The French court declined to entertain the case on the ground that Haiti's claims were related to the exercise of governmental power in Haiti and were, therefore, founded on foreign public law which the French courts would not enforce.

More recently, however, the French Court of Cassation has allowed judicial investigations into corruption charges against certain incumbent African heads of State (in relation to private assets owned by them in France) to proceed.[173] No charges have been preferred against the heads of State themselves, although some family property has been seized and an arrest warrant issued in respect of the son of the leader of Equatorial Guinea on charges of money laundering. On 26 September 2012 Equatorial Guinea instituted proceedings against France in the ICJ seeking an annulment of the investigative proceedings against the President and Vice-President (against whom an arrest warrant has also been issued) on the ground that such actions violate 'the principles of equality between States, non-intervention, sovereignty, and respect for immunity from criminal jurisdiction'.[174]

[172] *Republic of the Philippines v Marcos and others* (1986) 81 ILR 581; *Republic of the Philippines v Marcos and others (No 2)* (1987, 1988) 81 ILR 609, 642. See also *Republic of Haiti v Duvalier* [1990] 1 QB 202 (UK); and *Islamic Republic of Iran v Pahlavi* (1984) 81 ILR 557 when the new Government of Iran laid claim to assets owned or possessed by the former Shah in the US. The US Government left the matter to be determined on its merits by the court but notified the latter that any claim should not be barred by sovereign immunity principles or by the act of State doctrine.

[173] See Part 2, nn 190 and 275 above.

[174] See Press release <http://www.icj-cij.org>. No further action can take place unless France consents to the ICJ's jurisdiction in the matter.

5

International Responsibility of Heads of States and Other Senior State Representatives

The position of heads of State or other very senior officials under international law is not solely a matter of their powers or the special treatment to which they are entitled in foreign States. Such high officials can also engage the responsibility of their States and of themselves under international law.

1. State Responsibility

State responsibility is a concept fundamental to international law which is derived from the doctrines of State sovereignty and the equality of States. Article 1 of the International Law Commission's Articles on State Responsibility ('the ILC Articles') sets out the general rule, widely supported by practice, that every internationally wrongful act of a State entails responsibility. Article 2 provides that there is an internationally wrongful act of a State when conduct consisting of an act or omission is attributable to the State under international law and constitutes a breach of an international obligation of the State.

Typically, international law governs the rights and responsibilities of States and is, therefore, normally concerned with breaches of international legal obligations by those States and the consequences of such breaches. A State cannot, of course, in reality act on its own behalf and can only do so through its officials and representatives. The principle of State responsibility depends, therefore, on establishing the necessary link between the State and the person or persons who have actually committed the unlawful act or omission. Article 4 of the ILC Articles provides that the conduct of any State organ shall be considered an act of that State under international law, whether the organ exercises legislative, executive, judicial, or any other functions, whatever position it holds in the organization of the State and whatever its character as an organ of the central Government or of the territorial unit of the State. It is clear that this formulation covers acts of a head of State or other Government official, carried out in an official capacity. Such acts are attributable to the State and, if they involve a breach of the State's international obligations, it will bear international responsibility. Article 5 goes further and ensures that the conduct of a person or entity which is not an organ of the State in the above sense may nonetheless be attributed to the State if they are authorized to exercise governmental authority. Article 7 makes it clear that the conduct of a State organ or a person or entity empowered to exercise governmental authority, acting in an official capacity, is attributable to the State even if the organ or entity has exceeded its authority or acted contrary to instructions. It is clear, however, that State responsibility may co-exist with individual responsibility and that the two are not mutually exclusive.[1]

International crimes have been a particular area of controversy with regard to State responsibility. Article 19 of the ILC Draft Articles made a distinction between international crimes and international delicts within the context of internationally wrongful acts. International crimes were characterized as wrongful acts resulting from the breach of an international obligation considered to be so fundamental for the protection of the international community that they are recognized as crimes under international law. The examples given were aggression, colonial domination by force, slavery, genocide, apartheid, and pollution on a large scale of the atmosphere or the seas. Other internationally wrongful acts were termed international delicts. However, the question as to whether a State could be criminally responsible remained highly controversial with some doubting whether such a concept had any real meaning or legal value.[2] The debate threatened to derail the project as a whole and, as a result, the ILC decided to omit any mention of international crimes of States. Instead the Articles, as finally approved in 2001, concentrate on the consequences flowing from a breach by a State of obligations *erga omnes* or those arising under peremptory norms of international law (*ius cogens*). Moreover, Article 41 provides that States must cooperate to bring to an end, through lawful means, any serious breach[3] by a State of an obligation arising under a peremptory norm[4] of international law and must not recognize as lawful

[1] See Art 58 of the ILC Articles.

[2] See Crawford, *The International Law Commission's Articles on State Responsibility* (Cambridge University Press, 2002) 17–20 for analysis of the debate.

[3] Article 40(2) describes a breach as 'serious' if it involves a gross or systematic failure by the responsible State to fulfil the obligation.

[4] Examples given of peremptory norms are the prohibitions of aggression, slavery and the slave trade, genocide, racial discrimination and apartheid, torture, and the principle of self-determination: see ILC Commentary 2001, 283–4.

any such situation nor render aid or assistance in maintaining that situation. Peremptory norms are considered to have a higher status than other rules and may derive from custom or treaty. Article 53 of the Vienna Convention on the Law of Treaties 1969 defines such a norm as one 'accepted and recognized by the international community of States as a whole as a norm from which no derogation is permitted and which can be modified only by a subsequent norm of international law having the same character'.

2. Individual Responsibility

History and general principles

Typically, international law has been concerned with the rights and obligations of States and, until comparatively recently, international mechanisms for the holding to account of individuals for crimes committed directly under international law have been undeveloped. It has long been recognized, however, that international legal obligations can, in certain specialized areas, be imposed on individuals as opposed to States. Piracy is often invoked as the first international crime or the first offence to give rise to universal jurisdiction.[5] Those committing piracy have long been regarded as guilty of crimes against the international community as a whole for which they bear individual responsibility and for which they may be punished by an international tribunal or by any State at all.[6] In practice, the arrest and punishment of pirates has been left to national legal systems which are permitted to exercise jurisdiction over them provided that they have been apprehended on the high seas or in the territory of the forum State.[7] Such jurisdiction may be exercised regardless of the nationality of the pirate or the place where the crime was committed. Piracy *iure gentium* has been defined as illegal acts of violence, detention,

[5] Slave-trading is another example, although less longstanding than piracy. Currently Art 99 of the Law of the Sea Convention (UNCLOS) 1982 requires every State to take effective measures to prevent and punish the transport of slaves in ships authorized to fly its flag and to prevent the unlawful use of its flag for that purpose. Several earlier treaties existed for the suppression of the slave trade, eg one of 1862 between Britain and the US which established three mixed courts designed to condemn slavers and secure their ultimate trial before their own national courts. However, the courts did not hold any trials and in 1870, by an additional Convention, they were abolished. See 2 Moore, *International Law Digest* (1906) 469, 946.

[6] See eg *In re Piracy Iure Gentium* [1934] AC 586; and separate Opinion of Judge Guillaume in *Arrest Warrant of 11 April 2000 (DRC v Belgium)* (2002) ICJ Rep 3, 37–8, (2002) 128 ILR 60, 92–4; and *R v Jones* [2006] UKHL 16, (2006) 132 ILR 668.

[7] See Art 105 of UNCLOS 1982 (reproducing Art 19 of the Geneva Convention on the High Seas 1958). The recent upsurge of piracy off the coast of Somalia has prompted the establishment of a specialist court in Kenya (see BBC News, 24 June 2010, 'Kenya Opens Fast-track Piracy Court in

or depredation committed for private ends by the crew or passengers of a private ship or private aircraft and directed against another ship or aircraft (or persons or property therein) on the high seas or *terra nullius*.[8] The regulation of piracy entailed a recognition that individuals had personality in international law and could be held responsible for their crimes under that law but the essence of piracy was that it be committed for private objectives. As such there could be no overlapping responsibility of States.

Before 1945 the range of offences under international law for which individuals were regarded as bearing international responsibility was very narrow indeed. The approach to piracy was in strong contrast to the usual practice in regard to breaches of international law carried out by individuals in pursuit of State policies and objectives. Such individuals, including the most senior representatives were regarded as mere organs or agents of the State and their conduct could be punished, if punished at all, only at national level by States exercising normal territorial jurisdiction. Any responsibility for those breaches at international level lay on the State of the individual's nationality, employment, or allegiance.[9]

It is arguable that the first significant shift in this approach began with the actions of the Congress of Vienna in dealing with Napoleon. The Congress had declared that Napoleon, by his escape from Elba, had placed himself outside of civil and social relations, and that, as an 'Enemy and Disturber of the tranquillity of the world', he had delivered himself over to public prosecution for crime.[10] In practice, however, there was no trial and he was detained, as a preventive measure for the preservation of peace, on the island of St Helena until his death in 1821.[11]

Matters were taken a little further after the First World War when the Allies set up a 15-member Commission to investigate responsibility for the start of the War and any violations of the laws of war which had occurred.[12] The Commission's report, issued in March 1919, concluded that the central powers had been responsible for starting the War and that violations of the international laws of war and humanity had occurred. It recommended that high officials of those central powers, including Kaiser Wilhelm II, be prosecuted for ordering such crimes on the basis of command responsibility.[13] However,

Mombasa' <http://www.bbc.co.uk/news/10401413>) This court is not, however, of an international character, although some States have called for the establishment of such a court.

[8] See Art 101 of UNCLOS (and Art 15 of the 1958 High Seas Convention).

[9] See *Caroline case*, UK Law Officers Reports (1854) FO 83.2209 and p 138 above.

[10] 13 De Martens, *Recueil des Traites et Conventions conclus par Russie* (St Petersburg) 1905.

[11] A treaty was drawn up between Great Britain and the other Great Powers authorizing his imprisonment. See Brownlie, *International Law and the Use of Force By States* (Clarendon Press, 1963), 51.

[12] Report of the Commission to the Preliminary Peace Conference, reprinted in (1920) 14 AJIL 95.

[13] The Commission recommended that '...all persons belonging to enemy countries, however high their position may have been, without distinction of rank, including Chiefs of State, who have been guilty of offences against the laws and customs of war or the laws of humanity, are liable to criminal prosecution'.

the trial was opposed by the US, Japan, and Italy with arguments that the imposition of such responsibility on heads of State was unprecedented in international law and contrary to the sovereign equality of States. In this connection it was further argued that heads of State were essentially agents of their people and, therefore, responsible politically only to those people. As a compromise the Treaty of Versailles 1919 provided for the establishment of a special tribunal, to try the former Emperor for 'a supreme offence against international morality and the sanctity of treaties'.[14] No mention was made of any violation of the laws of war, nor of criminal responsibility. The tribunal, which was empowered to determine any appropriate sentence, was to be composed of judges appointed by the victorious powers; France, Great Britain, Italy, Japan, and the US. Any further development was prevented, however, by the refusal of the Netherlands Government to surrender the former Emperor on the ground that the charge did not refer to any punishable act according to the 1858 Dutch Penal Code or extradition treaties signed with the Allied Governments. It was added for good measure that the charge appeared to be more political than legal in nature. The former Emperor was never tried and remained in the Netherlands until his death in 1941. Other provisions of the Treaty[15] had provided for the prosecution of German nationals for war crimes before Allied courts, including mixed commissions where the victim had dual nationality. These were also never implemented although Germany, itself, did undertake some prosecutions in Leipzig between 1921 and 1923.[16]

It could be argued that little had been achieved but the Treaty was important in that it acknowledged (albeit in somewhat vague terms) the principle of individual responsibility for acts committed on the international plane and the responsibility of a head of State for acts committed under his or her authority. Moreover, although it might be claimed that the proposed trial lacked any clear legal basis, it did envisage the trial of a head of State in an internationally constituted court.

The Nuremberg International Military Tribunal

It is now accepted that heads of State, heads of Government, and other high-level officials bear a personal responsibility in international law for those acts which are so serious as to constitute international crimes. The idea that such conduct can only be attributed to the State is now seen by most as both unrealistic and contrary to common notions of justice. This acceptance is largely a result

[14] See Art 227. [15] See Arts 228 and 229.

[16] See *The Dover Castle* (1922)16 AJIL 704; and *The Landovery Castle* (1922)16 AJIL 708.

of the judgment at the International Military Tribunal at Nuremberg. At the end of the Second World War representatives of the victorious Allies—France, the UK, the US, and the USSR—met in London to draft the charter of an international military tribunal 'for the just and prompt trial and punishment of the major war criminals of the European Axis'. The Charter, which was an international agreement, was signed by the four Allies on 8 August 1945 and 19 other States later adhered to it.[17] The Tribunal had an ad hoc jurisdiction over international crimes against peace and attendant conspiracies, war crimes, and crimes against humanity 'for which there shall be individual responsibility'. It had eight judges, four principal judges from each of the four major Allies (France, the UK, the USSR, and the US) and four alternates drawn from the same four States. In effect only high-level German officials were tried[18] and the only trial was held in Nuremberg from 14 November 1945 to 1 October 1946. Given that the trial took place following the surrender of Germany and effective dismantling of its State apparatus, issues of personal immunity did not arise. It was, however, clear from the outset that the official position of the defendants, whether as heads of State, senior Ministers, or military commanders, would not free them from responsibility nor mitigate punishment.[19] The fact that a defendant acted in accordance with an order of his Government or of a superior officer would also not free him from responsibility but could be considered by the Tribunal in mitigation of punishment.

Three of the defendants (Schacht, a former President of the Reichsbank and Economics Minister, Fritzsche, a propaganda chief, and von Papen, a former Vice Chancellor and ambassador to Turkey) were acquitted while, of the remaining defendants, 12 were sentenced to death and seven to periods of imprisonment ranging from ten years to life. Those sentenced to death included Reich Marshall Goering,[20] Foreign Minister, von Ribbentrop, Field Marshall Keitel, General Jodl, Hans Frank, the former Governor-General in Poland, and Wilhelm Frick, a former Minister of the Interior and Reich Protector of Bohemia and Moravia. Those imprisoned included Hitler's deputy Rudolf Hess, Admiral Doenitz, Commander-in-Chief of the Navy, the former Commander-in-Chief of the Navy, Admiral Raeder, and Albert Speer, Minister for Armaments and Munitions.

[17] UNTS, vol 82, p 279; UKTS no 27 (1946).

[18] 24 individual defendants were indicted, as well as seven organizations.

[19] See Art 7 of the Charter. Watts notes that 'there can be little doubt that Adolf Hitler, if he had not died beforehand, would have been tried before the Nuremberg Tribunal notwithstanding his status as leader of Germany'. See Watts, 'The Legal Position in International law of Heads of States, Heads of Governments and Foreign Ministers' (1994) 247 III Recueil des Cours 83.

[20] (1946) Nuremberg IMT, Judgment and Sentences (1947) 41 AJIL 172. Goering committed suicide in his cell before his execution.

The principles set out in the Tribunal's Charter and judgment were affirmed by a resolution of the UN General Assembly[21] and, although some aspects of the Tribunal's decision remain controversial in international law, other elements have been very influential, particularly its clear affirmation of the fact that individuals may incur direct liability under international law. It was stated:

> crimes against international law are committed by men, not abstract entities, and only by punishing individuals who commit such crimes can the provisions of international law be enforced... individuals have international duties which transcend the national obligations of obedience imposed by the individual State.[22]

This has been described as 'a foundational statement in international criminal law'.[23]

The Tokyo International Military Tribunal

The ending of the Second World War also prompted the establishment of an International Military Tribunal for the Far East ('the Tokyo International Military Tribunal'). The Tribunal, which was composed of judges from 11 States,[24] was set up in January 1946 by a proclamation of General Douglas MacArthur.[25] The trial, in which 28 defendants were charged with crimes against peace and attendant conspiracies, war crimes, and murders, lasted almost two-and-a-half years and resulted in a majority judgment, delivered in 1948, which found all the defendants guilty on one or more of the charges levelled against them. Seven were sentenced to death[26] and the remainder to life imprisonment or, in two cases, to lesser terms of imprisonment. The judgment followed the reasoning adopted by the Nuremberg Tribunal on most aspects of the law, including the responsibility of individuals under international law and the abolition of the absolute defence of superior orders. However, the most striking aspect of the proceedings from the point of view of a study of the legal position of heads of State, is the fact that the Japanese Emperor Hirohito was not indicted by the Tribunal nor was he called as a witness.[27]

[21] See Resolution 95(I) UN Doc A/64/Add.1. See also the ILC's Report on Principles of the Nuremberg Tribunal, YBILC 1950, vol II, 195.

[22] 'Nuremberg International Military Tribunal: Judgment and Sentence' reprinted in (1947) 41 AJIL 172, 221.

[23] Cryer, Friman, Robinson, and Wilmshurst, *An Introduction to International Criminal Law and Procedure* (Cambridge University Press, 2007) 94.

[24] US, UK, USSR, Australia, Canada, China, France, India, the Netherlands, New Zealand, and the Philippines.

[25] Special Proclamation, Establishment of an International Military Tribunal for the Far East, 19 January 1946, TIAS No 1589, 3.

[26] Including former Prime Ministers, Tojo and Hirota.

[27] See *In re Hirota and others* (1948) 15 Ann Digest 356 and 373–4. Note also that Art 6 of the Charter of the Tokyo Tribunal contained a similar provision to that of the Nuremberg Tribunal regarding the official position of an accused (but without any specific reference to a head of State).

This was not on any legal ground of lack of responsibility or immunity but simply for political reasons relating to Japan's post-war stability.[28] The Emperor had appeared on the initial list of war criminals and some States, including the UK and the USSR, had argued in favour of his prosecution. However, General MacArthur had advised that such action could seriously damage the prospect of establishing an effective civilian government in Japan[29] and, led by the US, the decision was made not to prosecute. Matters were assisted by the formal position of the former Japanese Government, which it held to throughout the trial, that the Emperor's position as a constitutional monarch meant that he had been unable to oppose the decisions of the Government during the war in spite of his own preference for peace.[30] The decision did cause some concern amongst the judges. Justice Henri Bernard of France took the view that the failure to indict the Emperor was one of the serious defects undermining the credibility of the Tribunal, and the President of the Tribunal, William Webb of Australia, indicated that this failure meant that it would, in his view, be wrong for any of the Emperor's ministers to suffer the death penalty.[31]

Relevant international conventions

In 1946, the UN General Assembly affirmed the principles of the Nuremberg Charter and the decision of the Tribunal itself. It also declared that genocide was a crime under international law bearing individual responsibility.[32] This was reaffirmed in the Genocide Convention of 1948 which called for the prosecution of offenders by domestic courts or 'an international penal tribunal'. Article IV of the Genocide Convention provides that individuals who have committed genocide 'shall be punished whether they are constitutionally responsible rulers, public officials or private individuals'. In 1947, the International Law Commission (ILC) was established and directed by another General Assembly resolution to formulate the principles of international law recognized in the Charter of the Nuremberg Tribunal and in the judgment of the Tribunal and to prepare a draft code of offences against the peace and security of mankind. In response the ILC produced a Draft Code formulating certain specific crimes

28 See Cryer, Friman, Robinson, and Wilmshurst, *International Criminal Law and Procedure* (2nd edn, Cambridge University Press, 2011) 99.

29 See MacArthur to Chief of Staff, United States Army (Eisenhower), Tokyo 25 January 1946; *Foreign Relations of the US* (1946) 396.

30 See Beigbeder, *Judging War Criminals: The Politics of International Justice* (Macmillan, 1999) 57 although the author notes that one of the main defendants, former Prime Minister Tojo, at one point testified that 'there is no Japanese subject who would go against the will of His Majesty; more particularly, among high officials of the Japanese government or of Japan...' and then later sought to neutralize this by insisting on the Emperor's 'love for and desire for peace'.

31 But See n 26 above.

32 Resolution 96(I).

under international law and asserting that such 'offences against the peace and security of mankind as defined in this Code, are crimes under international law, for which the responsible individuals shall be punishable'.[33] The four 1949 Geneva Conventions, together with the 1977 Additional Protocols I and II which deal with armed conflicts, also affirm the responsibility of individuals with regard to grave breaches of those instruments. In principle any individual, regardless of official status or rank, may be personally liable for such grave breaches and, under the principle of command responsibility, any person in a position of authority, including a head of State or Government ordering the commission of such a grave breach, could be as accountable as the individual committing the crime. In the years following a number of international treaties were agreed, which defined particular international crimes and required parties to criminalize such offences and ensure the punishment of individual offenders. These included the 1973 Convention on the Suppression and Punishment of the Crime of Apartheid, the 1984 Convention Against Torture, and the 2006 Convention for the Protection of All Persons From Enforced Disappearance.

The Genocide Convention, the four Geneva Conventions, and some of the subsequent treaties affirming the responsibility of individuals for certain international crimes, deal with conduct of a kind which is often or indeed likely to be committed in an official capacity. In a few cases the official character of the crime forms part of its definition.[34] Prosecution and punishment of offenders is left to the national courts of the parties and although, in some cases, it might be argued that the primary focus is the prosecution of an official in his or her own national courts, it is clear that most of the relevant Conventions contemplate or require the assumption of extra-territorial jurisdiction over the international crime in question. As such, they clearly envisage the possibility of the prosecution of a State official in a foreign court. However, although it is clear that the official position of an offender does not, in itself, relieve him or her of responsibility, none of the Conventions addressed the issue of the international immunities to which such officials or former officials may be entitled in foreign courts. The now well-established principle that official capacity does not exclude individual responsibility does not, in itself, mean that an individual may not be immune from the jurisdiction of a particular

[33] Article 1 of the Draft Code of Offences Against the Peace and Security of Mankind 1954, A/2693 and (1954) 45 AJIL Supp 123. In 1996 this was followed up by the adoption of 20 Articles constituting a Code of Crimes Against the Peace and Security of Mankind (YBILC 1996 II (Part II) 15–56). The draft Code provided for individual responsibility with regard to aggression, genocide, crimes against humanity, crimes against the UN, and associated personnel and war crimes. The work has now been largely superseded by the Statute of the ICC, which sets out the international crimes within the jurisdiction of the Court. See pp 191–3 below.

[34] See Art 1 of the Convention Against Torture.

court or tribunal. The personal immunity enjoyed by an incumbent head of State, head of Government, or Minister for Foreign Affairs would, in the absence of any waiver by the home State, effectively preclude such prosecution before a foreign domestic court. The position is less clear with regard to the immunity *ratione materiae* enjoyed by former officials but, as we have seen, that current uncertainty can, in practice, pose considerable obstacles for any prosecutor, particularly if the home State objects to the proceedings.[35]

3. International Courts and Tribunals

These developments regarding the individual responsibility of officials meant that it could no longer be doubted that, as a matter of general customary international law, a head of State or other very senior official could be called to account for serious international crimes provided the necessary international legal mechanisms existed for their apprehension and trial. The Genocide Convention had contemplated trial of offenders before 'an international penal tribunal' but, in practice, States' enthusiasm for the establishment of such a court was limited. Political events at the end of the 1980s and in the early 1990s changed this, in particular the two conflicts arising from the break-up of the former State of Yugoslavia and the Rwandan genocide of 1990.

The International Criminal Tribunal for Yugoslavia

The conflict within what was then the Socialist Federal Republic of Yugoslavia began in 1991, although its roots go back much further. It involved the commission of a number of large-scale violations of international criminal law committed mainly against civilians, which prompted the UN Security Council to set up a special Commission to investigate allegations relating to those violations.[36] A series of Security Council resolutions (SCRs) had also expressed grave concern and affirmed the responsibilities of States with regard to breaches of international humanitarian law committed in the territory of the former Yugoslavia.[37] These resolutions also emphasized individual responsibility for grave breaches of the 1949 Geneva Conventions. Following the Commission's report in early 1993, which concluded that grave breaches and other violations of international humanitarian law had been committed, the Security Council adopted Resolution 808 (1993) calling for the establishment

[35] See Part 4 at 149–60. [36] SCR 780 (1992).
[37] See SCRs 764 (1992), 771 (1992), and 820 (1993).

of an international tribunal to prosecute 'persons responsible for serious violations of international humanitarian law committed in the territory of the former Yugoslavia since 1991'. The UN Secretary General then produced a report which incorporated a draft Statute and commentary. This was adopted by the Security Council, acting under Chapter VII of the UN Charter, in Resolution 827 (1993). This novel procedure for establishing the tribunal, which was not without its critics,[38] was chosen in preference to a treaty on the grounds that the negotiation of such an agreement would take too long and that there was no guarantee that all the relevant States, particularly those which had emerged from the former Yugoslavia, would ratify such a treaty.[39]

The Statute of the International Criminal Tribunal for Yugoslavia (ICTY) provides that it may prosecute persons responsible for grave breaches of the Geneva Conventions of 1949, violations of the laws or customs of war,[40] genocide, and crimes against humanity committed in the territory of the former Yugoslavia since 1991. There is no formal cut-off date, which means that, in practice, the later conflicts in Kosovo and the former Yugoslav republic of Macedonia can be the subject of prosecutions.[41] Article 7 of the Statute establishes that persons who 'planned, instigated, ordered, committed or otherwise aided and abetted in the planning, preparation or execution' of any of the crimes listed in the Statute shall be individually responsible for the crime. It goes on to declare:

> (2) the official position of any accused person, whether as head of State or Government or as a responsible Government official, shall not relieve such person of criminal responsibility nor mitigate punishment.
>
> (3) the fact that any of the acts referred to in Articles 2 to 5 of the present statute was committed by a subordinate does not relieve his superior of criminal responsibility if he knew or had reason to know that the subordinate was about to commit such acts or had done so and the superior failed to take the necessary and reasonable measures to prevent such acts or to punish the perpetrators thereof.

[38] In the *Tadic* case (see n 39 below) the Appeals Chamber of the ICTY reviewed the question of the legality of the establishment of the Tribunal, holding that the decision of the Security Council under Chapter VII was within the framework of its mandate to restore international peace and security and was binding on all Member States. The Dayton Peace Agreement which was signed subsequently contained a specific obligation for all states of the former Yugoslavia to cooperate with the Tribunal.

[39] Report of the Secretary General Pursuant to Security Council Resolution 880 (1993) UN Doc S/25704, para 20.

[40] The Appeals Chamber of the ICTY has confirmed that customary international law imposes criminal responsibility on individuals for serious breaches of humanitarian law in internal as well as international armed conflicts. See *Tadic* (1995) 105 ILR 149.

[41] See SCR 1160 (1998) and *Milutinovic*, ICTY, A Ch, 8 June 2004. See also *In re: The Republic of Macedonia* I, ICTY, T Ch, 4 October 2002.

(4) the fact that an accused person acted pursuant to an order of a Government or of a superior shall not relieve him of criminal responsibility, but may be considered in mitigation of punishment if the International Tribunal determines that justice so requires.

The Tribunal has concurrent jurisdiction with national courts but it has primacy over those courts and can, therefore, request that they defer to its competence.[42] States are obliged to cooperate with the Tribunal in the investigation and prosecution of persons accused of committing the crimes within its jurisdiction and, in particular, must comply with any request for assistance or order, including the identification or location of persons, the production of evidence and the taking of testimony, the arrest or detention of individuals, and the surrender of the accused to the Tribunal.[43]

On 27 May 1999, the Tribunal became the first international court to indict a serving head of State, Slobodan Milosevic, President of the Federal Republic of Yugoslavia (FRY) for crimes against humanity, and a violation of the laws or customs of war.[44] These charges were largely related to the deportation and murder of Kosovo Albanians but were later expanded by the ICTY prosecutor to include genocide, crimes against humanity, grave breaches of the 1949 Geneva Conventions, and violations of the laws or customs of war in Bosnia and Croatia as well as Kosovo. In 2000, Milosevic resigned from office and in June 2001, the FRY, somewhat reluctantly, surrendered its former President to the ICTY. However, matters were never concluded as Milosevic died shortly before his trial was due to finish. Nevertheless, his indictment, followed by arrest and trial, constitutes a clear precedent on the jurisdiction of a Security Council Tribunal over a head of State.[45]

In 2001, the Tribunal issued its first conviction for genocide of the Serb General Radislav Krstic for his part in the Srebrenica massacre. Since then it has convicted and sentenced numerous State officials from the region ranging from senior military leaders and Government politicians to relatively junior policemen. It is currently trying the former Bosnian Serb leader Radovan Karadzic, who was arrested in July 2008, and the former military chief Ratko Mladic, on charges including genocide, crimes against humanity, violations

[42] See Art 9, r 9 of the Tribunal's Rules of Procedure where such a request may be made where national proceedings have characterized the alleged crime as an ordinary crime, there is a lack of impartiality or independence, it appears that the alleged offender is being shielded from criminal responsibility, the matter is not being diligently prosecuted, or the national proceedings involve significant factual or legal issues with implications for other prosecutions before the Tribunal.

[43] Article 29.

[44] Also indicted for the same crimes were the Deputy Prime Minister of the FRY, the Chief of Staff of its Army, the President of Serbia, and the Minister of Internal Affairs of Serbia.

[45] See Cryer et al (n 28 above) at 439.

of the laws and customs of war, and grave breaches of the 1949 Geneva Conventions.

The International Criminal Tribunal for Rwanda (ICTR)

The establishment of the ICTY was followed by the establishment of a similar international tribunal in response to the Rwandan genocide of 1990. Again, a Commission of Experts was appointed to investigate atrocities[46] and the Security Council, acting under Chapter VII, established an international tribunal.[47] The Statute of the ICTR was modelled closely on that of the ICTY and, like that tribunal, it has jurisdiction over war crimes, crimes against humanity, and genocide. The definition of the last two crimes is slightly different, however, in particular 'crimes against humanity' which, as defined in Article 3 of the Statute, requires that such crimes be 'committed as part of a widespread or systematic attack against any civilian population on national, political, ethnic, racial or religious grounds'. Article 6 of the Statute has similar provisions to those of Article 7 of the ICTY Statute, in particular with regard to those persons holding official positions, command responsibility, and superior orders. The jurisdiction of the Tribunal is limited to serious violations of international humanitarian law committed in the territory of Rwanda and to Rwandan citizens responsible for such violations committed in the territory of neighbouring States between 1 January 1994 and 31 December 1994.[48] Its jurisdiction over war crimes is limited to those in non-international armed conflicts.[49] As in the case of the ICTY, the ICTR has primacy over domestic courts.[50]

The Tribunal has tried and convicted several high-level leaders, most notably Jean Kambanda, a former Prime Minister of Rwanda whose Government presided over the genocide. He pleaded guilty and was sentenced to life imprisonment.[51]

The International Criminal Court (ICC)

As we have seen, the 1948 Genocide Convention provided for persons charged with genocide to be tried either by a court in the territory where the crime was committed or by an 'international penal tribunal'. Accordingly, the UN General Assembly requested the ILC to look into the possibility of establishing an

[46] SCR 935 (1994). [47] SCR 955 (1994). [48] ICTR Statute, Art 1.

[49] ICTR Statute, Art 4. [50] ICTR Statute, Art 8(1).

[51] *Prosecutor v Kambanda*, ICTR T Ch I, 4 September 1998. This was the first time a former head of Government had been convicted of genocide. His appeal against sentence was dismissed (see *Kambanda* ICTR A Ch, 19 October 2000).

international court and, following its report, a draft statute for a permanent court was produced. Matters did not progress much further until 1989 when Trinidad and Tobago proposed that the creation of a permanent international criminal court be put back on the UN agenda. This request was prompted by a desire to develop international prosecution for drugs offences although the court that was finally established does not have jurisdiction over such offences. Nevertheless, in response to the proposal, the ILC was again asked to produce a draft statute. Matters then moved swiftly with production of a draft and the setting up of a Preparatory Committee to prepare the text of a possible draft Convention. This text served as the basis for negotiation at a conference convened in Rome, which concluded with the adoption of the ICC Statute[52] which came into force on 1 July 2002.

The Statute provides that the Court's jurisdiction is limited to the 'most serious crimes of concern to the international community as a whole'; namely genocide, crimes against humanity, war crimes, and aggression.[53] Article 25 confirms that a person who commits a crime within the jurisdiction of the court 'shall be individually responsible and liable for punishment'. The ICC only has jurisdiction with respect to crimes committed after the Statute came into force[54] and may exercise such jurisdiction only where the State, in whose territory the crime took place,[55] or the State of which the person accused of the crime is a national, is a party to the Statute. It is, however, open to a State which is not a party to declare that it accepts the jurisdiction of the court with respect to the crime in question.[56] The Court also has jurisdiction where a situation has been referred to it by the Security Council acting under Chapter VII of the Charter. As such the referral is binding and it is, therefore, unnecessary that a relevant State be a party to the Statute.[57]

It is clear that the Court is intended to supplement not replace national courts in the task of prosecuting those responsible for international crimes. The preamble to the ICC Statute expressly acknowledges that all States have a responsibility to exercise jurisdiction over such crimes and the principle of complementarity is firmly embedded in its Statute. The Court may not exercise its jurisdiction if a national authority is investigating or prosecuting

[52] The final text was adopted by a vote of 120 to 7 with 21 abstentions. The votes were not formally recorded but China, Israel, and the US declared that they had voted against.

[53] ICC Statute, Art 5(1).

[54] If a State becomes a party after its entry into force, the Court may exercise jurisdiction only with respect to crimes committed after the Statute entered into force for that State (Art 11) unless that State elects to make a declaration under Art 12(3) to fill this gap.

[55] If the crime took place on a vessel or aircraft, the State of registration of the vessel or aircraft must be a party.

[56] ICC Statute, Art 12(3).

[57] ICC Statute, Art 13(b).

the case or has already done so. National courts have primacy unless circumstances show that the State concerned is unwilling or unable to carry out proceedings 'genuinely'. It is for the ICC itself to decide whether these conditions are met. In practice, even where the Court itself has determined to exercise its jurisdiction over a particular case, it remains heavily dependent upon States insofar as the location, arrest, and surrender of defendants are concerned.

Article 27 of the Statute provides as follows:

> (1) This Statute shall apply equally to all persons without any distinction based on official capacity. In particular, official capacity as a Head of State or Government, a member of a Government or parliament, an elected representative or a government official shall in no case exempt a person from criminal responsibility under this Statute, nor shall it, in and of itself, constitute a ground for reduction of sentence.
>
> (2) Immunities or special procedural rules which may attach to the official capacity of a person, whether under national or international law, shall not bar the Court from exercising its jurisdiction over such a person.

However, Article 98(1) of the Statute provides that the Court cannot require a State to surrender a person or provide other assistance if, in so doing, it would breach its obligations under customary international law with respect to State or diplomatic immunity. The possible implications of these provisions with regard to the prosecution of heads of States and other high-level State officials before the ICC are discussed below.[58]

In practice, the Court has opened investigations into a number of situations: four were referred to it by the States parties themselves;[59] two were Security Council referrals;[60] and two were initiated by the Prosecutor *proprio motu*.[61] In 2013, the Court had indicted 30 individuals, including four incumbent heads of State.[62]

4. Hybrid Courts and Other Internationalized Domestic Courts and Tribunals

The establishment of a number of courts that contain a mixture of international and national elements is a relatively recent development. These so-called hybrid courts largely post-date the establishment of the ad hoc criminal

[58] At pp 199–202 below. [59] The Central African Republic, the Congo, Mali, and Uganda.

[60] Darfur (Sudan) and Libya. [61] Cote d'Ivoire and Kenya.

[62] President Omar Al-Bashir of Sudan was the first incumbent head of State to be indicted by the Court. Sudan, which is not a party to the Statute, has refused to surrender him to the Court.

tribunals for Yugoslavia and Rwanda and the ICC. Their emergence was prompted by the need to increase the political acceptability and legitimacy of criminal courts in sensitive post-conflict situations where reliance upon purely national institutions could fuel tensions further. At the same time, a purely international solution would have run the risk of being too costly and protracted. A number of different models have been adopted in different situations.

The Special Court for Sierra Leone (SCSL)

This Court was established, following a violent civil war in Sierra Leone, in order to prosecute persons 'bearing the greatest responsibility for serious violations of international humanitarian law and Sierra Leonean law committed in the territory of Sierra Leone since 30 November 1996'.[63] It was established under an agreement between the United Nations and Sierra Leone of 16 January 2002. The Court has jurisdiction with regard to crimes against humanity; violations of Article 3 common to the Geneva Conventions and Additional Protocol II; other serious violations of international humanitarian law; and some crimes under Sierra Leonean law. Its judges are divided between two Trial Chambers, composed of three judges each, and an Appeals Chamber, composed of five judges. The Government of Sierra Leone appoints one judge for each of the Trial Chambers and two for the Appeals Chamber. The rest are appointed by the UN Secretary-General. The Appeals Chamber hears appeals from persons convicted by the Trial Chambers or from the Prosecutor on grounds of procedural error. It can affirm, reverse, or amend the Trial Chamber's judgment and, in doing so, should be guided by the jurisprudence of the Appeals Chamber of the ICTY and ICTR. Where Sierra Leonean law is concerned it should be guided by the decisions of the Supreme Court of Sierra Leone.[64] The Prosecutor, who is assisted by a Sierra Leonean Deputy Prosecutor, acts as an independent organ of the Court and is appointed for a three-year term by the UN Secretary-General. The SCSL has primacy over the national courts of Sierra Leone and, under Article 8 of its Statute, may request them to defer to its competence.

Subsequently, the Court indicted Libya's leader Muammar Gadaffi, who was killed before he could be brought to trial, and President Uhuru Kenyatta of Kenya and Deputy President William Ruto, whose trials are pending. Laurent Gbagbo was indicted while he was still President of Cote d'Ivoire and is now in ICC custody pending trial while his wife, Simone Gbagbo, who has also been indicted, has yet to be surrendered to the Court and may be tried in Cote d'Ivoire. Cote d'Ivoire is not a party to the Statute but accepted the jurisdiction of the Court on 18 April 2003. This acceptance was reaffirmed on 14 December 2010.

[63] SCR 1315 (2000). [64] Statute of the SCSL, Art 20.

Section 6(2) of the Statute of the Special Court mirrors equivalent provisions in the ICTY and ICTR Statutes and Article 27(2) of the ICC Statute to the effect that the official position of any accused persons, whether as head of State or Government or as a responsible Government official, shall not relieve them of criminal responsibility or mitigate punishment.

Since its establishment, the SCSL has prosecuted several leaders of the warring factions involved in the civil war in Sierra Leone, including the former President of Liberia, Charles Taylor, who was sentenced to 50 years in prison in 2012. He was indicted in 2003 while still serving as President of Liberia. The indictment contained charges of crimes against humanity and grave breaches of the 1949 Geneva Conventions committed with the purpose of obtaining access to the mineral wealth of Sierra Leone and destabilizing that State. Taylor applied to quash the indictment on the ground that, at the time it was issued, he was an incumbent head of State and, therefore, enjoyed full immunity from criminal prosecution. This was rejected by the Court on the basis that it was clear from Security Council Resolution 1315 that the Special Court was established by treaty for the purposes of fulfilling an international mandate and qualified, therefore, as an 'international criminal tribunal' before which a serving head of State can be tried.[65] These arguments are examined in more detail below.

The Extraordinary Chambers of Cambodia

In 2003, the UN General Assembly approved a draft Agreement between the UN and Cambodia providing for the establishment of Extraordinary Chambers in the courts of Cambodia with the aim of prosecuting leaders of the Khmer Rouge and others responsible for the crimes and serious violations of international humanitarian law committed during the period from 17 April 1975 and 6 January 1979. The Agreement was ratified by Cambodia on 19 October 1994. The jurisdiction of the Chambers is set out in a Cambodian law and covers genocide as defined in the 1948 Genocide Convention, crimes against humanity as defined in the ICC Statute, grave breaches of the 1949 Geneva Conventions, and certain other crimes as defined under Cambodian law. The Chambers apply both international and national law and this is reflected in their mixed composition with a majority of Cambodian judges and a smaller number of international judges.

[65] *Prosecutor v Taylor*, Decision on Immunity from Jurisdiction, Case No SCSL-2003-01-1 ICL 25 (SCSL 2004).

The Special Tribunal for Lebanon (STL)

In 2006, the UN Security Council adopted a resolution calling upon the Secretary-General to negotiate an agreement with the Government of Lebanon aimed at establishing a tribunal of an international character to prosecute those accused of assassinating Rafiq Hariri, the former Prime Minister of Lebanon. Following a report from the Secretary-General, the Council, acting under Chapter VII of the Charter, reached an agreement with Lebanon which established the STL. This agreement, together with the Statute of the STL, was annexed to the resolution.[66] The Tribunal applies Lebanese criminal law and is composed of a mixture of Lebanese and international judges (one Lebanese judge and two international judges in its Trial Chamber and two Lebanese judges and three international judges in its Appeals Chamber). The Tribunal enjoys primacy over local courts and has jurisdiction not only over those responsible for the assassination of Rafik Hariri but also with regard to those responsible for other attacks in Lebanon between 1 October 2004 and 12 December 2005. This date may be extended to encompass other attacks that are seen as connected and of a similar nature and gravity as the assassination by agreement between the parties and with the consent of the Security Council.

Other internationalized tribunals

In addition to the above, there have been a number of specialized courts and tribunals set up from time to time.[67] Such courts have often been established in connection with a period of UN interim administration of a territory which has experienced severe conflict or disturbance. These are essentially local courts, operating within a domestic framework but with some international judges. Examples of these are the Regulation 64 panels set up by the UN Interim Administration Mission in Kosovo (UNMIK),[68] the East Timor Special Panels for Serious Crimes established by the UN Transitional Administration (UNTAET) there, and the War Crimes Chambers set up under the auspices of the Office of the High Representative in Bosnia with the support of the Security Council.[69] The Iraqi High Tribunal established

[66] SCR 1757 (2007).

[67] A recent example are the Extraordinary African Chambers in the courts of Senegal. The Chambers were established by treaty between Senegal and the African Union for the purpose of prosecuting the 'person or persons' most responsible for international crimes committed in Chad between 1982 and 1990. On 2 July 2013, Hissene Habre, the former President of Chad was charged with crimes against humanity, torture, and war crimes.

[68] UNMIK Regulation 2000/64.

[69] SCR 1503 (2003).

under the authorization of the Coalition Provisional Authority[70] is of a slightly different order. It was established to hear crimes alleged against persons serving in the regime of the former Iraqi leader, Saddam Hussein. According to its 2005 Statute it has jurisdiction over genocide, crimes against humanity, and war crimes committed between 16 July 1968 and 1 May 2003. The definitions of the crimes, as incorporated into Iraqi law, are based upon the provisions of the ICC Statute. The Tribunal has primacy over national courts and is required to appoint international advisers to assist the Iraqi judges with respect to international law and the application of due process. In the first trial to be concluded by the Tribunal, the former Iraqi leader, Saddam Hussein, and seven others were convicted of crimes committed in Dujail in 1982. Saddam Hussein was sentenced to death and executed by hanging on 30 December 2006.

5. Immunities before International Courts

Personal immunity

In the *Arrest Warrant* case, the ICJ emphasized that immunity from criminal jurisdiction and individual criminal responsibility are separate concepts and that the former does not exonerate the person to whom it may apply. It noted that this fact, combined with the fact that the immunities enjoyed by a Minister for Foreign Affairs (or head of State or head of Government) may, in certain circumstances, not be a bar to criminal prosecution, means that such persons do not enjoy impunity. The circumstances listed in which immunity may not bar prosecution by the Court included proceedings before 'certain international criminal courts, where they have jurisdiction'.[71] In this connection the Court referred to the ICTY, the ICTR, and the ICC, noting in particular the terms of Article 27(2) of the ICC Statute.

As discussed in earlier parts of this book, the special position of heads of State and certain other very high-level representatives under international law is derived from well-settled principles as to the independence and equality of States and the resulting acceptance that no State should claim jurisdiction over another. In modern times, this has been further elaborated into a functional rationale by which such treatment, particularly with regard to personal immunities, is justified as necessary in order to enable such representatives to carry out

[70] Order No 48.

[71] *Arrest Warrant of 11 April 2000 (DRC v Belgium)* (2002) ICJ Rep 3. The other examples given were: prosecution before the individual's own State's courts; prosecution before a foreign court where a waiver has been given by the individual's State; and prosecution after the individual has left office in respect of acts committed prior to or subsequent to that period of office; and 'acts committed during that period of office in a private capacity'.

their functions free from interference. These justifications have been deployed largely within the context of proceedings before national courts. It has been argued, however, that such considerations do not become irrelevant merely because the court or tribunal seeking to exercise jurisdiction is of an international character.[72] On this basis, the extent to which immunity may still be a practical obstacle will depend upon the universality, constitution, and mandate of the court or tribunal concerned and, in particular, whether or not the relevant States are bound by provisions setting aside immunity.[73] A properly established international court which has been established with the consent of the relevant States should, in principle, require no further consent from those States. No question of immunity or waiver should arise, therefore, in regard to officials or former officials of those States. Where officials of States which have not consented are concerned, however, matters may be less straightforward. An important consideration in this regard is the fact that international courts do not generally possess their own enforcement machinery and, in practice, must rely upon State police and judicial authorities to arrest and transfer alleged criminals. In this context it is, therefore, necessary to consider not only whether the court itself may lawfully indict and try the individual concerned but also whether States may lawfully arrest and surrender such individuals to the requesting court or tribunal.

Immunity before the ICTY and ICTR

When establishing the ICTY and ICTR, the Security Council, acting under Chapter VII of the UN Charter, clearly incorporated the principle that the official position of the defendant should not be a bar to prosecution. It also required all States to cooperate with the Tribunals and comply with any requests for surrender. No reference was made in the relevant resolutions or Statutes to any exception for surrender requests relating to persons enjoying immunities. It is well settled that, in the event of a conflict between Member States' obligations under the UN Charter and their obligations under any

[72] See Akande, 'International Law Immunities and the International Criminal Court' (2004) 98 AJIL 407. See also Lynch and Misa Zgonec-Rozej, 'The ICC Intervention in Kenya', Chatham House (February 2013) and Misa Zgonec-Rozej, '*Kenya and the ICC: A Test for Both*' (Chatham House, 2013) where it is noted that the indictment of a president and vice-president could impede them in carrying out their official duties and that the range and importance of their role and functions make this a serious concern. Both accused have requested permission to be excused from continuous attendance at their trials in the Hague and, although the precise modalities have yet to be settled, it is possible that the sessions will be organized so as to ensure that the two leaders are not absent at the same time.

[73] See Dissenting Opinion of Judge Shahabuddeen in *Prosecutor v Krstic* ICTY (IT-98-33-T) 17 September 2003 where he noted that 'A presumption of continuance of their immunities as those exist under international law is only offset where some element in the decision to establish such a court shows that they agreed otherwise'.

other agreement, the former shall prevail.[74] A UN Member State is therefore, obliged to comply with ICTY and ICTR surrender requests even if such requests are in conflict with its duty to respect the immunities enjoyed by a particular individual. Conversely the Member State from which the immunity is derived is estopped from raising those immunities on behalf of the individual concerned, by reason of its obligations under the UN Charter.[75] This analysis is not entirely satisfactory in regard to the ICTY as some doubts have been raised as to whether the Federal Republic of Yugoslavia (FRY) itself was recognized as a UN Member State at the relevant time. It was, however, a party to the Dayton Accords, which imposed upon it a specific obligation to cooperate with the Tribunal.[76] Given the specific mandate of that Tribunal it would not, therefore, be unreasonable to assume that the FRY had waived any immunities in respect of officials whose surrender was requested. The FRY did in fact eventually cooperate, most notably with the surrender of the former President Milosevic in 2001,[77] and both Tribunals have, in practice, conducted proceedings with regard to several senior Government officials.[78]

Immunity before the ICC

The approach taken to immunity in the ICC Statute is more explicit, although not without potential for uncertainty in some areas. Article 27(2) provides expressly that immunities or special procedural rules 'which may attach to the official capacity of a person... shall not bar the Court from exercising its jurisdiction'. ICC States Parties must cooperate with the Court and surrender individuals in accordance with the Statute, without reservation.[79] On this basis, it is clear that State parties have agreed that the immunities which their officials, including heads of State, may enjoy will not bar prosecution before the ICC. As we have seen, States which are not party may, nevertheless, undertake to cooperate 'fully' with the ICC through unilateral declarations. It is reasonable to assume that such an undertaking will put a State in the same position as a State party in this regard.

However, Article 98(1) also provides that requests for surrender shall not proceed when they would:

> require the requested State to act inconsistently with its obligations under international law with respect to the State or diplomatic immunity of a person or property

[74] See UN Charter, Arts 25, 41, 49, and esp 103.

[75] See Cryer et al (n 28 above) at 439.

[76] Article IX Dayton Peace Accords, 21 November 1995.

[77] Milosevic was indicted by the ICTY while he was still President. See *Milosevic*, ICTY Decision on preliminary motions, Trial Chamber III, Decision of 8 November 2001, paras [226]–[33].

[78] See eg *Prosecutor v Kambanda* ICTR Trial Chamber, 14 September 1998.

[79] See Arts 86, 89, and 120.

of a third State, unless the Court can first obtain the cooperation of that third State for the waiver of the immunity.

The practice of States Parties suggests that the combined effect of Article 27(2) and Article 98(1) has been to create a regime by which ICC States Parties have agreed to relinquish all immunities in relation to ICC requests concerning their own officials[80] and representatives but remain bound to respect the relevant immunities of a State which is not party to the ICC Statute.[81] If, therefore, a requested State is faced with a request relating to the head of State of *another* State Party, there would be no need to obtain any waiver of the immunity enjoyed by that individual.[82] This conclusion is usually justified on the grounds that, by ratifying the Statute or undertaking to cooperate 'fully' with the ICC, States have effectively waived any immunities against ICC prosecution and that there are, therefore, no 'obligations under international law' in terms of Article 98(1) which can prevent surrender.[83]

Article 98(1) does, however, require States Parties to respect the immunities of the head of State (or other high-level official enjoying personal immunity) of a non-State Party and, unless that State agrees to waive immunity, surrender of such a person should not proceed. In the normal course of events, it is contemplated that the ICC will have obtained the necessary waiver, but, where such waiver has been refused, the position becomes complicated and somewhat uncertain.[84] In this connection, questions have arisen in relation to the Court's exercise of jurisdiction where a situation has been referred to it by the Security Council acting under Chapter VII of the UN Charter.

Where this occurs, the Court has jurisdiction even if the State or States concerned are not parties to the Statute and have not given consent. In these circumstances what is the position where the person whose arrest is

[80] See statement by Lord Avebury on behalf of the UK Government: 'in accepting Article 27, a State party to the ICC Statute has already agreed that the immunity of its representatives, including its head of State, may be waived before the International Criminal Court and that their status is not a barrier to their arrest and surrender to the court' (HL, Hansard vol 622, col 11 (12 February 2001).

[81] Under s 23 of the UK ICC Act 2001 it is provided that any immunity, including those arising under customary international law, attaching to a person by reason of a connection with a State Party to the ICC Statute does not bar surrender proceedings. If the immunity derives from a non-State Party, any waiver obtained by the ICC will be treated as extending to such proceedings.

[82] See Broomhall, *International Justice and the ICC: Between Sovereignty and the Rule of Law* (Oxford University Press, 2003) 144 where an informal paper produced by Canada and the UK for discussion at meetings of the ICC Preparatory Commission is referred to. The paper concluded, 'Having regard to the terms of the Statute, the Court shall not be required to obtain a waiver of immunity with respect to the surrender by one State party, of a head of State or government, or diplomat of another State party'.

[83] Others have reached the same conclusion but by a different interpretative route arguing that 'third State' in Art 98(1) refers only to non-States Parties. See Cryer et al (n 28 above) at 441.

[84] In such circumstances, s 23(4) of the UK ICC Act 2001 confers a discretion on the Secretary of State to discontinue the proceedings although it is unclear how this would operate in practice.

sought enjoys personal immunity under customary international law? This has already happened twice in the relatively short history of the Court with the issue of ICC arrest warrants in respect of the incumbent President Omar Al-Bashir of Sudan and the Libyan leader Muammar Gaddafi.[85] In both cases, the Security Council had referred the situation in those countries to the Prosecutor under Article 13 of the Statute.

It is clear that the Security Council reference confers on the Court, itself, the necessary authority to exercise its jurisdiction in accordance with the provisions of its Statute. This includes Article 27(2), which becomes thereby applicable to the office-holders of non-parties. This was certainly the view of the ICC Pre-Trial Chamber, which noted that 'Al-Bashir's official capacity as a sitting head of State does not exclude his criminal responsibility, nor does it grant him immunity against prosecution before the ICC'. It also noted that the Security Council had accepted that investigations and prosecutions arising from its referral will take place 'in accordance with the statutory framework provided for in the Statute, the Elements of Crimes and the Rules as a whole'.

It is arguable that such referral would, of itself, oblige the State of the office-holder concerned to cooperate with the Court to the same extent required of States Parties. In referring a situation to the ICC, the Security Council has always determined that the State concerned shall 'cooperate fully' with the Court.[86] This was the same formula adopted in creating the ICTY and ICTR[87] and reinforces the view that the State concerned must be bound *vis-à-vis* the Court to waive any immunity.

The position with regard to the surrender obligations of States Parties is is a little more problematic but the requirement to 'cooperate fully' carries the implication that the State concerned has been placed under an obligation identical to that of a State party.[88] If so, it could be said that the State concerned, like any State Party, can no longer claim immunity for its officials *vis-à-vis* other States Parties. In these circumstances, the requested State has no 'obligations under international law' in terms of Article 98(1) which would bar surrender and must comply with any request from the Court. This would be based upon the premise that such referral would require that the ICC's statutory framework as a whole must be applied to the State which is the subject of referral.[89] Widely different views have been expressed on this

[85] At the time of his indictment Gaddafi held no formal position within the Libyan Government but was generally accepted as *de facto* head of State. See Ch 2 at 45 above.

[86] See eg SCR 1593 (2005).

[87] See SCR 1970 (2001), para 5 and SCR 1953 (2005), para 2.

[88] See Dapo Akande 'The Legal Nature of Security Council Referrals to the ICC and its Impact on Al Bashir's Immunities' (2009) 7 JICJ 333 at 341–2.

[89] But see Gaeta, 'Does President Bashir Enjoy Immunity From Arrest?' (2009) 7(2) J Int'l Crim Justice 315.

issue but the ICC itself appears to have no doubts on the matter. In this context, its Pre-Trial Chamber has made findings of non-compliance by States Parties in regard to their failure to arrest President Bashir when visiting their territory.[90] The decision issued in relation to Malawi directly addressed the issue of his immunity as a serving head of State. It did not, however, base its decision in this regard upon the existence of the Security Council referral but, instead stated simply:

> customary international law creates an exception to head of State immunity when international courts seek a head of State's arrest for the commission of international crimes. There is no conflict between Malawi's obligations towards the court and its obligations under customary international law; therefore, article 98(1) of the Statute does not apply.[91]

It has been pointed out that there are a number of problems in asserting such a broad exception.[92] Most notably the fact that there is no internationally accepted definition of an 'international court' and, in principle, the Pre-Trial Chamber's reference could encompass a court established by only a few States. Even if it is accepted that such a general rule applies as regards prosecution by an international court itself, it is difficult to understand how national authorities can be relieved of their obligations in regard to non-States Parties. In this context, the question must arise as to what purpose Article 98(1) was intended to serve.

It is clear that the ICC may request non-States Parties to surrender alleged criminals who are in their territory. However, as such States are not bound by the Statute, they are not obliged to comply. In this connection it is notable that, in the two cases in which the Security Council has referred a situation to the Court, it has not sought to impose obligations on non-States Parties other than the State or States directly concerned. Instead, it has simply 'urged' them to cooperate.[93] Unlike the position in regard to the ICTY and ICTR, such States do not, therefore, have an obligation to arrest and surrender pursuant to their obligations under the UN Charter which could be said to prevail over conflicting obligations. The question arises, therefore, whether such States could lawfully choose to hand over the head of State concerned or whether they are, in fact, bound to respect the personal immunities he or she enjoys

[90] See eg Al Bashir (ICC–02/05-01/09)ICC PTC-I, 13 December 2011 (Malawi and Chad).

[91] At para 43. The PCT also referred to the growing number of States parties to the ICC Statute, concluding that a 'critical mass' had been reached whereby immunities under customary international law no longer applied in this context (para [42]).

[92] See Dapo Akande <http://www.ejiltalk.org/icc-issues>.

[93] See (2005) SCR 1593 at para [2].

under customary international law. The question is, as yet, unresolved and can only be clarified through further practice and jurisprudence. There is an argument, however, that a State which chose to surrender would not be committing a wrongful act under international law provided it is accepted that the Security Council reference has the effect of imposing the same obligations on the State of the office holder as does on a State party.

Immunity before the SCSL

The question as to whether or not a head of State may be entitled to personal immunity before an international tribunal was raised directly before the Special Court for Sierra Leone (SCSL).[94] In 2003, it issued a warrant for the arrest of Charles Taylor, who at the time was President of Liberia and was visiting Ghana for peace talks. He returned to Liberia and accepted a offer from Nigeria to grant him asylum provided he resigned from office and took no further part in Liberian politics.[95] However, before he stepped down from office, his lawyers made an application to declare the arrest warrant null and void on the ground that as a serving head of State he enjoyed full immunity from criminal prosecution.

It was argued on his behalf that the SCSL, which was set up by agreement between the United Nations and Sierra Leone, does not constitute an 'international criminal court' of the kind referred to in the *Arrest Warrant* case. In this connection, it was noted that exceptions to immunity can only be derived from other rules of international law which bind the State concerned. As we have seen, these may arise from the constitutive instrument establishing the court (for State Parties) or from Security Council resolutions under Chapter VII of the Charter. The SCSL was not authorized under Chapter VII, although the agreement establishing it was negotiated pursuant to Security Council Resolution 1315, which had reiterated that the situation in Sierra Leone continued to constitute a threat to international peace and security. It was contended that the Court's lack of explicit Chapter VII powers meant that its orders were no different in character from those of a national judicial authority.

The SCSL dismissed the application to quash the warrant, holding that it was an international court and, as such, entitled to prosecute serving heads of State.[96] In doing so it relied heavily on statements made by the ICJ in the

[94] *Prosecutor v Taylor* Decision on Immunity from Jurisdiction, Case No SCSL-2003-01-1ICL 25 (SCSL, 2004).

[95] He was arrested in 2006, after repeatedly failing to honour this undertaking, and transferred to the SCSL for trial.

[96] See also decision of ICC PTC in *Al Bashir* (discussed at pp 201–2 above).

Arrest Warrant case and by the UK House of Lords in *Pinochet No 3* which referred in very general terms to the possibility of prosecution before international courts. The wording of those statements suggests, however, that the courts concerned were merely observing that there are some international courts with the power to set aside personal immunities in accordance with settled principles of international law. It is far less likely that they were referring to a general principle of customary international law that such immunities do not apply before any court which can be characterized as an 'international court'. The fact that there is no universally accepted definition of an international criminal court makes it very doubtful that such an exception exists.

In dismissing the application, the SCSL also placed some weight on its view that 'the Agreement between the United Nations and Sierra Leone is thus an Agreement between all members of the United Nations and Sierra Leone'.[97] This view appeared to be based on the argument that, in authorizing the UN Secretary-General to negotiate the agreement with Sierra Leone, the Security Council was acting 'on behalf of all members of the United Nations'. The reasoning on this point is, again, open to doubt as the UN has a distinct legal personality and is not synonymous with its individual Member States.

It remains doubtful whether the SCSL had a specific grant of power to set aside the personal immunities of an incumbent head of State and Ghana was, therefore, probably correct in not acting on the arrest warrant.

6. Conclusion

Personal immunities, which can only protect an incumbent head of State or other very high-level representative, remain opposable against an international court unless the relevant States are bound by provisions setting aside such immunity in regard to that court. Even where such provision exists, as, for example, in the ICC Statute, personal immunities, are, as we have seen, still capable of causing difficulty, or, at least, uncertainty with regard to the surrender obligations of States *vis-à-vis* officials from non-States Parties. However, where the Security Council acting under Chapter VII has referred a matter to a court established under a treaty, it is reasonable for States to proceed on the basis that such referral would require the relevant court's statutory framework as a whole, including any provisions setting aside immunity, to be applied to the State which is the

[97] See *Prosecutor v Taylor* (see n 94 above) at para [38].

subject of referral. The provisions setting aside immunity in Article 27(2) of the ICC Statute do not distinguish between personal immunities and the functional immunity enjoyed by all officials and former officials in respect of acts carried out in their official capacity. In principle, therefore, it might be assumed that the same considerations should apply but, as we have seen, there is now considerable support for the view that functional immunity should not bar prosecution for serious international crimes even in national courts, although there remains some doubt as to whether such an exception has yet attained the status of a rule of customary international law. The arguments which are deployed to justify such a development would apply *a fortiori* to most international criminal courts, with the additional fact that the rationale underlying immunity *ratione materiae* makes less sense within the context of an international tribunal specifically set up to prosecute serious international crimes.

Functional immunity exists to ensure that individual officials are not held responsible in foreign courts for acts which are, in effect, those of their State and to prevent the circumvention of the immunity of that State through proceedings brought against those who act on its behalf. In this way it prevents national courts from exercising jurisdiction over the acts of a foreign State. Since the Nuremberg judgment it has been generally accepted that State officials, including heads of State and other high-level officials, bear personal responsibility under international law for certain international crimes.[98] Moreover, one of the key purposes of immunity *ratione materiae*—to prevent the conduct of one State from being judged by another—may be significantly diminished in the context of an independent international judicial body with jurisdiction and a specific mandate to prosecute crimes universally condemned by all States and which, it is widely recognized, all States have a legal interest in suppressing. This is in contrast to the modern rationale underlying personal immunity which is based upon the practical and sometimes urgent necessity to ensure the effective conduct of relations between States. Any trial, whether before a foreign or international court, is capable of impeding a head of State or other senior representative in the exercise of his or her functions.

The practice of international courts and tribunals from the Nuremberg Military Tribunal (IMT) to the ICC tends to support the inherent inapplicability of immunity *ratione materiae* to international crimes prosecuted before them. In the *Blaskic* case[99], the ICTY has specifically held that there is no functional immunity under international law for genocide, crimes against

[98] This judgment is sometimes cited in support of the proposition that functional immunity can no longer apply to the prosecution of such crimes in national courts but is far more apposite in its proper context of prosecution before international courts.

[99] *Prosecutor v Blaskic* (ICTY) IT-95-14 AR 108 (1997); 110 ILR 607.Ugiti dolorem ullum eos ut

humanity, or war crimes. It is reasonably clear, therefore, that even, in the absence of specific provisions setting aside such immunity, immunity *ratione materiae* would not bar the prosecution of a former head of State or other high-level representative before an international court with the appropriate jurisdiction.

The question of whether States could lawfully arrest and surrender officials or former officials to the ICC where a non-State Party has actively invoked functional immunity on their behalf is less clear. In principle, the same considerations as for personal immunity would apply. Again, Article 98(1) of the ICC Statute makes no distinction, referring to 'State or diplomatic immunity of a person or property of a third State', and that surrender should not proceed if it would require the requested State to act inconsistently with regard to its obligations in that respect. As we have seen, however, a State's obligations in regard to functional immunity where the prosecution of international crimes is concerned is now the subject of debate. While many States remain unwilling to prosecute former high level foreign officials in their own domestic courts, it is clear that some no longer consider functional immunity to be an obstacle in such circumstances.

Selected Bibliography

BOOKS AND ARTICLES

Akande, 'International Law Immunities and the International Criminal Court' (2004) 98 AJIL 407

Akande, 'The Legal Nature of Security Council Referrals to the ICC and its impact on Al Bashir's Immunities' (2009) 7 Journal International Criminal Justice 333

Akande and Shah, 'International Crimes, Human Rights Violations and Foreign Domestic Courts' (2010) 21 EJIL 815

Alebeek, van, 'The Pinochet Case: International Human Rights Law on Trial' (2000) 71 BYIL 29

Alebeek, van, *The Immunity of States and Their Officials in International Criminal Law and International Human Rights Law* (Oxford University Press, 2008)

Aust, *Modern Treaty Law and Practice* (3rd edn, Cambridge University Press, 2006) 13

Baldwin, 'The Proposed Trial of the Former Kaiser' (2010) reprint from (1919) 29 Yale Law Journal 75

Barker, 'State Immunity, Diplomatic Immunity, and Act of State: A Triple Protection Against Legal Action?' (1998) 47 ICLQ 950

Barker, 'The Future of Former Head of State Immunity after ex parte Pinochet' (1999) 48 ICLQ 937

Beigbeder, *Judging War Criminals: The Politics of International Justice* (Macmillan Press,1999)

Bianchi, 'Immunity Versus Human Rights: The *Pinochet* Case' (1999) 10 EJIL 237

Broomhall, *International Justice and the ICC: Between Sovereignty and the Rule of Law* (Oxford University Press, 2003)

Brownlie, *Principles of Public International Law* (7th edn, Oxford University Press, 2008)

Buzzini, 'Lights and Shadows of Immunities and Inviolability of State Officials in International Law: Some Comments on the *Djibouti v France* Case' (2009) 22 Leiden Journal of Int'l Law 455

Byers, 'The Law and Politics of the *Pinochet* Case' (2000) 10 Duke J Comp and Int'l Law 415

Caplan, 'State Immunity, Human Rights and Ius Cogens: A Critique of the Normative Hierarchy Theory' (2003) 97 AJIL 741

Cassese, 'When May Senior State Officials Be Tried for International Crimes? Some Comments on the *Congo v Belgium* Case' (2002) 13 EJIL 853

Collins, 'Recovery of Stolen Property From Deposed Rulers', in Dominice, Parry, and Reymond (eds), *Etudes de droit international en l'honneur de Pierre Lalive* (1993) 221

Cosnard, 'Quelques observations sur les decisions de la Chambre des Lords dans l'affaire *Pinochet*' (1999) 103 RGDIP 309

Crawford, *The International Law Commission's Articles on State Responsibility* (Cambridge University Press, 2002)

Crawford, *The Creation of States in International Law* (2nd edn, Oxford University Press, 2006)

Cryer, 'Current Developments, Public International Law: II Implementation of the ICC Statute in England and Wales' (2002) 51 ICLQ 733

Cryer, Friman, Robinson, and Wilmshurst, *International Criminal Law and Procedure* (2nd edn, Cambridge University Press, 2011)

Damgaard, *Individual Criminal Responsibility for Core International Crimes: Selected Pertinent Issues* (Springer, 2008)

Denza, 'Ex parte Pinochet: Lacuna or Leap?' (1999) ICLQ 949

Denza, *Diplomatic Law* (3rd edn, Oxford University Press, 2008)

Dominice, 'Quelques observations sur l'immunite de jurisdiction penale de l'ancien Chef d'Etat' (1999) 103 RGDIP 297

Fox, 'The Pinochet (No3) Case' (1999) 48 ICLQ 687

Fox, 'Access to Justice and State Immunity' (2001) 117 LQR 10

Fox, 'The Resolution of the Institute of International Law on the Immunities of Heads of State and Government' (2002) 119 ICLQ 51

Fox, *The Law of State Immunity* (2nd edn, Oxford University Press, 2008)

Franey, *Immunity, Individuals and International Law* (Lambert Academic Publishing, 2011)

Gaeta, 'Ratione Materiae Immunities of Former Heads of State and International Crimes: The Hissene Habre Case' (2003) J Int'l Criminal Justice 186

Gaeta, 'Does President Bashir Enjoy Immunity from Arrest?' (2009) 7(2) J Int'l Criminal Justice 315

Gallagher, 'Universal Jurisdiction in Practice: Efforts to hold Donald Rumsfeld and Other High-level United States Officials Accountable for Torture' (2009) 7 J Int'l Criminal Justice 1087

Hafner, Kohen, and Breau (eds), *State Practice Regarding State Immunities: La pratique des Etats concernant les immunites des Etats* (Martinus Nijhoff, 2006)

Henzelin, 'L'immunite penale des chefs d'Etats en matiere financiere' (2002) RSDIE 179

Higgins, *Problems and Process: International Law and How We Use It* (Clarendon Press, 1994)

Jennings, 'Jurisdiction and Immunity in the ICJ decision in the *Yerodia* Case' (2002) 4 International Law Forum 99

Jennings and Watts, *Oppenheim's International Law* vol 1 (9th edn, Longman, 1992)

Jorgensen, *The Responsibility of States for International Crimes* (Oxford University Press, 2000)

Kalb, 'Immunities, Special Missions' *Max Planck Encyclopedia of Public International Law* V (Oxford University Press) 94–8

Kaleck, 'From Pinochet to Rumsfeld: Universal Jurisdiction in Europe 1998–2008' (2009) 30 Mich J Int'l L 927

Keitner, 'Foreign Official Immunity and the "Baseline" Problem' (2011) 80 Fordham Law Rev 605

Kiss (ed), *Repertoire de la pratique francaise en matiere de droit international* (1965) III, 262

Kofele-Kale, *International Law of Responsibility for Economic Crimes: Holding Heads of State and Other High Ranking Officials Individually Liable for Acts of Fraudulent Enrichment* (Kluwer Academic Publishers, 1995)

Koh, 'Foreign Official Immunity After Samantar: A US Government Perspective' (2011) 44 Vand J of Transnational Law 1141

Koller, 'Immunities of Foreign Ministers: Paragraph 61 of the Yerodia Judgment as it pertains to the Security Council and the International Criminal Court' (2004) 20 American U Int'l Law Rev 7

Lewis, *The Trial of Mary, Queen of Scots: A Brief History With Documents* (Bedford/St Martins, 1999)

Lutz and Reiger (eds), *Prosecuting Heads of State* (Cambridge University Press, 2009)

Mallory, 'Resolving the Confusion over Head of State Immunity: The Defined Right of Kings' (1986) 86 Col Law Rev 169

McGregor, 'State Immunity and *Ius Cogens*' (2006) 55 ICLQ 437

Meagher, 'Act of State and Sovereign Immunity: The Marcos Cases' (1988) 29 Harvard Int Law J 127

Murty, *The International Law of Diplomacy* (Martinus Nijhoff, 1989)

O'Donnell, 'Certain Criminal Proceedings in France (Republic of Congo v France) and Head of State Immunity: How Impenetrable Should the Immunity Veil Remain?' (2008) 26 Boston University Int'l Law J 375

O'Keefe, 'The European Convention on State Immunity and International Crimes' (1999) 2 Cambridge YB European Legal Studies 507

O'Keefe, 'State Immunity and Human Rights: Heads and Walls, Hearts and Minds' (2011) 44 Vanderbilt J of Transnational Law 999

O'Keefe and Tams (eds), *The United Nations Convention on Jurisdictional Immunities of States and Their Property: A Commentary* (Oxford University Press, 2012)

O'Neill, 'A New Customary Law of Head of State Immunity?: Hirohito and Pinochet' (2002) 38 Stanford Law J of Int'l Law 289

Oppenheim's International Law (9th edn, Oxford University Press, 1992) 1033–44

Rousseau, *Droit international public* IV (1980)

Salmon, *Manuel de droit diplomatique* (Bruylant, 1986) 591–610

Sanger, 'Immunity of State Officials from the Criminal Jurisdiction of a Foreign State' (2013) 62 ICLQ 193

Satow's Guide to Diplomatic Practice (5th edn, Longman, 1979) (ed Gore-Booth)

Satow's Diplomatic Practice (6th edn, Oxford University Press, 2009) (ed Roberts)

Stephens, 'The Modern Common Law of Foreign Official Immunity' (2011) 79 Fordham Law Rev 2669

Stewart, 'The Immunity of State Officials Under the UN Convention on Jurisdictional Immunities of States and Their Property' (2011) 44 Vanderbilt J of Transnational Law 1047

Talmon, *Recognition of Governments in International Law* (Oxford University Press, 1998)

Thalmann, 'French Justice's Endeavours to Substitute for the ICTR' (2008) 6 J Int'l Criminal Justice 995

Tomuschat, 'The International Law of State Immunity and its Development by National Institutions' (2011) 44 Vanderbilt J of Transnational Law 1105

Totten, 'Head of State and Foreign Official Immunity in the United States After Samantar: A Suggested Approach' (2011) 34 Fordham Int Law J 332

Trapp, *State Responsibility for International Terrorism* (Oxford University Press, 2011)

Tunks, 'Diplomats or Defendants? Defining the Future of Head of State Immunity' (2002) 52 Duke Law J 651

Varughese George, 'Head of State Immunity in the United States Courts: Still Confused After All These Years' (1995) 64 Fordham Law Rev 1051

Warbrick, 'The Pinochet Cases in the UK' (1999) 2 YB International Humanitarian Law 91

Warbrick, 'Immunity and International Crimes in English Law' (2004) 53 ICLQ 769

Watts, 'The Legal Position in International Law of Heads of States, Heads of Governments and Foreign Ministers' (1994) 247 III Recueil des Cours

Watts and Foakes, 'Heads of Governments and Other Senior Officials' and 'Heads of State' *Max Planck Encyclopedia of International Law* IV, 754–64

Weller, 'On the Hazards of Foreign Travel for Dictators and Other International Criminals' (1999) 75(3) International Affairs 599

Whomersley, 'Some Reflections on the Immunity of Individuals for Official Acts' (1992) ICLQ 848

Wickremasinghe, 'Immunities Enjoyed by Officials of States and International Organisations' in *International Law* (Cambridge University Press, 2003) (ed Evans)

Wilmshurst, 'Executive Certificates in Foreign Affairs: The United Kingdom' (1986) 35 ICLQ 157

Wirth, 'Immunity for Core Crimes? The ICJ's Judgment in the *Congo v Belgium* Case' (2002) 13 EJIL 877

Wood, 'The Immunity of Official Visitors' (2012) 16 Max Planck Yearbook of United Nations Law 35

Wouters, 'The Judgment of the ICJ in the *Arrest Warrant* Case: Some Critical Remarks' (2003) 16 Leiden Journal of Int'l Law 256

Wuerth, 'Foreign Official Immunity Determinations in the US Courts: The Case Against the State Department' (2011) 51 Vanderbilt J of Transnational Law 915

Wuerth, 'Pinochet's Legacy Reassessed' (2012) 106 AJIL 731

Young, 'Immunity in Hong Kong for Kleptocrats and Human Rights Violators' (2011) 41 Hong Kong Law J 421

Zappala, 'Do Heads of State Enjoy Immunity from Jurisdiction for International Crimes?: The *Gadaffi* Case before the French *Cour de Cassation*' (2001) 12 EJIL 595

Zegfeld, 'The *Bouterse* Case' (2001) 32 Netherlands YBIL 97

SELECT DOCUMENTS

Institut de droit international, 'Immunities from Jurisdiction and Execution of Heads of State and of Government in International Law' (2000/2001) 69 AIDI 441–755

ILC Secretariat Memorandum, 'Immunity of State Officials from Foreign Criminal Jurisdiction' (31 March 2008) UN Doc A/CN.4/596

ILC Special Rapporteur Kolodkin, *Preliminary Report on Immunity of State Officials from Foreign Criminal Jurisdiction* (29 May 2008) UN Doc A/CN.4/601

ILC Report on the Work of its Sixtieth Session (2008) UN Doc A/63/10

ILC Special Rapporteur Kolodkin, *Second Report on Immunity of State Officials from Foreign Criminal Jurisdiction* (10 June 2010) UN Doc A/CN.4/631

ILC Special Rapporteur Kolodkin, *Third Report on Immunity of State Officials from Foreign Criminal Jurisdiction* (24 May 2011) UN Doc A/CN.4/646

ILC Report on the Work of its Sixty-Third Session (2011) UN Doc A/66/10

ILC Special Rapporteur Escobar Hernandez, *Preliminary Report on Immunity of State Officials from Foreign Criminal Jurisdiction* (31 May 2012) UN Doc A/CN.4/654

ILC Special Rapporteur Escobar Hernandez, *Second Report on Immunity of State Officials from Foreign Criminal Jurisdiction* (. ..) UN Doc A/CN.4/661

ILC *Immunity of State Officials from Foreign Criminal Jurisdiction.* Text of draft articles 1, 3, and 4 provisionally adopted by the Drafting Committee at the Sixty-fifth Session A/CN.4/L.814.

Netherlands Advisory Committee on Issues of Public International Law (CAVV) Report No 20 (May 2011) and Netherlands Government Response

Index

abdication 32, 48, 106
abduction *see* **kidnapping**
Abdullah, King of Saudi Arabia 107
absolute doctrine
  State immunity 16
absolute personal immunity 88
Abu Dhabi 47, 84
  ruler of 46–7, 84, 88, 107
abuse of privilege 60
accidents 145
  investigation of 106
accountability
  heads of State 187
  violations of international law 3
'act of public power' 143
act of State 31, 36, 137, 147, 171, 178
***acta iure imperii/acta iure gestionis* distinction** 83, 88
acting in accordance with orders
  war crimes defence 184
acts of a private character 8
Adamov, Evgeny 177
adjudication 86
administrative proceedings
  Foreign Minister 124–5
  head of Government 124–5
  heads of State 124–5
  immunity from 83–98
Advisory Committee on Issues of Public International Law (CAVV) 135, 156
affiliation proceedings 91
agencies
  State 139
aggravated damages 169
aggression 180
Ahmadinejad, Mahmoud 60
aircrafts 182
Al Bashir, Omar 3, 200–1
al-Assad, Bashar 34
al-Assad, Hafez [1930–2000] 34
Al-Khasawneh, Judge 79
Al-Megrahi, Abdelbaset [1953–2012] 161
Albert, King of Belgium [1875–1934] 50
Albert II, King of the Belgians 106
Algeria 156
Alien Tort Statute (ATS) 170–1
Allende, Salvador Guillermo [1908–73] 56
Allied Governments
  diplomatic privileges granted to 50
Almatov, Zokirjon 157
Almog, Doron 134
ambassadors 144–5
  equated with foreign heads of State 99
  family members forming part of household 104, 108
  household 104
  newly appointed 43
  respect and 68
Amin, Idi [1925–2003] 34
Andorra
  head of State 29–30
Anglo-American Act of State doctrine 137
apartheid 180
appointment
  head of State 34
archives
  inviolability of 77
Aristide, Jean-Bertrand 31, 44–5, 52–3, 61, 114
armed conflict 37, 49
arrest 77
  Germany 160
***Arrest Warrant* case** 5, 22, 25–6, 127, 130, 132, 136, 197
arrest warrants 159 *see also* **European arrest warrant**
  International Criminal Court (ICC) 200
Articles on State Responsibility (ILC Articles) 179–80
Asquith, Herbert Henry [1852–1928] 60
assault 103, 169
assets
  enemy property 101
assumption of office
  lack of formal 45
asylum 166
attribution of conduct to State 138
Audiencia Nacional 24, 83
Australia 72–3, 92, 99, 105
  former heads of State 137
Austria 83, 90–1, 106, 145

authority
presumption of 39
autonomy
federal States 46
Aylwin, Patricio 56

Baez, Buenaventura [1812–84] 166
baggage
customs 101–2
Banda, Hastings [1898–1997] 34
bank accounts
freezing 100
Bank of Credit and Commerce International (BCCI) 84, 88
bankrupt estates 100
banners 73
Barak, Ehud 26, 130
Bayelsa State 48
Beatrix, Queen of the Netherlands 106
Belgium 99, 106, 124, 155
exile of king 50
Ben Said, Khaled 158
Benedict XVI, Pope 106
Benes, Edvard [1884–1948] 52
Bernard, Justice Henri 186
Bhutan 34–5
Bhutto, Benazir [1953–2007] 177
bilateral relations 10
bilateral treaties 39
Bo Xilai 26
body 'politic' 12
bona vacantia 100
Bongo, Ali 67, 80
Bosnia 190
US intervention in 38
War Crimes Chamber 196
Bouterse, Desi 155
breach of promise 16, 90, 98
Brunei, Sultan of 68
Bush, President George Herbert Walker 38
Bush, President George Walker 38, 156

cabinet ministers 132
Cambodia
crimes against humanity 195
Cameroon 40
Canada 61
Canadian rebellion (1837) 138
capacity
to enter legal relations 30
Caroline, The case 138
Castro, Fidel 82
Cedras, Joseph Raoul 114
ceremonial 62
certificates of recognition
FCO 47–8
Chad 155
Charles, Prince of Wales 105–6
skiing accident in Switzerland 106
Charles I, Emperor of Austria [1887–1922] 90
children 104, 108
removal from jurisdiction 146–7
Chile 55–6
torture 150–1
China 26, 43, 65, 73, 170
Minister for Commerce 131
civil claims 106–8
torture 170
civil law
immunity 84, 90
civil liability
criminal responsibility compared 141–2
international crimes 169–72
civil partners 104
civil proceedings *see* heads of State immunity from civil jurisdiction
Foreign Minister 124–5
heads of Government 124–5
heads of State 85–96
immunity 9, 83–98, 166–72
refusing immunity in 173
civil war
Sierra Leone 194–5
Clinton, President William Jefferson 38
coats of arms 61
codification
absence of 18
collective heads of State 29
colonial domination by force 180
Colonial Office 16
comity 109
commercial activities 83, 92, 94
commercial law 83
Committee on Jurisdictional Immunities of States and their Property 115
Commonwealth 30, 112
Commonwealth Relations Office 112
communication
freedom of 60–1
Communist Party
General Secretary 111
complementarity
International Court of Justice 192
Conference of Heads of State of Africa and France 65
Conference of Rulers 33–4

Congo *see* **Democratic Republic of the Congo**
Congress
power to declare war 37
Congress of Vienna 182
conspiracy 57
to torture 151
Constantine II, King of Greece 33
constituent territories
federal States 46–8
constitution
State 29
constitutional monarchy 186
constitutional role
head of State 110–1
consular immunity 162
Convention against Torture and Other Cruel, Inhuman or Degrading Treatment or Punishment (United Nations Convention against Torture) 144, 151–2, 155–6, 169–70, 187
Convention for the Protection of All Persons from Enforced Disappearance 153, 187
Convention on the Jurisdictional Immunities of States and Their Property 164
Convention on the Prevention and Punishment of the Crime of Genocide 186
Convention on the Prevention and Punishment of Crimes Against Internationally Protected Persons, including Diplomatic Agents (1973) 119–20, 126
Convention on the Suppression and Punishment of the Crime of Apartheid 187
Convention on Special Missions (1969) 113, 115–6, 118, 120, 122, 125–6
convictions
in absentia 158
Cook, Robin [1946–2005] 52
copyright
breach of 107
corruption 177
counter-measures
legal injury 100
counterclaims 91, 98
courtesies
international 68
Credentials *see* **Letters of Credence**
crimes
committed in forum State 6, 160–5
crimes against humanity 149, 171
Cambodia 195
international crimes 6, 82, 183–4
ordinary crimes 28, 148–50, 160–1, 154
Sierra Leone 194–5
Yugoslavia 189–90
criminal jurisdiction 23
exemption from local 13
immunity from foreign 21
criminal proceedings 176
comparison with civil proceedings 122, 141–2
Foreign Minister 123–4
foreign State officials 147–65
heads of Government 123–4
heads of State 124
immunity from 81–3
criminal responsibility
civil liability compared 141–2
State 141
Croatia 190
Crown Prosecution Service 56
cruel, inhuman, or degrading treatment or punishment 171
Cuba 82
customary international law 13, 23–5, 102, 108–9, 134, 154, 157, 170, 172
customs 101–2
exemption from inspection 102, 126
customs duties
exemption from 101–2
Cyprus 34

Dah, Ely Ould 158
Dalai Lama
no general recognition of 43
damages
international crimes 3
Dayton Accords 199
de Gaulle, Charles [1890–1970] 52, 61
De Legationibus 13
declaratory judgments 91
defamation 70, 146
Defence Ministers 25–6
comparison with Foreign Minister 26, 130–1
immunities 130–1
similarity to Foreign Minister 26, 130–1
defences
war crimes 184
defendant
State as 85–6
Delvalle, Eric Arturo 52
Democratic Republic of the Congo 23, 66–7, 80, 120, 128, 130, 134, 158
immunity of Vice President 130

departure
facilitating for Foreign Ministers 126
facilitating for heads of Government 126
deposition
head of State 48–53
deputies
head of State 32
deputy heads of State 32
designated heads of State 31–2
detention 77
dignity 15, 61–76
appropriate steps to prevent attack 67, 74
attacks on 64–5, 68
duty to protect 62, 74
foreign heads of State 69–71
Foreign Ministers 118–20
foreign missions 72
heads of Government 118–20
heads of State 3, 68
impairment 72
private litigation 3–4, 6
protecting 6
service of legal process 78, 96
specific offences or penalties 69–70, 75–6, 119, 148, 151, 157–8, 182, 186–7, 192
violation of 63
Dikko, Umaro 161–2
Diplomatic agents 4, 21, 62, 65, 75, 77, 88, 97, 101–2, 109, 119–20, 126, 135
Diplomatic business 111
diplomatic envoys 13, 15
diplomatic immunity 9, 13, 162, 168
akin to head of State immunity 43–7, 54, 67–8, 84, 88, 92, 102
common origin 11, 42, 90, 95
exceptions 92–3
former diplomats 9, 137, 140, 143
waiver 97–8
diplomatic missions 60, 93–4, 99, 105
immunity 83
diplomatic relations 19
severance 159
diplomatic representatives
appointment and reception 40–2
diplomats 9, 78, 146
family 95–6, 104
immunity 84, 97
kidnapping 74
scope of protection 95
Director of Public Prosecutions 144
District of Columbia Code 73
divine appointment
sovereign 12
divorce proceedings 84, 146–7
Djibouti 65–6, 79, 173
Djukanovic, Milo 46
documents
inviolability of 77
Dominican Republic 166
drug trafficking 176
dues
exemption from 101–2
Dutch Penal Code 1858 183
Duvalier, Jean-Claude 34, 178

East Timor 72
East Timor Special Panels for Serious Crimes 196
Eastern Europe
absolute doctrine 17
Edward VII, King of England [1841–1910] 60
Eichmann, Adolf [1906–62] 149–50
Elba 182
election
head of State 34
Elizabeth I, Queen of England [1533–1603] 13
embarrassment 4
Employment Minister
immunities 130
endorsement
by ICJ 24
specific rules 22–9
enemy property
assets 101
enforced disappearance 153
enforcement proceedings *see* **immunity from**
international arrest warrant 121
England
relationship with Scotland 14
entourage
of head of State 6, 102–8
entry
facilitating for Foreign Ministers 126
facilitating for heads of Government 126
envoys 105
equality of States 4, 16, 179, 183, 197
Equatorial Guinea 24, 67, 80, 178
espionage 163
Ethiopia
Italian invasion of 51
European arrest warrant 163
European Convention on State Immunity (1972) 165
European Court of Human Rights 70, 165
European Court of Justice (ECJ) 58–9
European Economic Community (EEC)
treaty establishing 39

European Union (EU) 59
obligations on member States 59–60
senior officials 1
evidence
sought through diplomatic channels 66
exchange of notes 39
execution
against property of heads of State 62
immunity from *see* **immunity** from execution
Executive
immunity from 88
role of 53–5
executive branch, role of 53–5, 146
former heads of State 145
sitting heads of State 54
UK practice 53–5
US practice 58, 145–6
exemptions
Foreign Ministers 125–6
heads of Government 125–6
exile, position of head of State 31, 34, 43, 45, 48, 50–3, 114
belligerent occupation 49–52
family members and Government officials 51
heads of State 45, 48–53
internal opposition 48, 52
problems associated with 52
prolonged 50–1
express waiver 98
expression
freedom of 70
expropriation 92
extortion 74
extra-territorial jurisdiction 2
international crime 187
international crimes 153
extradition 3, 27–8, 55–7, 145, 153, 155
treaties 183
'extrajudicial killing' 171
Extraordinary Chambers of Cambodia 195
'extraordinary rendition' 162

Fahd Bin Abdul Aziz, King of Saudi Arabia 68
Faisal, King of Saudi Arabia [1906–75] 54
false name
immunity and 98
Falun Gong 79, 170
family life 91
family members
accompanying head of State 2, 4, 6, 32, 51, 68, 94, 102–9, 126–7
ambassador's family analogy with 104, 108
diplomats 95–6, 104
exiled heads of State 51
heads of Government and Foreign Ministers 126–7
heads of State 4, 6, 59, 102–9
household, meaning of 105
immunity 103–9
private visits 15, 25, 35, 58, 75, 105, 108, 118, 120, 124–7
spouses 103–8
unaccompanied by head of State 103
Federal Republic of Germany 10, 143, 148
Federal Republic of Yugoslavia (FRY) 199
federal States 46–8
Federated Malay States *see* **Malaysia**
financial misconduct 176–7
First World War *see* **World War I**
flag burning 72
flags 61, 73
foreign affairs 36
Foreign and Commonwealth Office (FCO) 47, 56, 131, 134, 157
certificates of recognition 47–8
foreign courts 83
immunity from suit before 80–98
foreign criminal jurisdictions
limitations on immunity from 132
foreign heads of State 69, 89
ambassadors equated with 99
immunity 91–6
insulting 70
protection of 50, 74–6
foreign jurisdiction
immunity from criminal 21
foreign military bases 146
Foreign Ministers 1, 5, 20–2, 24–5, 35, 39, 78
changing role of 116
civil and administrative proceedings 124–5
criminal proceedings 123–4
exemptions and privileges 125–6
facilitating entry and departure of 126
family 126–7
freedom of communication 117–8
freedom of movement 117
ICJ ruling on status of 120–1
immunities 25, 79, 123, 130
immunity from suit before foreign courts 122–3
inviolability 120–2
jurisdictional immunities 23, 61, 66–7, 76, 86
official visits 127
position in international law 131
powers 112–3
private visits 127

Foreign Ministers (*cont.*):
protection of dignity, person and property 118–20
recognition 113–4
role of powers 111–2
similarity to Defence Minister 26
foreign missions
dignity 72
protecting 71
Foreign Sovereign Immunities Act 1976 (US) 17, 58, 93, 139, 171
foreign States
recognizing 36
form of address 61
former diplomats 9
former heads of State 6, 28
immunity 57, 84
international courts 6
reluctance to prosecute 157–8
status of 55–8
Former Yugoslav Republic of Macedonia 189
forms and titles 4, 29–33, 45, 110
heads of Government and Foreign Ministers 29–36, 61
heads of State 29–36, 61
forum State
crimes committed in 160–5
Fourth Geneva Convention 130
France 23, 65–7, 85, 90–1, 157–8, 161, 173, 178
arrest warrants 159
nuclear tests 40
refusal of entry into 58
Franco, General Francisco [1892–1975] 33
Free French 52
Free Tibet protests 73
freedom of communication 60–1
heads of Government and Foreign Ministers 117–8
freedom of expression 70
freedom of movement 58–60
heads of Government and Foreign Ministers 117
heads of State 58–60, 117
special missions 117
freezing orders 177
'Full Powers' 39
functional immunity 23, 59, 85, 137–40, 148, 150, 153–4, 167, 172–5, 203, 205
crimes committed in forum state 160–5
distinguished from personal immunity 6, 16, 18, 25–6, 28, 32, 49, 78, 80–6, 90–1, 95–6, 124–5, 128–31, 133
exceptions 6, 83, 92–3, 95, 160
international crimes 3, 154–7
international courts 197–204
necessity to invoke 172–5
rationale 6–11, 18, 20–4, 35, 49, 81, 84–6, 88, 92, 115–6, 129, 131–2, 149, 153, 159, 161–3, 172, 174
relation to State immunity 8–9, 16–7, 26, 47–8, 55, 83, 85–90, 95, 99, 109, 130, 137–9, 144, 147, 150, 152, 161, 164–5, 167–9, 171
relation to State responsibility 139–41, 179–81

Gabon 67, 80
Gadaffi, Muammar [1942–2011] 3, 45, 59
Gantz, Benny 134
Gbagba, Laurent 3
Geneva Conventions 187
breaches of 188–90, 195
genocide 149, 155, 180
individual responsibility for 189–90
Rwanda 158, 191
Yugoslavia 189–90
Gentili, Alberico [1552–1608] 13
German Democratic Republic 147–8
Germany 149–50, 152, 155, 160, 166 *see also* **Federal Republic of Germany; German Democratic Republic**
gift 100
'Glorious Revolution' (1688) 52
goods
customs 101
Gorbachev, Mikhail 157
government affairs
conducting from distance 61
Government ministers
distinguishing between different 131
Governments
competing 44
recognition of States compared to recognition of 43
recognizing 36
waiver of immunity 97–8
Governors
immunity 48
Governors-General 30
Greece 34
abolition of monarchy 33
Greenpeace 161
Grenada
US intervention in 38
Grotius, Hugo [1583–1645] 13
guarantee
office of head of State 34

Guatemala 74
murder of West German ambassador in 74

Habre, Hissene case 3, 155
Haile Selassie, Emperor of Ethiopia [1892–1975] 51
Haiti 31, 44–5, 53, 83, 176–8
rival Prime Ministers in 114
Hans-Adam II, Prince of Liechtenstein 91, 107
Hariri, Rafiq [1944–2005]
assassination of 196
Hassan II, King of Morocco [1929–99] 70
Hatton, Sir Christopher [1540–91] 15
headquarters
UN 60
head of State immunity 43–7, 54, 67–8, 84, 88, 92, 102
rationale 121, 125, 137–8, 152–3, 162, 166, 197, 204
heads of Government
changing role of 116
civil and administrative proceedings 124–5
criminal proceedings 123–4
exemptions and privileges 125–6
facilitating entry and departure of 126
family 126–7
freedom of communication 117–8
freedom of movement 117
Haiti 114
head of State as 36
head of State distinguished 110
heads of State compared 114–7
immunity 122
from suit before foreign courts 122–3
inviolability 120–2
jurisdictional immunities 23, 61, 66–7, 76, 86, 96
official visits 122, 127
Papua New Guinea 114
position in international law 131
powers 112–3
private visits 122–3, 127
protection of dignity, person and property 118–20
recognition 113–4
role and powers 112–3
heads of State
absolute personal immunity 28, 78, 80, 88, 91
authority to waive 97
dignity, duty to prevent attack 62, 74
entourage of 102–9
exemptions and privileges 125–6
family 2, 4, 6, 32, 51, 68, 94, 102–9, 126–7
former heads of State 6, 28, 55–8, 84, 157–8
freedom of communication 60–1
freedom of movement 58–60
inviolability 79
jurisdictional immunities 23, 61, 66–7, 76, 86
property of 100–1, 118–20
protection 3, 118–20
recognition 42–58
heirs apparent 32, 106
Hernandez, Concepcion Escobar 3, 132
high-level meetings 1
high-level officials
immunity 25–8
high-level representatives
immunity 6
Hirohito, Emperor [1901–89] 185–6
Holy See 30
Home Secretary 144
immunities 130
Hong Kong 103
hostage-taking 74
Hotman, Jean [1552–1636] 13
households, family members forming part of 105
ambassadors 104
ambiguity of term 105
heads of mission, analogy with 26, 55, 59, 62, 93–5
heads of State 109
human rights 2
violations of 3, 152
Hungary 58–9
Hussein, Saddam [1937–2006] 196–7

illegal arrests 85
immunity 2, 4–5, 19, 55, 130, 177
absence of 163–4
absolute personal 88
administrative proceedings 83–98
authority to waive 97
civil law 84, 90
civil proceedings 9, 83–94, 96, 166–72
criminal proceedings 81–3
Defence Ministers 130–1
determining 53
diplomatic 83, 162, 168
diplomats 9, 13, 84, 92–3, 97
Employment Minister 130
exceptions 6, 83, 92–3, 95, 160
false name 98
family of heads of State 103–9
foreign criminal jurisdictions 21, 132

immunity (*cont.*):
foreign heads of State 91–6
Foreign Ministers 25, 79, 121–3, 130
former heads of State 6, 57, 84, 136–78
formulation of general rule on 15
from execution 77
from Executive 88
from prosecution 67–8
from requisition 77
from search 77
from suit before foreign courts 80–98, 122–3
functional 10, 23, 59, 85, 137–40, 148, 150, 153–4, 167, 172–5, 203, 205
Governors 48
head of Government 122–3
heads of State 43–7, 54, 67–8, 84, 88, 92, 102
high-level officials 6, 25–8
historical background 12–8
Home Secretary 130
infringement 100
international courts 197–204
international crimes 3, 154–7
International Criminal Court (ICC) 199–202
International Criminal Tribunal for Rwanda (ICTR) 198–9
International Criminal Tribunal for the Former Yugoslavia (ICTY) 198–9
jurisdictional 23, 61, 66–7, 76, 86, 96
military forces 148–9
Minister for Atomic Energy 129
Minister of Justice 129
Ministers for Commerce and Industry 130
Ministers of State 130
personal 5, 11, 16, 18, 23, 49, 59, 81, 128, 197–8
private acts 91–2, 175–8
property 98–101
ratione materiae 6–9, 11, 18, 21–4, 49, 84–6, 137–8, 140–1, 147, 149, 153, 159, 161–3, 172, 174, 204–5
endorsement by ICJ 23–4
endorsement by national courts 27–8
ratione personae 7, 10–1, 20–1, 35, 81, 86, 88, 92, 115–6, 129, 131–2, 137, 163
endorsement by ICJ 22–3
endorsement by national courts 24–7
high-level officials 25–7
recognition 15
refusal of grant to head of State 88
refusing 145
restrictive theory of State 83
scope of 83–4
semi-sovereign States 46
Special Court for Sierra Leone (SCSL) 202–3
special missions 103–4, 134
State 8–9, 16–8, 20, 23–4, 58–9, 85, 87, 90–2, 99, 137–41, 167, 169
State officials 21
status-based 57
statutory provisions 55
types of 7–10
United Kingdom 92–3
waiver 89, 97–8
witness summons 79–80
Immunity of State Officials from Foreign Criminal Jurisdiction 163
implied waiver 98
in absentia
convictions 158
prosecutions 148, 156
inauguration 32
incapacity
head of State 32
incognito 90, 98
independence
State 12
States 15
India 34, 103
Princely States 30, 34
individual responsibility 181–8
industrial property 100
infringement
immunity 100
inheritance 83
inquests 84
inspection
customs 101–2
Institut de Droit International *see* **Institute of International Law**
Institute of International Law 10–1, 15, 62, 81, 91, 100, 123, 154
2001 resolution 82, 108, 123
2009 resolution 154
instrumentalities
State 139
insult
foreign head of State 70
in vicinity of foreign missions 72
intellectual property 100
intelligence services 161
interests of justice
rights of individual and 68

international arrest warrant 120
enforcement 121
International Court of Justice (ICJ) 2, 5, 22–3, 35, 40, 64–7, 76, 81, 120, 125, 165, 171, 173, 178
endorsement of specific rules by 22–4
international courts 188–93
former heads of State 6
immunities 197–204
international crimes 6, 82, 183–5
civil liability 169–72
extra-territorial jurisdiction 153, 187
former State officials 149–60
immunity 3, 154–7
international delicts distinguished 180
jurisdiction 153
prosecution 154–5, 187
punishment 182
International Criminal Court (ICC) 3, 45, 191–3, 197, 205
arrest warrants 200
complementarity 192
establishment 2, 192
immunities 199–202
jurisdiction 192, 200
obligations on non-State parties 202
Pre-Trial Chamber 201
referral to 201
statutory framework 201
international criminal law
developments in 2
International Criminal Tribunal for Rwanda (ICTR) 191
immunities 198–9
jurisdiction 191
International Criminal Tribunal for the Former Yugoslavia (ICTY) 23, 137, 149, 188–90, 205
establishment 188–9
immunities 198–9
jurisdiction 189
international criminal tribunals 2
international delicts
international crimes distinguished 180
international humanitarian law
violations of 3, 188–9, 194–5
international law
applicability of rules of 18–28
customary 13, 18–21, 23–5, 102, 108–9, 134, 154, 157, 170, 172
immunities 123
International Law Commission (ILC) 3, 5, 10, 21, 81, 132–3, 143, 145, 160, 163, 165, 173, 179–80, 186
articles on State responsibility 179–80
draft articles immunity of State officials from foreign criminal jurisdiction 5, 21, 48, 82, 96, 132, 141, 165, 180, 211
international obligations 64
breach of 180
international personality 30
international relations
conducting 1
international responsibility 182
international trade
officers of State 131
international waters 148
internationally protected person 75
internet 2
invasion 48
investigations
accidents 106
inviolability 76–80
Foreign Ministers 120–2
heads of Government 120–2
heads of State 79
limits on 77
personal 77–8
scope of 76–7
Iran
title of head of State 29
Iraq 148
occupation of Kuwait 50
US intervention in 38
Iraqi High Tribunal 196–7
Israel 25–6, 149–50, 156, 158, 171
Italy 46, 90, 101, 148, 152, 155, 162
invasion of Ethiopia 51
iure gestionis 8, 17, 164
iure imperii 8, 17, 140, 146, 148, 150, 164
***ius cogens* rules** 152, 156, 172, 174, 180
ius repraesentationis omnimodae 41–2

James II, King of England [1633–1701] 52
Japan
World War II 185–6
Jiang Zemin 73, 79, 157
Johore, Sultan of 90, 98
joint heads of State 29
Jordan 107
judicial restraint 86
jurisdiction 4–5
assertion of 78
extra territorial extensions of 2, 153, 187
immunity as bar to exercise of 10, 15–6, 81
immunity from foreign criminal 21
International Court of Justice 192

jurisdiction (*cont.*):
  international crimes 153
  International Criminal Court (ICC) 200
  non-justiciable 86
  personal 83–4
  removal of children from 146–7
  relationship of immunity to 10, 15–6, 81
  submission to 16
  territorial 89
  treaty-based extensions 153
jurisdictional immunity 23, 61, 66–7, 76, 86
  State 96
justiciability *see* **non justiciability**

Kabbah, Alhaji Ahmad Tejan 45, 52
Kabuye, Rose 159
Kagame, Paul 24
Kaiser Wilhelm II [1859–1941]
  proposed trial of 182–3
Kambanda, Jean 3, 191
Karadzic, Radovan 190
Kenyatta, Uhuru 3
Khmer Rouge 195
kidnapping 75, 161–2
  diplomats 74
Kim Il-Sung [1912–94] 34
Kim Jong-Il [1941–2011] 34
Kim Jong-un 34
Kolodkin, Roman 133, 160
Kosovo 189
Krenz, Egon 147
Krstic, Radislav 190
Kuwait
  occupation by Iraq 50

leaders in exile 31
Lebanon 196
  US intervention in 38
legal injury
  counter-measures 100
legal process
  heads of State inviolability to 79
legal status
  heads of State 3
legality 143
legitimacy
  head of State 49
Letters of Credence 40–1
liability
  war crimes 185
libel 70
Liberia 158, 195, 202
Libya 45, 161
  US intervention in 38
Libyan People's Bureau 71
Liechtenstein 83, 91, 106
litigation
  third parties and 68
Livni, Tzipi 157
Lockerbie **case** 161
loss of office
  position after 136–78
Louis XIV, King of France [1638–1718] 12, 52

MacArthur, General Douglas [1880–1964] 185–6
Malawi 202
Malaysia 30, 34, 47, 87
  elected monarch 33–4
manslaughter 147, 161
Marcos, President Ferdinand [1917–89] 177
Maroua Declaration 40
Mary, Queen of Scots [1542–87] 13, 15
  trial of 14
Mauretania 158
Maximilian, Emperor [1832–67] 91
Mbasogo, Teodoro Obiang Nguema 67, 80
McLeod Case *see* **Caroline Case**
media scrutiny 2
Mendoza, Bernardino de [1540–1604] 13
Metropolitan Police 166
military bases
  foreign 146
military forces 37, 148–9
  status of 149
military occupation 152
military orders 161
Milosevic, Slobodan [1941–2006]
  trial of 2, 190
Minister for Atomic Energy
  immunities 129
Minister for Commerce
  China 131
Minister for Foreign Affairs *see* **Foreign Ministers**
Minister of Justice
  immunities 129
Ministers for Commerce and Industry
  immunities 130
Ministers of State
  immunities 130
Mladic, Ratko 190
Mobutu, Sese Seko [1930–97] 58, 90, 92
mock execution 72
Mofaz, General Shaul 130
monarch *see* **heads of State**
monarchy
  abolition 33

elective 33–4
hereditary, position of family members 105
overthrow 33
republics contrasted 29
titles 35
Monde, Le 70
Mongolia 129
Montenegro 35, 46
Morocco 24, 70
movable property 100
movement
freedom of 58–60
Mudenge, Isaak Stanislaus Gorerazvo [1941–2012] 78, 125
Mugabe, Grace 103
Mugabe, Robert 78
murder 151, 156

Naples 46
Napoleon Bonaparte [1769–1821] 182
national courts
immunities of Foreign Ministers and 25
immunity and 2
national emergency 37
national law
violation 38–9
National Security Council of Mongolia 129
negligence 169
Netherlands 135, 155–6
Lockerbie case 161
New Zealand 158, 161, 170
Nezzar, Khaled 156
Nguesso, Denis Sassou 80
Nigeria 40, 48, 161–2
Nigerian High Commission 162
Niyazov, Saparmurat Atayevich [1940–2006] 34
Nkrumah, Kwame [1909–72] 34
non-governmental organizations (NGOs) 2
non-justiciability 87
non-official acts 89–96
non-sovereign acts 140
Noriega, General Manuel 31, 44, 111, 146, 176
normative hierarchy theory *see* ***ius cogens***
North Korea 34
Norway
immunity *ratione personae* 131
nuclear tests
France 40
Nuremberg International Military Tribunal 149–50, 183–5, 205
affirmation of principles of Charter 186
Charter 184–5

Obama, President Barak 38
occupation 48–9, 51–2
military 152
sovereignty and 50
offensive behaviour
near foreign missions 72
towards heads of State 69
office
assuming 43
lack of formal assumption of 45
officers of State
international trade 131
travel 131
offices of State
determining which should benefit from personal immunity 128
official acts 85–7
definition 142–7
distinguished from private acts 175–8
official and sovereign acts 85–7, 140
official but non-sovereign acts 87–9, 140
official but non-sovereign acts 87–9, 140
official capacity 8
acts performed in 142–75
official duties 32
official visits 102, 105
Foreign Ministers 127
head of Government 122–3, 127
private visits compared 6
Omar, Abu 162
Orders in Council 37, 47
overthrow
monarchy 33

Pahang 47
Pakistan 177
Panama 31, 44, 176
US intervention in 38
Papua New Guinea
head of Government 114
par in parem non habet imperium 10
paternity suits 83
peace 34
power to make 37–8
penalties
international crimes 3
peremptory norms *see* ***ius cogens***
personal immunity 5, 11, 16, 18, 23, 49, 59, 81, 128
diplomatic exceptions 92–3
distinguished from functional immunity 6, 16, 18, 25–6, 28, 49, 76, 80–6, 88, 90–1, 95–6, 124–5, 128–31, 133
international courts 197, 199

personal immunity (*cont.*):
  rationale 6–11, 20–4, 35, 49, 81, 84–5, 88, 92, 115–6, 129, 131–2, 149, 153, 159, 161–3, 174
personal inviolability 77–8
personal jurisdiction 83–4
personal life 91
personal services
  exemption from 126
personalization
  politics 2
Petain, Marshall Henri Philippe Benoni Omer Joseph [1856–1951] 52
Philippines 177
Pinochet, Augusto [1915–2006] 7, 26–8, 81, 148, 150–3, 160, 164
  request for extradition of 55–6
***Pinochet* case** 27, 55, 81, 93, 137, 160, 162
piracy 181–2
Poincare, Raymond [1860–1934] 50
politics
  personalization 2
pollution 180
Pope
  as head of State 30
power
  Foreign Ministers 112–3
  head of State 34
  internationally relevant 36–42
  seizure of 30–1
  State 12
Pre-Trial Chamber
  International Criminal Court (ICC) 201
prejudice 66–7
premises
  inviolability of 77
President-elect 31–2
Presidential powers
  United States 37
Prime Minister *see* **heads of Government**
private acts 83, 89–96, 100, 175–8
  distinguished from official acts 175–8
  former heads of State, heads of Government and Foreign Ministers 175–8
  immunity 91–2
  sitting heads of State, heads of Government and Foreign Ministers 81, 83, 86, 90–2, 94, 96, 124–5, 146
private conduct 100, 145, 172
  ambassadors 145
private law 83
private property
  acquiring 89
private visits 103, 105, 108
  Foreign ministers 127
  head of Government 122–3, 127
  official visits compared 6
privileges 18–9
  Foreign Ministers 125–6
  head of State 102
  heads of Government 125–6
  heads of State 3
  special missions 103–4
  statutory provisions 92–3
professional activities 83
property 100–1
  administration of 100
  Foreign Ministers 118–20
  heads of Government 118–20
  immunity 98–101
  inviolability of 77
property of head of State 98–101
prosecution
  evidence for 158
  international crimes 187
prosecution *in absentia* 148, 156
prosecutions 82, 153
  immunity from 67–8
  international crimes 154–5
  likelihood of success 157
  reluctance over former high-level officials 157–8
protection *see also* **security**
  diplomats 95
  foreign heads of State 74–6
  Foreign Ministers 118–20
  heads of Government 118–20
  heads of State 3
protocol 62
provisional measures 66–7
public capacity 89
public international law 138
public policy 47
punishment
  international crimes 182
'puppet' rulers 51–2

Qatar, Amir of 92
Quebec
  secessionist movement 61
Queen
  powers in UK 36

Rainbow Warrior 161
Rajapaksa, Percy Mahendra 24
ratification 32

ratione materiae 6–9, 11, 18, 21–4, 49, 84–6, 137–8, 140–1, 147, 149, 159, 161–3, 172, 174, 204–5
endorsement by ICJ 23–4
endorsement by national courts 27–8
ratione personae 7, 10–1, 20–1, 35, 81, 86, 88, 92, 115–6, 129, 132, 137, 163
endorsement by ICJ 22–3
endorsement by national courts 24–7
high-level officials 25–7
Norway 131
Switzerland 131
Reagan, President Ronald Wilson [1911–2004] 38, 123
real property 83
recognition
Foreign Ministers 113–4
head of State 42–58
heads of Government 113–4
role of Executive Branch 53–5
withdrawal 51
regents 32–3
regimes
change of 52
recognition of 43–4
Report on the Abuse of Diplomatic Immunities and Privileges 71
representation
acts relating to a treaty 115
representatives 78
duty of State to protect 119
immunities 128–33
republics
monarchies contrasted 29
Republika Srpska 43
requisition
immunity from 77
resignation 48
Resolution on Immunities from Jurisdiction and execution of Heads of State and of Government in International Law 123
Resolution on the Immunity from Jurisdiction of the State and of Persons Who Act on Behalf of the State 154
respect
heads of State 69
responsibility
individual 181–8
international 179–205
State 139–41, 179–81
restrictive doctrine
State immunity 16–8
retirement
activity after 2
rights of individual
interests of justice and 68
rival claims 48
royal households 94
Royal Pleasure 36
rules
endorsement of specific 22–9
Rumsfeld, Donald 157
Russia 85, 177
Rwanda 24, 54, 128, 159–60
genocide 158, 191

sabotage 163
sale of property
head of State 87
Samantar, Mohamed Ali 57, 173–4
San Marino
head of State 30
Santo Domingo 166
Sassou Ngueso, Denis 66–7
Saudi Arabia 9, 94, 107, 151, 169
Scilingo, Adolfo 158
Scotland
relationship with England 14
search
immunity from 77
Second World War *see* **World War II**
secret service agents 162
security *see also* **protection**
visiting heads of State 74
Security Council *see* **United Nations, Security Council**
self-defence 77
semi-sovereign States 46
Senegal 3, 155
Serbia 46
service of process 78, 96
Sharon, Ariel 124, 155
Shin Bet 156
ships 182
Siad Barre, Mohamed [1919–95] 57, 173
Sierra Leone 45, 52, 202–3
civil war 194–5
slavery 180
Slovakia 58–9
social security legislation
exemption from 125–6
Somalia 57, 173
US intervention in 38
Somare, Sir Michael 114
South African Embassy
demonstrations outside 71

South America
kidnapping 74
South Korea 54
sovereign *see* **heads of State**
abdication 32
death 32
doctrine of two bodies 12
sovereign acts 85–7, 140
sovereign authority 8, 17
sovereign capacity 89
sovereignty 35, 166–7
occupation and 50
territorial 61
United States 168
Soviet Union
absolute doctrine 17
Spain 56, 82–3, 155, 158, 164
arrest warrants 159
Audiencia Nacional 24
head of State 33
Spanish Civil War 33
Special Court for Sierra Leone (SCSL) 194–5
composition 194
immunity before 202–3
special missions 20, 62, 77, 103–4, 113, 115, 126–7, 133–5
duty on State to protect 119
freedom of movement 117
immunity status 134
special treatment
justifications for 10–1
Special Tribunal for Lebanon (STL) 196
spouses 104–5
heads of State 103, 107–8
St Helena 182
State 44, 47
acts performed on orders of 138
agencies and instrumentalities 139
ceasing to exist 48
constitutional structure 29
definition of to include representatives 86, 139
development of territorial 12
federal 46–8
immunity and 8, 58
independence 12, 15
international obligations 64
jurisdictional immunity 96
legal personality 110
personal embodiment of 127
power 12
recognition of Governments compared to recognition of 43
refusal of entry into 59–60
relations with other States 63–4
treaty-making capacity 38
uncertainty over existence of 43
State criminal responsibility 141
State Department 173–4
State immunity 9, 20, 23–4, 59, 85, 87, 90–2, 99, 139, 167, 169
absolute doctrine 16
relation to functional immunity 8–9, 16–17, 26, 47–8, 55, 83, 85–90, 92–3, 95–9, 109, 130, 137–9, 144, 147, 150, 152, 161, 164–6, 167–9, 171
restrictive doctrine 16–8
restrictive theory of 16–8, 83, 87
State responsibility 139–41
State officials
criminal proceedings against 147–65
immunity 21
State representatives
heads of State distinguished 75
travel 1
treaty-making capacity 39
State responsibility 179–81
ICL Draft Articles 5, 21, 48, 82, 96, 132, 141, 165, 180, 211
relationship with immunity 139–41
State immunity 139–41
statement of interest 57
States
representation for acts relating to a treaty 115
vassal 103
Status of Forces agreements 149
status-based immunity 57
Statute of the International Criminal Court 192–3, 197, 199–200, 204
succession 32, 34, 42–3, 100
Suggestion of Immunity 54, 145
Sultanates
Malaysia 47
Suriname 155
torture 151
Swiss Criminal Code 50
Switzerland 50, 81, 91, 103, 106, 109, 156, 158, 177
head of State 29
immunity *ratione personae* 131
symbols 61

Tate letter 17
taxation
exemption from 126
taxes
exemption from 101–2
heads of Government and Foreign Ministers 101–2
heads of State 101

Taylor, Charles 2, 158–9, 195, 202
term of office 34
extending 32
territorial jurisdiction 89
territorial sovereignty 61
territorial tort exception 165
territory
acquiring and ceding 36
terrorism 163
Thatcher, Margaret Hilda [1925–2013] 123
third parties
litigation and 68
non-immune 78–9
Tibet
status of 43
title 61
head of State 29, 34
Tito, Marshall Josip Broz [1892–1980] 34
Tokyo International Military Tribunal 185–6
torture 57, 144, 155–8, 162, 169
Chile 150–1
civil claims against 170
Saudi Arabia 9
Suriname 151
Torture Convention 144, 151–2, 155–6, 169–70, 187
Torture Victim Protection Act (US) 171
Transparency International 80
travel
officers of State 131
State representatives 1
treaties 20, 113, 131
concluding 36
extradition 183
guaranteeing office of head of State 34
powers to make 38–40
ratification 39
signature 39
United States 38
treaty 38–41, 112–3
automatic presumption of authority 39
definition 38
Treaty of Rome 39
treaty-based extensions of jurisdiction 153
treaty-making powers
informal 39
tribunals 188–93
trust property 100
Tunisia 158
Turkey 34

***ultra vires* acts** 143
UN Interim Administration Mission in Kosovo (UNMIK) 196
UN Millennium Summit 78
unification 48
United Arab Emirates 47, 88, 94
elected monarch 34
head of State 34
United Kingdom 34, 99
former heads of State 137
immunity 92–3
powers of the Queen 36
refusal of entry into 59
restrictive doctrine 17
visiting heads of State 74
United Nations (UN) 53
headquarters 60
Security Council 34
United Nations Convention on the Jurisdictional Immunities of States and Their Property 2004 164
United States 24, 36, 53, 57, 65, 73, 79, 84, 107, 148, 159
abuse of privilege 60
Presidential powers 37
refusal of entry into 58
restrictive doctrine 17
sovereignty 168
State Department 173–4
treaty-making 38
war power 37
US State Department 54

vassal States 103
Vatican City 30
Venezuela 145, 176
Vichy Government 51–2
Victor Emmanuel III, King of Italy [1869–1947] 101
Vienna Convention on Diplomatic Relations (1961) 112, 118–9, 127, 147, 162
Vienna Convention on the Law of Treaties (1969) 113, 115
Vietnam War 37
violation
national law 38–9
visiting heads of State 60, 77–8
inviolability 76–80
security 75

waiver
authority to waive 97
immunity 97–8
implied and express 39, 98
Waldheim, Kurt Josef [1918–2007] 58

war 37
  laws of 182–3, 189
  power to make 37–8
war crimes 58, 149, 156–7, 160, 171, 183
  defences 184
  individual responsibility for 181–8
  liability 185
  punishment 183–5
War Crimes Chambers 196
war, power to make 37–8
  United States 37
War Powers Resolution 37
Watts, Sir Arthur [1931–2007] 1, 21
West Germany 74
wilful damage 161
Wilhelm II, Kaiser [1859–1941] *see* **Kaiser, Wilhlem II [1859–1941]**
Wilhelmina, Queen of the Netherlands [1880–1962] 50
Willem-Alexander, King of the Netherlands 106
winding up 100
witness summons
  immunity from 79–80
women
  subordinate status 14
World War I 182–3
World War II 50, 52, 58, 101, 149–50, 183–5
  Japan 185–6

Ya'alon, Moshe 158
Yaron, Amos 155
Yerodia Case *see* ***Arrest Warrant*** **Case**
Yerodia Ndombasi, Abdoulaye 76, 120–1
Yugoslavia 35, 145
  conflict in 188–90
  crimes against humanity 189
  genocide 189

Zaire 58, 92, 106
Zayed bin Sultan Al Nahyan, Sheikh [1918–2004] 88
Zimbabwe 103, 125

The manufacturer's authorised representative in the EU for product safety is Oxford University Press España S.A. of el Parque Empresarial San Fernando de Henares, Avenida de Castilla, 2 – 28830 Madrid (www.oup.es/en or product.safety@oup.com). OUP España S.A. also acts as importer into Spain of products made by the manufacturer.

www.ingramcontent.com/pod-product-compliance
Lightning Source LLC
LaVergne TN
LVHW011756200926
848484LV00003B/716
9780199640287